BOOKS FOR PUBLIC LIBRARIES

Second Edition

Nonfiction for Small Collections

BOOKS FOR PUBLIC LIBRARIES

Second Edition
Nonfiction for Small Collections

Compiled by the Starter List for New Branch & New Libraries Collection Committee of the Public Library Association, a division of the American Library Association

R. R. Bowker Company
A Xerox Education Company
New York & London, 1975

Published by R. R. Bowker Co. (A Xerox Education Company)
1180 Avenue of the Americas, New York, N.Y. 10036
Copyright © 1975 by Xerox Corporation
All rights reserved.
Printed and bound in the United States of America.

Second Printing, January 1976

Library of Congress Cataloging in Publication Data

Public Library Association. Starter List for New
  Branch & New Libraries Collection Committee.
  Books for public libraries: nonfiction for small
  collections.

  1. Bibliography—Best books.   2. Public libraries.
I. Title.
Z1035.P93 1975   011   74-20606
ISBN 0-8352-0733-1

CONTENTS

PREFACE xiii

PROFESSIONAL TOOLS 1

000 GENERAL WORKS 3
    001   Knowledge, Research, Bibliographies 3
    001.5   Cybernetics, Bionics 3
    001.9   UFOs, the Unexplained 4
    028   Reading, Reading Guides 4
    029   Computers 4
    070   Journalism, Newspapers 4

100 PHILOSOPHY, PSYCHOLOGY 5
    100   Philosophy 5
    133   Astrology, ESP, Magic, Witchcraft 5
    135   Dreams 6
    150   Psychology, Psychoanalysis 6
    155   Child Psychology 7
    160   Logic 8
    170   Ethics 8
    180   Historical and Geographical Philosophy 8
    190   Modern Western Philosophy 8

200 RELIGION 10
    200   General Religious Philosophy 10
    215   Religion and Science 10

220	Bible	10
230	Christianity	11
240	Applied Christianity	11
260	Christian Church Functions	12
270	Christian Church History	13
280	Denominations & Sects	13
290	Comparative Religion	13
292	Mythology	14
294	Oriental Religions	14
296	Judaism	14
297	Islam	15
299	American Indian Religion	15
300	**SOCIAL SCIENCE**	**16**
301	Sociology	16
301.1	Social Psychology	16
301.3	Population	17
301.4	Groups	17
301.41	Women	17
301.42	Family	18
301.43	Aging, Retirement	19
301.45	Ethnic Groups	19
320	Political Science	20
323.4	Civil Rights, City Problems	20
325	Immigration	21
326	Afro-Americans	21
327	International Relations	21
328	Parliamentary Procedure	21
329	Politics, Elections	22
330	Economics	22
331	Labor, Careers	23
332	Investment, Personal Finance	23
333	Real Estate	24
333.7	Conservation	24
335	Communism, Socialism	24
338	Consumers and Products	24
340	Law	24
341	United Nations	25
342	Constitutional Law	25
347	Criminal Law, Everyday Law, the Courts	25
351.3	Civil Service Examinations	26

351.7	Police, Espionage	26
353	American Government	26
355	Military	27
360	Social Agencies	27
364	Crime, Prisons	27
367	Social Clubs	28
368	Insurance	28
370	Education	28
380	Transportation, Communication	29
389	Weights and Measures	29
391	Costume	30
392	Customs, Rites, Holidays	30
395	Etiquette, Grooming	30
398	Folklore	31

400 LANGUAGE **32**
401	General	32
423	Dictionaries	32
425	Grammar	32
428	Usage	33
428.4	Reading Improvement	33
430	German	33
440	French	33
450	Italian	33
460	Spanish, Portuguese	34
470	Latin	34
480	Greek	34
490	Russian	34
495	Oriental Languages	34
496	African Languages	34

500 SCIENCE **35**
500	General	35
510	Mathematics	35
520	Astronomy	37
526	Surveying, Mapping	38
530	Physics	38
540	Chemistry	38
550	Earth Science, Geology	39
560	Paleontology	40
572	Human Races, Anthropology	40

574	Biology	41
575	Evolution, Genetics	41
576	Microbiology	42
579	Taxidermy	42
580	Botany	42
590	Zoology	43
594	Mollusks, Seashells	44
595	Insects	44
597	Fishes, Amphibians	44
598	Reptiles, Birds	45
599	Mammals	45
600	**APPLIED SCIENCE**	**47**
600	Technology, Inventions	47
610	Medical Sciences	47
612	Anatomy, Physiology	47
613	Health, Safety	48
615	Drugs, Alcohol, Smoking	49
616	Medicine, Disease	49
616.8	Mental Health	50
617	Eyes, Ears, Teeth	51
618	Gynecology, Obstetrics	51
620	Engineering	51
621	Electronics, Electricity, Radio, TV	52
622	Mining	53
623.4	Guns	53
623.8	Boats, Seamanship	53
628	Pollution, Ecology	53
629.1	Flight	54
629.2	Motor Vehicles	54
629.3	Bicycles	56
629.4	Space	56
630	Agriculture	56
636	Pets, Livestock	57
641	Homemaking, Cooking	58
642	Beauty	59
643	Household Equipment	59
646	Sewing	60
649	Child Care	60
650	Business, Office Practice and Procedure	60
660	Industry, Metals, Manufacturing	61

680   Furniture, Upholstery, Woodworking 62
690   Home Repairs, Construction, Remodeling, etc. 62

700   ARTS, SPORTS **64**
701   Arts—General 64
709   Art History 64
711   City Design 65
716   Gardening, Landscaping 65
720   Architecture 66
730   Sculpture, Plastics, Ceramics 67
740   Commercial Art, Cartoons, Drawing 67
745   Crafts, Design 67
747   Interior Decoration 69
749   Antiques 70
750   Painting 70
760   Prints, Cuts 71
770   Photography, Films 71
780   Music 72
782   Opera, Sacred Music 73
784   Vocal, Folk, Pop, Bands 73
786   Instruments 74
791   Movies 74
792   Theater, Dance 74
793   Games, Amusements 75
796   Athletics, Sports, Camping 76
797   Water Sports 77
798   Equestrian Sports 78
799   Hunting & Fishing 78

800   LITERATURE **79**
801   General, History 79
808   Writing Guides 80
808.1   Poetry 80
808.2   Drama 81
808.3   Fiction 81
808.5   Speech 82
810   American Literature—General 82
811   American Poetry 83
812   American Drama 83
813   American Fiction 84
817   American Satire and Humor 85

818	American Miscellany	85
820	English Literature	85
821	English Poetry	86
822	English Drama	87
822.3	Shakespeare	87
823	English Fiction	88
828	English Miscellany	88
830	German Literature	88
839	Scandinavian Literature	89
840	French Literature	89
850	Italian Literature	90
860	Spanish and Portuguese Literature	90
870	Latin Literature	90
880	Greek Literature	91
890	African and Asian Literature	91
891	Russian Literature	92

900	**GEOGRAPHY, BIOGRAPHY, HISTORY**	**93**
900	General and World History	93
910	Geography, Discovery	94
912	Atlases	94
913	Archaeology	94
914–919	Travel	94
920	Collective Biography	95
	Individual Biography	97
929	Names, Genealogy, Heraldry	108
930	Ancient World	109
937	Ancient Rome	109
938	Ancient Greece	110
940	Europe—General History	110
940.1	Europe: 476–1453	110
940.2	Europe: 1453–1914	111
940.3	Europe: World War I	111
940.5	Europe: 1918 to the Present; World War II	112
941	Ireland	113
942	Great Britain	113
943	Germany	114
944	France	114
945	Italy	114
946	Spain	115

947	Russia	115
948	Scandinavia	115
949	Other European Countries	116
950	Asia	116
951	China	116
951.9	Korea	117
952	Japan	117
954	India, Pakistan, Ceylon, Iran	117
955	Near East	117
959	Southeast Asia	118
960	Africa	118
970	Indians of North America	119
971	Canada	119
972	Mexico, Central America, Caribbean	120
973	United States—General	120
973.1	United States: to 1607	121
973.2	United States: 1607–1775	121
973.3	United States: 1775–1789	121
973.4	United States: 1789–1809	122
973.5	United States: 1809–1845	122
973.6	United States: 1845–1861	123
973.7	United States: 1861–1865	123
973.8	United States: 1865–1901	123
973.9	United States: 1901 to the Present	124
974–979	United States—Regional Areas	125
980	South America	125
990	Other Parts of the World	125
INDEX		**127**

PREFACE

The need for a frequently revised, concise list of good nonfiction titles in all subject areas has often been expressed by both small and large libraries. The first edition of *Books for Public Libraries* appeared in 1970, with the promise of a revision at a later date. A complete revision of the earlier list has been attempted in this publication.

Since over 50 percent of the library agencies in the nation are serving populations of less than 50,000 people, and frequently are staffed by part-time and/or volunteer help, it is hoped a list such as this will aid in updating, maintaining, or starting new collections.

No core or basic collection list can be compiled that would totally serve all libraries. The collection should represent the community it serves, be it rural, semi-rural, suburban, or urban—particularly in the most rapidly changing areas of human knowledge. This list hopefully will be an *aid* to selection; it is not intended to be an all-inclusive source. Included here are approximately 5,000 titles, at least 50 percent of which are new to this edition. A concerted effort was made to include as much new and updated material as possible. Generalization into broad subject areas is used in preference to a minute breakdown of subjects.

The arrangement of the list is by Dewey classification, based loosely on the 10th abridged edition of *Dewey*. When a question of two classifications occurred, a decision was made as to the more applicable subject heading. An author–title index has been added to facilitate use. All titles were in print at the time of compilation. While many titles are available in paperback as well as hardback, it is assumed that most libraries will prefer a hardbound book for an initial circulating collection. Therefore, hardbound editions are cited exclusively—except when paperback is the only available edition. It should be the decision of the local library whether use will warrant purchase of paper or hardbound editions. Prices have been rounded to the nearest higher dollar. Books commonly thought of as reference/noncirculating are not included.

Individual committee members took responsibility for specific areas, but the committee as a whole agreed on final choices. Most committee members had access to bibliographic resources as well as large and varied collections in their areas, resulting in opportunity to personally peruse and evaluate most of the titles included.

The present committee recommends the publication be kept up-to-date with regular supplements and that a revised edition of the main list appear as soon as needed.

JoAnn Kingston
Committee Chairman
August 1974

COMMITTEE MEMBERS

Helen Barron
Head, Arts Division
Indianapolis/Marion County Public
    Library
Indianapolis, Ind.

Robert Dillon
Assistant Adult Services Coordinator
Brooklyn Public Library
Brooklyn, N.Y.

George Harrell
Director
Floral Park Public Library
Floral Park, N.Y.

James C. Hathaway
Director
Leavenworth Public Library
Leavenworth, Kans.

Virginia Hefferman
Director
Scituate Public Library
Scituate, Mass.

Cordie Hines
Branch Coordinator
Dallas Public Library
Dallas, Tex.

Alma Jacobs
Director
Montana State Library
Helena, Mont.

Robert Joyce
Assistant Director
Fort Worth Public Library
Fort Worth, Tex.

Clayton Kilpatrick
Adult Services Coordinator
Annapolis Public Library
Annapolis, Md.

Jo Ann Kingston
Branch Librarian
Flint Public Library
Flint, Mich.

Louise E. Morrison
Director
Timberland Regional Library
Olympia, Wash.

Barbara Paul
Director
Chicago Heights Public Library
Chicago Heights, Ill.

Leila-Jane Roberts
Director
Winchester Public Library
Winchester, Mass.

Judy K. Rule
Assistant Director
Cabell County Public Library
Glenville, W. Va.

James Soester
Director
Central Kansas Library System
Great Bend, Kans.

PROFESSIONAL TOOLS

This section gives a listing of valuable tools which are excellent aids to book selection and librarianship. An asterisk (*) means essential.

Akers, Susan G. *Simple Library Cataloging*. 5th rev. ed. Scarecrow, 1969. $8.
*American Library Association. *Minimum Standards for Public Library Systems*. ALA, 1967. $2.
_____. *Reference Books for Small and Medium-sized Libraries*. 2nd ed. ALA, 1973. $6.
Barton, Mary N. *Reference Books: a Brief Guide*. 7th ed. Enoch Pratt, 1970. paper, $2.
Books in Print. 2 vols. Bowker, published annually. set, $65.
Bulletin boards *see* classification number 745.
Dewey Decimal Classification and Relative Index. 10th abr. ed. Wilson, 1971. $12.
El-Hi Textbooks in Print. Bowker, 1974. $20.
Esdaile, Arundell. *Esdaile's Manual of Bibliography*. 4th ed. B&N, 1967. $10.
Galin, Saul. *Reference Books: How to Select and Use Them*. Random, 1969. $8.
Literary Market Place. Bowker, published annually. $20.
Nueckel, Susan. *Selected Guide to Make It, Fix It, Do It Yourself Books*. Fleet, 1973. $15.
Paperbound Books in Print. Bowker, published three times per year. annual subscription, $53.
Periodicals:
  Kirkus Book Review Service. Kirkus, published twice monthly. annual subscription, $40.
  Library Journal. Bowker, published twice monthly except July and August. 1 year, $17; 2 years, $29; 3 years, $42.
  Publishers Weekly. Bowker, published weekly. 1 year, $20; 2 years, $37; 3 years, $54.

1

Sinclair, Dorothy. *Administration of the Small Public Library*. ALA, 1965. $5.
Subject Guide to Books in Print. 2 vols. Bowker, published annually. $47.
Warren, Jefferson T. *Exhibit Methods*. Sterling, 1972. $7.
Wheeler, Joseph L. *Practical Administration of Public Libraries*. Harper, 1962. $9.
Winchell, Constance. *Guide to Reference Books*. 8th ed. ALA, 1967. $15.

000

GENERAL WORKS

001 KNOWLEDGE, RESEARCH, BIBLIOGRAPHIES

Barzun, Jacques. *Modern Researcher*. rev. ed. Harcourt, 1970. $9

Bradley, Van Allen. *New Gold in Your Attic*. Fleet, 1968. $9.

Cheney, Frances N. *Fundamental Reference Sources*. ALA, 1971. $9.

Downs, Robert B. *How to Do Library Research*. 3rd ed. Scarecrow, 1971. $10.

French, Scott R. *New Earth Catalog*. Putnam, 1973. $4.

Good, Carter V. *Methods of Research*. Appleton, 1954. $10.

Leidy, W. Philip. *Popular Guide to Government Publications*. 3rd ed. Columbia, 1968. $12.

McWhirter, Norris. *Guinness Book of World Records*. latest ed. Sterling, rev. annually. $7.

Nicholson, Margaret. *Manual of Copyright Practice*. 2nd ed. Oxford, 1956. $8.

Rufsvold, Margaret I. *Guides to Educational Media*. 3rd ed. ALA, 1971. $3.

Snow, Charles P. *Two Cultures: And a Second Look*. Cambridge, 1969. $4.

Turabian, Kate L. *Manual for Writers of Term Papers, Theses, and Dissertations*. 4th ed. Chicago, 1973. $5.

001.5 CYBERNETICS, BIONICS

Fuchs, Walter R. *Cybernetics for the Modern Mind*. Macmillan, 1971. $7.

Marteka, Vincent. *Bionics*. Lippincott, 1965. $5.

Parsegian, V. L. *This Cybernetic World of Men, Machines and Earth*. Doubleday, 1972. $7.

Rothman, Milton A. *Cybernetic Revolution*. Watts, 1972. $6.

001.9   UFOs, THE UNEXPLAINED
Hynek, J. Allen. *UFO Experience*. Regnery, 1972. $7.
Klass, Philip J. *UFOs Identified*. Random, 1968. $8.
Sanderson, Ivan T. *Investigating the Unexplained*. Prentice, 1971. $8.

028   READING, READING GUIDES
Adler, Mortimer J. *How to Read a Book*. rev. ed. S&S, 1972. $9.
Arbuthnot, May H. *Children's Reading in the Home*. Lothrop, 1969. $9.
Burach, A. S. *Writer's Handbook*. rev. ed. Writer, 1971. $10.
Carlsen, Robert G. *Books and the Teenage Reader*. Harper, 1972. $7.
Fader, Daniel N. *Hooked on Books*. Putnam, 1968. $7.
Haight, Anne L. *Banned Books*. 3rd ed. Bowker, 1970. $10.
Haines, Helen E. *Living with Books*. 2nd ed. Columbia, 1950. $11.
Hazard, Paul. *Books, Children, and Men*. Horn, 1960. $7.

029   COMPUTERS
Benice, Daniel D. *Introduction to Computers and Data Processing*. Prentice, 1970. $11.
Cooper, M. J. *What the Computer Can Do: a Guide for the Plain Man*. Auerbach, 1969. $8.
Davidson, Charles H. *Computers*. Wiley, 1967. $15.
Diebold, John. *Man and the Computer*. Praeger, 1969. $6.
Farina, Mario V. *Computers: a Self-teaching Introduction*. Prentice, 1969. $9.
Feldzaman, A. N. *Intelligent Man's Easy Guide to Computers*. McKay, 1971. $8.
Saxon, James A. *Basic Principles of Data Processing*. Prentice, 1970. $11.
Sippl, Charles J. *Computer Dictionary and Handbook*. 2nd ed. Sams, 1972. $17.
Swallow, Kenneth P. *Elements of Computer Programming*. 2nd ed. Holt, 1970. $11.
Vickery, Brian. *Information Systems*. Shoe String, 1973. $18.

070   JOURNALISM, NEWSPAPERS
Barron, Jerome A. *Freedom of the Press for Whom?* Indiana, 1973. $9.
Glessing, Robert J. *Underground Press in America*. Indiana, 1970. $7.
Johnson, Michael L. *New Journalism*. Kansas, 1971. $7.
Mott, Frank L. *American Journalism*. 3rd rev. ed. Macmillan, 1962. $11.
Time-Life Books. *Photojournalism*. Morgan, 1971. $10.
Woods, Allan. *Modern Newspaper Production*. Harper, 1964. $7.

100

PHILOSOPHY AND PSYCHOLOGY

100   PHILOSOPHY

Brennan, Joseph. *Meaning of Philosophy*. 2nd ed. Harper, 1967. $9.

Durant, Will. *Story of Philosophy*. rev. ed. S&S, 1961. $8.

James, Will. *Essays on Faith and Morals*. Peter Smith. $6.

Jaspers, Karl. *Great Philosophers*. 2 vols. Harcourt, 1962, 1966. set, $19.

Kaplan, Abraham. *New World of Philosophy*. Random, 1961. $9.

Magill, Frank N. *Masterpieces of World Philosophy in Summary Form*. Harper, 1961. $13.

133   ASTROLOGY, ESP, MAGIC, WITCHCRAFT

Adams, Evangeline. *Astrology for Everyone*. Dodd, 1970. $5.

_____. *Astrology: Your Place Among the Stars*. Dodd, 1930. $7.

_____. *Astrology: Your Place in the Sun*. Dodd, 1969. $5.

Angoff, Allan. *Psychic Force*. Putnam, 1970. $8.

Brown, Wenzell. *How to Tell Fortunes with Cards*. Sterling, 1963. $4.

Burland, Cottie A. *Beyond Science*. Grosset, 1973. $10.

Christopher, Milbourne. *ESP, Seers and Psychics*. Crowell, 1970. $7.

Cohen, Daniel. *ESP*. Harcourt, 1973. $6.

Ford, Arthur A. *Life Beyond Death*. Putnam, 1971. $7.

Freedland, Nat. *Occult Explosion*. Putnam, 1972. $7.

Godwin, John. *Occult America*. Doubleday, 1972. $8.

Goodman, Linda. *Sun Signs*. Taplinger, 1969. $8.

Gray, Eden. *Complete Guide to the Tarot*. Crown, 1970. $7.

Hansen, Chadwick. *Witchcraft at Salem*. Braziller, 1969. $7.

Hart, Roger W. *Witchcraft*. Putnam, 1972. $6.

Holzer, Hans. *Power of Hypnosis*. Bobbs, 1973. $6.

Jennings, Gary. *Teenager's Realistic Guide to Astrology*. Association, 1971. $6.

Jones, Louis C. *Things That Go Bump in the Night*. Hill, 1959. $5.
Kaplan, Stuart R. *Tarot Classic*. Grosset, 1972. $6.
Lynde, Edward. *Astrology for Everyone*. rev. ed. Dutton, 1970. $6.
McConnell, Robert A. *ESP Curriculum Guide*. S&S, 1971. $5.
MacNiece, Louis, *Astrology*. Doubleday, 1964. $7.
Montgomery, Ruth. *Gift of Prophecy*. Morrow, 1965. $6.
_____. *World Beyond*. Coward, 1971. $6.
Nostradamus. *Complete Prophecies*. Crown, 1964. $6.
Rhine, Louise E. *Mind Over Matter*. Macmillan, 1970. $8.
Somerlott, Robert. *Here, Mr. Splitfoot*. Viking, 1971. $8.
Stearn, Jess. *Time for Astrology*. Coward, 1971. $10.
_____. *Edgar Cayce, the Sleeping Prophet*. Doubleday, 1967. $7.
Teltscher, Herry O. *Handwriting*. Hawthorn, 1971. $7.
Wilson, Colin. *Occult*. Random, 1971. $10.

135   DREAMS
Freud, Sigmund. *Interpretation of Dreams*. Mod. Library. $3.
Stewart, Walter A. *Secret of Dreams*. Macmillan, 1972. $6.

150   PSYCHOLOGY, PSYCHOANALYSIS
Dewey, John. *How We Think*. Heath, 1933. $10.
Fast, Julius. *Body Language*. Evans, 1970. $5.
Flesch, Rudolf F. *Art of Clear Thinking*. Harper, 1951. $6.
Freud, Sigmund. *Basic Writings*. Mod. Library. $5.
_____. *General Introduction to Psychoanalysis*. Liveright. $8.
Fromm, Erich. *Anatomy of Human Destructiveness*. Holt, 1973. $13.
_____. *Art of Loving*. Harper, 1956. $4.
_____. *Psychoanalysis and Religion*. Yale, 1950. $6.
Garrett, Henry E. *Great Experiments in Psychology*. 3rd ed. Appleton, 1951. $12.
Grier, William. *Black Rage*. Basic, 1968. $6.
Hayakawa, Samuel I. *Symbol, Status and Personality*. Harcourt, 1963. $6.
Hershey, Gerald L. *Living Psychology*. Macmillan, 1970. $8.
Highet, Gilbert. *Man's Unconquerable Mind*. Columbia, 1964. $6.
Hilgard, Ernest. *Introduction to Psychology*. 5th ed. Harcourt, 1971. $12.
Horney, Karen. *Our Inner Conflicts*. Norton, 1945. $7.
Jung, Carl G. *Analytical Psychology*. Pantheon, 1968. $7.
_____. *Portable Jung*. Viking, 1971. $8.
Koestler, Arthur. *Act of Creation*. Macmillan, 1964. $10.
Laing, R. D. *Self and Others*. 2nd rev. ed. Pantheon, 1970. $6.
Lorayne, Henry. *Memory Book*. Stein, 1974. $8.
Luce, Gay. *Body Time: Physiological Rhythms and Social Stress*. Pantheon, 1971. $7.

May, Rollo. *Love and Will*. Norton, 1969. $8.
_____. *Meaning of Anxiety*. Ronald, 1950. $8.
_____. *Power and Innocence: a Search for the Sources of Violence*. Norton, 1972. $8.
Menninger, Karl A. *Human Mind*. Knopf, 1945. $10.
_____. *Love Against Hate*. Harcourt, 1959. $9.
_____. *Man Against Himself*. Harcourt. $13.
Morgan, Clifford T. *Introduction to Psychology*. 4th ed. McGraw, 1971. $12.
Overstreet, Harry A. *Mature Mind*. Norton, 1959. $7.
Peale, Norman V. *Stay Alive All Your Life*. Prentice, 1957. $6.
Riesman, David. *Lonely Crowd*. rev. ed. Yale, 1969. $13.
Rogers, Carl. *Carl Rogers on Encounter Groups*. Harper, 1970. $6.
_____. *On Becoming a Person*. Houghton, 1970. paper, $4.
Singer, June. *Boundaries of the Soul*. Doubleday, 1972. $10.
Skinner, B. F. *Beyond Freedom and Dignity*. Knopf, 1971. $7.
Storr, Anthony. *Human Aggression*. Atheneum, 1968. $6.
Strecker, Edward A. *Discovering Ourselves*. 3rd ed. Macmillan, 1958. $5.
Tournier, Paul. *Escape from Loneliness*. Westminster, 1962. $4.
_____. *Whole Person in a Broken World*. Harper, 1964. $5.
Tyler, Leona E. *Psychology of Human Differences*. 3rd ed. Appleton, 1965. $10.
Watson, Robert I. *Great Psychologists: From Aristotle to Freud*. 2nd ed. Lippincott, 1968. $7.
Wilson, John R. *Mind*. Time, 1969. $6.

155   CHILD PSYCHOLOGY

Beadle, Muriel. *Child's Mind*. Doubleday, 1971. paper, $4.
Bettelheim, Bruno. *Love Is Not Enough*. Free Press, 1950. $8.
Button, Alan D. *Authentic Child*. Random, 1969. $6.
Egg, Maria. *When a Child Is Different*. John Day, 1964. $5.
Erickson, Erik H. *Identity: Youth and Crisis*. Norton, 1968. $9.
Gardner, George E. *Emerging Personality*. Delacorte, 1970. $7.
Gardner, Richard A. *Understanding Children*. Aronson, 1973. $10.
Gesell, Arnold. *The Infant and Child in the Culture of Today*. rev. ed. Harper, 1974. $10.
Grollman, Earl A. *Explaining Death to Children*. Beacon, 1969. $5.
Horrocks, John E. *Psychology of Adolescence*. 3rd ed. Houghton, 1969. $11.
Missildene, W. Hugh. *Your Inner Child of the Past*. S&S, 1963. $7.
Montessori, Maria. *Absorbent Mind*. Holt, 1967. $7.
_____. *From Childhood to Adolescence*. Schocken, 1973. $7.
Piaget, Jean. *Origins of Intelligence in Children*. International U. Pr., 1966. $13.

Pulaski, MaryAnn S. *Understanding Piaget*. Harper, 1971. $7.
Steinzor, Bernard. *When Parents Divorce*. Pantheon, 1969. $6.
Stewart, Mark A. *Raising a Hyperactive Child*. Harper, 1973. $9.
Wing, Lorna. *Autistic Children*. Brunner, 1972. $7.

160 LOGIC

Chase, Stuart. *Guides to Straight Thinking*. Harper, 1956. $6.
Copi, Irving M. *Introduction to Logic*. 4th ed. Macmillan, 1972. $9.
Lieber, Hugh. *Mits, Wits and Logic*. 3rd ed. Norton, 1960. $6.

170 ETHICS

Adler, Mortimer. *Time of our Lives: Ethics of Common Sense*. Holt, 1970.
$8.
Callahan, Daniel. *Abortion: Law, Choice and Morality*. Macmillan, 1970.
$15.
Dedek, John F. *Human Life*. Ward, 1972. $6.
Kennedy, Eugene C. *New Sexuality: Myths, Fables and Hang-ups*. Double-
day, 1972. $6.
Koestler, Arthur. *Insight and Outlook*. Peter Smith. $5.
Langone, John. *Death Is a Noun*. Little, 1972. $6.
Mace, David R. *Abortion*. Abingdon, 1972. $4.
Mannes, Marya. *Last Rights*. Morrow, 1974. $5.
Oraison, Marc. *Morality for Moderns*. Doubleday, 1972. $5.
Severn, William. *End of the Roaring Twenties: Prohibition and Repeal*.
Messner, 1969. $4.

180 HISTORICAL AND GEOGRAPHICAL PHILOSOPHY

Cornford, Francis M. *Before and After Socrates*. Cambridge, 1932. $6.
Creel, Herrlee G. *Chinese Thought from Confucious to Mao Tse-Tung*.
Chicago, 1971. $6.
I. Ching. *Book of Changes*. Peter Smith. $6.
Stearn, Jess. *Yoga, Youth and Reincarnation*. Doubleday, 1965. $7.
Zorn, William. *Body Harmony*. Hawthorn, 1971. $5.

190 MODERN WESTERN PHILOSOPHY

Camus, Albert. *Rebel*. Knopf, 1954. $6.
Collins, James D. *British Empiricists: Locke, Berkeley, Hume*. Bruce,
1967. $3.
Fisch, Max H. *Classic American Philosophers*. Appleton, 1966. $7.
Frankel, Charles. *Golden Age of American Philosophy*. Braziller, 1960. $9.
Frost, S. E. *Basic Teachings of the Great Philosophers*. Doubleday. $2.
Fuller, Buckminster. *Four D Time Lock*. Gannon. $6.
_____. *Ideas and Integrities*. Prentice, 1963. $11.
Hume, David. *Philosophy of David Hume*. Mod. Library, 1949. $3.

James, William. *Writings*. Mod. Library. $5.

Kant, Immanual. *Philosophy of Kant*. Mod. Library, 1949. $3.

Kierkegaard, Soren. *Kierkegaard Anthology*. Mod. Library, 1959. $3.

Koller, John M. *Oriental Philosophies*. Scribner, 1970. $9.

Munson, Thomas N. *Essential Wisdom of George Santayana*. Columbia, 1962. $8.

Nietzsche, Friedrich W. *Portable Nietzsche*. Viking, 1954. $6.

Russell, Bertrand. *Basic Writings*. S&S, 1961. $10.

Schopenhauer, Arthur. *Will to Live*. Ungar. $9.

Spinoza, Benedict De. *Chief Works*. 2 vols. Dover. each, $9.

White, Morton. *Science and Sentiment in America*. Oxford, 1972. $10.

Whitehead, Alfred N. *Anthology*. Macmillan, 1961. $7.

200

RELIGION

200   GENERAL RELIGIOUS PHILOSOPHY

Ford, Leighton. *One Way to Change the World*. Harper, 1970. paper, $2.

James, William. *Varieties of Religious Experience*. Mod. Library. $3.

Skinner, Tom. *How Black Is the Gospel?* Lippincott, 1970. $5.

Stroup, Herbert. *Four Religions of Asia*. Harper, 1968. $6.

Thomas, George F. *Religious Philosophies of the West*. Scribner, 1965. paper, $5.

Thurman, Howard. *Search for Common Ground*. Harper, 1971. $5.

Tillich, Paul. *What Is Religion?* Harper, 1973. paper, $3.

215   RELIGION AND SCIENCE

DeChardin, Pierre T. *Hymn of the Universe*. Harper, 1965. $4.

Koestler, Arthur. *Sleepwalkers*. Macmillan, 1968. $9.

220   BIBLE

Burke, Carl F. *God Is for Real, Man*. Association, 1966. $4.

Burrows, Millar. *Dead Sea Scrolls*. Viking, 1955. $8.

_____. *More Light on the Dead Sea Scrolls*. Viking, 1958. $7.

Chase, Mary E. *Bible and the Common Reader*. rev. ed. Macmillan, 1962. paper, $2.

_____. *Psalms for the Common Reader*. Norton, 1962. $6.

Cruden, Alexander. *Cruden's Concordance*. unabr. ed. Baker, $8.

Fox, Emmett. *Diagrams for Living*. Harper, 1968. $5.

Goodspeed, Edgar J. *Story of the Apocrypha*. Chicago, 1939. $5.

_____. *The Twelve*. Holt, 1957. $4.

Hastings, James. *Dictionary of the Bible*. rev. ed. Scribner, 1963. $18.

Herford, R. Travers. *Talmud and Apocrypha*. KTAV, 1929. $10.

HOLY BIBLE
Jerusalem Bible. Doubleday, 1967. $10.
King James Version. Nelson. $7.
Living Bible. Doubleday, 1971. $10.
New English Bible. 2nd ed. Oxford, 1970. $13.
Revised Standard Version. Zondervan. $4.
Kee, Howard C. *Understanding the New Testament*. 2nd ed. Prentice, 1965. $10.
Leitch, Addison H. *Readers Introduction to the New Testament*. Doubleday, 1971. $6.
Lindsey, Hal. *Late Great Planet Earth*. Zondervan, 1973. $4.
McKenzie, John L. *Dictionary of the Bible*. Macmillan, 1965. $18.
Maus, Cynthie. *Christ and the Fine Arts*. rev. ed. Harper, 1959. $8.
Neil, William. *Harper's Bible Commentary*. Harper, 1963. $8.
Oursler, Fulton. *Greatest Book Ever Written*. Doubleday, 1957. $7.
Price, Eugenia. *Learning to Live from the Acts*. Lippincott, 1970. $4.
Strong, James. *Exhaustive Concordance of the Bible*. Abingdon, 1958. $17.
Thompson, John A. *Bible and Archaeology*. Eerdmans, 1962. $8.
Wright, George E. *Westminster Historical Atlas to the Bible*. rev. ed. Westminster, 1956. $10.

230 CHRISTIANITY
Augustine, Saint. *City of God*. Mod. Library. $5.
Bishop, Jim. *Day Christ Died*. Harper, 1957. $8.
_____. *Day Christ Was Born*. Harper, 1960. $4.
Cassels, Louis. *Reality of God*. Doubleday, 1971. $5.
Goodspeed, Edgar J. *Life of Jesus*. Harper, 1968. paper, $2.
Hofmann, Hans. *Discovering Freedom*. Beacon, 1969. $6.
Kavanaugh, James J. *Modern Priest Looks at His Outdated Church*. new ed. Nash, 1973. paper, $4.
McGinley, Phyllis. *Saint Watching*. Viking, 1969. $6.
Oursler, Fulton. *Greatest Story Ever Told*. Doubleday, 1949. $7.
Thomas Aquinas. *Introduction to St. Thomas Aquinas*. Mod. Library, 1948. $3.
Tillich, Paul. *Future of Religions*. Harper, 1966. $3.
_____. *History of Christian Thoughts*. S&S. paper, $5.
Weatherhead, Leslie. *Christian Agnostic*. Abingdon, 1972. $3.

240 APPLIED CHRISTIANITY
Armor, Reginald C. *Magic of Love*. Dodd, 1967. $4.
Bailey, Albert E. *Gospel in Hymns*. Scribner, 1950. $14.
Berrigan, Daniel. *Absurd Convictions, Modest Hopes*. Random, 1972. $8.
_____. *False Gods, Real Men*. Macmillan, 1969. $5.
Bonhoeffer, Dietrich. *Letters and Papers from Prison*. Macmillan, 1972. $8.

Boyd, Malcolm. *Are You Running with Me, Jesus?* Holt, 1965. $4.

_____. *Human Like Me, Jesus*. S&S, 1971. $6.

Cain, Arthur H. *Young People and Religion*. John Day, 1970. $5.

Furfey, Paul H. *Morality Gap*. Macmillan, 1968. $5.

Goudge, Elizabeth. *Diary of Prayer*. Coward, 1966. $7.

Graham, Billy. *World Aflame*. Doubleday, 1965. $4.

Hunt, Gladys N. *Christian Way of Death*. Zondervan, 1971. $4.

Ikerman, Ruth C. *Devotional Programs for Every Month*. Abingdon, 1957. $3.

Irion, Mary J. *Yes, World*. R. W. Baron, 1970. $5.

Kauffman, Donald T. *For Instance*. Baker, 1970. paper, $3.

Kempis, Saint Thomas. *Imitation of Christ*. Wehman, 1969. $3.

King, Martin Luther, Jr. *Strength to Love*. Harper, 1963. $6.

Lair, Jess. *I Ain't Much, Baby—but I'm All I've Got*. Doubleday, 1972. $3.

Lewis, Clive S. *Screwtape Letters*. Macmillan, 1964. $5.

Marshall, Catherine. *Beyond Ourselves*. McGraw, 1961. $6.

Marshall, Peter. *Mr. Jones, Meet the Master*. Revell. $4.

Merton, Thomas. *No Man Is an Island*. Doubleday. paper, $2.

Miller, Keith. *Habitation of Dragons*. Word Bks, 1970. $5.

Palmer, Roger C. *Jesus Kids*. Judson, 1971. paper, $2.

Peale, Norman V. *Enthusiasm Makes the Difference*. Prentice, 1967. $6.

_____. *Power of Positive Thinking*. Prentice, 1954. $5.

Robinson, John A. *Christian Freedom in a Permissive Society*. Westminster, 1970. paper, $3.

Schweitzer, Albert. *Reverence for Life*. Harper. $5.

Sheen, Fulton J. *Power of Love*. S&S, 1965. $4.

Trueblood, Elton. *New Man for Our Times*. Harper, 1970. $3.

Wilkerson, David. *Cross and the Switchblade*. Geis, 1963. $5.

_____. *Hey Preach, You're Comin' Through*. Revell, 1971. $4.

260   CHRISTIAN CHURCH FUNCTIONS

Barrett, William E. *Red Laquered Gate*. Sheed. $7.

Benson, Dennis C. *Now Generation*. Knox, 1969. paper, $3.

Berton, Pierre. *Comfortable Pew*. Lippincott, 1965. $4.

Bestic, Alan. *Praise the Lord and Pass the Contribution*. Taplinger, 1971. $7.

Blake, Eugene C. *Church in the Next Decade*. Macmillan, 1966. $5.

Book of Common Prayer. Virginia, 1973. price not set.

Cox, Harvey. *The Secular City*. rev. ed. Macmillan, 1966. paper, $2.

Duckert, Mary. *Help! I'm a Sunday School Teacher*. Westminster, 1969. paper, $2.

Gilmore, J. Herbert. *When Love Prevails*. Eerdmans, 1971. paper, $4.

Holmes, Marjorie. *I've Got to Talk to Somebody, God*. Doubleday, 1969. $4.

_____. *Who Am I, God?* Doubleday, 1971. $4.

Kennedy, Eugene C. *People Are the Church*. Doubleday, 1969. $5.

Keyes, Frances P. *Tongues of Fire*. Coward, 1966. $7.

Kuhns, William. *Environmental Man*. Harper, 1969. $5.

Marshall, Peter. *Prayers of Peter Marshall*. McGraw, 1954. $6.

Oursler, Will. *Religion: Out or Way Out*. Stackpole, 1968. $6.

Poling, David. *Last Years of the Church*. Doubleday, 1969. $2.

Smith, Charles M. *How to Talk to God When You Aren't Feeling Religious*. Word Bks, 1971. $5.

Weiser, Francis X. *Handbook of Christian Feasts and Customs*. Harcourt, 1958. $7.

Wilkerson, David. *Little People*. Revell, 1969. $4.

270   CHRISTIAN CHURCH HISTORY

Bowie, Walter R. *Story of the Church*. Abingdon, 1955. $4.

Foxe, John. *Foxe Book of Martyrs*. Moody. $6.

Harris, Sara. *Sisters*. Bobbs, 1971. $8.

Hudson, Winthrop S. *American Protestantism*. Chicago, 1961. $7.

Hutchinson, Paul. *Twenty Centuries of Christianity*. Harcourt. $9.

Nigg, Walter. *Warriors of God*. Knopf, 1959. $9.

Simon, Edith. *Reformation*. Time, 1970. $7.

280   DENOMINATIONS AND SECTS

Bacon, Margaret H. *Quiet Rebels*. Basic, 1969. $6.

Bainton, Roland H. *Early Christianity*. Van Nostrand, 1960. paper, $2.

Book of Mormon. Deseret. $5.

Clark, Elmer T. *Small Sects in America*. rev. ed. P. Smith. $4.

Eddy, Mary B. *Science and Health with Key to the Scriptures*. First Church. $7.

Ellis, John T. *American Catholicism*. 2nd ed. Chicago, 1969. $9.

Ellwood, Robert S. *Religious and Spiritual Groups in Modern America*. Prentice, 1972. $9.

Graham, Billy. *Jesus Generation*. Zondervan, 1971. $5.

Hostetler, John A. *Amish Society*. rev. ed. Johns Hopkins, 1970. $8.

Judah, J. Stillson. *History and Philosophy of the Metaphysical Movements in America*. Westminster, 1967. $8.

Mead, Frank S. *Handbook of Denominations in the United States*. 5th ed. Abingdon, 1970. $4.

Sherrill, John L. *They Speak with Other Tongues*. Chosen. $5.

Stuber, Stanley I. *How We Got Our Denominations*. Association, 1965. $5.

West, Jessamyn. *Quaker Reader*. Viking, 1962. $8.

Whalen, William J. *Minority Religions in America*. Alba, 1972. paper, $2.

290   COMPARATIVE RELIGION

Bach, Marcus. *Major Religions of the World*. Abingdon, 1970. paper, $2.

Brandon, S. G. *Dictionary of Comparative Religion*. Scribner, 1970. $18.

Fairchild, Johnson E. *Basic Beliefs*. Sheridan. $7.
Gaer, Joseph. *What the Great Religions Believe*. Dodd, 1963. $5.
Haskins, James. *Religions*. Lippincott, 1973. $5.
Hume, Robert E. *World's Living Religions*. rev. ed. Scribner, 1959. $6.
Landis, Benson Y. *World Religions*. Dutton, 1965. $4.
Needleman, Jacob. *New Religions*. Doubleday, 1970. $6.
Noss, John B. *Man's Religions*. 5th ed. Macmillan, 1974. $10.
Parrinder, Geoffrey. *Faiths of Mankind*. Crowell, 1965, $5.
Smith, Huston. *Great Religions of the World*. National Geographic, 1971. $12.
_____. *Religions of Man*. Harper, 1958. $6.
Toynbee, Arnold. *Historian's Approach to Religion*. Oxford, 1956. $8.

292 MYTHOLOGY

Bach, Marcus. *Strangers at the Door*. Abingdon, 1971. $4.
Bulfinch, Thomas. *Bulfinch's Mythology*. 2nd rev. ed. Crowell, 1970. $7.
Frazer, James G. *Golden Bough*. abr. ed. Macmillan. $7.
Hamilton, Edith. *Mythology*. Little, 1942. $7.
Zimmerman, John E. *Dictionary of Classical Mythology*. Harper, 1964. $6.

294 ORIENTAL RELIGIONS

Anesaki, Masaharu. *History of Japanese Religion*. Tuttle, 1963. $9.
Buddha, Gautama. *Teachings of the Compassionate Buddha*. NAL, 1955. paper, $1.
Ch'en, Kenneth K. *Buddhism, the Light of Asia*. Barron, 1968. $6.
Fromm, Erich. *Zen Buddhism and Psychoanalysis*. Harper, 1970. paper, $2.
Garabedian, John H. *Eastern Religions in the Electric Age*. Grosset, 1969. $5.
Kaltenmark, Max. *Lao Tzu and Taoism*. rev. ed. Stanford, 1969. $6.
Suzuki, Daisetz T. *Essentials of Zen Buddhism*. Greenwood, 1973. $20.
Watts, Alan. *Art of Contemplation*. Pantheon, 1973. $3.
_____. *Spirit of Zen*. Paragon. $4.
_____. *Supreme Identity*. Pantheon, 1972. $6.
_____. *Way of Zen*. Pantheon, 1957. $7.
Zorn, William. *Yoga for the Mind*. F&W, 1969. $5.

296 JUDAISM

Brasch, R. *Judaic Heritage*. McKay, 1969. $8.
Buber, Martin. *I and Thou*. Lyceum, 1970. $6.
Dimont, Max. *Jews, God and History*. S&S, 1968. $8.
Hertzberg, Arthur. *Judaism*. Braziller, 1962. $4.
Neusner, Jacob. *Invitation to the Talmud*. Harper, 1973. $8.
Steinberg, Milton. *Basic Judaism*. Harcourt. $3.
Wouk, Herman. *This Is My God*. Doubleday, 1959. $7.

297   ISLAM

Fitch, Florence M. *Allah, the God of Islam*. Lothrop, 1950. $4.
Gibbs, Hamilton A. *Mohammedanism*. 2nd ed. Oxford, 1953. paper, $2.
Rodwell, J. M. ed. *Koran*. Dutton. $4.

299   AMERICAN INDIAN RELIGION

Hurdy, John M. *American Indian Religions*. Sherbourne, 1971. paper, $3.
Marriott, Alice. *American Indian Mythology*. Crowell, 1968. $8.
Underhill, Ruth M. *Red Man's Religion*. Chicago, 1965. $9.

300

SOCIAL SCIENCE

301   SOCIOLOGY
Alvarez, A. *Savage God.* Random, 1972. $8.
Berelson, Benard. *Human Behavior.* Harcourt, 1964. $12.
Chase, Stuart. *Proper Study of Mankind.* 2nd ed. Harper, 1962. $7.
Deutsch, Morton. *Theories in Social Psychology.* Basic, 1965. $5.
Dubos, René J. *So Human an Animal.* Scribner, 1968. $9.
Durkheim, Emile. *Suicide.* Free Press, 1951. $6.
Lippmann, Walter. *Public Opinion.* Free Press, 1965. paper, $3.
Marcuse, Herbert. *Reason and Revolution.* 2nd ed. Humanities, 1968. $9.
Ogburn, William F. *Sociology.* 4th ed. Houghton, 1964. $11.
Roszak, Theodore. *Making of a Counterculture.* Doubleday, 1969. $8.
Rousseau, Jean J. *Social Contract; and Discourses.* Dutton, 1950. $4.
Schlesinger, Arthur M. *Crisis of Confidence.* Houghton, 1969. $6.
Swift, Henry. *Community Groups and You.* Day, 1964. $5.
Theodorson, George A. *Modern Dictionary of Sociology.* Crowell, 1969.
    $10.
Weber, Max. *Basic Concepts in Sociology.* Greenwood, 1962. $8.
Yoors, Jan. *Gypsies.* S&S, 1967. $7.

301.1   SOCIAL PSYCHOLOGY
Bettelheim, Bruno. *Social Change and Prejudice.* Free Press, 1964. $9.
Commoner, Barry. *Closing Circle.* Knopf, 1971. $7.
Cook, Bruce. *Beat Generation.* Scribner, 1971. $7.
Drucker, Peter. *Age of Discontinuity.* Harper, 1969. $8.
Gardner, John W. *Self-Renewal.* Harper, 1964. $5.
Hardin, Garrett. *Stalking the Wild Taboo.* Kaufmann, 1973. $9.
Hoffer, Eric. *Ordeal of Change.* Harper, 1963. $5.
Howard, Jane. *Please Touch.* McGraw, 1970. $7.

Lens, Sidney. *Radicalism in America.* new ed. Crowell, 1969. $10.
Roberts, Ron. *The New Communes.* Prentice, 1971. paper, $2.
Somewhere Else: A Living-Learning Catalog. Swallow, 1973. $6.
Sorenson, Thomas C. *Word War: Story of American Propaganda.* Harper, 1968. $8.
Toffler, Alvin. *Future Shock.* Random, 1970. $9.
Winick, Charles. *Lively Commerce: Prostitution in the United States.* Quadrangle, 1971. $9.

301.3   POPULATION

Bettelheim, Bruno. *Children of the Dream.* Macmillan, 1969. $7.
Ehrlich, Paul R. *Population Bomb.* Sierra, 1969. $6.
Hart, Harold. *Population Control.* Hart, 1973. $8.
Hauser, Philip M. *Population Dilemma.* 2nd ed. Prentice, 1970. paper, $3.
Hollingshead, A. *Elmstown's Youth.* Wiley, 1949. $6.
Longgood, William. *Darkening Land.* S&S, 1972. $10.
Lynd, Robert. *Middletown.* Harcourt. paper, $4.
_____. *Middletown in Transition.* Harcourt. paper, $4.
Malthus, Thomas R. *Population.* Michigan, 1959. $5.
Morris, Desmond. *Human Zoo.* McGraw, 1969. $7.
Osburn, Fairfield. *Our Crowded Planet.* Doubleday, 1962. $5.
Packard, Vance O. *Nation of Strangers.* McKay, 1972. $8.
Reich, Charles A. *Greening of America.* Random, 1970. $8.
Ridley, Anthony. *Living in Cities.* John Day, 1972. $8.
Ward, Barbara. *Only One Earth.* Norton, 1972. $6.
Wood, Robert C. *Suburbia.* Houghton. $6.

301.4   GROUPS

Baltzell, E. Digby. *Protestant Establishment.* Random, 1964. $10.
Berne, Eric. *Games People Play.* Grove, 1964. $5.
Dollard, John. *Caste and Class in a Southern Town.* Peter Smith. $5.
Gans, Herbert J. *Levittowners.* Pantheon, 1967. $10.
Huenefeld, John. *Community Activist's Handbook.* Beacon, 1970. $6.
Mills, C. Wright. *White Collar.* Oxford, 1956. paper, $3.
Packard, Vance O. *Status Seekers.* McKay, 1959. $8.

301.41   WOMEN

Bird, Caroline. *Born Female.* McKay, 1970. $6.
Boston Women's Health Book Collective. *Our Bodies, Ourselves.* S&S, 1973. $9.
Cooke, Joanne. *New Women.* Bobbs, 1970. $6.
DeBeauvoir, Simone. *Second Sex.* Mod. Library, 1953. $5.
DeCrow, Karen. *Young Woman's Guide to Liberation.* Pegasus, 1971. $5.
Flezner, Eleanor. *Century of Struggle.* Harvard, 1959. $12.

Friedan, Betty. *Feminine Mystique*. Norton, 1963. $8.

Greer, Germaine. *Female Eunuch*. McGraw, 1971. $7.

Harris, Janet. *Single Standard*. McGraw, 1971. $5.

Janeway, Elizabeth. *Man's World, Woman's Place*. Morrow, 1971. $9.

Kanowitz, Leo. *Women and the Law*. New Mexico, 1969. $9.

Koedt, Anne. *Radical Feminism*. Quadrangle, 1973. $10.

Mill, John S. *On Liberty, Representative Government, the Subjugation of Women*. Oxford, 1912. $3.

Millet, Kate. *Sexual Politics*. Avon, 1971. paper, $3.

Montagu, Ashley. *Natural Superiority of Women*. rev. ed. Macmillan, 1968. $7.

Morgan, Robin. *Sisterhood Is Powerful*. Random, 1970. $9.

O'Brien, Patricia. *The Woman Alone*. Quadrangle, 1973. $8.

Reische, Diana. *Women and Society*. Wilson, 1972. $5.

Seaman, Barbara. *Free and Female*. Coward, 1972. $7.

Sullerot, Evelyne. *Woman, Society and Change*. McGraw, 1971. $5.

301.42 FAMILY

Blaine, Graham B. *Are Parents Bad for Children?* Coward, 1973. $6.

Bowman, Henry D. *Marriage for Moderns*. 6th ed. McGraw, 1970. $11.

Brothers, Joyce. *Brothers' System for Liberated Love and Marriage*. Wyden, 1972. $8.

Callahan, Sidney C. *Working Mother*. Macmillan, 1971. $6.

Cole, Larry. *Our Children's Keepers*. Grossman, 1972. $7.

Cotton, Dorothy W. *Case for the Working Mother*. Stein, 1965. $5.

DeCourcy, Peter. *Silent Tragedy*. Alfred, 1973. $8.

Fletcher, Grace N. *What's Right with Our Young People?* Morrow, 1966. $6.

Fontana, V. J. *Maltreated Child*. 2nd ed. Thomas, 1971. $7.

Gil, David. *Violence Against Children*. Harvard, 1970. $7.

Hechinger, Grace. *Teenage Tyranny*. Morrow, 1963. $7.

Helfer, Ray E. *Battered Child*. Chicago, 1968. $13.

Hunt, Morton M. *World of the Formerly Married*. McGraw, 1966. $9.

Kempe, C. H. *Helping the Battered Child and His Family*. Lippincott, 1972. $9.

Kenniston, Kenneth. *Uncommitted*. Harcourt, 1965. $9.

_____ . *Young Radicals*. Harcourt, 1968. $7.

Landis, Paul H. *Making the Most of Marriage*. 4th ed. Appleton, 1970. $11.

Lederer, William J. *Mirages of Marriage*. Norton, 1968. $10.

Lukas, J. Anthony. *Don't Shoot—We Are Your Children*. Random, 1971. $9.

McGinnis, Tom. *Your First Year of Marriage*. Doubleday. $6.

Mead, Margaret. *Culture and Commitment*. Natural History, 1970. $5.

Neisser, Edith. *Mothers and Daughters*. Harper, 1970. $10.

Nye, F. Ivan. *Family*. Macmillan, 1973. $11.

Packard, Vance O. *Sexual Wilderness*. McKay, 1968. $7.

Pierce, Ruth I. *Single and Pregnant.* Beacon, 1971. $6.

Richette, Lisa A. *Throwaway Children.* Lippincott, 1969. $8.

Rogers, Carl. *Becoming Partners.* Dell, 1972. $3.

Ryan, William. *Blaming the Victim.* Pantheon, 1970. $8.

Seligson, Marcia. *Eternal Bliss Machine.* Morrow, 1973. $8.

Sheen, Fulton J. *Children and Parents.* S&S, 1970. $5.

Sheresky, N., and Mannes, M. *Uncoupling: The Art of Coming Apart.* Viking, 1972. $7.

Spock, Benjamin. *Problems of Parents.* Houghton, 1962. $5.

Van de Velde, Theodore. *Ideal Marriage.* Random, 1965. $8.

Winter, Elmer. *Women at Work.* S&S, 1967. $6.

Young, Leontine. *Wednesday's Children.* McGraw, 1971. $6.

301.43 AGING, RETIREMENT

Buckley, Joseph C. *Retirement Handbook.* rev. ed. Harper, 1971. $8.

Collins, Thomas. *Complete Guide to Retirement.* Prentice, 1972. paper, $3.

Curtin, Sharon. *Nobody Ever Died of Old Age.* Little, 1973. $7.

Field, Minna. *Aging with Honor and Dignity.* Thomas, 1968. $9.

Hoffman, Adeline M. *Daily Needs and Interests of Older People.* Thomas, 1970. $17.

May, Siegmund H. *Crowning Years.* Lippincott, 1969. $4.

Nader, Ralph. *You and Your Pension.* Grossman, 1972. $6.

Pitkin, Walter B. *Life Begins at Fifty.* S&S, 1965. $5.

Stern, Edith M. *You and Your Aging Parents.* rev. ed. Harper, 1965. $6.

Stonecypher, D. D., Jr. *Getting Older and Staying Young.* Norton, 1974. $9.

Taylor, Robert E. *Feeling Alive After 65.* Arlington, 1974. $8.

301.45 ETHNIC GROUPS

Baldwin, James. *Notes of a Native Son.* Dial, 1955. $5.

Billingsley, Andrew. *Black Families in White America.* Prentice, 1968. $5.

Clark, Kenneth B. *Dark Ghetto.* Harper, 1965. $6.

DuBois, W. E. B. *Souls of Black Folk.* Dodd, 1970. $6.

Frazier, E. Franklin. *Negro Family in the United States.* abr. ed. Chicago, 1966. $6.

Griffin, John H. *Black Like Me.* Houghton, 1961. $5.

Johnson, James W. *Autobiography of an Ex-Coloured Man.* Knopf, 1927. $6.

Lester, Julius. *Look Out Whitey! Black Power's Gon' Get Your Mama.* Dial, 1968. $4.

Lewis, Oscar. *Children of Sanchez.* Random, 1961. $13.

Meier, Matt S. *Chicanos.* Hill, 1972. $7.

Parks, Gordon. *Born Black.* Lippincott, 1971. $9.

Rendon, Armando B. *Chicano Manifesto.* Macmillan, 1971. $8.

Seale, Bobby. *Sieze the Time.* Random, 1970. $7.

Silberman, Charles E. *Crisis in Black and White.* Random, 1964. $6.
Steiner, Stan. *La Raza.* Harper, 1970. $9.
Teague, Bob. *Letters to a Black Boy.* Walker, 1968. $5.
Young, Whitney. *Beyond Racism.* McGraw, 1969. $7.

320   POLITICAL SCIENCE

Arendt, Hannah. *Origins of Totalitarianism.* rev. ed. Harcourt, 1966. $10.
Barker, Elizabeth. *Cold War.* Putnam, 1972. $6.
Cohen, Carl. *Communism, Fascism and Democracy.* 2nd ed. Random, 1972. $7.
De Tocqueville, Alexis. *Democracy in America.* Oxford, 1947. $4.
Epstein, Jason. *Great Conspiracy Trial.* Random, 1970. $8.
Hecksher, Gunnar. *Study of Comparative Government and Politics.* Greenwood, 1973. $9.
Key, Vladimir O. *Public Opinion and American Democracy.* Knopf, 1961. $12.
Kohn, Hans. *Nationalism.* rev. ed. Van Nostrand, 1965. paper, $3.
Lester, Julius. *Revolutionary Notes.* R. W. Baron, 1969. $6.
Locke, John. *Two Treatises of Civil Government.* Dutton, 1960. $4.
Machiavelli, Niccolo. *Prince; and Discourses.* Mod. Library. paper, $2.
Magrath, C. Peter. *American Democracy.* Macmillan, 1969. $10.
Meyer, Franks. *What Is Conservatism?* Holt, 1964. $5.
Mill, C. Wright. *Power Elite.* Oxford, 1956. $11.
More, Thomas. *Utopia.* Dutton, 1973. paper, $3.
Rossiter, Clinton L. *Conservatism in America.* 2nd ed. Knopf, 1962. $7.
————. *Seedtime of the Republic.* Harcourt, 1953. $11.
Schwartz, Barry N. *White Racism.* Dell, 1970. paper, $2.
Skinner, B. F. *Walden Two.* Macmillan, 1960. paper, $3.
Verba, Sidney. *Small Groups and Political Behavior.* Princeton, 1961. $9.
Ward, Barbara. *Nationalism and Ideology.* Norton, 1966. $4.

323.4   CIVIL RIGHTS, CITY PROBLEMS

Bain, Carolyn. *It's Easy to Become a Citizen.* Hawthorn, 1968. $4.
Cohen, Carl. *Civil Disobedience.* Columbia, 1971. $8.
Conot, Robert E. *Rivers of Blood, Years of Darkness.* Morrow, 1968. $8.
Downs, Robert B. *First Freedom.* ALA, 1960. $9.
Ernst, Morris L. *Censorship.* Macmillan, 1964. $7.
Fraenkel, Osmond K. *Rights We Have.* Crowell, 1971. $6.
Isenberg, Irwin. *City in Crisis.* Wilson, 1968. $5.
Konvitz, Milton. *Expanding Liberties.* Viking, 1966. $9.
Lewis, Anthony. *Portrait of a Decade.* Random, 1964. $10.
Liston, Robert A. *Downtown.* Delacorte, 1970. $5.
McClellan, Grant S. *Censorship in the United States.* Wilson, 1967. $5.
————. *Civil Rights.* Wilson, 1964. $5.

Mumford, Lewis. *City in History.* Harcourt, 1968. $15.
Steffens, Lincoln. *Shame of the Cities.* Peter Smith, 1959. $4.
Thompson, Wilbur R. *Preface to Urban Economics.* Johns Hopkins, 1968. $9.

325   IMMIGRATION

Fellows, Donald K. *Mosaic of America's Ethnic Minorities.* Wiley, 1972. paper, $5.
Fermi, Laura. *Illustrious Immigrants.* 2nd ed. Chicago, 1971. $8.
Glazer, Nathan. *Beyond the Melting Pot.* 2nd ed. MIT, 1970. $10.
Handlin, Oscar. *Children of the Uprooted.* Braziller, 1966. $9.
Huthmacher, J. Joseph. *Nation of Newcomers.* Delacorte, 1969. $4.
Marden, Charles F. *Minorities in American Society.* 4th ed. Van Nostrand, 1973. $8.
Neidle, Cecyle S. *New Americans.* Twayne, 1968. $6.
Wittke, Carl. *We Who Built America.* rev. ed. Case Western, 1967. $8.

326   AFRO-AMERICANS

Elkins, Stanley M. *Slavery.* 2nd ed. Chicago, 1968. $5.
Fanon, Frantz. *Black Skins, White Masks.* Grove, 1967. $5.
Fishel, Leslie. *Black American: a Documentary History.* rev. ed. Morrow, 1970. $10.
Franklin, John H. *From Slavery to Freedom.* Knopf, 1967. $12.
Frazier, E. Franklin. *Negro in the United States.* rev. ed. Macmillan, 1957. $10.
Lester, Julius. *Search for the New Land.* Dial, 1969. $5.
_____. *To Be a Slave.* Dial, 1968. $5.

327   INTERNATIONAL RELATIONS

Fisher, Roger D. *International Conflict for Beginners.* Harper, 1969. $6.
Galbraith, John K. *Ambassador's Journal.* Houghton, 1969. $10.
Kennan, George F. *Russia and the West under Lenin and Stalin.* Little, 1961. $9.
Kohler, Foy D. *Understanding the Russians.* Harper, 1970. $10.
Plano, Jack C. *International Relations Dictionary.* Holt, 1969. paper, $5.
Salisbury, Harrison. *War between Russia and China.* Norton, 1969. $5.
Servan-Schreiber, J. J. *American Challenge.* Atheneum, 1968. $7.
Steel, Ronald. *Pax Americana.* rev. ed. Viking, 1967. $7.

328   PARLIAMENTARY PROCEDURE

Davidson, Henry A. *Handbook of Parliamentary Procedure.* 2nd ed. Ronald, 1968. $5.
Long, Fern. *All about Meetings.* Oceana, 1967. $5.
Robert, Henry M. *Robert's Rules of Order.* 3rd rev. ed. Morrow, 1971. $7.

329   POLITICS, ELECTIONS

Aristotle. *Politics.* Harvard, 1932. $5.

Barone, Michael. *Almanac of American Politics.* rev. ed. Houghton, 1973. $15.

Binkley, Wilfred E. *American Political Parties.* 4th rev. ed. Knopf, 1963. $8.

Chalmers, David M. *Hooded Americanism.* Doubleday, 1965. $6.

Chambers, William N. *Democratic Party in American Politics.* 2nd ed. Van Nostrand, 1972. paper, $3.

Chester, Lewis. *American Melodrama: Presidential Campaign of 1968.* Viking, 1969. $10.

Hamilton, Alexander. *Federalist.* Dutton. $4.

Hesseltine, William B. *Third Party Movements in the United States.* Van Nostrand, 1962. paper, $2.

Key, Vladimer O. *Politics, Parties and Pressure Groups.* 5th ed. Crowell. $10.

McGinniss, Joe. *Selling of the President, 1968.* Trident, 1969. $6.

Paine, Thomas. *Common Sense and Other Political Writings.* Bobbs, 1953. paper, $2.

Plano, Jack C. *American Political Dictionary.* Holt, 1967. $7.

Porter, Kirk H. *National Party Platforms, 1840–1968.* 4th ed. Illinois, 1970. $13.

Roseboom, Eugene H. *History of Presidential Elections.* rev. ed. Macmillan, 1970. $10.

Scammon, Richard M. *Real Majority.* Coward, 1970. $8.

White House Transcripts. Bantam, 1974. paper, $3.

Wynar, Lubomyr R. *American Political Parties.* Libs. Unl., 1969. $14.

330   ECONOMICS

Ashton, Thomas S. *Industrial Revolution, 1760–1830.* Oxford, 1948. paper, $4.

Chamberlain, John. *Enterprising Americans.* rev. ed. Harper, 1974. $9.

Chandler, Lester V. *America's Greatest Depression.* Harper, 1970. $8.

Faulkner, Harold U. *American Economic History.* Harper, 1960. $14

Friedberg, Robert. *Paper Money of the United States.* rev. ed. Coin & Currency, 1972. $14.

Galbraith, John K. *Affluent Society.* 2nd ed. Houghton, 1969. $7.

——. *Great Crash.* 3rd ed. Houghton, 1972. $6.

Harrington, Michael. *Other America: Poverty in the United States.* rev. ed. Macmillan, 1970. $7.

Heilbroner, Robert L. *Economic Problem.* 3rd ed. Prentice, 1972. $11.

——. *Primer on Government Spending.* 2nd ed. Random, 1970. $6.

——. *Worldly Philosophers.* S&S $8.

Kraus, Albert L. *New York Times Guide to Business and Finance.* Harper, 1972. $9.

Lekachman, Robert. *Age of Keynes.* Random, 1966. $9.
Lens, Sidney. *Poverty: America's Enduring Paradox.* Crowell, 1969. $9.
Paradis, Adrian. *Hungry Years.* Chilton, 1967. $5.
Ricardo, David. *Principles of Political Economy and Taxation.* Dutton, 1973. paper, $3.
Samuelson, Paul A. *Economics.* 9th ed. McGraw, 1973. $12.
Smith, Adam. *Wealth of Nations.* Mod. Library, 1937. $5.

331   LABOR, CAREERS

Broehl, Wayne G. *Molly Maguires.* Harvard, 1964. $11.
Brooks, Thomas R. *Toil and Trouble.* Delacorte, 1971. $8.
Cohen, Sanford. *Labor in the United States.* 3rd ed. Merrill, 1970. $12.
Dulles, Foster. *Labor in America.* 3rd ed. Crowell, 1966. $10.
Janeway, Eliot. *Economics of Crisis.* Weybright. $10.
Keynes, John M. *General Theory of Employment, Interest and Money.* Harcourt. $9.
Lens, Sidney. *Labor Wars.* Doubleday, 1973. $10.
Lovejoy, Clarence E. *Lovejoy's Career and Vocational Guide.* S&S, 1973. $8
Moore, Truman E. *Slaves We Rent.* Random, 1965. $8.
Peterson, Florence. *American Labor Unions.* 2nd ed. Harper, 1963. $7.
Schwartz, Alvin. *Unions.* Viking, 1972. $7.
Summer Employment Directory. Nat'l Dir. Serv., published annually. $6.
Terkel, Studs. *Working.* Pantheon, 1974. $10.
U.S. Bureau of Labor Statistics. *Occupational Outlook Handbook.* U.S. Govt. Printing Off., published annually. $7.
Veblen, Thorstein. *Theory of the Leisure Class.* Houghton, 1973. $7.

332   INVESTMENT, PERSONAL FINANCE

Berstein, Peter L. *Primer on Money, Banking and Gold.* Random, 1968. $5.
Dacey, Norman F. *How to Avoid Probate.* Crown, 1965. $5.
Engel, Louis. *How to Buy Stocks.* 5th rev. ed. Little, 1971. $8.
Graham, Benjamin. *Intelligent Investor.* 4th rev. ed. Harper, 1973. $8.
Kent, Raymond P. *Money and Banking.* 6th ed. Holt, 1972. $13.
Lasser, Jacob K. *Managing Your Family Finances.* rev. ed. Doubleday, 1973. $6.
_____. *Your Income Tax.* S&S, annual. paper, $2.
Loeb, Gerald M. *Battle for Stock Market Profits.* S&S, 1971. $7.
Low, Janet. *Understanding the Stock Market.* Little, 1968. $5.
Nuccio, Sal. *New York Times Guide to Personal Finance.* Harper, 1968. $5.
Smith, Adam. *Money Game.* Random, 1968. $7.
Smith, Carlton. *Time-Life Book of Family Finance.* Time, 1969. $12.
Watkins, Art. *Dollars and Sense.* Quadrangle, 1973. $8.

333   REAL ESTATE
Campbell, Don G. *Handbook of Real Estate Investment*. Bobbs, 1968. $8.
Dasmann, Raymond F. *Environmental Conservation*. 3rd ed. Wiley, 1972.
    $11.
Griffin, Al. *So You Want to Buy a House*. Regnery, 1970. $6.
_____. *So You Want to Buy a Mobile Home*. Regnery, 1970. $6.
McMichael, Stanley L. *How to Make Money in Real Estate*. 3rd ed. Prentice,
    1968. $9.
Semenow, Robert W. *Questions and Answers on Real Estate*. 7th ed. Pren-
    tice, 1972. $10.
Tyler, Poyntz. *Securities, Exchanges and the S.E.C.* Wilson, 1965. $5.

333.7   CONSERVATION
Marine, Gene. *America, the Raped*. S&S, 1969. $6.
Miller, Herman P. *Rich Man, Poor Man*. Crowell, 1971. $9.
Udall, Stewart L. *Quiet Crisis*. Holt, 1963. $7.
Zwick, David. *Water Wasteland*. Grossman, 1971. $8.

335   COMMUNISM, SOCIALISM
Daniels, Robert V. *Nature of Communism*. Random, 1962. $10.
Djilas, Milovan. *New Class*. Praeger, 1957. $6.
Ebenstein, William. *Today's Isms*. 7th ed. Prentice, 1973. $8.
Hedgepeth, William. *Alternative: Communal Life*. Macmillan, 1970. $8.
Houriet, Robert. *Getting Back Together*. Coward, 1971. $8.
Ketchum, Richard M. *What Is Communism?* Dutton, 1963. $7.
Lawson, Donna. *Brothers and Sisters All Over This Land*. Praeger, 1972. $7.
Marx, Karl. *Das Kapital*. abr. ed. Regnery. paper, $3.
_____. *Communist Manifesto*. Pantheon, 1967. $6.
Salvadori, Massimo. *Rise of Modern Communism*. rev. ed. Peter Smith,
    1963. $5.

338   CONSUMERS AND PRODUCTS
Ashabranner, Brent. *Moment in History*. Doubleday, 1971. $8.
Cochran, Willard W. *World Food Problem*. Crowell, 1969. $8.
Coles, Robert. *Still Hungry in America*. NAL, 1973. $9.
Freeman, Orville L. *World without Hunger*. Praeger, 1968. $6.
McClellan, Grant S. *Consuming Public*. Wilson, 1968. $5.
Packard, Vance O. *Waste Makers*. McKay, 1960. $8.
Ward, Barbara. *Rich Nations and Poor Nations*. Norton, 1962. paper, $2.

340   LAW
Bloom, Murray. *Trouble with Lawyers*. S&S, 1969. $7.
Bloomstein, Morris J. *Verdict: the Jury System*. rev. ed. Dodd, 1968. $4.
Boylan, Brian R. *The Legal Rights of Women*. Award, 1971. paper, $1.

Douglas, William O. *Anatomy of Liberty*. S&S, 1967. $5.
East, Sara T. *Law in American Society*. Wilson, 1963. $5.
Levine, Alan. *The Rights of Students*. R. W. Baron, 1973. $5.
McCart, Samuel W. *Trial by Jury*. Chilton, 1965. $5.
Norwick, Kenneth P. *Your Legal Rights*. John Day, 1972. $8.
Williams, Edward B. *One Man's Freedom*. Atheneum, 1962. $6.

341 UNITED NATIONS
Calder, Nigel. *Unless Peace Comes*. Viking, 1968. $6.
Eichelberger, Clark M. *U.N.: the First 25 Years*. 4th ed. Harper, 1970. $6.
Everyman's United Nations. 8th ed. United Nations, 1968. $6.
Wadsworth, James. *Glass House*. Praeger, 1966. $6.

342 CONSTITUTIONAL LAW
Beard, Charles A. *Economic Interpretation of the Constitution of the United States*. Macmillan, 1935. $7.
Bowen, Catherine D. *Miracle at Philadelphia*. Little, 1966. $10.
Cushman, Robert E. *Leading Constitutional Decisions*. 14th ed. Appleton, 1971. $8.
Garraty, John A. *Quarrels That Have Shaped the Constitution*. Harper, 1964. $5.
Kelly, Alfred H. *American Constitution*. 4th ed. Norton, 1972. $12.
Murphy, Paul L. *Constitution in Crisis Times*. Harper, 1972. $10.

347 CRIMINAL LAW, EVERYDAY LAW, THE COURTS
Aymar, Brandt. *Pictorial History of the World's Great Trials*. Crown, 1967. $10.
Bedau, Hugh A. *Death Penalty in America*. Aldine, 1968. $10.
Black, Henry C. *Black's Law Dictionary*. West, 1968. $15.
Brower, David. *Only a Little Planet*. McGraw, 1972. $13.
Callahan, Parnell. *Your Complete Guide to Estate Planning*. Oceana, 1971. $8.
Clark, Ramsey. *Crime in America*. S&S, 1970. $7.
Colby, Edward E. *Everything You Always Wanted to Know about the Law but Couldn't Afford to Ask*. Drake, 1972. $7.
Farmer, Robert. *How to Adopt a Child*. 2nd ed. Arco, 1968. $5.
——. *How to Avoid Problems with Your Will*. Arco, 1968. $5.
Horwitz, Elinor L. *Capital Punishment, U.S.A.* Lippincott, 1973. $5.
Kling, Samuel G. *Complete Guide to Everyday Law*. 3rd ed. Follett, 1973. $10
Leavy, Morton L. *Law of Adoption*. 3rd ed. Oceana, 1968. $4.
Lineberry, William P. *Justice in America*. Wilson, 1972. $5.
McCafferty, James A. *Capital Punishment*. Lieber, 1972. $8.
Mayer, Martin. *Lawyers*. Harper, 1967. $9.

Nelson, Jack. *FBI and the Berrigans.* Coward, 1972. $8.
Nizer, Louis. *Implosion Conspiracy.* Doubleday, 1973. $10.
_____. *My Life in Court.* Pyramid, 1972. paper, $2.
Ross, Martin J. *Handbook of Everyday Law.* Harper, 1973. $8
Sellin, Thorsten. *Capital Punishment.* Harper, 1967. $5.
Sparrow, John. *After the Assassination.* Chilmark, 1968. $4.
Time-Life Books. *Time-Life Family Legal Guide.* Time, 1971. $12.
Weeks, Robert P. *Commonwealth vs. Sacco and Vanzetti.* Prentice, 1958.
   $4.

351.3   CIVIL SERVICE EXAMINATIONS

The Arco series of Civil Service exams is excellent and is revised frequently.
Check publisher and/or BIP for latest editions of those titles which are
needed on individual job tests. The following are general:

Arco Publ. Co. *Civil Service Arithmetic and Vocabulary.* 6th ed. Arco, 1967
   $6.
_____. *Federal Service Entrance Examinations.* 8th ed. Arco, 1972. $8.
Turner, David R. *Homestudy Courses for Civil Service Jobs.* Arco, 1965. $8.
Turner, Edward R. *Practice for Clerical, Typing and Stenographic Tests.* 4th
   ed. Arco, 1972. $9.

351.7   POLICE, ESPIONAGE

Archer, Jules. *Treason in America.* Hawthorn, 1971. $6.
Chambers, Whittaker. *Witness.* Random, 1952. $10.
Cook, Fred J. *FBI Nobody Knows.* Pyramid, 1972. paper, $2.
Dulles, Allen. *Craft of Intelligence.* Harper, 1963. $8.
Reiss, Albert J. *Police and the Public.* Yale, 1971. $9.
Rosenthal, Abraham M. *38 Witnesses.* McGraw, 1964. $3.
Soderman, Harry. *Modern Criminal Investigation.* 5th ed. F&W, 1962. $10.
Tully, Andrew. *FBI's Most Famous Cases.* Morrow, 1966. $6.
Wilson, Orlando W. *Police Administration.* 3rd ed. McGraw, 1972. $12.

353   AMERICAN GOVERNMENT

Black, Charles L., Jr. *Impeachment: A Handbook.* Yale, 1974. $6.
Burns, James M. *Government by the People: National, State and Local
   Edition.* 8th ed. Prentice, 1972. $11.
Caldwell, Gaylon L. *American Government Today.* rev. ed. Norton, 1969.
   $8.
Corwin, Edward S. *President: Office and Powers.* 4th ed. NYU, 1957. $10.
Goodman, Walter. *Committee: the Extraordinary Career of the House Com-
   mittee on Un-American Activities.* Farrar, 1968. $14.
Griffith, Ernest S. *Congress.* 4th ed. NYU, 1967. $10.
Harris, Joseph P. *Congress and the Legislative Process.* McGraw, 1972. $6.

Koenig, Louis W. *Chief Executive*. Harcourt, 1968. $7.
Kotler, Milton. *Neighborhood Government*. Bobbs, 1969. $5.
Morrow, William L. *Congressional Committees*. Scribner, 1969. $7.
Neustadt, Richard E. *Presidential Power*. Wiley, 1960. $6.
Ogg, Frederic A. *Introduction to American National Government*. 13th ed. Appleton. $11.
Polsby, Nelson W. *Congress and the Presidency*. 2nd ed. Prentice, 1971. $7.
Rossiter, Clinton. *American Presidency*. Harcourt, 1960. paper, $3.
Schlesinger, Arthur M. *Imperial Presidency*. Houghton, 1973. $13.
United States Government Organization Manual. U.S. Govt. Printing Off., published annually. paper, $6.
White, Leonard D. *Jacksonians*. Macmillan, 1954. $7.
White, William S. *Citadel: Story of the U.S. Senate*. Houghton, 1968. $5.
Young, Donald. *American Roulette: History and Dilemma of the Vice Presidency*. Holt, 1965. $8.

355   MILITARY

Arco Publ. Co. *Practice for the Armed Forces Tests*. 8th ed. Arco, 1973. $8.
_____. *U.S. Service Academy Admission Tests*. 2nd ed. Arco, 1966. $6.
Just, Ward. *Military Men*. Knopf, 1971. $7.
Kannik, Preben. *Military Uniforms of the World in Color*. Macmillan, 1968. $5.
Kerrigan, Evans E. *American Badges and Insignia*. Viking, 1967. $8.
_____. *American War Medals and Decorations*. rev. ed. Viking, 1971. $7.
Tunis, Edwin. *Weapons: a Pictorial History*. World, 1954. $4. (May be updated with various Arco books and series like Bantam's *Knowledge Through Color*.)
Weigley, Russell F. *History of the United States Army*. Macmillan, 1967. $13.

360   SOCIAL AGENCIES

Davis, Kenneth S. *Paradox of Poverty in America*. Wilson, 1969. $5.
Greenberg, Selig. *Quality of Mercy*. Atheneum, 1971. $7.
Kennedy, Edward M. *In Critical Condition*. Pocket Bks, 1973. paper, $2.
Piven, Frances F. *Regulating the Poor*. Pantheon, 1971. $10.

364   CRIME, PRISONS

Capote, Truman. *In Cold Blood*. Random, 1966. $7.
Charriere, Henri. *Banco*. Morrow. $8.
_____. *Papillon*. Morrow, 1970. $9.
Epstein, Edward J. *Inquest*. Viking, 1966. $5.
Gage, Nicholas. *Mafia Is Not an Equal Opportunity Employer*. McGraw, 1971. $6.
Lewin, Stephen. *Crime and Its Prevention*. Wilson, 1968. $5.

Maas, Peter. *Valachi Papers*. Putnam, 1968. $7.
Menninger, Karl. *Crime of Punishment*. Viking, 1968. $7.
Mitford, Jessica. *Kind and Usual Punishment*. Knopf, 1973. $8.
Sands, Bill. *My Shadow Ran Fast*. Prentice, 1964. $7.
Sereny, Gitta. *Case of Mary Bell*. McGraw, 1973. $8.
Talese, Guy. *Honor Thy Father*. World, 1971. paper, $2.
Wambaugh, Joseph. *Onion Field*. Delacorte, 1973. $9.

367   SOCIAL CLUBS

Hegarty, Edward J. *How to Run Better Meetings*. McGraw, 1957. $10.
MacKenzie, Norman. *Secret Societies*. Holt, 1968. $10.
Seymour, Harold J. *Designs for Fund Raising*. McGraw, 1966. $8.
Stern, Renee B. *Club Handybook*. rev. ed. Sterling, 1973. $4.

368   INSURANCE

Chernik, Vladimir P. *Consumer's Guide to Insurance Buying*. Sherbourne,
     1970. $7.
Gillespie, Paul. *No-Fault*. Praeger, 1972. $6.
U.S. News & World Report, eds. *Social Security and Medicare Simplified*.
     Macmillan, 1970. $6.

370   EDUCATION

Arco Publ. Co. *High School Equivalency Diploma Tests*. Arco, published
     biannually. $9.
Barron's Guide to the Two-Year Colleges. rev. ed. Barron, 1972. $8.
Barron's How to Prepare for College Entrance Examinations. 5th ed. Bar-
     ron, 1973. $9.
Barzun, Jacques. *American University*. Harper, 1968. $8.
Bond, Guy L. *Teaching the Child to Read*. 4th ed. Macmillan, 1966. $10.
Bruner, Jerome S. *Process of Education*. Harvard, 1960. $3.
Cass, James. *Comparative Guide to American Colleges 1973–74*. 6th ed.
     Harper, 1973. $6.
Conant, James B. *Comprehensive High School*. McGraw, 1967. $4.
Cruickshank, William M. *Education of Exceptional Children and Youth*.
     2nd ed. Prentice, 1967. $13.
Dewey, John. *Democracy and Education*. Free Press, 1966. paper, $3.
_____. *On Education*. Mod. Library. $3.
Ehrlich, Eugene H. *How to Study Better and Get Higher Marks*. Crowell,
     1961. $6.
Fine, Benjamin. *Underachievers*. Dutton, 1967. $7.
Ginott, Haim G. *Teacher and Child*. Macmillan, 1972. $6.
Good, Harry G. *History of American Education*. 2nd ed. Macmillan, 1962.
     $10.

Guide to Summer Camps and Summer Schools. Sargent, published annually. $5.

Hart, Jane. *Where's Hannah?* Hart, 1970. $9.

Herndon, James. *Way It 'Spozed to Be*. S&S, 1968, $5.

Holt, John. *How Children Fail*. Pitman, 1964. $5.

―――. *How Children Learn*. Pitman, 1969. $5.

―――. *What Do I Do Monday?* Dutton, 1970. $8.

Hutchins, Robert M. *Learning Society*. Praeger, 1968. $5.

Keeslar, Oreon. *National Catalog of Financial Aids for Higher Education*. 6th ed. W. C. Brown, 1974. $9.

Kohl, Herbert. *36 Children*. Norton, 1968. $6.

Kozol, Jonathan. *Death at an Early Age*. Houghton, 1967. $6.

Kraus, Philip E. *Yesterday's Children*. Wiley, 1973. $10.

LeShan, Eda J. *Conspiracy against Childhood*. Atheneum, 1967. paper, $4.

Lindgren, Henry C. *Educational Psychology in the Classroom*. 4th ed. Wiley, 1972. $11.

Lovejoy, Clarence E. *Lovejoy's Career and Vocational School Guide*. S&S, 1973. $8.

―――. *Lovejoy's College Guide*. 13th ed., rev. biannually. S&S, 1974. $8.

Neill, Alexander S. *Summerhill*. Hart, 1960. $8.

Pines, Maya. *Revolution in Learning*. Harper, 1967. $6.

Roose, Kenneth D. *Rating of Graduate Programs*. Ace, 1970. $4.

Silberman, Charles E. *Crisis in the Classroom*. Random, 1970. $10.

Smith, Bert K. *Your Non-Learning Child*. Beacon, 1968. $5.

Totten, W. Fred. *Power of Community School Education*. Pendell, 1970. $8.

380 TRANSPORTATION, COMMUNICATION

Brown, Les. *Television*. Harcourt, 1971. $9.

Dunlap, Orrin E. *Communications in Space*. rev. ed. Harper, 1964. $8.

Ellis, Hamilton. *Pictorial Encyclopedia of Railways*. Crown, 1968. $10.

Hertz, Louis H. *Complete Book of Model Railroading*. rev. ed. Crown, 1971. $10.

Jacobs, David. *Bridges, Canals, and Tunnels*. Hale, 1968. $5.

Lineberry, William P. *Mass Communications*. Wilson, 1969. $5.

Sandman, Peter M. *Media*. Prentice, 1972. $9.

Skornia, Harry J. *Television and Society*. McGraw, 1965. $8.

Tunis, Edwin. *Wheels*. World, 1955. $7.

389 WEIGHTS AND MEASURES

DeSimone, Daniel V. *Metric America; a Decision Whose Time Has Come*. U.S. Govt. Printing Off., 1971. $3.

Donovan, Frank. *Prepare Now for a Metric Future*. Weybright, 1970. $6.

Gilbert, Thomas F. *Thinking Metrics*. Wiley, 1973. paper, $3.
Kelly, Gerard W. *Metric System Simplified*. Sterling, 1973. $3.

391   COSTUME
Evans, Mary. *Costume through the Ages*. 3rd ed. Lippincott, 1950. $9.
Gorsline, Douglas. *What People Wore*. Viking, 1952. $13.
Jackson, Sheila. *Simple Stage Costumes and How to Make Them*. Watson, 1969. $9.
Laver, James. *Concise History of Costume and Fashion*. Abrams, 1969. $9.
Snook, Barbara. *Costumes for Children*. Branford, 1970. $4.
Wilcox, E. Turner. *Five Centuries of American Costume*. Scribner, 1963. $13.

392   CUSTOMS, RITES, HOLIDAYS
Arisian, Khoren. *New Wedding*. Knopf, 1973. $8.
Bride's Magazine, eds. *Bride's Book of Etiquette*. rev. ed. Grosset. $6.
Brill, Mordecai L. *Write Your Own Wedding*. Association, 1973. $8.
Bryant, Flora F. *It's Your Wedding*. Regnery, 1970. $7.
Collier, John. *American Indian Ceremonial Dances*. new ed. Crown, 1972. $4.
Douglas, George W. *American Book of Days*. 2nd ed. Wilson, 1948. $10.
Gaster, Theodor H. *Festivals of the Jewish Year*. Peter Smith, 1962. $5.
Greer, Rebecca. *Book for Brides*. Arco, 1965. $4.
Hazeltine, Mary E. *Anniversaries and Holidays*. 2nd ed. ALA, 1944. $7.
Ickis, Marguerite. *Book of Religious Holidays and Celebrations*. Dodd, 1967. $5.
Leach, William H. *Cokesbury Marriage Manual*. Abingdon, 1959. $3.
Mitford, Jessica. *American Way of Death*. S&S, 1963. $5.
Spicer, Dorothy. *Book of Festivals*. Gale, 1969. $13.
Washington, Joseph R. *Marriage in Black and White*. Beacon, 1970. $8.
Waugh, Dorothy. *Festive Decorations the Year 'Round*. Macmillan, 1962. $4.
Wernecke, Herbert H. *Christmas Customs around the World*. Westminster, 1959. $4.
Wilson, Barbara. *Complete Book of Engagement and Wedding Etiquette*. Hawthorn, 1970. $7.

395   ETIQUETTE, GROOMING
Esquire, eds. *Book of Good Grooming for Men*. Grosset, 1969. $7.
————. *Esquire's Guide to Modern Etiquette*. rev. ed. Lippincott, 1969. $8.
Free, Anne R. *Social Usage*. 2nd ed. Appleton, 1970. $8.
Post, Emily P. *Etiquette*. F&W, 1969. $10.
Vanderbilt, Amy. *Amy Vanderbilt's Etiquette*. rev. ed. Doubleday, 1972. $8.

398   FOLKLORE

Ausubel, Nathan. *Treasury of Jewish Folklore*. Crown, 1948. $6.

Dorson, Richard. *American Folklore*. Chicago, 1959. $9.

Hughes, Langston. *Book of Negro Folklore*. Dodd, 1958. $8.

Maple, Eric. *Superstition and the Superstitious*. B&N, 1972. $9.

400

LANGUAGE

401   GENERAL

Chase, Stuart. *Power of Words.* Harcourt, 1954. $8.

Hayakawa, Samuel I. *Language in Thought and Action.* 3rd ed. Harcourt, 1972. $7.

Laird, Charlton. *Language in America.* World, 1970. $15.

Martinet, Andre. *Elements of General Linguistics.* Chicago, 1964. $7.

Ogg, Oscar. *26 Letters.* rev. ed. Crowell, 1971. $7.

Pei, Mario. *How to Learn Languages and What Languages to Learn.* rev. ed. Harper, 1973. $7.

――. *Language Today.* F&W, 1967. $6.

――. *Story of Language.* rev. ed. Lippincott, 1965. $8.

――. *Story of the English Language.* rev. ed. Lippincott, 1967. $8.

423   DICTIONARIES

American Heritage Dictionary of the English Language. Houghton, 1969. $9.

Funk & Wagnalls. *Standard College Dictionary.* new ed. F&W, 1968. $7.

Johnson, Burgess. *New Rhyming Dictionary and Poets' Handbook.* rev. ed. Harper, 1957. $6.

Roget's International Thesaurus. 3rd ed. Crowell, 1962. $6.

Webster, Noah. *Webster's Dictionary of Synonyms.* Merriam. $7.

Webster's New Collegiate Dictionary. rev. ed. Merriam, 1973. $9.

425   GRAMMAR

Aurbach, Joseph. *Transformational Grammar.* Eng. Lang., 1969. paper, $4.

Gerould, Gordon H. *Patterns in English.* Russell, 1966. $11.

Myers, Louis M. *Guide to American English.* 5th ed. Prentice, 1972. $8.

Opdycke, John B. *Harper's English Grammar.* Harper, 1966. $6.

Pence, Raymond W. *Grammar of Present-Day English.* 2nd ed. Macmillan, 1963. $8.

Roberts, Paul. *Understanding Grammar.* Harper, 1954. $8.

428   USAGE

Dillard, Joey L. *Black English.* Random, 1972. $10.

Fowler, Henry W. *Dictionary of Modern Usage.* 2nd ed. Oxford, 1965. $8.

Funk, Peter V. *It Pays to Increase Your Word Power.* F&W, 1968. $5.

Jordan, June M. *Soulscript.* Doubleday, 1970. $4.

Landy, Eugene E. *Underground Dictionary.* S&S, 1971. $6.

Lewis, Norman. *Thirty Days to Better English.* Doubleday, 1973. $5.

_____. *Word Power Made Easy.* Doubleday, 1949. $5.

Mencken, H. L. *American Language.* 4th ed., 3 vols. 2 suppls. Knopf, 1936/ 48. set, $45.

Morsberger, Robert E. *Commonsense Grammar and Style.* 2nd rev. ed. Crowell, 1972. $9.

Nurnberg, Maxwell. *All about Words.* Prentice, 1966. $7.

Onions, C. T. *Modern English Syntax.* St. Martin, 1971. $6.

Partridge, Eric. *Dictionary of Slang and Unconventional English.* 7th ed. Macmillan, 1970. $19.

Pei, Mario A. *Double-Speak in America.* Hawthorn, 1973. $7.

_____. *Many Hues of English.* Knopf, 1967. $6.

428.4   READING IMPROVEMENT

Leedy, Paul. *Key to Better Reading.* McGraw, 1968. $6.

Lewis, Norman. *How to Read Better and Faster.* 3rd ed. Crowell, 1958. $6.

430   GERMAN

Cassell's New Compact German Dictionary. F&W, 1966. $5.

Curme, George O. *Grammar of the German Language.* 2nd rev. ed. Ungar, 1952. $13.

Langenscheidt Staff. *New Pocket German Dictionary.* Hippocrene, 1970. $4.

Madrigal, Margarita. *Invitation to German.* S&S, 1971. $5.

440   FRENCH

Cassell's New Compact French Dictionary. F&W, 1968. $5.

Hendrix, William S. *Beginning French, a Cultural Approach.* 4th ed. Houghton, 1970. $11.

Madrigal, Margarita. *Invitation to French.* S&S, 1962. paper, $2.

Micks, Wilson. *New Fundamental French.* Oxford, 1953. $6.

450   ITALIAN

Madrigal, Margarita. *Invitation to Italian.* S&S, 1965. $4.

Pei, Mario. *Getting Along in Italian.* Harper, 1957. $5.

Vittorini, Domenico. *Italian Grammar.* McKay, 1947. $4.

460   SPANISH, PORTUGUESE
Barlow, Joseph W. *Basic Elements of Spanish.* Appleton, 1955. $9.
Cassell's New Compact Spanish Dictionary. F&W, 1969. $5.
Cortina Method Language Series. *Conversational Brazilian-Portuguese.*
    Doubleday. $5.
Ibarra, Francisco. *Spanish Self-Taught.* Random, 1941. $7.
Madrigal, Margarita. *Invitation to Spanish.* S&S, 1962. paper, $2.

470   LATIN
Cassell's New Compact Latin Dictionary. F&W, 1971. $5.
Wheelock, Frederic M. *Latin: an Introductory Course.* 3rd ed. B&N, 1963.
    $5.

480   GREEK
Pring, Julian T. *Phrase Book of Modern Greek, in English and Greek.*
    McKay, 1967. $3.
Smyth, Herbert W. *Greek Grammar.* rev. ed. Harvard, 1956. $10.

490   RUSSIAN
Cornyn, William S. *Beginning Russian.* rev. ed. Yale, 1961. $7.
Smirnitsky, A. I. *Russian-English Dictionary.* rev. ed. Dutton, 1973. $12.

495   ORIENTAL LANGUAGES
Cooper, Lee. *Chinese Language for Beginners.* Tuttle, 1971. paper, $2.
Cortina Method Language Series. *Conversational Japanese.* rev. ed. Double-
    day, 1963. $5.
Martin, Samuel. *Basic Japanese Conversation Dictionary.* Tuttle, 1957. $3.
Swadesh, Morris. *Conversational Chinese for Beginners.* Dover, 1948. paper,
    $2.

496   AFRICAN LANGUAGES
Chuks-Orji, Ogonna. *Names from Africa: Their Origin, Meaning, and Pro-
    nunciation.* Johnson, 1972. $5.
Gilmore, Theopolis L. *Swahili Phrase Book.* Ungar, 1963. $5.

500

SCIENCE

500   GENERAL

Barber, Bernard. *Sociology of Science.* Free Press, 1962. $11.

Bernal, J. D. *Science in History.* 4 vols. MIT, 1971. paper, each, $4.

Brooks, Stewart M. *Integrated Basic Science.* 3rd rev. ed. Mosby, 1970. $12.

Commoner, Barry. *Science and Survival.* Viking, 1966. paper, $2.

Daniels, George H. *Science in American Society.* Knopf, 1971. $10.

Dilson, Jesse. *Curves and Automation: the Scientist's Plot.* Lippincott, 1971. $6.

Dubos, René. *Reason Awake: Science for Man.* Columbia, 1970. $8.

Eiseley, Loren. *Invisible Pyramid.* Scribner, 1972. $7.

Farb, Peter. *Face of North America.* Harper, 1964. $9.

Hogben, Lancelot. *Science for the Citizen.* rev. ed. Norton, 1957. $15.

Hoyle, Fred. *New Face of Science.* Norton, 1971. $7.

Moore, A. D. *Invention, Discovery and Creativity.* Doubleday, 1969. $5.

Simak, Clifford D. *March of Science.* Harper, 1971. $8.

Singer, Charles. *Short History of Scientific Ideas to 1900.* Oxford, 1959. $16.

Time-Life Books. *Life Nature Library.* 25 vols. Time, 1961/67. each, $7.

———. *Life Science Library.* 26 vols. Time, 1961/67. each, $7.

The above-listed Time-Life series books cover material in the whole spectrum of 500s classification. Consult publisher's list/BIP for complete list of latest titles. Index volume to each set is available.

Weinberg, Alvin M. *Reflections on Big Science.* MIT, 1968. $7.

510   MATHEMATICS

Adler, Henry. *Introduction to Probability and Statistics.* 5th ed. Freeman, 1972. $9.

Adler, Irving. *New Look at Geometry.* John Day, 1966. $10.
——. *New Mathematics.* rev. ed. John Day, 1972. $8.
——. *Probability and Statistics for Everyman.* rev. ed. John Day, 1963. $8.
——. *Thinking Machines.* rev. ed. John Day, 1973. $7.
Allendoerfer, Carl B. *Fundamentals of College Algebra.* McGraw, 1967. $9.
——. *Fundamentals of Freshman Mathematics.* 3rd ed. McGraw, 1972.
$11.
Armstrong, James W. *Elements of Mathematics.* Macmillan, 1970. $9.
Behr, Merlyn J. *Fundamentals of Elementary Mathematics: Number Systems and Algebra.* Academic, 1971. $10.
Bell, Eric T. *Men of Mathematics.* S&S, 1961. $8.
Boyer, Carl T. *History of Mathematics.* Wiley, 1968. $15.
Brumfel, Charles F. *Principles of Arithmetic.* Addison, 1963. $10.
Campbell, Hugh G. *Introduction to Matrices, Vectors and Linear Programming.* Appleton, 1965. $10.
Comrie, Leslie J. *Barlow's Tables of Squares, Cubes, Square Roots, Cube Roots, and Reciprocals.* 4th ed. Halstead, 1965. $6.
Cooke, Nelson M. *Basic Mathematics for Electronics.* 3rd ed. McGraw,
1970. $11.
Cooley, Hollis R. *Introduction to Mathematics.* 3rd ed. Houghton, 1968.
$10.
Courant, Richard. *What Is Mathematics?* Oxford, 1941. $11.
Coxeter, H. S. M. *Introduction to Geometry.* 2nd ed. Wiley, 1969. $13.
Dantzig, Tobias. *Number, the Language of Science.* 4th ed. Macmillan,
1954. $8.
Davis, Philip J. *3.1414 and All That.* S&S, 1969. $6.
Eves, Howard. *Introduction to the History of Mathematics.* 3rd ed. Holt,
1969. $11.
Gamow, George. *One, Two, Three-Infinity.* rev. ed. Viking, 1963. paper, $3.
Gardner, Martin. *New Mathematical Diversions.* S&S, 1966. paper, $3.
Harris, Charles O. *Slide Rule Simplified.* 3rd ed. Am. Technical, 1961. $7.
Hartkopf, Roy. *Math Without Tears.* Emerson, 1970. $7.
Hogben, Lancelot T. *Mathematics for the Millions.* rev. ed. Norton, 1968.
$10.
Huff, Darrell. *How to Lie with Statistics.* Norton, 1954. $4.
Jacobs, Harold R. *Mathematics.* Freeman, 1970. $9.
Jones, Burton W. *Elementary Concepts of Mathematics.* 3rd ed. Macmillan,
1970. $10.
Lang, Serge. *Basic Mathematics.* Addison, 1971. $10.
Langley, Russell. *Practical Statistics Simply Explained.* Dover, 1972. $3.
Newman, James R. *World of Mathematics.* 4 vols. S&S, 1956/60. set, $30.
Niven, Ivan. *Introduction to the Theory of Numbers.* 3rd ed. Wiley, 1966.
$11.
Nunz, Gregory. *Electronics Mathematics.* comb. vol. McGraw, 1967. $12.

Rees, Paul K. *Principles of Mathematics*. Prentice, 1970. $11.

Rosenberg, Nancy. *How to Enjoy Mathematics with Your Child*. Stein, 1970. $7.

Singer, E. J. *Basic Mathematics for Electricity and Electronics*. 3rd ed. McGraw, 1972. $11.

Stein, Edwin I. *Fundamentals of Mathematics*. Allyn, 1972. $7.

_____. *Practical Applications in Mathematics*. new ed. Allyn, 1972. $3.

Stuart, Fredric. *Fortran Programming*. rev. ed. Wiley, 1970. $11.

Whipkey, Kenneth L. *Power of Calculus*. Wiley, 1972. $10.

520   ASTRONOMY

Abell, George. *Exploration of the Universe: Brief Updated Edition*. Holt, 1973. $10.

Alter, Dinsmore. *Practical Astronomy*. 3rd ed. Crowell, 1969. $10.

_____. *Pictorial Guide to the Moon*. rev. ed. Crowell, 1967. $9.

Asimov, Isaac. *Solar System and Back*. Doubleday, 1970. $6.

_____. *Stars in their Courses*. Doubleday, 1971. $6.

_____. *Universe*. rev. ed. Walker, 1971. $7.

Baker, Robert H. *Astronomy*. 9th ed. Van Nostrand, 1971. $14.

Gamow, George. *Moon*. rev. ed. Abelard, 1971. $5.

Howard, Neale E. *Telescope Handbook and Star Atlas*. Crowell, 1967. $12.

Inglis, Stuart J. *Planets, Stars and Galaxies*. 3rd ed. Wiley, 1972. $12.

Irwin, Keith G. *Three Hundred Sixty-Five Days*. Crowell, 1963. $6.

Jackson, Joseph H. *Pictorial Guide to the Planets*. 2nd ed. Crowell, 1974. $10.

Jastrow, Robert. *Astronomy*. Wiley, 1972. $13.

_____. *Red Giants and White Dwarfs*. rev. ed. Harper, 1970. $7.

Ley, Willy. *Watchers of the Skies*. Viking, 1963. $9.

Menzel, Donald H. *Astronomy*. Random, 1970. $18.

_____. *Field Guide to the Stars and Planets*. Houghton, 1964. $7.

Moore, Patrick. *New Guide to the Planets*. 3rd ed. Norton, 1972. $8.

Neely, Henry M. *Stars by Clock and Fist*. rev. ed Viking, 1972. $6.

Nourse, Alan. *Nine Planets*. rev. ed. Harper, 1970. $9.

Olcott, William T. *Field Book of the Skies*. 4th ed. Putnam, 1954. $6.

Page, Thornton, ed. Sky and Telescope. *Library of Astronomy*. 8 vols. Macmillan, 1965–69. each, $8.

Rey, Hans A. *Stars*. 3rd ed. Houghton, 1967. $7.

Richardson, Robert S. *Stars and Serendipity*. Pantheon, 1971. $6.

Shapley, Harlow. *Galaxies*. 3rd ed. Harvard, 1972. $10.

Texereau, Jean. *How to Make a Telescope*. Wiley, 1963. $8.

Whitney, Charles A. *Discovery of our Galaxy*. Knopf, 1971. $10.

Wyatt, Stanley P. *Principles of Astronomy*. 2nd ed. Allyn, 1971. $15.

Young, Louise B. *Exploring the Universe*. 2nd ed. Oxford, 1971. $13.

526   SURVEYING, MAPPING

Brown, Lloyd A. *Map Making.* Little, 1960. $7.

Greenhood, David. *Mapping.* rev. ed. Chicago, 1964. $6.

Rayner, William H. *Fundamentals of Surveying.* Van Nostrand, 1969. $10.

Robinson, Arthur. *Elements of Cartography.* 3rd ed. Wiley, 1969. $13.

Tannenbaum, Beulah. *Understanding Maps.* McGraw, 1969. $6.

Tooley, R. V. *Maps and Map-Makers.* Crown, 1971. $8.

530   PHYSICS

Atkins, Kenneth R. *Physics.* Wiley, 1969. $14.

Backus, John. *Accoustical Foundations of Music.* Norton, 1969. $10.

Barnett, Lincoln. *Universe and Dr. Einstein.* 2nd ed. Morrow, 1957. $6.

Bernal, J. D. *Extension of Man: History of Physics before the Modern Age.* MIT, 1972. $13.

Bova, Ben. *Fourth State of Matter.* St. Martin, 1971. $6.

Bulman, A. D. *Model Making for Physicists.* Crowell, 1968. $5.

Burnham, Robert W. *Color.* Wiley, 1963. $13.

Coleman, James A. *Relativity for the Layman.* William-F., 1958. $3.

Einstein, Albert. *Meaning of Relativity.* 5th ed. Princeton, 1956. $8.

Frisch, Otto. *Nature of Matter.* Dutton, 1972. $8.

Gardner, Martin. *Relativity for the Millions.* Macmillan, 1962. $7.

Gottlieb, Milton. *Seven States of Matter.* Walker, 1966. $7.

Heisenberg, Werner. *Physics and Beyond.* Harper, 1971. $8.

Kavaler, Lucy. *Freezing Point.* Day, 1970. $9.

Kittel, Charles. *Introduction to Solid State Physics.* 4th ed. Wiley, 1971. $17.

Lieber, Lillian. *Einstein Theory of Relativity.* Holt, 1945. $4.

Manning, Henry. *Fourth Dimension Simply Explained.* Peter Smith. $4.

Needham, George H. *Microscope, a Practical Guide.* Thomas, 1968. $7.

Rosenfeld, Sam. *Science Experiments with Water.* Harvey, 1966. $7.

Sterland, E. G. *Energy into Power.* Doubleday. $4.

Taylor, John G. *New Physics.* Basic, 1972. $9.

VanHeel, Abraham. *What Is Light?* McGraw, 1968. paper, $3.

540   CHEMISTRY

Beiser, Germaine. *Story of Cosmic Rays.* Dutton, 1962. $4.

Bennett, Alan. *Crystals: Perfect and Imperfect.* Walker, 1966. $7.

Benson, Sidney W. *Chemical Calculations.* 3rd ed. Wiley, 1971. $5.

Davis, George E. *Radiation and Life.* Iowa, 1967. $8.

Depuy, Charles H. *Introduction to Organic Chemistry.* Wiley, 1967. $11.

Farber, Eduard. *Evolution of Chemistry.* 2nd ed. Ronald, 1969. $10.

Holden, Alan. *Crystals-Crystal Growing.* Doubleday. paper, $3.

Masterson, William L. *Chemical Principles.* Saunders, 1973. $13.

Mortimer, Charles E. *Chemistry.* 2nd ed. Reinhold, 1971. $13.

Pauling, Linus. *College Chemistry.* 3rd ed. Freeman, 1964. $10.

Sanderson, R. T. *Inorganic Chemistry.* Reinhold, 1967. $16.

Sienko, Michell. *Chemistry.* 3rd ed. McGraw, 1966. $10.

Smith, Richard F. *Chemistry for the Million.* Scribner, 1972. $8.

Weeks, Mary E. *Discovery of the Elements.* 7th ed. Chemical Ed., 1968. $13.

550   EARTH SCIENCE, GEOLOGY

Adams, George F. *Landforms.* Western, 1971. $5.

Atkinson, Bruce W. *Weather Business.* Doubleday, 1969. $7.

Bardach, John. *Harvest of the Sea.* Harper, 1968. $7.

Bates, Marston. *Forest and the Sea.* Random, 1970. $7.

Brooks, Maurice. *Appalachians.* Houghton, 1965. $8.

Calder, Nigel. *Restless Earth.* Viking, 1972. $10.

Clare, Patricia. *Struggle for the Great Barrier Reef.* Walker, 1972. $8.

Cotter, Charles H. *Physical Geography of the Oceans.* Am. Elsevier, 1966. $7.

Cousteau, Jacques Y. *Life and Death in a Coral Sea.* Doubleday, 1971. $9.

———. *Silent World.* Harper, 1953. $8.

Day, John A. *Science of Weather.* Addison, 1966. $9.

Deeson, A. F. L. *Collector's Encyclopedia of Rocks and Minerals.* Potter, 1973. $13.

Desautels, Paul E. *Mineral Kingdom.* Grosset, 1972. $8.

Fairbridge, Rhodes W. *Encyclopedia of Oceanography.* Reinhold, 1966. $28.

Fenton, Carroll L. *Rock Book.* Doubleday, 1970. $13.

Fisher, P. J. *Science of Gems.* Scribner, 1972. $10.

Fletcher, Edward. *Pebble Collecting and Polishing.* Sterling, 1973. $4.

Gilluly, James. *Principles of Geology.* 3rd ed. Freeman, 1968. $13.

Hay, John. *Atlantic Shore.* Harper, 1966. $7.

Hillcourt, William. *New Field Book of Nature Activities and Hobbies.* rev. ed. Putnam, 1970. $6.

Hunt, Charles B. *Physiography of the United States.* Freeman, 1967. $10.

Hurlbut, Cornelius S. *Minerals and Man.* Random, 1968. $18.

Idyll, Clarence P. *Abyss.* rev. ed. Crowell, 1971. $8.

Jaeger, Edmund. *North American Deserts.* Stanford, 1957. $7.

Klots, Elsie. *New Field Book of Freshwater Life.* Putnam, 1966. $6.

Kraus, Edward H. *Gems and Gem Materials.* 5th ed. McGraw, 1947. $11.

Landsberg, Helmut E. *Weather and Health.* Doubleday, 1969. $5.

Leopold, Aldo. *Sand County Almanac.* Oxford, 1966. $8.

Loomis, Frederick B. *Field Book of Common Rocks and Minerals.* rev. ed. Putnam, 1948. $6.

MacGinitie, G. E. *Natural History of Marine Animals.* 2nd ed. McGraw, 1968. $14.

Mather, Kirtley F. *Earth beneath Us*. Random, 1964. $18.

Matthews, William H., III. *Invitation to Geology*. Doubleday, 1971. $6.

Moore, Ruth. *Earth We Live On*. 2nd ed. Knopf, 1971. $9.

Ogburn, Charlton, Jr. *Forging of Our Continent*. Hale, 1968. $5.

Pough, Frederick H. *Field Guide to Rocks and Minerals*. 3rd ed. Houghton, 1953. $6.

Raikes, Robert. *Water, Weather, and Prehistory*. Humanities, 1967. $10.

Reid, George. *Pond Life*. Western, 1967. $5.

Sears, Paul B. *Living Landscape*. Basic, 1966. $6.

Shepherd, Francis P. *Earth beneath the Sea*. 2nd ed. Johns Hopkins, 1967. $7.

Silverberg, Robert. *Challenge of Climate*. Hawthorn, 1969. $7.

———. *World within the Ocean Wave*. Weybright, 1972. $7.

———. *World within the Tidal Pool*. Weybright, 1972. $7.

Stokes, William L. *Introduction to Geology*. Prentice, 1967. $13.

Tarling, Don. *Continental Drift*. Doubleday. $6.

Teale, Edwin. *Autumn across America*. Dodd, 1956. $8.

———. *Journey into Summer*. Dodd, 1960. $8.

———. *North with the Spring*. Dodd, 1951. $8.

———. *Wandering through Winter*. Dodd, 1965. $8.

Tennissen, Anthony. *Colorful Mineral Identifier*. Sterling, 1971. $4.

Tricker, R. A. R. *Science of Clouds*. Am. Elsevier, 1970. $8.

Uman, Martin. *Understanding Lightning*. Sterling, 1972. $7.

Zim, Herbert S. *Rocks and Minerals*. Western, 1957. $5.

———. *Seashores*. Western, 1955. $5.

560   PALEONTOLOGY

Beerbower, James R. *Search for the Past*. 2nd ed. Prentice, 1968. $15.

Cohen, Daniel. *Age of Giant Mammals*. Dodd, 1969. $4.

Colbert, Edwin H. *Dinosaurs*. Dutton, 1961. $10.

DeCamp, L. S. *Day of the Dinosaur*. Doubleday, 1968. $8.

Eisley, Loren. *Night Country*. Scribner, 1971. $8.

Fenton, Carroll L. *Fossil Book*. Doubleday, 1959. $18.

———. *Tales Told by Fossils*. Doubleday, 1966. $7.

MacFall, Russell P. *Fossils for Amateurs*. Van Nostrand, 1972. $11.

572   HUMAN RACES, ANTHROPOLOGY

Ardrey, Robert. *African Genesis*. Atheneum, 1961. $10.

Barnett, Samuel A. *Instinct and Intelligence*. Prentice, 1967. $9.

Beals, Ralph L. *Introduction to Anthropology*. 4th ed. Macmillan, 1971. $11.

Benedict, Ruth. *Patterns of Culture*. Houghton. $7.

Cohen, Robert. *Color of Man*. Random, 1968. $4.

Goldsby, Richard A. *Race and Races*. Macmillan, 1971. $6.

Hoebel, Edward A. *Anthropology*. 4th ed. McGraw, 1972. $12.

Mead, Margaret. *Coming of Age in Samoa*. Peter Smith. $5.

———. *Growing up in New Guinea*. Peter Smith. $5.

Megaw, Vincent. *Dawn of Man*. Putnam, 1972. $6.

Moore, Ruth. *Man, Time and Fossils*. 2nd rev. ed. Knopf, 1961. $9.

Morris, Desmond. *Naked Ape*. McGraw, 1968. $6.

Patton, A. Rae. *Chemistry of Life*. Random. $4.

Spinar, Zdenek V. *Life before Man*. McGraw, 1972. $9.

Steward, Julian. *Native Peoples of South America*. McGraw, 1959. $14.

Thomas, Elizabeth M. *Harmless People*. Knopf, 1959. $6.

Time-Life Books. "Emergence of Man" series. 9 vols. Time, 1972. each, $8.

Turnbull, Colin M. *The Mountain People*. S&S, 1972. $8.

Vlahos, Olivia. *African Beginnings*. Viking, 1967. $7.

Von Daniken, Erich. *Chariots of the Gods: Unsolved Mysteries of the Past*. Putnam, 1970. $6.

———. *Gods from Outer Space*. Putnam, 1971. $6.

———. *In Search of Ancient Gods*. Putnam, 1974. $9.

Wilson, Clifford. *Crash Go the Chariots; an Alternative to Chariots of the Gods*. Lancer, 1973. paper, $2.

574 BIOLOGY

Baer, Adela S. *Central Concepts of Biology*. Macmillan, 1971. $9.

Beaver, William C. *General Biology*. 8th ed. Mosby, 1970. $12.

Carlson, Elof A. *Modern Biology*. Braziller, 1967. $8.

Chedd, Graham. *New Biology*. Basic, 1972. $9.

Colbert, Edwin H. *Evolution of the Vertebrates*. 2nd ed. Wiley, 1969. $15.

Curtis, Helene. *Biology*. Worth, 1968. $12.

Farago, Peter. *Life in Action: Biochemistry Explained*. Knopf, 1972. $7.

Farris, Edmond J. *Care and Breeding of Laboratory Animals*. Wiley, 1950. $20.

Gray, Peter. *Dictionary of the Biological Sciences*. Reinhold, 1968. $16.

———. *Student Dictionary of Biology*. Van Nostrand, 1973. $8.

Keeton, William. *Biological Science*. 2nd ed. Norton, 1972. $12.

Milne, Lorus. *Arena of Life*. Doubleday, 1972. $15.

Moore, Ruth. *Coil of Life*. Knopf, 1961. $8.

Neill, Wilfred. *Geography of Life*. Columbia, 1969. $15.

Otto, James. *Modern Biology*. Holt, 1965. $9.

Simpson, George. *Life: an Introduction to Biology*. 2nd ed. Harcourt, 1965. $12.

Taylor, William T. *General Biology*. 2nd ed. Van Nostrand, 1968. $12.

Vishniac, Roman. *Building Blocks of Life*. Scribner, 1971. $7.

575 EVOLUTION, GENETICS

Asimov, Isaac. *Genetic Code*. Grossman, 1963. $5.

Borek, Ernest. *Code of Life*. Columbia, 1965. $8.

Darwin, Charles. *Origin of the Species; and Descent of Man*. Mod. Library, 1936. $5.

Ehrlich, Paul. *Process of Evolution*. McGraw, 1963. $13.

Eiseley, Loren. *Darwin's Century*. Doubleday, 1958. paper, $3.

Koestler, Arthur. *Case of the Midwife Toad*. Random, 1972. $6.

Kroeber, Theodora. *Ishi in Two Worlds*. California, 1961. $8.

Krutch, Joseph W. *Great Chain of Life*. Houghton, 1957. $6.

Montagu, Ashley. *Man's Most Dangerous Myth: the Fallacy of Race*. rev. ed. World, 1965. paper, $5.

Paterson, David. *Applied Genetics*. Doubleday, 1968. $7.

Scheinfeld, Amram. *Your Heredity and Environment*. Lippincott, 1965. $21.

Watson, James D. *Double Helix*. Atheneum, 1968. $8.

Wendt, Herbert. *From Ape to Adam*. Bobbs. $15.

Winchester, A. M. *Genetics*. 4th ed. Houghton, 1972. $12.

576   MICROBIOLOGY

Afzelius, Bjorn. *Anatomy of the Cell*. Chicago, 1966. $7.

Andrewes, Christopher H. *Natural History of Viruses*. Norton, 1967. $10.

Carpenter, Philip L. *Microbiology*. 3rd ed. Saunders, 1972. $10.

Gillie, Oliver. *Living Cell*. F&W, 1971. $7.

Smith, Alice L. *Principles of Microbiology*. 4th ed. Mosby, 1973. $11.

Stanier, Roger Y. *Microbial World*. 3rd ed. Prentice, 1970. $17.

Swanson, Carl P. *Cell*. 3rd ed. Prentice, 1969. paper, $4.

Thompson, Paul D. *Virus Realm*. Lippincott, 1968. $5.

Wyss, Orville. *Microrganisms and Man*. Wiley, 1971. $10.

579   TAXIDERMY

Grantz, Gerald J. *Home Book of Taxidermy and Tanning*. Stackpole, 1970. $8.

Labrie, Jean. *Amateur Taxidermist*. Hart, 1972. $8.

Moyer, John W. *Practical Taxidermy*. Ronald, 1953. $6.

580   BOTANY

Alexander, Taylor R. *Botany*. Western, 1970. $4.

Baker, Herbert G. *Plants and Civilization*. 2nd ed. Wadsworth, 1970. paper, $4.

Brockman, C. Frank. *Trees of North America*. Western, 1968. $6.

Christensen, Clyde M. *Molds and Man*. 3rd ed. Minnesota, 1965. $9.

Cobb, Boughton. *Field Guide to the Ferns*. Houghton, 1956. $6.

Coulter, Merle C. *Story of the Plant Kingdom*. 3rd rev. ed. Chicago, 1964. $8.

Duddington, C. L. *Beginner's Guide to Botany*. Drake, 1971. $6.

Ewan, Joseph. *Short History of Botany in the United States*. Hafner, 1969. $8.

Gibbons, Euell. *Stalking the Wild Asparagus*. McKay, 1970. $8.

Kavaler, Lucy. *Mushrooms, Molds and Miracles*. John Day, 1965. $9.

King, Lawrence J. *Weeds of the World*. Halsted, 1966. $18.

Klein, Richard M. *Discovering Plants*. Natural History, 1968. $5.

Krieger, Louis C. *Mushroom Handbook*. Dover, 1967. paper, $4.

Mathews, F. Schuyler. *Field Book of American Wild Flowers*. Putnam, 1966. $6.

———. *Field Book of American Trees and Shrubs*. Putnam, 1951. $6.

Muller, Walter H. *Botany*. 2nd ed. Macmillan, 1969. $10.

Novak, F. A. *Pictorial Encyclopedia of Plants and Flowers*. Crown, 1965. $10.

Peattie, Donald C. *Natural History of Trees of Eastern and Central North America*. Houghton, 1966. $9.

———. *Natural History of Western Trees*. Houghton, 1953. $10.

Petrides, George A. *Field Guide to Trees and Shrubs*. 2nd ed. Houghton, 1972. $6.

Pohl, Richard W. *How to Know the Grasses*. 2nd ed. W. C. Brown, 1968. $5.

Reisigel, Herbert. *World of Flowers*. Viking, 1966. $13.

Salisbury, Frank B. *Biology of Flowering*. Natural History, 1971. $6.

Sinnott, Edmund W. *Botany*. 6th ed. McGraw, 1963. $12.

Thomas, William S. *Field Book of Common Mushrooms*. 3rd rev. ed. Putnam, 1948. $7.

Wilson, Carl L. *Botany*. 5th ed. Holt, 1971. $14.

590   ZOOLOGY

Barnes, Robert D. *Invertebrate Zoology*. 2nd ed. Saunders, 1968. $11.

Brown, Leslie. *Life of the African Plains*. McGraw, 1972. $5.

Buchsbaum, Ralph. *Animals without Backbones*. rev. ed. Chicago, 1948. $9.

Dembeck, Hermann. *Animals and Men*. Doubleday. $8.

Dempsey, Michael. *Concise Color Encyclopedia of Nature*. Crowell, 1972. $8.

Elliott, Alfred M. *Zoology*. 4th ed. Appleton, 1968. $13.

Fisher, James. *Zoos of the World*. Doubleday, 1967. $7.

Guggisberg, C. A. *Man and Wildlife*. Arco, 1970. $13.

Hyman, Libbie H. *Comparative Vertebrate Anatomy*. 2nd ed. Chicago, 1942. $7.

Jarman, Cathy. *Atlas of Animal Migration*. John Day, 1972. $10.

Ley, Willy. *Dawn of Zoology*. Prentice, 1968. $10.

Ley, Willy. *Exotic Zoology*. rev. ed. Viking, 1959. $6.

MacArthur, Robert H. *Geographical Ecology*. new ed. Harper, 1972. $14.

McCauley, William J. *Vertebrate Physiology*. Saunders, 1971. $10.

Milne, Lorus. *Nature of Animals*. Lippincott, 1969. $6.

Murie, Olaus J. *Field Guide to Animal Tracks*. Houghton, 1954. $6.
Nayman, Jacqueline. *Atlas of Wildlife*. John Day, 1972. $10.
Pedersen, Alwin. *Polar Animals*. Taplinger, 1966. $6.
Romer, Alfred S. *Vertebrate Body*. 4th ed. Saunders, 1970. $11.
Storer, Tracy I. *General Zoology*. 5th ed. McGraw, 1972. $12.
Wendt, Herbert. *Sex Life of the Animals*. S&S, 1965. $8.
Young, John Z. *Life of Vertebrates*. 2nd ed. Oxford, 1962. $13.

594   MOLLUSKS, SEASHELLS

Johnstone, Kathleen Y. *Sea Treasure*. Houghton, 1957. $5.
Morris, Percy A. *Field Guide to the Shells of Our Atlantic and Gulf Coasts*.
    rev. ed. Houghton, 1951. $6.
_____. *Field Guide to the Shells of the Pacific Coast and Hawaii*. rev. ed.
    Houghton, 1966. $6.
Schmitt, Waldo L. *Crustaceans*. Michigan, 1965. $6.

595   INSECTS

Bates, Marston. *Natural History of Mosquitoes*. Peter Smith. $6.
Dines, Arthur. *Honeybees from Close Up*. Crowell, 1968. $9.
Evans, Howard. *Life on a Little Known Planet*. Dutton, 1968. $9.
Fabre, J. Henri. *Life of the Spider*. Horizon, 1971. $8.
Hutchins, Ross E. *Insects*. Prentice, 1966. $9.
Kalmus, H. *101 Simple Experiments with Insects*. Doubleday. $6.
Klots, Alexander. *Field Guide to the Butterflies*. Houghton, 1951. $6.
_____. *Insects of North America*. Doubleday, 1971. $10.
Little, Van Allen. *General and Applied Entomology*. 3rd ed. Harper, 1972.
    $10.
Lutz, Frank E. *Field Book of Insects*. rev. ed. Putnam, 1948. $6.
Oldroyd, Harold. *Elements of Entymology*. Universe, 1972. $9.
Wigglesworth, Vincent. *Life of Insects*. Universe, 1972. $13.

597   FISHES, AMPHIBIANS

Axelrod, Herbert R. *Color Guide to Tropical Fish*. Sterling, 1969. $6.
_____. *Encyclopedia of Tropical Fish*. TFH Pubns., 1957. $10.
_____. *Tropical Fish as a Hobby*. rev. ed. McGraw, 1969. $9.
_____. *Tropical Fish in Your Home*. Sterling. $4.
Budker, Paul. *Life of Sharks*. Columbia, 1971. $13.
Carr, Archie. *Handbook of Turtles*. Comstock, 1952. $17.
Cousteau, Jacques Y. *Octopus and Squid*. Doubleday, 1973. $10.
_____. *Shark*. Doubleday, 1970. $9.
Herlad, Earl S. *Fishes of North America*. Doubleday, 1972. $10.
Innes, William T. *Exotic Aquarium Fish*. 19th ed. Dutton. $6.
Janus, Horst. *Pond Life in the Aquarium*. Van Nostrand, 1966. paper, $2.
Lagler, Karl. *Ichthyology*. Wiley, 1962. $16.

McCormick, Harold. *Shadows in the Sea*. Chilton, 1963. $9.

Marshall, N. B. *Life of Fishes*. Universe, 1966. $13.

Porter, George. *World of the Frog and the Toad*. Lippincott, 1967. $6.

Schiotz, Arne. *Guide to Aquarium Fishes and Plants*. Lippincott, 1972. $7.

Schultz, Leonard P. *Wondrous World of Fishes*. National Geographic, 1969. $10.

Straughan, Robert P. *Salt-Water Aquarium in the Home*. 2nd rev. ed. B&N, 1969. $15.

Vogt, Dieter. *Complete Aquarium*. Arco, 1963. $8.

Walker, Braz. *Tropical Fish Identifier*. Sterling, 1971. $4.

598   REPTILES, BIRDS

Audubon, John J. *Birds of America*. Macmillan, 1947. $13.

Barbour, Roger W. *Bats of America*. Kentucky, 1969. $18.

Barker, Will. *Familiar Reptiles and Amphibians of America*. Harper, 1964. $7.

Bellairs, Angus. *World of Reptiles*. Am. Elsevier, 1966. $6.

Conant, Roger. *Field Guide to Reptiles and Amphibians*. Houghton, 1958. $6.

Ditmars, Raymond L. *Reptiles of North America*. rev. ed. Doubleday, 1936. $15.

Goin, Coleman J. *Introduction to Herpetology*. 2nd ed. Freeman, 1971. $10.

Hanzak, Jan. *Pictorial Encyclopedia of Birds*. Crown, 1965. $10.

Harrison, Hal H. *World of the Snake*. Lippincott, 1971. $6.

Kaufman, John. *Wings, Sun, and Stars*. Morrow, 1969. $6.

Leviton, Alan E. *Reptiles and Amphibians of North America*. Doubleday, 1972. $10.

Minton, Sherman. *Venomous Reptiles*. Scribner, 1969. $8.

Peterson, Roger T. *Field Guide to the Birds*. rev. ed. Houghton, 1947. $6.

_____. *Field Guide to Western Birds*. rev. ed. Houghton, 1961. $6.

Pough, Richard. *Audubon Water Bird Guide*. Doubleday, 1951. $7.

Schmidt, Karl P. *Field Book of Snakes of U.S. and Canada*. Putnam, 1941. $6.

Stebbins, Robert. *Field Guide to the Western Reptiles and Amphibians*. Houghton, 1966. $6.

Wetmore, Alexander. *Song and Garden Birds of North America*. National Geographic, 1965. $12.

_____. *Water, Prey, and Game Birds of North America*. National Geographic, 1965. $12.

599   MAMMALS

Adamson, Joy. *Born Free*. Pantheon, 1960. $7.

_____. *Forever Free*. Harcourt, 1963. $9.

_____. *Living Free*. Harcourt, 1961. $9.

Barker, Will. *Familiar Animals of America*. Harper, 1956. $7.

Bourne, Geoffrey H. *Ape People*. Putnam, 1971. $8.

Burt, William H. *Field Guide to the Mammals*. 2nd ed. Houghton, 1964. $6.

Cousteau, Jacques Y. *Whale*. Doubleday, 1972. $10.

Curry-Lindahl, Kai. *Let Them Live*. Morrow, 1972. $10.

Dorst, Jean. *Field Guide to Larger Mammals of Africa*. Houghton, 1970. $9.

Droscher, Vitus B. *Friendly Beast*. Dutton, 1971. $9.

Fitter, Richard. *Vanishing Wild Animals of the World*. Watts, 1969. $8.

Gray, Robert. *Great Apes*. Grosset, 1969. $5.

Haas, Emmy. *Pride's Progress*. Harper, 1967. $6.

Hahn, Emily. *On the Side of the Apes*. Crowell, 1971. $8.

Jenkins, Marie M. *Animals without Parents*. Holiday, 1970. $5.

Jordan, Emil L. *Animal Atlas of the World*. Hammond, 1969. $17.

Milne, Lorus. *Cougar Doesn't Live Here Anymore*. Prentice, 1971. $11.

Morris, Desmond. *Mammals*. Harper, 1965. $13.

Morris, Ramona. *Men and Pandas*. McGraw, 1967. $8.

National Geographic Society. *Marvels of Animal Behavior*. National Geographic, 1972. $12.

National Geographic Society. *Wild Animals of North America*. National Geographic, 1971. $8.

Olsen, Jack. *Night of the Grizzlies*. Putnam, 1969. $7.

Roedelberger, Franz. *African Wildlife*. Viking, 1965. $9.

Rood, Ronald. *Animals Nobody Loves: Varmit Ecology*. Greene, 1971. $7.

Rowell, Thelma. *Social Behavior of Monkeys*. Gannon. $5.

Rue, Leonard. *Pictorial Guide to the Mammals of North America*. Crowell, 1967. $9.

Sanderson, Ivan. *Living Mammals of the World*. Doubleday, 1955. $16.

Scheffer, Victor B. *Year of the Seal*. Scribner, 1970. $8.

Stonehouse, Bernard. *Animals of the Antarctic*. Holt, 1972. $11.

_____. *Animals of the Arctic*. Holt, 1971. $11.

VanLawick-Goodall, Jane. *My Friends the Wild Chimpanzees*. National Geographic, 1967. $5.

600

APPLIED SCIENCE

600   TECHNOLOGY, INVENTIONS

Byrd, E. *How Things Work*. Prentice, 1973. $9.

Crispin, Frederic S. *Dictionary of Technical Terms*. rev. ed. Macmillan, 1970. $7.

Derry, T. K. *Short History of Technology from the Earliest Times to A.D. 1900*. Oxford, 1961. $13.

Fenner, Terrence W. *Inventor's Handbook*. Chemical Pub., 1968. $9.

Freeman, Mitchell. *Practical and Industrial Formulary*. Chemical Pub., 1962. $9.

Jones, Stacy V. *Inventor's Patent Handbook*. rev. ed. Dial, 1966. $6.

Usher, Abbott P. *History of Mechanical Inventions*. rev. ed. Harvard, 1954. $15.

610   MEDICAL SCIENCES

Blakiston's New Gould Medical Dictionary. 3rd ed. McGraw, 1972. $15.

Dorland, William A. N. *Dorland's Illustrated Medical Dictionary*. 24th ed. Saunders, 1965. $14.

Hartog, Jan de. *Hospital*. Atheneum, 1964. $6.

Longmore, Donald. *Machines in Medicine*. Doubleday, 1970. $7.

Nolen, William A. *Making of a Surgeon*. Random, 1970. $7.

Rapier, Dorothy. *Practical Nursing*. 4th rev. ed. Mosby, 1970. $9.

612   ANATOMY, PHYSIOLOGY

Asimov, Isaac. *Human Body*. Houghton, 1963. $8.

Charles, Anton J. *Machinery of the Body*. 5th rev. ed. Chicago, 1961. $8.

Child Study Assn. of America. *What to Tell Your Children about Sex*. Hawthorn, 1968. $4.

Dublin, Louis I. *Factbook on Man*. 2nd ed. Macmillan, 1965. $10.

Frohse, Franz. *Atlas of Human Anatomy*. 6th ed. B&N, 1961. $5.

Gray, Madeline. *Changing Years: Menopause without Fear*. rev. ed. Doubleday, 1967. $5.

Johnson, Eric W. *Love and Sex in Plain Language*. rev. ed. Lippincott, 1974. $6.

———. Sex: *Telling It Straight*. Lippincott, 1970. $4.

Kimber, Diana C. *Anatomy and Physiology*. 15th ed. Macmillan, 1966. $10.

Locke, David M. *Enzymes: Agents of Life*. Crown, 1969. $6.

McCary, James L. *Human Sexuality*. Van Nostrand, 1973. $11.

Nourse, Alan S. *The Body*. Time, 1964. $6.

Pomeroy, Wardell B. *Boys and Sex*. Delacorte, 1968. $5.

———. *Girls and Sex*. Delacorte, 1970. $5.

———. *Your Child and Sex: A Guide for Parents*. Delacorte, 1974. price not set.

Tanner, James M. *Growth*. Time, 1965. $6.

613   HEALTH, SAFETY

Aaron, James E. *First Aid and Emergency Care*. Macmillan, 1972. paper, $5.

American Red Cross. *First Aid Textbook*. rev. ed. Doubleday. $2.

Benjamin, Bry. *In Case of Emergency, What to Do until the Doctor Arrives*. rev. ed. Doubleday, 1965. $6.

Bogert, L. Jean. *Nutrition and Physical Fitness*. 9th ed. Saunders, 1973. $10.

Cahill, Kevin M. *Medical Advice for the Traveler*. Holt, 1970. $4.

Chaney, Margaret S. *Nutrition*. 8th ed. Houghton, 1971. $10.

Cooper, Kenneth H. *New Aerobics*. Evans, 1970. $6.

Craig, Marjorie. *21-Day Shape-up Program for Men and Women*. Random, 1968. $7.

Diehl, Harold S. *Healthful Living*. 9th ed. McGraw, 1973. $10.

Falls, Harold B. *Foundations of Conditioning*. Academic, 1970. $4.

Fleck, Henrietta. *Introduction to Nutrition*. 2nd ed. Macmillan, 1971. $10.

Galton, Lawrence. *Outdoorsman's Fitness and Medical Guide*. Harper, 1967. $5.

Gardner, Archibald W. *New Essential First Aid*. Little, 1971. $5.

Gibbons, Joe. *Feast on a Diabetic Diet*. rev. ed. McKay, 1973. $3.

Haggerty, James J. *Food and Nutrition*. Time, 1967. $6.

Henderson, John. *Emergency Medical Guide*. 3rd ed. McGraw, 1973. $9.

Hittleman, Richard L. *Yoga Way to Figure and Facial Beauty*. Hawthorn, 1968. $6.

Kiphuth, Robert. *How to Be Fit*. Yale, 1963. $7.

Pauling, Linus. *Vitamin C and the Common Cold*. Freeman, 1970. $4.

Royal Canadian Air Force. *RCAF Exercise Plans for Physical Fitness*. Essandess, 1962. paper, $2.

Stone, Irwin. *Healing Factor, Vitamin C*. Grosset, 1972. $7.

Wagman, Richard J. *New Concise Family Health and Medical Guide*.
Doubleday, 1972. $10.
Weiner, Michael. *Earth Medicine—Earth Food*. Macmillan, 1972. $9.

615   DRUGS, ALCOHOL, SMOKING

Andrews, Matthew. *Parent's Guide to Drugs*. Doubleday, 1972. $7.
Bloch, Marvin A. *Alcoholism*. John Day, 1965. $8.
Bloomquist, E. R. *Marijuana*. Glencoe, 1968. $7.
Brecher, Edward M. *Licit and Illicit Drugs*. Little, 1972. $13.
Cohen, Sidney. *Drug Dilemma*. McGraw, 1969. $6.
Diehl, Harold S. *Tobacco and Your Health*. McGraw, 1969. $5.
Endore, Guy. *Synanon*. Doubleday, 1968. $7.
Fort, Joel. *Pleasure Seekers*. Bobbs, 1969. $7.
Grinspoon, Lester. *Marijuana Reconsidered*. Harvard, 1971. $13.
Harms, Ernest. *Drugs and Youth*. Pergamon, 1973. $13.
Hyde, Margaret O. *Mind Drugs*. McGraw, 1969. $5.
———. *Alcohol: Drink or Drug?* McGraw, 1974. $5.
Louria, Donald B. *Overcoming Drugs*. McGraw, 1971. $7.
Marin, Peter. *Understanding Drug Use*. Harper, 1971. $6.
Modell, Walter. *Drugs*. Time, 1972. $6.
Ochsner, Alton. *Smoking*. S&S, 1971. $5.
Oursler, Will. *Marijuana*. rev. ed. Eriksson, 1970. $6.
Rice, Julius. *Ups and Downs*. Macmillan, 1972. $6.

616   MEDICINE, DISEASE

Baldry, P. E. *Battle against Bacteria*. Cambridge, 1966. $8.
———. *Battle against Heart Disease*. Cambridge, 1971. $13.
Berland, Theodore. *Living with Your Ulcer*. St. Martin, 1971. $6.
Bobroff, Arthur. *Acne and Related Disorders of Complexion and Scalp*.
Thomas, 1964. $6.
Boettcher, Helmuth M. *Wonder Drugs: a History of Antibiotics*. Lippincott, 1964. $6.
Boylan, Brian R. *New Heart*. Chilton, 1969. $5.
Brams, William A. *Managing Your Coronary*. Arc, 1966. $7.
Brookes, Vincent J. *Poisons*. 2nd ed. Van Nostrand, 1958. $13.
Brooks, Stewart M. *V. D. Story*. B&N, 1971. $7.
Clark, Randolph L. *Book of Health*. 3rd ed. Coward, 1970. $25.
Cruikshank, William M. *Cerebral Palsy*. Syracuse, 1966. $11.
Danowski, T. S. *Diabetes as a Way of Life*. 3rd ed. Coward, 1970. $5.
Dolger, Henry. *How to Live with Diabetes*. 3rd ed. Norton, 1972. $7.
Duke, Mark. *Acupuncture*. Pyramid, 1972. $7.
Fast, Julius. *You and Your Feet*. St. Martin, 1971. $6.
Faust, Ernest C. *Animal Agents and Vectors of Human Disease*. 3rd ed. Lea
& Febiger, 1968. $12.

Fishbein, Morris. *Ask the Doctor*. McKay, 1973. $7.

———. *Handy Home Medical Adviser and Concise Medical Encyclopedia*. rev. ed. Doubleday, 1973. $6.

———. *Modern Family Health Guide*. rev. ed. Doubleday, 1968. $10.

Glemser, Bernard. *Man against Cancer*. F&W, 1969. $8.

Grover, John W. *V. D.: the ABC's*. Prentice, 1971. $5.

Hyman, Harold T. *Complete Home Medical Encyclopedia*. rev. ed. Hawthorn, 1973. $13.

Karelitz, Samuel. *When Your Child Is Ill*. rev. ed. Random, 1969. $8.

Kavaler, Lucy. *Cold against Disease*. John Day, 1972. $7.

Lamb, Lawrence E. *Your Heart and How to Live with It*. Viking, 1969. $8.

Longmore, Donald. *Spare-Part Surgery*. Doubleday, 1968. $7.

Medical Aid Encyclopedia for the Home. rev. ed. Nelson, 1972. $15.

Merck Manual of Diagnosis and Therapy. 12th ed. Merck, 1972. $8.

Miller, Robert A. *How to Live with a Heart Attack and How to Avoid One*. rev. ed. Chilton, 1973. $7.

Nicholas, Leslie. *How to Avoid Social Diseases*. Stein, 1973. $6.

Nourse, Alan E. *Ladies Home Journal Family Medical Guide*. Harper, 1973. $15.

Obley, Fred A. *Emphysema*. Beacon, 1970. $8.

Palos, Stephan. *Chinese Art of Healing*. McGraw, 1971. $7.

Prescott, Frederick. *Control of Pain*. Crowell, 1965. $5.

Rapaport, Howard G. *Complete Allergy Guide*. S&S, 1971. $9.

Rosenberg, Nancy. *Vaccine and Virus*. Grosset, 1971. $5.

Rubin, Harold. *Ulcer Diet Cookbook*. Evans, 1963. $6.

Sacks, Oliver W. *Migraine*. California, 1970. $10.

Sarno, John E. *Stroke*. McGraw, 1969. $7.

Schmitt, George F. *Diabetes for Diabetics*. 3rd ed. Diabetes Pr., 1971. $9.

Scott, Donald F. *About Epilepsy*. rev. ed. International U. Pr., 1973. $9.

Taylor, Norman. *Plant Drugs that Changed the World*. Dodd, 1965. $5.

VanRiper, Charles. *Speech Correction*. 5th ed. Prentice, 1972. $11.

Waksman, Selman A. *Conquest of Tuberculosis*. California, 1965. $7.

Williams, Greer. *Virus Hunters*. Knopf, 1959. $8.

Wilson, David. *Body and Antibody*. Knopf, 1972. $9.

Zinsser, Hans. *Rats, Lice and History*. Little, 1935. $7.

616.8   MENTAL HEALTH

Alvarez, Walter C. *Live at Peace with Your Nerves*. Prentice, 1958. $7.

Anonymous. *Go Ask Alice*. Prentice, 1971. $7.

Berne, Eric. *Layman's Guide to Psychiatry and Psychoanalysis*. 3rd ed. S&S, 1968. $7.

Fleming, Alice. *Psychiatry*. Regnery, 1972. $5.

Fromm, Erich. *Crisis of Psychoanalysis*. Holt, 1970. $6.

Harris, Thomas A. *I'm OK, You're OK*. Harper, 1969. $6.

Killilea, Marie. *Karen*. Prentice, 1962. $7.
Laing, R. D. *Divided Self*. Pantheon, 1969. $6.
Schreiber, Flora R. *Sybil*. Regnery, 1973. $9.
Stern, Edith M. *Mental Illness*. 5th ed. Harper, 1968. $5.
Thigpen, Corbett. *Three Faces of Eve*. Regent. $10.

617   EYES, EARS, TEETH
Baker, Jeffrey. *Truth about Contact Lenses*. Putnam, 1970. $6.
Berland, Theodore. *Your Children's Teeth*. Hawthorn, 1968. $7.
McDonald, Linda. *Contact Lenses*. Doubleday, 1972. $7.
McGuire, Thomas. *Tooth Trip*. Random, 1972. $7.
Seeman, Bernard. *Your Sight*. Little, 1968. $6.
Wright, David. *Deafness*. Stein, 1970. $6.

618   GYNECOLOGY, OBSTETRICS
Boston Children's Medical Center. *Pregnancy, Birth and the Newborn Baby*.
    Delacorte, 1972. $10.
Demarest, Robert J. *Conception, Birth and Contraception*. McGraw, 1969.
    $9.
Dick-Read, Grantly. *Childbirth without Fear*. 4th ed. Harper, 1972. $8.
Eastman, Nicholas J. *Expectant Motherhood*. 5th rev. ed. Little, 1970. $3.
Gifford-Jones, W. *On Being a Woman*. rev. ed. Macmillan, 1971. $7.
Kaufman, Sherwin A. *New Hope for the Childless Couple*. S&S, 1970. $5.
Lader, Lawrence. *Foolproof Birth Control*. Beacon, 1973. $7.
Lamaze, Fernand. *Painless Childbirth: LaMaze Method*. Regnery, 1970. $6.
Lieberman, E. James. *Sex and Birth Control*. Crowell, 1973. $6.
Liley, H. I. *Modern Motherhood*. rev. ed. Random, 1969. $6.
Rugh, Roberts. *From Conception to Birth*. Harper, 1971. $12.
Seaman, Barbara. *Doctor's Case against the Pill*. Wyden, 1969. $6.

620   ENGINEERING
Black, Perry. *Pumps*. 2nd ed. Audel, 1970. $6.
Brady, George S. *Materials Handbook*. 10th ed. McGraw, 1971. $25.
Calder, Ritchie. *Evolution of the Machine*. Hale, 1968. $5.
Canfield, D. T. *Business, Legal, and Ethical Phases of Engineering*. 2nd ed.
    McGraw, 1954. $14.
Jones, Franklin D. *Engineering Encyclopedia*. 3rd ed. Industrial, 1963. $18.
Kemper, John D. *Engineer and His Profession*. Holt, 1967. paper, $7.
Kirby, Richard S. *Engineering in History*. McGraw, 1956. $11.
LaLonde, William S. *Professional Engineer's Examination Questions and
    Answers*. 2nd ed. McGraw, 1966. $12.
McNickle, L. S. *Simplified Hydraulics*. McGraw, 1956. $11.
National Geographic Society. *Those Inventive Americans*. National Geo-
    graphic, 1971. $5.

Perry, Robert H. *Engineering Manual*. 2nd ed. McGraw, 1967. $14.

Woodruff, Everett B. *Steam Plant Operation*. McGraw, 1967. $14.

621   ELECTRONICS, ELECTRICITY, RADIO, TV

American Radio Relay League. *Radio Amateur's Handbook*. Am. Radio, published annually. $5.

Anderson, Edwin P. *Electric Motors*. 2nd ed. Audel, 1971. $6.

Black, Perry O. *Machinist's Library*. 2nd ed., 3 vols. Audel, 1970. set, $17.

Boyd, Waldo T. *World of Cryogenics*. Putnam, 1969. $4.

Brotherton, Manfred. *Masers and Lasers*. McGraw, 1964. $10.

Brown, Ronald. *Lasers*. Doubleday, 1969. $7.

_____. *Telecommunications: Booming Technology*. Doubleday, 1970. $7.

Buban, Peter. *Understanding Electricity and Electronics*. 2nd ed. McGraw, 1969. $9.

Buchsbaum, Walter H. *Color TV Servicing*. 2nd ed. Prentice, 1968. $10.

Carroll, John M. *Story of the Laser*. rev. ed. Dutton, 1970. $6.

Collins, A. Frederick. *Radio Amateur's Handbook*. 12th rev. ed. Crowell, 1970.

Crouse, William H. *Small Engines*. McGraw, 1974. $6.

Crowhurst, Norman H. *Servicing Modern Hi-Fi-Stereo Systems*. TAB, 1970. $8.

Daniels, Farrington. *Direct Use of the Sun's Energy*. Yale, 1964. $13.

Day, Richard. *Electrical Repairs and Projects for the Handyman.* Arco, 1973. $5.

Ewers, William. *Sincere's Air Conditioning Service*. Sincere, 1972. $9.

Graham, Kennard C. *Interior Electric Wiring: Residential*. 6th ed. Am. Technical, 1962. $6.

Grob, Bernard. *Basic Electronics*. 3rd ed. McGraw, 1971. $13.

Halacy, D. S., Jr. *Coming Age of Solar Energy*. rev. ed. Harper, 1973. $8.

Hertzberg, Robert. *So You Want to Be a Ham*. 6th ed. Sams, 1973. paper, $6.

Lytel, Allan. *ABCs of Lasers and Masers*. 3rd ed. Sams, 1972. $4.

Mages, Loren J. *Electric Generating Systems*. Audel, 1970. $6.

Mandl, Matthew. *Fundamentals of Electronics*. 2nd ed. Prentice, 1965. $14.

Marcus, Abraham. *Basic Electricity*. 3rd ed. Prentice, 1969. $12.

_____. *Basic Electronics*. 2nd ed. Prentice, 1971. $11.

Middleton, Robert G. *Practical Electricity*. 2nd ed., Audel, 1971. $6.

_____. *Tape Recorder Servicing Guide*. Sams, 1970. $4.

National Fire Protection Assn. *NFPA Handbook of the National Electrical Code*. 3rd rev. ed. McGraw, 1972. $14.

Novick, Sheldon. *Careless Atom*. Houghton, 1969. $6.

Nunz, Gregory J. *Electronics in Our World*. Prentice, 1972. $14.

Oberg, Erik. *Machinery's Handbook*. 19th ed. Industrial, 1971. $15.

Olney, Ross R. *Simple Gasoline Engine Repair*. Doubleday, 1972. paper, $3.

Orr, William I. *Radio Handbook*. 19th ed. Sams, 1972. $15.

Palmquist, Roland E. *House Wiring*. Audel, 1971. $6.

Pipe, Ted. *Basic Electricity Training Manual*. Sams, 1973. paper, $7.

Reynolds, John. *Windmills and Watermills*. Praeger, 1970. $14.

Richter, H. P. *Practical Electrical Wiring, Residential, Farm, and Industrial*. 8th ed. McGraw, 1970. $13.

Timbie, William H. *Essentials of Electricity*. 3rd ed. Wiley, 1963. $10.

622   MINING

Gibson, Ulric P. *Water Well Manual*. Premier, 1971. paper, $6.

Herndon, Booton. *Great Land*. Weybright, 1971. $7.

LeGaye, E. S. *Gold . . . ABCs of Panning*. Western Her., 1970. $3.

Nichols, Herbert. *Moving the Earth*. 2nd ed. North Castle, 1962. $25.

623.4   GUNS

Chapel, Charles E. *Complete Book of Gun Collecting*. Coward, 1961. $6.

_____. *Complete Guide to Gunsmithing, Gun Care, and Repair*. 2nd rev. ed. ABC, 1962. $7.

_____. *Gun Collector's Handbook of Values*. 10th rev. ed. Coward, 1972. $13.

Olsen, John. *Shooter's Bible*. Follett, published annually (65th ed., 1973). paper, $5.

Smith, Walter H. *Small Arms of the World*. 10th ed. Stackpole, 1973. $8.

Tunis, Edwin. *Weapons: Pictorial History*. World, 1954. $5.

623.8   BOATS, SEAMANSHIP

Benford, Jay. *Practical Ferro-Cement Boatbuilding*. 3rd ed. Int. Marine, 1972. $10.

Chapman, Charles F. *Piloting, Seamanship and Small Boat Handling*. Motor Boating, 1971. $9.

Crawford, William P. *Mariner's Notebook: a Guide to Boating Fundamentals*. 5th ed. Haessner. $11.

Gibbs, Tony. *Practical Sailing*. Motor Boating. $6.

Graumont, Raoul. *Encyclopedia of Knots and Fancy Rope Work*. 4th ed. Tidewater, 1952. $15.

Jobe, Joseph. *Great Age of Sail*. Viking, 1971. $17.

Polmar, Norman. *Atomic Submarines*. Van Nostrand, 1963. $11.

Technical Publications, Inc. *Outboard Motor Service Manual*. 6th ed., 2 vols. Sams, 1973. set, $11.

Watts, Alan. *Instant Weather Forecasting*. Dodd, 1968. $4.

628   POLLUTION, ECOLOGY

Baron, Robert A. *Tyranny of Noise*. St. Martin, 1970. $9.

Behrman, Abraham S. *Water Is Everybody's Business*. Doubleday, 1968. $6.

Carr, Donald E. *Breath of Life*. Norton, 1965. $6.

_____. *Death of the Sweet Waters*. Norton, 1971. $7.

Carson, Rachel. *Edge of the Sea*. Houghton, 1955. $7.

_____. *Sea around Us*. rev. ed. Oxford, 1961. $8.

_____. *Silent Spring*. Houghton, 1970. $7.

Esposito, John C. *Vanishing Air*. Grossman, 1970. $8.

Graham, Frank, Jr. *Since Silent Spring*. Houghton, 1970. $7.

Graves, John. *Water Hustlers*. Sierra, 1973. rev. ed. paper, $3.

Lewis, Howard R. *With Every Breath You Take*. Crown, 1965. $5.

McClellan, Grant S. *Protecting Our Environment*. Wilson, 1970. $5.

Odum, Eugene P. *Fundamentals of Ecology*. 3rd ed. Saunders, 1971. $12.

Popkin, Roy. *Desalination: Water for the World's Future*. Praeger, 1968. $8.

Small, William E. *Third Pollution*. Praeger, 1971. $7.

Stewart, George R. *Not So Rich as You Think*. Houghton, 1967. $7.

Wright, Jim. *Coming Water Famine*. Coward, 1966. $7.

Zwick, David. *Water Wasteland*. Grossman, 1971. $8.

629.1 FLIGHT

Ahnstrom, D. N. *Complete Book of Helicopters*. rev. ed. World, 1971. $7.

Gablehouse, Charles. *Helicopters and Autogyros*. rev. ed. Lippincott, 1969. $7.

Godson, John. *Unsafe at Any Height*. S&S, 1971. $6.

Guerny, Gene. *Pilot's Handbook of Weather*. Aero, 1966. $9.

Gunston, William T. *Hydrofoils and Hovercraft*. Doubleday, 1970. $7.

Laumer, Keith. *How to Design and Build Flying Models*. rev. ed. Harper, 1970. $6.

McEntee, Howard G. *Model Aircraft Handbook*. 5th ed. Crowell, 1968. $7.

Musciano, Walter A. *Building and Flying Model Airplanes*. F&W, 1972. $7.

_____. *Building and Flying Scale Model Aircraft*. rev. ed. Cahners, 1970. $8.

Simonson, Leroy. *Private Pilot Study Guide*. 2 vols. Aviation, 1970. set, $13.

Stine, G. Harry. *Handbook of Model Rocketry*. 3rd rev. ed. Follett, 1970. $7.

Van Sickle, Neil D. *Modern Airmanship*. 4th ed. Reinhold, 1971. $16.

629.2 MOTOR VEHICLES

American Automobile Assn. *Sportsmanlike Driving*. 6th ed. McGraw, 1970. $7.

Arctander, Erik. *New Book of Motorcycles*. Arco, 1968. $4.

Chilton's Auto Repair Manual. Chilton, published annually. $11.

Chilton's Import Car Repair Manual. 2 vols. Chilton, 1973. set, $19.

Chilton's Motorcycle Repair Manual. Chilton, published annually. $23.

Chilton's Repair and Tune-up Guide for Snowmobiles. Chilton, 1972. $7.

Chilton's Repair and Tune-up Guide for the Volkswagen. Chilton, 1973. $9.

Chilton's Truck Manual. Chilton, 1971. $18.

Cleary, Malachy. *Woman's Guide to Fixing the Car*. Walker, 1973. $6.

Crouse, William H. *Automotive Chassis and Body*. 4th ed. McGraw, 1971. $10.

———. *Automotive Electric Equipment*. 7th ed. McGraw, 1971. $8.

———. *Automotive Emission Control*. McGraw, 1971. $4.

———. *Automotive Engines*. 4th ed. McGraw, 1971. $9.

———. *Automotive Transmissions and Power Trains*. 4th ed. McGraw, 1971. $11.

Day, Dick. *Complete Book of Karting*. Prentice, 1961. $8.

———. *How to Service and Repair Your Own Car*. Harper, 1973. $11.

Dipboye, Jessie J. *Trailer Owners Handbook*. Trail-R-Club, 1969. $4.

Eliel, Lambert. *Trailer Owner's Manual*. Trail-R-Club, 1969. $4.

Eshelman, Philip V. *Tractors and Crawlers*. 2nd ed. Am. Technical, 1967. $9.

Ewers, William. *Sincere's Mini Bike Service*. Sincere, 1971. $10.

Georgano, G. N. *Complete Encyclopedia of Motor Cars: 1885–1968*. Dutton, 1968. $25.

Glenn, Harold T. *Automechanics*. 2nd rev. ed. Bennett, 1969. $10.

———. *Automobile Engine Rebuilding and Maintenance*. 2nd rev. ed. Chilton, 1967. $13.

Graham, Frank D. *Truck and Tractor Guide*. Audel, 1960. $8.

Hull, Clinton R. *How to Select, Buy, and Enjoy a Motor Home, Van, Camper, Tent-Top, or Tent*. Trail-R-Club, 1970. $5.

Johnson, Larry. *Fix Your Volkswagen*. rev. ed. Goodheart, published annually. $5.

Kearney, Paul W. *How to Drive Better and Avoid Accidents*. 3rd ed. Crowell, 1969. $7.

Motor's Auto Repair Manual. Motor Books, published annually. $11.

Motor's Automobile Trouble Shooter. 10th ed. Motor Books, 1973. $4.

Motor's Truck and Diesel Repair Manual. Motor Books, published annually. $17.

Nader, Ralph. *Unsafe at Any Speed*. rev. ed. Grossman, 1972. $8.

———. *What to Do with Your Bad Car*. Grossman, 1971. $9.

Ritch, OCee. *Chilton's Motorcycle Carburetion Systems*. Chilton, 1969. $7.

———. *Chilton's Motorcycle Electrical Systems*. Chilton, 1969. $7.

Roeing, Richard S. *Auto Engine Tune-up*. 2nd ed. Audel, 1970. $6.

Sargent, Robert L. *Automobile Sheet Metal Repair*. 2nd rev. ed. Chilton, 1969. $10.

Smith, LeRoi. *How to Fix Up Old Cars*. Dodd, 1968. $5.

Spicer, Edward D. *Automotive Collision Work*. 4th ed. Am. Technical, 1964. $9.

Stapley, Ray. *Car Owner's Handbook*. Doubleday, 1971. $7.

Stockel, Martin W. *Auto Mechanics Fundamentals*. Goodheart, 1969. $9.

_____. *Auto Service and Repair*. Goodheart, 1969. $11.

Toboldt, William K. *Auto Body Repairing and Repainting*. Goodheart, 1972. $6.

_____. *Fix Your Chevrolet*. Goodheart, published annually. $5.

_____. *Fix Your Ford*. Goodheart, published annually. $5.

Weissler, Paul. *Auto Repairs You Can Make*. rev. ed. Arco, 1972. $7.

Wheatley, Richard C. *Restoration of Antique and Classic Cars*. Bentley, 1967. $9.

629.3 BICYCLES

Complete Bicycle Book–Buyer's Guide. Petersen, published annually. $4.

Cuthbertson, Tom. *Anybody's Bike Book*. Ten Speed, 1971. $7.

Ewers, William. *Sincere's Bicycle Service Book*. Sincere, 1970. $9.

Frankel, Lillian. *Bikeways*. rev. ed. Sterling, 1972. $4.

McIntyre, Bibs. *Bike Book*. Harper, 1972. $7.

629.4 SPACE

Caidin, Martin. *Destination Mars*. Doubleday, 1972. $8.

Clarke, Arthur C. *Man and Space*. Time, 1968. $6.

_____. *Promise of Space*. Harper, 1968. $9.

Ley, Willy. *Rockets, Missiles and Men in Space*. 4th rev. ed. Viking, 1968. $11.

McLaughlin, Charles. *Space Age Dictionary*. 3rd ed. Van Nostrand, 1974. $12.

Newlon, Clarke. *1001 Questions Answered about Space*. 3rd ed. Dodd, 1971. $8.

Von Braun, Wernher. *History of Rocketry and Space Travel*. Crowell, 1966. $18.

_____. *Space Frontier*. rev. ed. Holt, 1971. $7.

630 AGRICULTURE

Abraham, George. *Green Thumb Book of Fruit and Vegetable Gardening*. Prentice, 1970. $8.

Blake, Claire. *Greenhouse Gardening for Fun*. Barrows, 1972. $8.

Dowdell, Dorothy. *Tree Farms*. Bobbs, 1965. $4.

Ewers, William. *Sincere's Lawn Mower Service Book*. 2nd ed. Sincere, 1973. $10.

Foss, E. W. *Construction and Maintenance for Farm and Home*. Wiley, 1960. $11.

Free, Montague. *Plant Propagation in Pictures*. Doubleday, 1957. $7.

Garner, Robert J. *Grafter's Handbook*. 3rd ed. Oxford, 1968. $8.

Karolevitz, Robert F. *Everything's Green . . . But My Thumb*. North Plains, 1971. $6.

Knott, James E. *Handbook for Vegetable Growers*. rev. ed. Wiley, 1962. $8.

Mortenson, William P. *Farm Management Handbook*. Interstate, 1972. $6.

Peterson, Franklynn. *Handbook of Lawn Mower Repair*. Emerson, 1973. $7.

Pirone, Pascal P. *Tree Maintenance*. 4th ed. Oxford, 1972. $15.

Platt, Rutherford H. *Great American Forest*. Prentice, 1965. $9.

Rudd, Rubert L. *Pesticides and the Living Landscape*. Wisconsin, 1964. $10.

Saunby, T. *Soilless Culture*. Transatlantic, 1970. $5.

Shurtleff, Malcolm C. *How to Control Plant Diseases in Home and Garden*. 2nd ed. Iowa, 1966. $11.

Smith, Harris P. *Farm Machinery and Equipment*. 5th ed. McGraw, 1964. $14.

Westcott, Cynthia. *Gardener's Bug Book*. 3rd ed. Doubleday, 1964. $10.

Wigginton, B. Eliott. *Foxfire Book*. Doubleday. $10.

_____. *Foxfire Two*. Doubleday. $9.

Zimmerman, Josef D. *Irrigation*. Wiley, 1966. $23.

636   PETS, LIVESTOCK

American Kennel Club. *Complete Dog Book*. rev. ed. Doubleday, 1972. $8.

Bateman, James A. *Animal Traps and Trapping*. Stackpole, 1971. $9.

Clear, Val. *Common Cagebirds in America*. Bobbs, 1966. $6.

Dangerfield, Stanley. *International Encyclopedia of Dogs*. McGraw, 1971. $20.

Davis, Henry P. *New Dog Encyclopedia*. Stackpole, 1970. $25.

Free, James L. *Training Your Retriever*. 3rd ed. Coward, 1970. $7.

Goodall, Daphne M. *Horses of the World*. Macmillan, 1965. $11.

Guthrie, Esther L. *Home Book of Animal Care*. Harper, 1966. $6.

Hapgood, Ruth. *First Horse*. Chronicle, 1972. $7.

Lampert, Lincoln N. *Modern Dairy Products*. Chemical Pub., 1970. $17.

McCoy, J. J. *Complete Book of Dog Training and Care*. rev. ed. Coward, 1970. $7.

Mather, Helen. *Light Horsekeeping*. Dutton, 1970. $7.

Merck Veterinary Manual. 4th ed. Merck, 1973. $15.

Morse, Roger A. *Complete Guide to Beekeeping*. Dutton, 1972. $7.

Pond, Grace. *Complete Cat Encyclopedia*. Crown, 1972. $15.

Robinson, D. G., Jr. *Know Your Gerbils*. Doubleday, 1973. paper, $1.

Rogers, Cyril H. *Parakeet Guide*. Doubleday, 1971. $4.

Self, Margaret C. *Horseman's Encyclopedia*. Arco, 1963. $10.

Sports Illustrated. *Dog Training*. rev. ed. Lippincott, 1972. $4.

Stamm, Gustav W. *Veterinary Guide for Farmers*. rev. ed. Hawthorn, 1963. $7.

Strickland, Winifred G. *Expert Obedience Training for Dogs*. rev. ed. Macmillan, 1969. $8.

Summerhays, Reginald. *Summerhays' Encyclopedia for Horsemen*. rev. ed. Warne, 1970. $8.

Taynton, Mark. *Successful Kennel Management*. rev. ed. Beech Tree, 1966. $9.

Templeton, George. *Domestic Rabbit Production*. Interstate, 1968. $6.

Thatcher, William. *Caring for Your Cat*. Arco, 1972. $2.

Whitney, Leon F. *Complete Book of Cat Care*. Doubleday, 1953. $6.

———. *First Aid for Pets*. Vanguard, 1954. $5.

———. *Pets*. McKay, 1971. $7.

Tropical/Aquarium fish books are listed in 597.

641   HOMEMAKING, COOKING

Angier, Bradford. *Feasting Free on Wild Edibles*. Stackpole, 1972. $8.

Beard, James. *Menus for Entertaining*. Delacorte, 1965. $9.

Better Homes & Gardens, eds. *Casserole Cook Book* (and many others). Meredith, 1969. $4 each.

———. *Creative Table Settings*. Meredith, 1973. $4.

———. *New Cook Book*. rev. ed. Better Homes, 1968. $7.

Bowen, Angela J. *Diabetic Gourmet*. Harper, 1970. $7.

Bowring, Jean. *New Cake Decorating Book*. Arco, 1974. $8.

Brown, Sam. *Cooking Creatively with Natural Foods*. Hawthorn, 1972. $7.

Cadwallader, Sharon. *Whole Earth Cook Book*. Houghton, 1972. $6.

Child, Julia. *Mastering the Art of French Cooking*. 2 vols. Knopf, 1961/70. set, $25.

Claiborne, Craig. *New York Times International Cook Book*. Harper, 1971. $13.

Crocker, Betty. *Betty Crocker's Cook Book*. Western, 1969. $6.

———. *Betty Crocker's Cooky Book*. Western, 1963. $3.

Davis, Adelle. *Let's Eat Right to Keep Fit*. rev. ed. Harcourt, 1970. $6.

Engel, Lyle K. *Complete Book of Mobil Home Living*. Arco, 1973. $6.

Farm Journal, eds. *Freezing and Canning Cookbook*. Doubleday, 1973. $7.

———. *Homemade Bread*. Doubleday, 1969. $5.

Farmer, Fannie M. *Fannie Farmer Cookbook*. 11th ed. Little, 1965. $8.

Fowler, Sina F. *Food for Fifty*. 5th ed. Wiley, 1971. $13.

Herrmann, Martin K. *Art of Making Good Candies at Home*. Doubleday, 1966. $6.

Hewitt, Jean. *New York Times Natural Foods Cookbook*. Quadrangle, 1971. $10.

Hull, Raymond. *Home Book of Smoke-Cooking Meat, Fish, and Game*. Stackpole, 1971. $8.

Hunter, Beatrice T. *Natural Foods Cookbook*. S&S, 1961. $5.

———. *Natural Foods Primer*. S&S, 1972. $5.

Keys, Ancel. *Eat Well and Stay Well*. rev. ed. Doubleday, 1963. $6.

Kohn, Bernice. *Organic Living Book*. Viking, 1972. $5.

Lee, Nata. *Complete Book of Entertaining*. rev. ed. Hawthorn, 1968. $7.

Margolius, Sidney. *Innocent Consumer vs. the Exploiters*. Trident, 1967. $7.

Meyer, Hazel. *Complete Book of Home Freezing*. rev. ed. Lippincott, 1970. $8.

Moore, Alma C. *How to Clean Everything*. 3rd ed. S&S, 1968. $5.

New York Times. *New York Times Cookbook*. Claiborne, Craig, ed. Harper, 1961. $10.

Nidetch, Jean. *Weight Watchers Program Cook Book*. Hearthside, 1973. $7.

Oaks, Marian C. *Fell's Guide to Mobile Home Living*. Fell, 1965. $6.

Orton, Mildred E. *Cooking with Wholegrains*. Farrar, 1971. $5.

Payne, Alma S. *Fat and Sodium Control Cookbook*. 3rd rev. ed. Little, 1966. $6.

Percivall, Julia. *Household Ecology*. Prentice, 1972. $6.

Rodale Cookbook. new ed. Rodale, 1973. $11.

Rombaur, Irma S. *Joy of Cooking*. rev. ed. Bobbs, 1951. $7.

Sandler, Sandra. *Home Bakebook of Natural Breads and Goodies*. Stackpole, 1972. $8.

Sullivan, Betty. *Blender Way to Better Cooking*. Western, 1966. $8.

Sunset. Various cookbook titles, including *Fondue, Spices and Herbs*, etc. Lane, 1972/4. each, $3.

642   BEAUTY

Brauer, Earle W. *Your Skin and Hair*. Macmillan, 1969. $8.

Glamour Magazine. *Glamour Beauty and Health Book*. S&S, 1972. $10.

Sternberg, Thomas H. *More Than Skin Deep*. Doubleday, 1970. $8.

643   HOUSEHOLD EQUIPMENT

Anderson, Edwin P. *Audel's Home Appliance Servicing*. Audel, 1971. $7.

_____. *Home Refrigeration and Air Conditioning Guide*. 2nd ed. Audel, 1966. $7.

Belt, Forest H. *Easi-Guide to Color TV*. Sams, 1973. paper, $4.

Ewers, William. *Sincere's Sewing Machine Service Book*. 3rd ed. Sincere, 1971. $10.

_____. *Sincere's Vacuum Cleaner and Small Appliance Service Manual*. Sincere, 1973. $10.

Hertzberg, Robert. *Repairing Small Electrical Appliances*. Arco, 1968. $4.

Lemons, Wayne. *Major Appliance Repair Manual*. TAB, 1971. $9.

_____. *Small Appliance Repair Guide*. TAB, 1970. $8.

Margolis, Art. *Make Your Own TV Repairs*. Arco, 1968. $4.

Peet, Louise J. *Household Equipment*. 6th ed. Wiley, 1970. $12.

Squeglia, Michael. *All about Repairing Small Appliances*. Hawthorn, 1973. paper, $5.

Tricomi, Ernest. *How to Repair Major Appliances*. 2nd ed. Sams, 1968. paper, $5.

Ward, Kay B. *Feminine Fix-it Handbook*. Grosset, 1972. $6.

646   SEWING

Bishop, Edna B. *Super Sewing*. 3rd ed. Lippincott, 1974. $7.

Cunningham, Gladys. *Singer Sewing Book*. Random, 1972. $9.

Doerr, Catherine M. *Smart Sewing.* Macmillan, 1967. $8.

Ficarotta, Phyllis. *Sewing without a Pattern*. Sterling, 1971. $3.

Johnson, Mary. *Sewing the Easy Way*. rev. ed. Dutton, 1966. $7.

McCalls. *McCall's Sewing Book*. rev. ed. Random, 1968. $7.

McCunn, Donald H. *How to Make Your Own Sewing Patterns*. Hart, 1973.
$10.

Margolis, Adele P. *Design Your Own Dress Patterns*. Doubleday, 1971. $9.

_____. *Dressmaking Book*. Doubleday, 1972. $5.

Rosenberg, Sharon. *Illustrated Hassle-Free Make Your Own Clothes Book*.
Straight Arrow, 1971. $8.

649   CHILD CARE

Broadribb, Violet. *Modern Parent's Guide to Baby and Child Care*. Lippincott, 1973. $10.

Cattell, Psyche. *Raising Children with Love and Limits*. Nelson, 1973. $7.

Dodson, Fitzhugh. *How to Parent*. Nash, 1970. $8.

Ginott, Haim G. *Between Parent and Child*. Macmillan, 1965. $6.

_____. *Between Parent and Teenager*. Macmillan, 1969. $6.

Gordon, Thomas. *Parent Effectiveness Training*. Wyden, 1970. $7.

Gruenberg, Sidonie M. *New Encyclopedia of Child Care and Guidance*.
Doubleday, 1968. $13.

Hurlock, Elizabeth B. *Child Growth and Development*. 4th ed. McGraw,
1970. $9.

Hymes, Jesild, Jr. *Child under Six*. Prentice, 1963. $7.

Narramore, Bruce. *Help! I'm a Parent*. Zondervan, 1972. $4.

Spock, Benjamin M. *Baby and Child Care*. new rev. ed. Hawthorn, 1968. $7.

Vanderpoel, Sally. *Care and Feeding of Your Diabetic Child*. Fell, 1968. $6.

Wright, Erna. *Common Sense in Child Rearing*. Hart, 1973. $6.

650   BUSINESS, OFFICE PRACTICE AND PROCEDURE

Angel, Juvenal L. *Why and How to Prepare an Effective Job Resume*. rev.
ed. World Trade, 1972. $13.

Arnold, Robert R. *Modern Data Processing*. 2nd ed. Wiley, 1972. $11.

Bartee, Thomas C. *Digital Computer Fundamentals*. 3rd ed. McGraw, 1972.
$12.

Boynton, Lewis D. *20th Century Bookkeeping and Accounting*. 23rd ed.
Southwestern, 1968. $7.

Burton, Philip W. *Advertising Fundamentals*. Intext, 1970. $13.

Dearden, John. *Cost Accounting and Financial Control System*. Addison,
1973. $12.

Dible, Donald M. *Up Your Own Organization*. Hawthorn, 1973. $15.

Dixon, Robert L. *Executive's Accounting Primer*. McGraw, 1971. $10.

Duncan, Delbert J. *Modern Retailing Management*. Irwin, 1972. $12.

Eddings, Claire N. *Secretary's Complete Model Letter Handbook*. Prentice, 1965. $8.

Gavin, Ruth E. *Reference Manual for Stenographers and Typists*. 4th ed. McGraw, 1970. $5.

Holmes, Arthur W. *Basic Auditing Principles*. 4th ed. Wylie, 1972. $11.

How to Start Your Own Small Business. Drake, 1973. $4.

Hutchinson, Lois. *Standard Handbook for Secretaries*. 8th ed. McGraw, 1969. $8.

Ivey, Paul W. *Successful Salesmanship*. 4th ed. Prentice, 1961. $11.

Janis, Jack H. *New Standard Reference for Secretaries and Administrative Assistants*. Macmillan, 1972. $10.

Jucius, Michael J. *Introduction to Business*. 3rd ed. Irwin, 1966. $11.

Kelley, Pearce C. *How to Organize and Operate a Small Business*. 4th ed. Prentice, 1968. $12.

Kleppner, Otto. *Advertising Procedure*. 6th ed. Prentice, 1973. $12.

Lasser, Jacob K. *Business Management Handbook*. 3rd ed. McGraw, 1968. $17.

―――. *How to Run a Small Business*. 3rd ed. McGraw, 1963. $10.

Leslie, Louis A. *Gregg Notehand*. 2nd ed. McGraw, 1968. $7.

―――. *Gregg Shorthand Functional Method*. 2nd ed. McGraw, 1971. $7.

Lessenberry, David D. *Clerical Office Typing*. Southwestern, 1972. $4.

Levine, Nathan. *Typing for Everyone*. Arco, 1972. $4.

Lloyd, Alan C. *Personal Typing*. 3rd ed. McGraw, 1969. $6.

Packard, Vance. *Hidden Persuaders*. McKay, 1957. $8.

Peter, Laurence J. *The Peter Principle*. Morrow, 1969. $6.

Phillips, Charles F. *Marketing: Principles and Methods*. 6th ed. Irwin, 1968. $12.

Rowe, John L. *Gregg Typing*. 2nd ed. McGraw, 1967. $6.

Shook, Robert L. *How to Be the Complete Professional Salesman*. Fell, 1973. $10.

Townsend, Robert. *Up the Organization*. Knopf, 1970. $6.

Weeks, Bertha. *Filing and Records Management*. 3rd ed. Ronald, 1964. $7.

Wylie, Harry L. *Office Management Handbook*. 2nd ed. Ronald, 1958. $14.

660   INDUSTRY, METALS, MANUFACTURING

Althouse, Andrew D. *Modern Welding*. Goodheart, 1970. $10.

Begeman, Myron L. *Manufacturing Processes*. 6th ed. Wiley, 1968. $16.

Blumberg, Robert S. *Fine Wines of California*. Doubleday, 1974. paper, $4.

Feirer, John L. *General Metals*. McGraw, 1974. $11.

Giachino, J. W. *Welding Technology*. 2nd ed. Am. Technical, 1973. $8.

Lappin, Alvin R. *Plastics―Projects and Techniques*. McKnight, 1965. $7.

Linton, George E. *Modern Textile and Apparel Dictionary*. 4th rev. ed. Textile, 1973. $24.

Milby, Robert V. *Plastics Technology*. McGraw, 1973. $13.

Newcomb, Ellsworth. *Miracle Metals*. Putnam, 1962. $4.

Newman, Thelma. *Plastics as Design Form*. Chilton, 1972. $18.

Rogers, Bruce A. *Nature of Metals*. MIT. paper, $3.

Simon, André. *International Wine and Food Society's Encyclopedia of Wines*. Quadrangle, 1973. $15.

Stout, Evelyn E. *Introduction to Textiles*. 3rd ed. Wiley, 1970. $12.

Walker, John R. *Modern Metalworking*. Goodheart, 1973. $9.

680   FURNITURE, UPHOLSTERY, WOODWORKING

Adams, Jeanette. *Complete Woodworking Handbook*. Arco, 1960. $6.

Bast, Herbert. *New Essentials of Modern Upholstery*. Bruce, 1970. $6.

Bergen, John. *All about Upholstering*. Hawthorn, 1962. $6.

Berger, Robert. *All about Antiquing and Restoring Furniture*. Hawthorn, 1971. $7.

Feirer, John L. *Advanced Woodwork and Furniture Making*. Scribner, 1973. $15.

Gottshall, Franklin H. *How to Make Colonial Furniture*. Macmillan, 1971. $10.

————. *Reproducing Antique Furniture*. Crown, 1971. $10.

Grotz, George. *From Gunk to Glow*. Random, 1973. paper, $2.

Hammond, James J. *Woodworking Technology*. rev. ed. McKnight, 1972. $8.

Hand, Jackson. *How to Do Your Own Wood Finishing*. rev. ed. Popular Science, 1968. $4.

Luna, Benjamin C. *Upholstery*. Am. Technical, 1969. $6.

Peters, Geoff. *Woodturning*. Arco, 1961. $5.

Schremp, William E. *Designer Furniture Anyone Can Make*. S&S, 1972. $7.

Spielman, Patrick E. *Make Your Own Sport Gear*. Macmillan, 1970. $8.

Sunset Magazine, eds. *Furniture Finishing and Refinishing*. Lane, 1969. $2.

————. *Furniture Upholstery and Repair*. Lane, 1970. $2.

Wolansky, William D. *Woodworking Made Easy*. Scribner, 1972. $7.

690   HOME REPAIRS, CONSTRUCTION, REMODELING, ETC.

Audel & Co. *Builders Encyclopedia*. Audel, 1971. $8.

Babbitt, Harold E. *Plumbing*. 3rd ed. McGraw, 1960. $20.

Better Homes & Gardens, eds. *Handyman's Book*. rev. ed. Better Homes, 1970. $8.

Brimer, John B. *Homeowner's Complete Outdoor Building Book*. Popular Science, 1971. $9.

Bruner, Wally. *Wally's Workshop*. S&S, 1973. $8.

Carrell, Al. *Super Handyman's Encyclopedia of Home Repair Hints*. Prentice, 1971. $8.

Dalzell, J. Ralph. *Simplified Concrete Masonry Planning and Building.* 2nd rev. ed. McGraw, 1972. $9.

Daniels, George. *How to Use Hand and Power Tools.* Harper, 1964. $4.

Day, Richard. *Remodeling Rooms.* Arco, 1968. $4.

Family Handyman. *America's Handyman Book.* Scribner, 1970. $10.

French, Thomas E. *Fundamentals of Engineering Drawing.* 3rd ed. McGraw, 1972. $12.

_____. *Mechanical Drawing.* 8th ed. McGraw, 1974. $10.

Giesecke, Frederick E. *Technical Drawing.* 5th ed. Macmillan, 1967. $11.

Gladstone, Bernard. *New York Times Complete Manual of Home Repair.* Macmillan, 1966. $8.

Hand, Jackson. *Complete Book of Home Repairs and Maintenance.* Harper, 1971. $9.

Harmon, A. J. *Guide to Home Remodeling.* Grosset, 1971. $8.

Hasenau, J. James. *Building Your Own Home.* Holland, 1973. paper, $6.

Huff, Darrell. *Complete Book of Home Improvement.* Harper, 1970. $12.

McCabe, Francis T. *Mechanical Drafting Essentials.* Prentice, 1967. $8.

Merritt, Frederick S. *Building Construction Handbook.* 2nd ed. McGraw, 1965. $25.

Schuler, Stanley. *Householder's Encyclopedia.* Sat. Rev., 1973. $10.

_____. *How to Fix Almost Everything.* Evans, 1963. $5.

Schwartz, Robert. *Complete Homeowner.* Macmillan, 1965. $6.

Stanforth, Deidre. *Buying and Renovating a House in the City.* Knopf, 1972. $10. paper, $5.

Sunset. Various titles on: outdoor lighting, outdoor building, walks, fireplaces, fences, barbecues, etc. Lane. paper, $2.

Wagner, Willis. *Modern Carpentry.* Goodheart, 1973. $7.

Watkins, Arthur M. *Complete Book of Home Remodeling, Improvement, and Repair.* Doubleday, 1963, paper, $2.

_____. *Homeowner's Survival Kit.* Hawthorn, 1971. $7.

Woodin, James C. *Home and Building Maintenance.* McKnight, 1969. $8.

700

ARTS, SPORTS

701   ARTS–GENERAL

Canady, John E. *Keys to Art*. Tudor, 1963. $13.

Chamberlain, Betty. *Artist's Guide to His Market*. Watson, 1970. $6.

Gombrich, Ernst H. *Story of Art*. 12th rev. ed. Phaidon, 1972. $15.

Holden, Honal. *Art Career Guide*. rev. ed. Watson, 1973. $8.

Jameson, Kenneth. *Art and the Young Child*. Viking, 1969. $7.

Kramer, Edith. *Art as Therapy with Children*. Viking, 1969. $10.

Kuh, Katharine. *Break-Up: the Core of Modern Art*. NYGS, 1969. $9.

_____. *Open Eye: in Pursuit of Art*. Harper, 1971. $9.

Lucas, E. Louise. *Art Books: a Basic Bibliography on the Fine Arts*. NYGS, 1968. $5.

Meyers, Hans. *150 Techniques in Art*. Reinhold, 1963. $9.

Munro, Eleanor C. *Encyclopedia of Art*. rev. ed. Western, 1964. $15.

Munro, Thomas. *Arts and Their Interrelations*. rev. ed. Case Western, 1967. $10.

Nahm, Milton C. *Readings in the Philosophy of Art and Aesthetics*. Appleton, 1973. $12.

Whittick, Arnold. *Symbols, Signs and Their Meaning*. Branford, 1971. $21.

Wold, Milo. *Introduction to Music and Art in the Western World*. 4th ed. Brown Bk., 1972. $6.

709   ART HISTORY

Amaya, Maris. *Pop Art and After*. Viking, 1972. $9.

Chipp, Herschel B. *Theories of Modern Art*. California, 1968. $17.

Janson, Horst W. *History of Art*. rev. ed. Prentice, 1969. $15.

_____. *History of Art and Music*. Abrams, 1968. $15.

Larkin, Oliver W. *Art and Life in America*. rev. ed. Holt, 1960. $15.

Lee, Sherman E. *History of Far Eastern Art*. Prentice, 1974. $15.

Mendelowitz, Daniel M. *History of American Art*. 2nd ed. Holt, 1970. $18.

Pavola, Rene. *Optical Art: Theory and Practice*. Reinhold, 1969. $15.

Rice, Tamara T. *Concise History of Russian Art*. Praeger, 1963. $9.

Russell, John. *Pop Art Redefined*. Praeger, 1969. $9.

Willett, Frank. *African Art*. Praeger, 1971. $9.

711   CITY DESIGN

Bacon, Edmund N. *Design of Cities*. rev. ed. Viking, 1973. $20.

Fairbrother, Nan. *New Lives, New Landscapes: Planning for the 21st Century*. Knopf, 1970. $13.

Holland, Lawrence B. *Who Designs America?* Peter Smith. $4.

Jacobs, Jane. *Death and Life of Great American Cities*. Random, 1961. $10.

Nairn, Ian. *American Landscape*. Random, 1967. $4.

Rudofsky, Bernard. *Streets for People*. Doubleday, 1969. $15.

716   GARDENING, LANDSCAPING

Abraham, George. *Green Thumb Book of Indoor Gardening*. Prentice, 1967. $8.

_____. *Green Thumb Garden Handbook*. Prentice, 1961. $8.

Atkinson, Robert E. *Complete Book of Groundcovers*. McKay, 1970. $8.

Better Homes & Gardens, eds. *Flower Arranging*. Better Homes, 1957, $4.

_____. *Better Homes & Gardens House Plants*. 2nd ed. Better Homes, 1971. $3.

Coats, Peter. *Great Gardens of the Western World*. Putnam, 1963. $23.

Compton, Joan. *House Plants*. Grosset, 1973. $5.

Crockett, James U. *Landscape Gardening*. Time, 1971. $8.

Cruso, Thalassa. *Making Things Grow Outdoors*. Knopf, 1971. $8.

Culpeper, Nicholas. *Culpeper's Complete Herbal*. Sterling, 1959. $7.

Doole, Louise E. *Herb Magic & Garden Craft*. Sterling, 1973. $4.

Fitch, Charles M. *Complete Book of Houseplants*. Hawthorn, 1972. $10.

Fox, Helen M. *Gardening with Herbs*. Sterling, 1970. $5.

Griffith, Anna N. *Guide to Rock Garden Plants*. Dutton, 1965. $8.

Haage, Walter. *Cacti and Succulents*. rev. ed. Dutton, 1963. $13.

Ireys, Alice R. *How to Plan and Plant Your Own Property*. Morrow, 1967. $8.

Kramer, Jack. *Gardening and Home Landscaping*. Harper, 1971. $10.

_____. *1000 Beautiful House Plants and How to Grow Them*. Morrow, 1969. $13.

Kranz, Frederick H. *Gardening Indoors under Lights*. new ed. Viking, 1971. $8.

Lamb, Brian. *Pocket Encyclopedia of Cacti and Succulents*. Macmillan, 1970. $5.

McCalls. *McCalls' Garden Book*. S&S, 1968. $10.

McDonald, Elvin. *Low-Upkeep Book of Lawns and Landscape.* Hawthorn, 1971. $7.

Meyer, Joseph E. *Herbalist.* rev. ed. Sterling, 1968. $5.

New York Times Book of Home Landscaping. Knopf, 1964. $5.

Reader's Digest. *Reader's Digest Complete Book of the Garden.* Norton, 1966. $10.

Rockwell, Frederick F. *Rockwell's Complete Guide to Successful Gardening.* Doubleday, 1965. $9.

Schery, Robert W. *Lawn Book.* Macmillan, 1961. $6.

Schuler, Stanley. *Gardener's Basic Book of Trees and Shrubs.* S&S, 1973. $10.

Simmons, Adelma G. *Herbs to Grow Indoors.* Hawthorn, 1969. $6.

Sunset Magazine, eds. Lane, 1968–72. each, $2–$3: *Basic Gardening Illustrated; Bonsai; Color in Your Garden; Desert Gardening; Garden and Patio Building Book; Garden Pools, Fountains and Waterfalls; Gardening in Containers; How to Grow African Violets; How to Grow and Use Annuals; How to Grow Bulbs; How to Grow Herbs; How to Grow House Plants; How to Grow Roses; Ideas for Landscaping; Lawns and Ground Covers; Pruning Handbook; Succulents and Cactus; Terrariums and Miniature Gardens.*

Taylor, Norman. *Encyclopedia of Gardening.* rev. ed. Houghton, 1961. $13.

———. *Guide to Garden Shrubs and Trees.* Houghton, 1965. $10.

Wilson, Helen. *Helen V. Wilson's African Violet Book.* Hawthorn, 1970. $8.

Wyman, Donald. *Trees for American Gardens.* rev. ed. Macmillan, 1965. $11.

———. *Wyman's Gardening Encyclopedia.* Macmillan, 1971. $18.

720   ARCHITECTURE

In recent years there have been many excellent guides and descriptions of the architecture of particular cities, towns, states, and regions. Individual libraries are urged to search these out for their collections.

Baumgart, Fritz. *History of Architectural Styles.* Praeger, 1970. $12.

Goodban, W. T. *Architectural Drawing and Planning.* McGraw, 1965. $8.

Hague, William E. *Your Vacation Home.* Doubleday, 1972. $7.

Halse, Albert O. *Architectural Rendering.* 2nd ed. McGraw, 1972. $22.

Hamlin, Talbot. *Architecture through the Ages.* rev. ed. Putnam, 1953. $10.

Hepler, Donald E. *Architecture: Drafting and Design.* 2nd ed. McGraw, 1971. $10.

Hoag, Edwin. *American Houses.* Lippincott, 1964. $6.

Kaufmann, Edgar, Jr. *Rise of an American Architecture.* Praeger, 1970. $10.

Meinhardt, Carl. *So You Want to Be an Architect.* Harper, 1969. $5.

Millon, Henry A. *Key Monuments of the History of Architecture.* Prentice, 1964. $11.

Mirsky, Jeannette. *Houses of God.* Viking, 1965. $9.

Pevsner, Nikolaus. *Outline of European Architecture*. Gannon, 1960. $6.

Scully, Vincent. *American Architecture and Urbanism*. Praeger, 1969. paper, $6.

Spence, William P. *Architecture*. 2nd ed. McKnight, 1972. $11.

Stern, Robert. *New Directions in American Architecture*. Braziller, 1969. $6.

Whiffen, Marcus. *American Architecture since 1780*. Arch. Bk., 1968. $9.

Wills, Royal B. *More Houses for Good Living*. Arch. Bk., 1968. $9.

730   SCULPTURE, PLASTICS, CERAMICS

Cheney, Sheldon. *Sculpture of the World*. Viking, 1968. $13.

DiValentin, Maria M. *Sculpture for Beginners*. Sterling, 1969. $5.

Gross, Chaim. *Technique of Wood Sculpture*. Arco, 1957. $5.

Gruber, Elmar. *Metal and Wire Sculpture*. Sterling, 1969. $3.

Harman & Parmelee. *Ceramic Glazes*. Cahners, 1973. $15.

Hoppe, H. *Whittling and Wood Carving*. Sterling, 1969. $3.

Isenstein, Harald. *Creative Claywork*. Sterling. $4.

Morely-Fletcher, Hugo. *Investing in Pottery and Porcelain*. Potter, 1968. $8.

Nelson, Glenn C. *Ceramics*. 3rd ed. Holt, 1971. $9.

Newman, Thelma R. *Plastics as an Art Form*. rev. ed. Chilton, 1969. $13.

Percy, H. M. *New Materials in Sculpture*. 2nd ed. Transatlantic, 1966. $7.

Priolo, Joan B. *Ceramics—and How to Decorate Them*. Sterling. $7.

Read, Herbert. *Concise History of Modern Sculpture*. Praeger, 1964. $9.

Schegger, Theresia M. *Make Your Own Mobiles*. Sterling. $3.

Sunset. *Ceramics*. Lane, 1971. paper, $2.

_____. *Sculpture with Simple Materials*. Lane, 1971. paper, $2.

Williams, Guy R. *Making Mobiles*. Emerson, 1969. $5.

740   COMMERCIAL ART, CARTOONS, DRAWING

Gollwitzer, Gerhard. *Drawing from Nature*. Sterling, 1969. $4.

_____. *Express Yourself in Drawing*. Sterling, 1960. $4.

Herter, Christine. *Dynamic Symmetry*. Norton, 1966. $10.

Jaxtheimer, Bodo W. *Reinhold Drawing and Painting Book*. Reinhold, 1962. $11.

Nelson, Roy P. *Fell's Guide to Commercial Art*. Fell, 1966. $7.

Richardson, H. Wilmont. *Freehand Lettering*. Sterling, 1970. $5.

Sloane, Eunice M. *Illustrating Fashion*. Harper, 1968. $16.

Wolchonok, Louis. *Art of Pictorial Composition*. Peter Smith, 1961. $7.

Zaidenberg, Arthur. *How to Draw and Compose Pictures*. Abelard, 1971. $5.

Many other drawing titles available by this author.

745   CRAFTS, DESIGN

Amlick, Barbara A. *Dried Flower Craft*. Macmillan, 1971. $3.

Aytes, Barbara. *Adventures in Crocheting*. Doubleday, 1972. $8.

_____. *Knitting Made Easy*. Doubleday, 1970. $5.

Beitler, Ethel J. *Hooked and Knotted Rugs*. Sterling, 1973. $3.

Better Homes & Gardens. *Stitchery and Crafts*. Better Homes, 1966. $7.

Boulay, Roger. *Make Your Own Elegant Jewelry*. Sterling, 1972. $3.

Bowers, Melvyn K. *Easy Bulletin Boards*. Scarecrow, 1966. $4.

Bressard, M. J. *Creating with Burlap*. Sterling, 1970. $3.

Bucher, Jo. *Complete Guide to Embroidery Stitches and Crewel*. Better Homes, 1971. $9.

Butler, Anne. *Embroidery Stitches*. Praeger, 1968. $6.

Carey, Mary. *Candlemaking*. Western, 1972. $5.

Choate, Sharr. *Creative Casting*. Crown, 1966. $8.

Clapper, Edna N. *Pack-O-Fun Treasury of Crafts, Gifts, and Toys*. Hawthorn, 1971. $5.

Comins, Jeremy. *Getting Started in African Crafts*. Macmillan, 1971. paper, $3.

Coplan, Kate. *Poster Ideas and Bulletin Board Techniques*. Oceana, 1962. $10.

Dendel, Esther W. *Needleweaving: Easy as Embroidery*. Doubleday, 1972. $8.

DiValentin, Maria M. *Practical Encyclopedia of Crafts*. Sterling, 1971. $20.

Duncan, Ida R. *Complete Book of Progressive Knitting*. rev. ed. Liveright, 1972. $7.

Duncan, Molly. *Spin, Dye, and Weave Your Own Wool*. Sterling, 1973. $4.

Golden Hands Handicrafts. Random, 1973. $5.

Green, Sylvia. *Patchwork for Beginners*. Watson, 1972. $8.

Griswold, Lester E. *New Handicraft; Processes and Projects*. 10th ed. Van Nostrand, 1972. $10.

Guild, Vera P. *Good Housekeeping New Complete Book of Needlecraft*. Hearst, 1971. $9.

Hellegers, Louisa F. *Family Book of Crafts*. Sterling, 1973. $17.

Honda, Isao. *World of Origami*. Japan, 1965. $15.

Horowitz, Elinor L. *Mountain People, Mountain Crafts*. Lippincott, 1974. $7.

Howard, Sylvia. *Tin Can Crafting*. rev. ed. Sterling, 1964. $4.

Hutton, Helen. *Practical Gemstone Craft*. Viking, 1972. $9.

Jacobsen, Charles W. *Oriental Rugs*. Tuttle, 1962. $17.

Johnson, Pauline. *Creating with Paper*. Washington, 1966. $9.

Kenny, Carla. *Art of Papier Mache*. Chilton, 1968. $13.

LaCroix, Grethe. *Creating with Beads*. Sterling, 1969. $3.

Laury, Jean R. *Handmade Rugs from Practically Anything*. Doubleday, 1972. $8.

Lozier, Herbert. *Model Making*. Chilton, 1967. $8.

Lynch, John. *How to Make Collages*. Viking, 1961. $6.

McCall's Needlework Treasury. Random, 1965. $9.

Meilach, Dona Z. *Creating Art from Anything*. Reilly, 1968. $7.

Mirow, Gregory. *Treasury of Designs for Artists and Craftsmen*. Peter Smith, 1969. $5.

Monroe, Ruth. *Kitchen Candlecrafting*. B&N, 1969. $8.

Nimocks, Patricia. *Decoupage*. Scribner, 1968. $10.

Nussbaumer, Hanny. *Lacquer and Crackle*. Sterling, 1972. $3.

Pahlman, William. *Book of Interior Design*. 3rd ed. Viking, 1968. $11.

Papanek, Victor. *Design for the Real World*. Pantheon, 1972. $9.

Phillips, Mary W. *Step-by-Step Macrame*. Western, 1970. $5.

Rottger, Ernst. *Creative Wood Design*. Van Nostrand, 1972. $6.

Sanford, William R. *Jewelry, Queen of Crafts*. Macmillan, 1970. $9.

Scobey, Jean. *Do-it-all-Yourself Needlepoint*. S&S, 1971. $6.

Sunset Magazine, eds. Lane, 1969-73. paper, each, $2-$3: *Crafts for Children; Crafts You Can Make; Decorative Stitchery; Macrame; Needlepoint; Papier Mache; Quilting and Patchwork; Things to Make with Leather*.

Taylor, Gertrude. *America's Crochet Book*. Scribner, 1972. $10.

———. *America's Knitting Book*. Scribner, 1968. $10.

Timmons, Virginia G. *Designing and Making Mosaics*. Davis, 1971. $9.

Van Zandt, Eleanor. *Crafts for Fun and Profit*. Doubleday, 1974. $7.

Wildman, Emily. *Step-by-Step Crochet*. Western, 1972. $6.

Wing, Frances S. *Complete Book of Decoupage*. rev. ed. Coward, 1970. $7.

Wiseman, Ann. *Rag Tapestries and Wool Mosaics*. Van Nostrand, 1969. $8.

Wood, Paul W. *Stained Glass Crafting*. rev. ed. Sterling, 1971. $5.

Young, Jean. *Woodstock Craftsman's Manual*. Praeger, 1972. $10.

———. *Woodstock Craftsman's Manual Two*. Praeger, 1973. $10.

Zimmerman, Elizabeth. *Knitting without Tears*. Scribner, 1971. $8.

Znamierowski, Nell. *Step-by-Step Weaving*. Western, 1967. $5.

747 INTERIOR DECORATION

Aaronson, Joseph. *Encyclopedia of Furniture*. rev. ed. Crown, 1965. $8.

Better Homes & Gardens, eds. *Creative Decorating on a Budget*. Better Homes, 1970. $3.

———. *Decorating Ideas under $100*. Better Homes, 1973. $4.

———. *Hundreds of Ideas*. Better Homes, published annually. $5.

Comstock, Helen. *100 Most Beautiful Rooms in America*. rev. ed. Crowell, 1965. $15.

Doyle, Robert V. *Your Career in Interior Design*. Messner, 1969. $5.

Draper, Dorothy. *365 Shortcuts to Home Decorating*. Dodd, 1968. $7.

Farm Journal. *How to Make Your Home More Convenient*. Doubleday, 1972. $7.

Faulkner, Ray N. *Inside Today's Home*. 3rd ed. Holt, 1968. $13.

House & Garden. *Complete Guide to Interior Decoration*. 7th ed. S&S, 1970. $18.

Katz, Marjorie. *Instant-Effect Decorating*. Evans, 1972. $9.

Rodgers, Dorothy. *My Favorite Things*. Crown, 1972. $5.

Sunset Magazine, eds. Lane, rev. often. paper, each, $2–$3: *Children's Rooms and Play Yards; Ideas for Recreation Rooms; Ideas for Remodeling Your Home; Ideas for Storage; Planning and Remodeling Bathrooms; Planning and Remodeling Kitchens.*

749   ANTIQUES

Beedell, Suzanne. *Restoring Junk*. McKay, 1971. $4.

Browning, Elizabeth L. *With Love and Elbow Grease*. S&S, 1968. $5.

Cole, Ann K. *Golden Guide to American Antiques*. Western, 1967. $4.

Comstock, Helen. *Concise Encyclopedia of American Antiques*. Hawthorn, 1965. $17.

Connoisseur. *Complete Encyclopedia of Antiques*. Hawthorn, 1962. $18.

Durant, Mary B. *American Heritage Guide to Antiques*. American Heritage, 1970. $7.

Flayderman, Norman. *Collecting Tomorrow's Antiques Today*. Doubleday, 1972. $8.

Gros-Galliner, Gabriella. *Glass: a Guide for Collectors*. Stein, 1970. $8.

Grotz, George. *Antiques You Can Decorate With*. rev. ed. Doubleday, 1971. $7.

_____. *New Antiques*. rev. ed. Doubleday, 1970. $6.

Kettell, Russell H. *Early American Rooms*. Peter Smith, 1967. $7.

Kovel, Ralph M. *Directory of American Silver, Pewter, and Silver Plate*. rev. ed. Crown, 1961. $6.

McClinton, Katharine M. *Antiques Past and Present*. Potter, 1971. $10.

Marsh, Moreton. *Easy Expert in Collecting and Restoring American Antiques*. Lippincott, 1968. $7.

Phillips, Phoebe. *Collector's Encyclopedia of Antiques* Crown, 1973. $20.

Rockmore, Cynthia. *Room-by-Room Book of American Antiques*. Hawthorn, 1970. $11.

Salter, Stefan. *Joys of Hunting Antiques*. Hart, 1971. $10.

Savage, George. *Dictionary of Antiques*. Praeger, 1970. $18.

Stillinger, Elizabeth. *Antiques' Guide to Decorative Arts in America, 1600–1875*. Dutton, 1972. $11.

Warner, Dorothy, D. *Adapting American Antiques*. Macmillan, 1971. $9.

750   PAINTING

Baigell, Matthew. *History of American Painting*. Praeger, 1971. paper, $5.

Birren, Faber. *History of Color in Painting*. Reinhold, 1965. $25.

Brooks, Leonard. *Painter's Workshop*. Van Nostrand, 1969. $15.

Cherepov, George. *Discovering Oil Painting*. Watson, 1971. $12.

Country Beautiful, eds. *Beauty of America in Great American Art*. Country Beautiful, 1965. $10.

DiValentin, Maria M. *Color in Oil Painting*. Sterling, 1965. $7.

Fabri, Ralph. *Color: a Complete Guide for Artists*. Watson, 1967. $14.
Gaunt, William. *Concise History of English Painting*. Thames, 1967. paper, $4.
Gettens, Rutherford J. *Painting Materials*. Dover, 1965. paper, $3.
Hours, Madeleine. *Secrets of the Great Masters*. Putnam, 1968. $13.
Jaffe, Hans. *20,000 Years of World Painting*. Abrams, 1967. $25.
Keck, Caroline K. *Handbook on the Care of Paintings*. Watson, 1967. $8.
Laidman, Hugh. *Complete Book of Drawing and Painting*. Viking, 1974. $16.
Massey, Robert. *Formulas for Painters*. Watson, 1967. $7.
Mayer, Ralph. *Artists' Handbook of Materials and Techniques*. 3rd ed. Viking, 1970. $13.
Myers, Bernard S. *Encyclopedia of Painting*. 3rd rev. ed. Crown, 1970. $15.
Reynolds, Graham. *Concise History of Watercolors*. Abrams, 1971. $9.
Richardson, Edgar P. *Painting in America, from 1502 to the Present*. Crowell, 1965. $18.
Soyer, Moses. *Oil Painting in Progress*. Van Nostrand, 1972. $8.
Time-Life Books. *American Painting, 1900-1970*. Time, 1971. $8.
Torche, Judith. *Acrylic and Other Water-Base Paints*. Sterling, 1966. $7.
Werner, Alfred. *German Painting: Old Masters*. McGraw, 1964. $10.
Whitney, Edgar A. *Complete Guide to Watercolor Painting*. Watson, 1965. $13.
Woody, Russell O. *Painting with Synthetic Media*. Reinhold, 1965. $15.

760   PRINTS, CUTS

Antreasian, Garo Z. *Tamarind Book of Lithography*. Abrams, 1971. $28, paper, $15.
Banister, Manly. *Lithographic Prints from Stone and Plate*. Sterling, 1972. $7.
_____. *Prints–from Linoblocks and Woodcuts*. Sterling, 1967. $7.
Birkner, Heinrich. *Screen Printing*. Sterling, 1971. $5.
Hayter, Stanley W. *New Ways of Gravure*. 2nd ed. Oxford, 1966. $18.
Monk, Kathleen. *Fun with Fabric Printing*. Taplinger, 1969. $9.
Peterdi, Gabor. *Printmaking*. rev. ed. Macmillan, 1971. $15.
Tokuriki, Tomikichiro. *Woodblock Print Primer*. Japan, 1970. $5.
Zigrosser, Carl. *Guide to the Care and Collecting of Original Prints*. Crown, 1965. $4.

770   PHOTOGRAPHY, FILMS

Adams, Ansel. *Print*. Morgan, 1968. $6.
_____. *Artificial Light Photography*. Morgan, 1968. $6.
_____. *Camera and Lens*. rev. ed. Morgan, 1969. $12.
_____. *Natural Light Photography*. Morgan, 1969. $6.
_____. *Negative*. Morgan, 1968. $6.

Andersen, Yvonne. *Make Your Own Animated Movies*. Little, 1970. $7.

Atkins, Jim. *Filming TV News and Documentaries*. Amphoto, 1965. $7.

Baddeley, W. Hugh. *Technique of Documentary Film Production*. 3rd rev. ed. Hastings, 1963. $13.

Croy, D. R. *Complete Art of Printing and Enlarging*. Amphoto, 1970. $10.

Eastman Kodak Co. *Home Movies Made Easy*. Amphoto, 1972. $5.

Eisenstaedt, Alfred. *Eye of Eisenstaedt*. Viking, 1969. $8.

Feininger, Andreas. *Basic Color Photography*. Amphoto, 1972. $7.

_____. *Complete Photographer*. Prentice, 1965. $10.

Ferguson, Robert. *How to Make Movies*. Viking, 1969. $7.

Foldes, Joe. *Large-Format Camera Practice*. Chilton, 1969. $6.

Jacobson, C. I. *Enlarging*. 21st rev. ed. Amphoto, 1972. $14.

Jonas, Paul. *Manual of Darkroom Procedures and Techniques*. 4th ed. Amphoto, 1971. $8.

Lipton, Lenny. *Independent Filmmaking*. Straight Arrow, 1972. $13.

Mascelli, Joseph V. *Five C's of Cinematography*. 4th ed. Cine/Grafic, 1970. $15.

Moholy-Nagy, Laszlo. *Painting, Photography, Film*. new ed. MIT, 1973. $8.

Neblette, Carroll B. *Fundamentals of Photography*. Van Nostrand, 1970. $11.

Newhall, Beaumont. *History of Photography*. Museum of Mod. Art, 1972. $15.

_____. *Latent Image*. Doubleday, 1967. $3.

Petzold, Paul. *Light on People*. Amphoto, 1971. $10.

Provisor, Henry. *8mm/16mm Movie Making*. Amphoto, 1970. $9.

Smallman, Kirk. *Creative Film Making*. Macmillan, 1969. $8.

Souto, H. Mario. *Technique of the Motion Picture Camera*. rev. ed. Hastings, 1967. $16.

Steichen, Edward. *Life in Photography*. Doubleday, 1968. $10.

Sussman, Aaron. *Amateur Photographer's Handbook*. 8th ed. Crowell, 1973. $9.

Weiner, Peter. *Making the Media Revolution*. Macmillan, 1973. $9.

Woolley, A. E. *Creative 35mm Techniques*. Amphoto, 1970. $9.

780   MUSIC

Ammer, Christine. *Harper's Dictionary of Music*. Harper, 1972. $10.

Austin, William. *Music in the 20th Century*. Norton, 1966. $11.

Barnes, R. A. *Fundamentals of Music*. McGraw, 1964. $8.

Bernstein, Leonard. *Infinite Variety of Music*. S&S, 1966. $7.

Bernstein, Martin. *Introduction to Music*. 4th ed. Prentice, 1972. $11.

Brye, Joseph C. *Basic Principles of Music Theory*. Ronald, 1965. $7.

Castellini, John. *Rudiments of Music*. Norton, 1962. $7.

Chase, Gilbert. *America's Music*. McGraw, 1955. $12.

Collier, James L. *Practical Music Theory*. Grosset, 1970. $5.

Einstein, Alfred. *Short History of Music*. Knopf, 1954. $7.
Feather, Leonard. *Encyclopedia of Jazz*. Horizon, 1955. $15.
———. *Encyclopedia of Jazz in the Sixties*. Horizon, 1966. $15.
Gaston, E. Thayer. *Music in Therapy*. Macmillan, 1968. $10.
Goldman, Richard F. *Harmony in Western Music*. Norton, 1965. $9.
Grout, Donald J. *History of Western Music*. rev. ed. Norton, 1973. $10.
Lang, Paul H. *Music in Western Civilization*. Norton, 1941. $15.
Levarie, Seigmund. *Tone*. Kent, 1968. $8.
Lilienfeld, Robert. *Learning to Read Music*. F&W, 1968. $5.
Machlis, Joseph. *Introduction to Contemporary Music*. Norton, 1961. $10.
Nanry, Charles. *American Music*. Transaction, 1972. $8.
Nordoff, Paul. *Music Therapy in Special Education*. John Day, 1971. $7.
Oliver, Paul. *Story of the Blues*. Chilton, 1969. $13.
Persichetti, Vincent. *20th Century Harmony*. Norton, 1961. $8.
Shemel, Sidney. *More about This Business of Music*. Watson, 1967. $7.
———. *This Business of Music*. rev. ed. Watson, 1971. $15.
Southern, Eileen. *Music of Black Americans: a History*. Norton, 1971. $10.
Wiora, Walter. *Four Ages of Music*. Norton, 1965. $6.

782   OPERA, SACRED MUSIC

Engel, L. *Words with Music*. Macmillan, 1972. $8.
Ewen, David. *New Encyclopedia of the Opera*. Hill, 1971. $15.
Jacobs, Arthur. *Opera*. Drake, 1972. $10.
Routley, Erik. *Twentieth Century Church Music*. Oxford, 1964. $6.
Simon, Henry W. *Victor Book of Opera*. 13th ed. S&S, 1968. $10.
Wienandt, Elwyn. *Choral Music of the Church*. Free Press, 1965. $9.

784   VOCAL, FOLK, POP, BANDS

Aldridge, Alan. *Beatles Illustrated Lyrics*. 2 vols. Delacorte, 1969/71. each, $6.
Atwater, Constance. *Baton Twirling*. Tuttle, 1964. $7.
Bekker, Paul. *Orchestra*. Norton, 1963. paper, $3.
Belz, Carl. *Story of Rock*. 2nd ed. Oxford, 1972. $8.
Coh, Nik. *Rock, from the Beginning*. Stein, 1969. $6.
Dylan, Bob. *Bob Dylan Song Book*. Grosset, 1971. paper, $5.
Ewen, David. *American Popular Songs from the Revolutionary War to the Present*. Random, 1966. $10.
Gershwin, George. *George and Ira Gershwin Songbook*. S&S, 1960. $10.
Green, Stanley. *World of Musical Comedy*. 2nd rev. ed. B&N, 1973. $15.
Goldstein, Richard. *Poetry of Rock*. Bantam, 1969. paper, $1.
Lawless, Ray M. *Folksingers and Folksongs in America*. Duell, 1965. $13.
Lovell, John, Jr. *Black Song*. Macmillan, 1972. $15.
Nettl, Bruno. *Folk and Traditional Music on the Western Continents*. 2nd ed. Prentice, 1973. $9.

Nettl, Paul. *National Anthems.* 2nd ed. Ungar, 1967. $8.
Porter, Cole. *Cole Porter Song Book.* S&S, 1959. $13.
Roxon, Lillian, *Rock Encyclopedia.* Grosset, 1969. $10.
Schitz, Askel. *Singer and His Art.* Harper, 1970. $7.
Shaw, Arnold. *Rock Revolution.* Macmillan, 1969. $6.
Simon, George T. *Big Bands.* rev. ed. Macmillan, 1971. $10.
Simon, Henry. *Treasury of Christmas Songs and Carols.* rev. ed. Houghton, 1973. $7.
Simon, Paul. *Songs of Paul Simon.* Knopf, 1972. $13.

786   INSTRUMENTS

Andersen, Paul G. *Organ Building and Design.* Oxford, 1969. $21.
Bachman, Aberto. *Encyclopedia of the Violin.* 2nd ed. DaCapo, 1967. $13.
Dolan, Robert E. *Music in Modern Media.* Schirmer, 1967. $5.
Gieseking, Walter. *Piano Technique.* Peter Smith. $5.
Grunfeld, Frederick V. *Art and Times of the Guitar.* Macmillan, 1969. $10.
Hubbard, Frank T. *Three Centuries of Harpsichord Making.* Harvard, 1965. $15.
Judd, F. C. *Electronic Music and Musique Concrete.* Dufour, 1961. $5.
Lincoln, Harry B. *Computer and Music.* Cornell, 1970. $15.
Mathews, M. V. *Technology of Computer Music.* MIT, 1969. $12.
Mehegan, John. *Jazz Improvisation.* 4 vols. Watson, 1968. each, $5.
Ritchie, Jean. *Dulcimer Book.* Quick Fox. paper, $3.
Sachs, Curt. *History of Musical Instruments.* Norton, 1940. $10.
Sloane, Irving. *Classic Guitar Instruction.* Dutton, 1966. $7.

791   MOVIES

Bazin, Andre. *What Is Cinema?* 2 vols. California, 1967/71. set, $14.
Blum, Daniel. *New Pictorial History of the Talkies.* Grosset, 1970. $10.
Dickinson, Thorold. *Discovery of Cinema.* Oxford, 1973. $9.
Levin, G. Roy. *Documentary Explorations.* Doubleday, 1971, $10.

792   THEATER, DANCE

Austell, Jan. *What's in a Play?* Harcourt, 1968. $4.
Buchman, Herman. *Stage Makeup.* Watson, 1971. $15.
DeMille, Agnes. *To a Young Dancer.* Little. $5.
Denby, Edwin. *Looking at the Dance.* Horizon, 1968. $8.
Denis, Paul. *Opportunities in Dancing.* Universal, 1966. $4.
Dolman, John. *Art of Acting.* Greenwood, 1949. $15.
––––. *Art of Play Production.* 3rd ed. Harper, 1973. $10.
Geisinger, Marion. *Plays, Players, and Playwrights: an Illustrated History of the Theatre.* Hart, 1971. $20.
Gilbert, Pia. *Music for the Modern Dance.* W. C. Brown, 1961. $5.
Kerensky, Oleg. *World of Ballet.* Coward, 1970. $8.
Kraus, Richard G. *Folk Dancing.* Macmillan, 1962. $9.

Lawson, Joan. *European Folk Dances.* Pitman, 1955. $10.

McDonagh, Don. *Rise and Fall and Rise of Modern Dance.* Outerbridge, 1970. $7.

Maynards, Olga. *Children and Dance and Music.* Scribner, 1968. $7.

Parker, W. Oren. *Scene Design and Stage Lighting.* 2nd ed. Holt, 1968. $14.

Sachs, Curt. *World History of the Dance.* Norton, 1963. paper, $3.

Stearns, Marshall. *Jazz Dance.* Macmillan, 1968. $10.

Terry, Walter. *Ballet Companion.* Dodd, 1968. $7.

Theatre Student Series. Rosen Pr. $7-$13 per vol. Purchase those subjects needed: *Acting; Costuming; Directing; Film Making; Makeup; Music and Sound Effects; Musicals; Practical Stage Lighting; Preparing the Classics; Producing Plays for Children; Properties and Dressing the Stage; Publicity and Management; Puppetry; Scenery; Scenes to Perform.*

Westmore, Michael. *Art of Theatrical Makeup for Stage and Screen.* McGraw, 1973. paper, $5.

793   GAMES, AMUSEMENTS

American Heritage Publ. Co. *Great Days of the Circus.* Harper, 1962. $6.

Cabeen, Richard M. *Standard Handbook of Stamp Collecting.* 2nd ed. Crowell, 1965. $9.

Carlson, Bernice W. *Party Book for Boys and Girls.* Abingdon, 1963. $3.

Depew, Arthur M. *Cokesbury Game Book.* rev. ed. Abingdon. $5.

———. *Cokesbury Party Book.* rev. ed. Abingdon. $5.

Foster, Robert F. *Foster's Complete Hoyle.* rev. ed. Lippincott, 1963. $7.

Freeman, Louis M. *Betty Crocker's Parties for Children.* Western, 1964. $3.

Gibson, Walter B. *Family Games America Plays.* Doubleday, 1969. $6.

———. *Hoyle's Simplified Guide to the Popular Card Games.* rev. ed. Doubleday, 1971. $8.

Gleeson, Margaret. *Complete Shower Party Book.* Doubleday, 1971. $6.

Goren, Charles H. *Goren's New Contract Bridge in a Nutshell.* rev. ed. Doubleday, 1972. $5.

———. *Modern Backgammon.* Doubleday, 1974. $8.

Gregg, Elizabeth M. *What to Do When "There's Nothing to Do."* Delacorte, 1968. $5.

Harbin, Elvin O. *Fun Encyclopedia.* Abingdon, 1968. $7.

Harkness, Kenneth. *Official Chess Handbook.* rev. ed. McKay, 1972. $8.

———. *Official Chess Rulebook.* McKay, 1970. $4.

Harris, Jane A. *Dance Awhile: Handbook of Folk, Square, and Social Dance.* rev. ed. Burgess, 1968. $7.

Hay, Henry. *Amateur Magician's Handbook.* rev. ed. Crowell, 1972. $8.

Kelsey, H. W. *Improve Your Bridge.* Hart, 1971. $5.

Mulac, Margaret E. *Party Fun.* Harper, 1960. $8.

Reinfeld, Fred. *Catalogue of the World's Most Popular Coins.* rev. ed. Doubleday, 1971. $9.

———. *Chess for Young People.* Holt, 1961. $5.

_____. *Chess in a Nutshell.* Doubleday, 1958. $5.

_____. *Complete Chessplayer.* Prentice, 1953. $7.

_____. *Easiest Way to Learn Chess.* S&S, 1960. $4.

Rigney, Francis J. *Beginner's Book of Magic.* Devin, 1963. $5.

Scarne, John. *Scarne's Complete Guide to Gambling.* S&S, 1971. $10.

Scott Publications. *Scott's Standard Postage Stamps of the World.* 3 vols.
   S&S, published annually. set, $26.

796   ATHLETICS, SPORTS, CAMPING

Angier, Bradford. *Home in Your Pack.* Collier, 1972. $5.

Associated Press. *Century of Sports.* Hammond, 1971. $10.

Bartlett, Eric G. *Judo and Self Defense.* Arc, 1971. paper, $2.

Beddoes, Richard. *Hockey!* 3rd rev. ed. Macmillan, 1973. $10.

Brasch, Rudolph. *How Did Sports Begin?* McKay, 1969. $10.

Burton, Nelson. *Bowling.* Atheneum, 1973. $6.

Burrill, Bob. *Who's Who in Boxing.* Arlington, 1973. $8.

Colby, Carroll B. *Today's Camping.* new ed. Coward, 1973. $4.

Cousy, Robert. *Basketball.* Allyn, 1970. $11.

Douglas, Bob. *Wrestling.* Cornell, 1972, $9.

Dryden, Ken. *Face-off at the Summit.* Little, 1973. $6.

Edmonds, I. G. *Minibikes and Minicycles for Beginners.* Macrae, 1973. $5.

_____. *Motorcycling for Beginners.* Macrae, 1972. $5.

Engel, Lyle K. *Complete Book of Motor Camping.* rev. ed. Arco, 1973. $6.

_____. *Complete Book of Trailering.* Arco, 1973. $6.

_____. *Indianapolis 500.* rev. ed. Four Winds, 1972. $8.

Eskenazi, Gerald. *Thinking Man's Guide to Pro Hockey.* Dutton, 1972. $7.

Fletcher, Colin. *Complete Walker.* Knopf, 1968. $8.

Gilbert, Rod. *Playing Hockey the Professional Way.* Harper, 1972. $8.

Glanville, Brian. *Soccer.* Crown, 1968. $6.

Griffin, Al. *Motorcycles.* Regnery, 1972. $8.

Hanley, Reid M. *Who's Who in Track and Field.* Arlington, 1973. $8.

Harrington, A. P. *Every Boy's Judo.* Emerson, 1960. $5.

Helmker, Judith A. *Manual of Snowmobiling.* B&N, 1971. $7.

Kariher, Harry C. *Who's Who in Hockey.* Arlington, 1973. $8.

Karst, Gene. *Who's Who in Professional Baseball.* Arlington, 1973. $13.

Keith, Harold. *Sports and Games.* 5th ed, Crowell, 1969. $6

Kirkley, George W. *Weight Lifting and Weight Training.* Arc, 1966. paper,
   $1.

_____. *Modern Weight Lifting.* Wehman, 1961. $5.

Kovac, Steve. *Learn to Bowl.* Rand, 1969. $2.

Kozuki, Russell. *Junior Karate.* Sterling, 1971. $3.

Landers, Chris. *Learn to Ski.* Rand, 1969. $2.

Liebers, Arthur. *Complete Book of Winter Sports.* Coward, 1971. $7.

Loken, Newton C. *Gymnastics.* Sterling, 1969. $4.

Lombardi, Vince. *Run to Daylight.* Prentice, 1967. $7.

Lowell, Frederick P. *Jui-jitsu.* Ronald, 1942. $5.

Lund, Morten. *Pleasures of Cross Country Skiing.* Dutton, 1972. $7.

McFarlane, Brian. *Everything You Want to Know about Hockey.* rev. ed. Scribner, 1973. $8.

McKay, Jim. *My Wide World.* Macmillan, 1973. $7.

McWhirter, Norris. *Guinness Sports Record Book.* rev. ed. Sterling, 1973. $4.

Malo, John W. *Snowmobiling.* Macmillan, 1971. $8.

Mendell, Ronald. *Who's Who in Basketball.* Arlington, 1973. $8.

Merrins, Eddie. *Swing the Handle, Not the Clubhead.* S&S, 1973. $7.

Morrill, William K. *Lacrosse.* rev. ed. Ronald, 1966. $6.

Musker, Frank F. *Guide to Gymnastics.* Macmillan, 1968. $8.

Namath, Joe. *Matter of Style.* Little, 1973. $13.

National Football League. *First Fifty Years.* S&S, 1971. $15.

Nicklaus, Jack. *Golf My Way.* S&S, 1974. $10.

———. *Take a Tip from Me.* S&S, 1968. $5.

Palmer, Arnold. *Go for Broke.* S&S, 1973. $8.

Pezzano, Chuck. *Guide to Better Bowling.* S&S, 1974. $9.

Plagenhoef, Stanley. *Fundamentals of Tennis.* Prentice, 1970. $8.

Prudden, Bonnie. *Bonnie Prudden's Fitness Book.* Ronald, 1959. $5.

Riviere, William A. *Camper's Bible.* rev. ed. Doubleday, 1970. $3.

Ryan, Frank. *Weight Training.* Viking, 1969. $7.

Seaton, Don C. *Physical Education Handbook.* 5th ed. Prentice, 1969. $9.

Sloane, Eugene A. *New Complete Book of Bicycling.* Trident, 1974. $13.

Sports Illustrated, eds. Lippincott, varied dates, revised often. each, $4 (average): *Badminton; Baseball; Basketball; Football; Golf; Ice Hockey; Skiing; Soccer; Table Tennis; Tennis; Training with Weights; Track and Field; Volleyball.*

Stainback, Berry. *Pro Football Heroes of Today.* Random, 1973. $4.

Tegner, Bruce. *Complete Book of Judo.* rev. ed. Thor, 1973. $6.

———. *Complete Book of Karate.* 2nd rev. ed. Thor, 1970. $6.

———. *Karate.* Thor, 1973. paper, $3.

Thomas, James L. *Safe Snowmobiling.* Sterling, 1971. $5.

Tokle, Art. *Complete Guide to Cross Country Skiing and Touring.* Holt, 1973. $7

Tuite, James J. *Snowmobiles and Snowmobiling.* Regnery, 1969. $6.

Wells, George S. *Modern ABC's of Family Camping.* Stackpole, 1967. $5.

797   WATER SPORTS

Borgeson, Lillian. *Skin and Scuba Diver.* Arco, 1962. $4.

Kenealy, James P. *Boating from Bow to Stern.* Hawthorn, 1973. $5.

Klein, H. Arthur. *Surf-Riding.* Lippincott, 1972. $4.

Lanoue, Fred R. *Drownproofing.* Prentice, 1963. $7.

Liebers, Arthur. *Complete Book of Water Sports.* rev. ed. Coward, 1972. $7.

_____. *Encyclopedia of Pleasure Boating.* rev. ed. B&N, 1973. $12.

Malo, John. *Complete Guide to Canoeing and Canoe-Camping.* Quadrangle, 1969. $7.

_____. *Complete Guide to House Boating.* Macmillan, 1974. $9.

Sava, Charles. *How to Teach Yourself and Your Family to Swim Well.* S&S, 1960. $6.

Sports Illustrated, eds. Lippincott, varied dates, revised often. each, $4, (average): *Better Boating; Diving; Skin Diving and Snorkeling; Swimming.*

Tyll, Al. *Complete Beginner's Guide to Water Skiing.* Doubleday, 1970. $7.

Zadig, Ernest A. *Complete Book of Boating.* Prentice, 1972. $13.

798 EQUESTRIAN SPORTS

Kulesza, Severyn R. *Modern Riding.* Arco, 1966. $6.

Sports Illustrated, eds. *Horseback Riding.* Lippincott, 1971. $4.

799 HUNTING, FISHING

Barrett, Jean A. *Archery.* 2nd ed. Goodyear, 1973. paper, $2.

Bateman, James A. *Animal Traps and Trapping.* Stackpole, 1971. $9.

Butler, David F. *New Archery.* rev. ed. B&N, 1973. $6.

Evanoff, Vlad. *Complete Guide to Fishing.* Crowell, 1961. $5.

_____. *Freshwater Fisherman's Bible.* Doubleday, 1964. $3.

Morris, Dan. *Fisherman's Almanac.* Macmillan, 1970. $5.

Ormond, Clyde. *Complete Book of Hunting.* rev. ed. Harper, 1972. $7.

_____. *Outdoorsman's Handbook.* Popular Science, 1971. $6.

_____. *Small Game Hunting.* Dutton, 1970. $5.

Power, John. *Fisherman's Handbook.* Scribner, 1972. $8.

Roberts, Daniel. *Archery for All.* Drake, 1971. $6.

Waterman, Charles F. *Hunting in America.* Holt, 1973. $17.

800

LITERATURE

801 GENERAL, HISTORY

Benet, William R. *Reader's Encyclopedia.* Crowell, 1965. $10.

Daiches, David. *Critical Approaches to Literature.* Prentice, 1956. $10.

———. *Study of Literature for Readers and Critics.* Norton, 1964. paper, $2.

Eliot, T. S. *Essays.* Columbia, 1963. $12.

Hall, Vernon. *Short History of Literary Criticism.* NYU, 1963. $8.

Hamilton, Edith. *Ever-Present Past.* Norton, 1964. $5.

Highet, Gilbert. *Classical Tradition.* Oxford, 1949. $15.

———. *People, Places and Books.* Oxford, 1953. $7.

Holman, C. Hugh. *Handbook to Literature.* 3rd ed. Odyssey, 1972. $6.

Praz, Mario. *Romantic Agony.* Oxford, 1970. $8.

Priestly, J. B. *Literature and Western Man.* Harper, 1960. $11.

Ross, James B. *Portable Medieval Reader.* Viking. $6.

———. *Portable Renaissance Reader.* Viking, 1953. $6.

Seymour-Smith, Martin. *Guide to Modern World Literature.* F&W, 1973. $14.

Smith, James H. *Great Critics.* 3rd ed. Norton, 1951. $10.

Trilling, Lionel. *Opposing Self.* Viking, 1959. paper, $2.

Van Nostrand, Albert. *Literary Criticism in America.* Bks for Libs, 1957. $15.

Wellek, Rene. *History of Modern Criticism, 1750-1950.* 4 vols. Yale, 1955/65. set, $46.

———. *Theory of Literature.* rev. ed. Harcourt. paper, $3.

Wilson, Edmund. *Axel's Castle.* Scribner, 1939. $7.

———. *Classics and Commercials.* Farrar, 1950. $10.

Woolf, Virginia. *Room of One's Own.* Harcourt, 1929. paper, $2.

Zitner, Sheldon. *Preface to Literary Analysis.* Scott, 1964. paper, $5.

808   WRITING GUIDES

Allen, Walter. *Writers on Writing.* Writer, 1959. $6.

Aristotle. *Poetics; Rhetoric.* Dutton, 1963. $4.

Brooks, Cleanth. *Fundamentals of Good Writing.* Harcourt. $11.

Burack, Abraham. *Writer's Handbook.* rev. ed. Writer, 1973. $13.

Engle, Paul. *On Creative Writing.* Dutton, 1964. $7.

Foerster, Norman. *Writing and Thinking.* 5th ed. Houghton, 1952. $6.

Gunther, Max. *Writing the Modern Magazine Article.* Writer, 1973. $8.

Harral, Stewart. *Feature Writer's Handbook.* Oklahoma, 1966. $7.

Hilliard, Robert L. *Writing for TV and Radio.* 2nd ed. Hastings, 1967. $8.

Hodges, John. *Harbrace College Handbook.* 7th ed. Harcourt, 1972. $6.

Kierzek, John M. *Macmillan Handbook of English.* 5th ed. Macmillan, 1965. $6.

Marchwardt, Albert. *Scribner Handbook of English.* 4th ed. Scribner, 1967. $4.

Niggli, Josefina. *New Pointers on Playwriting.* rev. ed. Writer, 1967. $5.

Riebel, John P. *How to Write Reports, Papers, Theses, Articles.* 2nd ed. Arco, 1972. $8.

Rose, Camille D. *How to Write Successful Magazine Articles.* Writer, 1967. $7.

Shapiro, Karl. *Prosody Handbook.* Harper, 1965. $6.

Strunk, William. *Elements of Style.* Macmillan, 1972. $4.

Weeks, Edward. *Breaking into Print.* Writer, 1962. $5.

Zeiger, Arthur. *Encyclopedia of English.* Arco, 1957. paper, $3.

808.1   POETRY

Auslander, Joseph. *Winged Horse.* Doubleday, 1949. $6.

Brinnin, John M. *Modern Poets.* 2nd ed. McGraw, 1970. $6.

Brooks, Cleanth. *Understanding Poetry.* 3rd ed. Holt, 1960. $11.

Ciardi, John. *How Does a Poem Mean?* Houghton, 1960. $6.

Creekmore, Hubert. *Little Treasury of World Poetry.* Scribner, 1952. $10.

Deutsch, Babette. *Poetry Handbook.* 3rd rev. ed. F&W, 1969. $6.

Drew, Elizabeth A. *Poetry.* Norton, 1959. $6.

Eastman, Max. *Enjoyment of Poetry.* Scribner, 1951. $8.

Ellman, Richard. *Norton Anthology of Modern Poetry.* Norton, 1973. $15.

Ferris, Helen. *Favorite Poems Old and New.* Doubleday, 1957. $7.

Highet, Gilbert. *Powers of Poetry.* Oxford, 1960. $9.

Hillyer, Robert. *First Principle of Verse.* Writer, 1950. $5.

Hodnett, Edward. *Poems to Read Aloud.* rev. ed. Norton, 1967. $7.

Roethke, Theodore. *On the Poet and His Craft.* Washington, 1965. $5.

Stevenson, Burton E. *Home Book of Modern Verse.* 2nd ed. Holt, 1953. $10.

———. *Home Book of Verse.* 9th ed., 2 vols. Holt, 1953. $30.

Untermeyer, Louis. *Forms of Poetry.* rev. ed. Harcourt, 1926. $5.

_____. *Treasury of Great Poems.* rev. ed. S&S, 1955. $13.
Van Doren, Mark. *Anthology of World Poetry.* Harcourt. $15.
Walsh, Chad. *Today's Poets.* Scribner, 1964. $4.
Williams, Oscar. *Little Treasury of Great Poetry.* rev. ed. Scribner, 1955. $6.
_____. *Little Treasury of Modern Poetry.* rev. ed. Scribner, 1955. $6.
_____. *Master Poems of the English Language.* Trident, 1966. $13.
Yeats, W. B. *Oxford Book of Modern Verse.* Oxford, 1936. $8.

808.2 DRAMA

Abramson, Doris E. *Negro Playwrights in the American Theatre.* Columbia, 1969. $13.
Bentley, Eric. *Classic Theatre.* 4 vols. Anchor. set, $14.
_____. *Life of the Drama.* Atheneum, 1964. $4.
_____. *Modern Theater.* 6 vols. Peter Smith. set, $24.
Best Plays of 19--. editor varies. Dodd, published annually. each, $10-$15.
Brustein, Robert S. *Theatre of Revolt.* Little, 1964. $9.
Cerf, Bennett A. *24 Favorite One-Act Plays.* Doubleday. $7.
Clark, Barrett H. *World Drama.* 2 vols. Peter Smith, 1933. paper, each, $4.
Clurman, Harold. *Seven Plays of the Modern Theatre.* Grover, 1962. paper, $5.
Dickinson, Thomas H. *Chief Contemporary Dramatists.* 2nd ser. Houghton, 1930. $11.
Esslin, Martin. *Theatre of the Absurd.* rev. ed. Overlook, 1973. $13.
Fergusson, Francis. *Idea of a Theater.* Princeton, 1968. $10.
Gassner, John. *Introducing the Drama.* Holt, 1963. $6.
_____. *Masters of the Drama.* 3rd ed. Dover, 1953. $9.
_____. *Treasury of the Theatre.* 3 vols. S&S, 1963. set, $30.
Nicoll, Allardyce. *World Drama.* Harcourt, 1949. $10.
Richards, Stanley. *Best Mystery and Suspense Plays of the Modern Theatre.* Dodd, 1971. $10.
_____. *Best Plays of the Sixties.* Doubleday, 1970. $10.
Swortzell, Lowell. *All the World's a Stage.* Delacorte, 1972. $13.
Williams, Raymond. *Drama from Ibsen to Brecht.* Oxford, 1969. $7.

808.3 FICTION

Brooks, Cleanth. *Understanding Fiction.* 2nd ed. Appleton, 1959. $9.
Cowley, Malcolm. *Lesson of the Masters.* Scribner, 1971. paper, $5.
Daiches, David. *Novel and the Modern World.* Chicago, 1960. $6.
Drew, Ellen. *Novel.* Norton, 1964. $6.
Forster, E. M. *Aspects of the Novel.* Harcourt. $7.
Haines, Helen E. *What's in a Novel.* Columbia, 1942. $10.
Pritchett, Victor S. *Living Novel, and Later Appreciations.* Random, 1964. $9.
Van Nostrand, Albert. *Denatured Novel.* Greenwood, 1973. $10.

808.5   SPEECH

Baird, A. Craig. *American Public Addresses.* McGraw, 1956. $9.

_____. *Essentials of General Speech Communication.* 4th ed. McGraw, 1973. $6.

Carnegie, Dale. *Quick and Easy Way to Effective Speaking.* Association, 1962. $5.

Copeland, Lewis. *World's Greatest Speeches.* 3rd rev. ed. Dover, 1958. $5.

Gorrell, Robert M. *Modern English Handbook.* 5th ed. Prentice, 1972. $7.

Hurd, Charles. *Treasury of Great American Speeches.* rev. ed. Hawthorn, 1970. $13.

McBurney, James R. *Argumentation and Debate.* 2nd ed. Macmillan, 1964. $8.

Prochnow, Herbert V. *Public Speaker's Treasure Chest.* rev. ed. Harper, 1964. $8.

_____. *Successful Toastmaster.* Harper, 1966. $7.

Sandford, William P. *Principles of Effective Speaking.* 6th ed. Ronald, 1963. $6.

Summers, Harrison B. *How to Debate.* 3rd ed. Wilson, 1963. $6.

810   AMERICAN LITERATURE–GENERAL

Allen, Gay W. *American Prosody.* Octagon, 1966. $11.

Bryer, Jackson R. *Sixteen Modern American Authors.* Norton, 1973. paper, $6.

Cambridge History of American Literature. 3 vols. Macmillan, 1943. $13.

Canby, Henry S. *Classic Americans.* Russell, 1931. $13.

Cowley, Malcolm. *After the Genteel Tradition.* rev. ed. S. Illinois, 1964. $5.

Foerster, Norman. *American Poetry and Prose.* 2 vols. Houghton, 1962. each, $9.

Gayle, Addison. *Black Expressions.* McKay, 1969. $5.

Hart, James D. *Oxford Companion to American Literature.* 4th ed. Oxford, 1965. $15.

Kazin, Alfred. *Contemporaries.* Little, 1962. $10.

_____. *On Native Grounds.* Harcourt, 1973. $9.

Leyda, Jay. *Portable Melville.* Viking. $6.

Margolis, Edward. *Native Sons.* Lippincott, 1969. $6.

Matthiessen, Francis O. *American Renaissance.* Oxford, 1941. $13.

Miller, Perry. *Major Writers of America.* 2 vols. Harcourt, 1962, each, $10.

Parrington, Vernon L. *Main Currents in American Thought.* Harcourt, 1939. $12.

Quinn, Arthur H. *Literature of the American People.* Appleton, 1951. $14.

Spiller, Robert, ed. *Literary History of the United States.* 3rd ed., 2 vols. Macmillan, 1963. set, $20. *Bibliography,* 1964, $17. *Supplement,* 1972, $15.

811 **AMERICAN POETRY**

Adoff, Arnold. *Poetry of Black America*. Harper, 1973. $13.

Aiken, Conrad P. *Twentieth Century American Poetry*. Mod. Library. $3.

Allen, Donald M. *New American Poetry 1945–1960*. Peter Smith. $6.

Allen, Gay W. *American Poetry*. Harper, 1965. $11.

Bontemps, Arna. *American Negro Poetry*. Hill, 1963. $5.

Bryant, William C. *Poetical Works*. AMS, 1969. $15.

Carruth, Hayden. *The Voice that Is Great within Us*. Bantam, 1970. paper, $2.

Ciardi, John. *Mid-Century American Poetry*. Twayne, $6.

Chester, Laura. *Rising Tides; 20th Century American Women Poets*. Washington Sq., 1973. paper, $2.

Cronyn, George W. *American Indian Poetry*. new ed. Liveright, 1970. $8.

Cummings, E. E. *Collected Poems*. Harcourt. $8.

Dickinson, Emily. *Complete Poems*. Little, 1960. $15.

Eliot, Thomas S. *Complete Poems and Plays*. Harcourt, 1952. $10.

Felleman, Hazel. *Best Loved Poems of the American People*. Doubleday, 1936. $6.

Frost, Robert. *Complete Poetry*. Holt, 1969. $11.

Hughes, Langston. *New Negro Poets*. Indiana, 1964. $6.

Johnson, James W. *God's Trombones*. Viking, 1927. $4.

Longfellow, Henry W. *Complete Poetical Works*. Houghton. $10.

Lowell, James R. *Complete Poetical Works*. Houghton. $10.

Lowenfels, Walter. *Poets of Today*. International, 1964. paper, $2.

Masters, Edgar L. *Spoon River Anthology*. Macmillan, 1916. $5.

Mazzaro, Jerome. *Modern American Poetry*. McKay, 1970. $8.

Matthiessen, F. O. *Oxford Book of American Verse*. Oxford, 1950. $10.

Rexroth, Kenneth. *American Poetry in the Twentieth Century*. new ed. Seabury, 1973. paper, $3.

Sandburg, Carl. *Selected Poems*. Harcourt, 1954. $7.

Service, Robert. *Collected Poems*. Dodd, 1944. $6.

Shapiro, Karl. *American Poetry*. Crowell, 1960. $7.

Waggoner, Hyatt H. *American Poets*. Dell, 1970. paper, $3.

Ward, Herman M. *Poems for Pleasure*. Hill, 1963. $3.

Whitman, Walt. *Leaves of Grass*. Harper, 1949. $3.

_____. *Portable Walt Whitman*. Viking, 1945. $6.

Williams, Oscar. *Little Treasury of American Poetry*. rev. ed. Scribner, 1955. $10.

_____. *Mentor Book of Major American Poets*. NAL. paper, $2.

812 **AMERICAN DRAMA**

Albee, Edward. *Who's Afraid of Virginia Woolf?* Atheneum, 1963. $3.

_____. *Zoo Story, Sandbox, Death of Bessie Smith*. Coward, 1960. paper, $3.

Amacher, Richard E. *Edward Albee*. Twayne, 1968. $6.

Gassner, John. *Best American Plays, 1939–1945*. 2nd ser. Crown, 1947. $7.

———. *Best American Plays, 1945–1951*. 3rd ser. Crown, 1952. $8.

———. *Best American Plays, 1951–1957*. 4th ser. Crown, 1958. $8.

———. *Best American Plays, 1957–1963*. 5th ser. Crown, 1963. $8.

———. *Best American Plays, 1963–1967*. 6th ser. Crown, 1971. $8.

———. *Best American Plays, 1918–1958 Suppl. Vol.* Crown, 1961. $8.

———. *Best Plays of the Early American Theater (to 1916)*. Crown, 1967. $8.

———. *Best Plays of the Modern American Theater*. 2nd ser. Crown, 1947. $8.

———. *Fifty Best Plays of the American Theater*. 4 vols. Crown, 1969. set, $30.

———. *Twenty-five Plays of the Modern American Theater*. early ser. Crown, 1949. $8.

Gaver, Jack. *Critics Choice*. Bks for Libs, 1955, $25.

Hellman, Lilliam. *Collected Plays*. Little, 1972. $15.

Inge, William M. *Four Plays*. Random, 1958. $8.

Lewis, Allan. *American Plays and Playwrights of the Contemporary Theater*. rev. ed. Crown, 1970. $6.

MacLeish, Archibald. *JB*. Houghton, 1958. $5.

Miller, Arthur. *Collected Plays*. Viking, 1957. $7.

———. *Portable Arthur Miller*. Viking, 1971. $9.

Miller, Jordan Y. *American Dramatic Literature*. McGraw, 1961. $10.

O'Neill, Eugene. *Nine Plays*. Mod. Library. $5.

Quinn, Arthur H. *History of American Drama*. rev. ed. Appleton, 1943/46. each, $12.

Wilder, Thornton N. *Three Plays*. Bantam. paper, $1.

Williams, Tennessee. *Theater of Tennessee Williams*. 4 vols. New Directions, 1971/72. each, $10.

813   AMERICAN FICTION

Auchincloss, Louis. *Pioneers and Caretakers*. Minnesota, 1965. $6.

Bone, Robert A. *Negro Novel in America*. rev. ed. Yale, 1965. $9.

Eisinger, Chester E. *Fiction of the Forties*. Chicago, 1963. $9.

Faulkner, William. *Portable Faulkner*. rev. ed. Viking, 1967. $7.

Gloster, Hugh M. *Negro Voice in American Fiction*. Russell, 1965. $13.

Hawthorne, Nathaniel. *Portable Hawthorne*. Cowley, Malcolm, ed. Viking, 1969. $7.

Hoffman, Daniel G. *Form and Fable in American Fiction*. Oxford, 1961. $10.

Quinn, Arthur H. *American Fiction*. Appleton, 1947. $12.

Steinbeck, John. *Portable Steinbeck*. 2nd ed. Viking, 1971. $6.

Van Doren, Carl. *American Novel, 1789–1939*. rev. ed. Macmillan, 1940. $7.

Wagenknecht, Edward. *Cavalcade of the American Novel*. Holt, 1952. $12.

817 AMERICAN SATIRE AND HUMOR

Adams, Joey. *Encyclopedia of Humor*. Bobbs, 1969. $8.

Benchley, Robert. *Benchley Roundup*. Harper, 1954. $6.

Bombeck, Erma. *At Wit's End*. Doubleday, 1967. $5.

_____. *Just Wait Till You Have Children of Your Own*. Doubleday, 1971. $6.

Irving, Washington. *Sketch Book*. Dutton. $4.

Kerr, Jean. *Please Don't Eat the Daisies*. Doubleday. $4.

_____. *Snake Has All the Lines*. Fawcett, 1961. paper, $1.

Lardner, Ring. *Ring Lardner Reader*. Scribner. $13.

Marquis, Don. *Lives and Times of Archy and Mehitabel*. Doubleday. $6.

Twain, Mark. *Complete Humorous Sketches and Tales*. Doubleday, 1961. $7.

_____. *Innocents Abroad*. Harper, 1869. $7.

_____. *Life on the Mississippi*. Harper. $6.

Van Dyke, Dick. *Faith, Hope and Hillarity*. Doubleday, 1970. $5.

Woods, Ralph L. *Modern Handbook of Humor*. McGraw, 1967. $12.

Yates, Norris W. *American Humorist*. Iowa, 1964. $10.

818 AMERICAN MISCELLANY

Emerson, Ralph W. *Essays*. Dutton. $4.

_____. *Portable Emerson*. Viking, 1946. $6.

Fitzgerald, F. Scott. *Fitzgerald Reader*. Scribner, 1963. $9.

James, Henry. *Portable Henry James*. Viking, 1956. $7.

Mencken, Henry L. *Mencken Chrestomathy*. Knopf, 1949. $9.

Poe, Edgar A. *Complete Stories and Poems*. Doubleday. $7.

_____. *Portable Poe*. Viking, 1945. $6.

Stein, Gertrude. *Selected Writings*. Random, 1972. paper, $4.

Thoreau, Henry D. *Portable Thoreau*. rev. ed. Viking, 1947. $7.

_____. *Walden*. Dodd, 1972. $6.

Thurber, James. *Thurber Album*. S&S. $7.

_____. *Thurber Carnival*. Harper, 1945. $6.

Twain, Mark. *Complete Essays*. Doubleday, 1963. $8.

_____. *Portable Mark Twain*, Viking, 1946. $6.

820 ENGLISH LITERATURE

Abrams, Meyer H. *Norton Anthology of English Literature*. 2 vols. rev. ed. Norton, 1968. set, $10.

Baugh, Albert C. *Literary History of England*. 2nd ed., 4 vols. Appleton, 1967. each, $7.

Daiches, David. *Critical History of English Literature*. 2nd ed., 2 vols. Ronald, 1970. set, $15.

Greenfield, Stanley B. *Critical History of Old English Literature*. NYU, 1965. $9.

Haight, Gordon S. *Portable Victorian Reader*. Viking, 1972. $7.

Harvey, Paul. *Oxford Companion to English Literature*. 4th ed. Oxford, 1967. $15.

Haydn, Hiram H. *Portable Elizabethan Reader*. Viking. $6.

Legouis, Emile H. *History of English Literature*. 18th ed. Rowman, 1973. $12.

Osgood, Charles G. *Voice of England*. 2nd ed. Harper, 1952. $10.

Sampson, George. *Concise Cambridge History of English Literature*. 3rd rev. ed. Cambridge, 1970. $12.

Spencer, Hazelton. *British Literature*. 2nd ed., 2 vols. Heath, 1963. each, $12.

821   ENGLISH POETRY

Auden, Wystan H. *Poets of the English Language*. 5 vols. Viking, 1950. each, $6.

Bateson, Frederick W. *English Poetry: a Critical Introduction*. 2nd ed. B&N, 1966. $5.

Browning, Elizabeth B. *Complete Poetical Works*. Houghton. $7.

Browning, Robert. *Poems and Plays*. 2 vols. Dutton. each, $4.

Burns, Robert. *Complete Poetical Works*. Houghton. $7.

Chaucer, Geoffrey. *Canterbury Tales*. Oxford, $3; Dutton, $4; Penguin, $2.

_____. *Modern Reader's Chaucer*. Macmillan, 1967. $8.

_____. *Portable Chaucer*. Morrison, Theodore, ed. Viking, 1949. $6.

Child, Francis J. *English and Scottish Popular Ballads*. 5 vols. Peter Smith, 1965. set, $35.

Coleridge, Samuel. *Portable Coleridge*. Viking, 1950. $6.

Houseman, A. E. *Collected Poems*. rev. ed. Holt, 1971. $7.

Kennedy, Charles W. *Anthology of Old English Poetry*. Oxford, 1960. $6.

_____. *Earliest English Poetry*. Rowman, 1971. $14.

_____. *Early English Christian Poetry*. Oxford, 1963. paper, $3.

Lear, Edward. *Complete Nonsense Book*. Dodd, 1948. $5.

New Oxford Book of English Verse 1250–1950. Oxford, 1972. $10.

Palgrave, Francis. *Golden Treasury*. 5th ed. Oxford, 1964. $8.

Quiller-Couch, Arthur T. *Oxford Book of Ballads*. 2 vols. Somerset, 1955. set, $35.

Reeves, James. *Short History of English Poetry, 1340–1940*. Dutton, 1964. $6.

Shelley, Percy B. *Complete Poetical Works*. Houghton. $8.

Spenser, Edmund. *Complete Poetical Works*. Houghton, 1908. $10.

Tennyson, Alfred. *Poems and Plays*. Oxford, 1953. $6.

Thomas, Dylan. *Collected Poems*. New Directions, 1971. $5.

Wilde, Oscar. *Portable Oscar Wilde*. Viking, 1946. $7.

Williams, Oscar. *Mentor Book of Major British Poets*. NAL. paper, $2.

Wordsworth, William. *Poetical Works*. Oxford, 1950. $8.

822   ENGLISH DRAMA

Adams, Joseph Q. *Chief Pre-Shakespearean Drama*. Houghton, 1924. $10.

Barrie, James M. *Plays*. Scribner, 1928. $9.

Cohen, Ruby. *Twentieth Century Drama*. Random, 1966. $5.

Donoghue, Dennis. *Third Voice*. Princeton. $8.

Gassner, John. *Medieval and Tudor Drama*. Bantam, 1968. paper, $2.

Nicoll, Allardyce. *British Drama*. 5th ed. B&N, 1963. $7.

O'Casey, Sean. *Selected Plays*. Braziller, 1956. $8.

Pollard, Alfred W. *English Miracle Plays, Moralities, and Interludes*. 8th rev. ed. Oxford, 1927. $9.

Popkin, Henry. *Modern British Drama*. Grove, 1964. $6.

Rowell, George. *Nineteenth Century Plays*. 2nd ed. Oxford, 1972. paper, $3.

Schelling, Felix E. *Elizabethan Playwrights*. Blom, 1925. $13.

Shaw, George B. *Seven Plays*. Dodd, 1951. $10.

Tatlock, John S. *Representative English Plays*. 2nd rev. ed. Appleton, 1938. $14.

Twelve Famous Plays of the Restoration and 18th Century. Mod. Library, 1960. $4.

822.3   SHAKESPEARE

Recommended edition of Shakespeare's plays: one play to a volume, edited by G. L. Kittredge, revised by Irving Ribner, published by Blaisdell in paperback only.

American Heritage. *Shakespeare: His Life, His Times, His Works*. McGraw, 1970. $5.

Bradley, Andrew C. *Shakespearean Tragedy*. St. Martin, 1905. $12.

Campbell, Oscar J. *Reader's Encyclopedia of Shakespeare*. Crowell, 1966. $15.

Chambers, Edmund K. *Short Life of Shakespeare*. Oxford, 1933. $4.

Chute, Marchette. *Introduction to Shakespeare*. Dutton. $4.

_____. *Shakespeare of London*. Dutton. $8.

_____. *Stories from Shakespeare*. World, 1956. $6.

Halliday, F. E. *Shakespeare Companion*. rev. ed. Schocken, 1964. $12.

Harbage, Alfred. *Shakespeare: the Tragedies*. Prentice, 1964. $6.

Hazlitt, William. *Characters of Shakespeare's Plays*. Oxford, 1929. $3.

Lamb, Charles. *Tales from Shakespeare*. Macmillan. $4.

Masefield, John. *William Shakespeare*. B&N, 1969. $4.

Nicoll, Allardyce. *Studies in Shakespeare*. Folcroft. $10.

Raleigh, Walter. *Shakespeare's England*. 2 vols. Oxford, 1916. set, $22.

Shakespeare, William. *Complete Pelican Shakespeare*. Penguin, 1969. $15.

_____. *Complete Works*. Oxford, 1943. $5.

_____. *Complete Works of Shakespeare*. Crowell, 1966. $15.

_____. *Sonnets, Songs and Poems*. Schocken, 1964. $7.
Thorndike, Ashley. *Shakespeare's Theater*. Macmillan, 1928. $7.
Van Doren, Mark. *Shakespeare*. Doubleday, 1953. paper, $2.
Wilson, John D. *What Happens in Hamlet*. 3rd ed. Cambridge, 1951. $12.

823   ENGLISH FICTION
Allen, Walter E. *English Novel*. Dutton, 1955. $7.
_____. *Modern Novel*. Dutton, 1964. paper, $2.
Conrad, James. *Portable Conrad*. Viking, 1968. $7.
Joyce, James. *Portable James Joyce*. Viking, 1966. $7.
Karl, Frederick R. *Reader's Guide to Great 20th Century English Novels*.
    Octagon, 1972. $11.
Wagenknecht, Edward C. *Cavalcade of the English Novel*. Holt, 1954. $12.
Williams, Raymond. *English Novel from Dickens to Lawrence*. Oxford,
    1970. $8.

828   ENGLISH MISCELLANY
Arnold, Matthew. *Portable Matthew Arnold*. Viking, 1949. $6.
Bacon, Francis. *Essays*. Houghton, 1923. $4.
Beckwith, Lillian. *Rope—In Case*. Dutton, 1969. $5.
_____. *Sea for Breakfast*. Dutton. $5.
Blake, William. *Portable Blake*. Viking. $6.
Carlyle, Thomas. *Selected Works*. Harvard, 1970. $12.
Fielder, Leslie. *Art of the Essay*. 2nd ed. Crowell, 1969. paper, $5.
Greene, Graham. *Portable Graham Greene*. Viking, 1973. $8.
Huxley, Aldous L. *Collected Essays*. Harper, 1971. paper, $3.
Kronenberger, Louis, ed. *Portable Johnson and Boswell*. Viking. $6.
Lamb, Charles. *Portable Charles Lamb*. Viking, 1949. $5.
Lawrence, D. H. *Portable D. H. Lawrence*. Viking. $7.
Loomis, Roger. *Medieval English Verse and Prose*. Appleton, 1948. $10.
Milton, John. *Portable Milton*. Viking. $6.
Russell, Diarmuid. *Portable Irish Reader*. Viking, 1946. $7.
Swift, Jonathan. *Portable Swift*. Viking, 1948. $5.
Wann, Louis. *Century Readings in the English Essay*. rev. ed. Appleton,
    1939. $8.

830   GERMAN LITERATURE
Bentley, Eric R. *Classic Theater, Vol. 2: Five German Plays*. Doubleday.
    paper, $3.
Bithell, Jethro. *Modern German Literature, 1880–1950*. Ungar. $10.
Brecht, Bertolt. *Seven Plays*. Grove, 1961. $9.
Goethe, Johann W. *Faust*. Mod. Library. $3.
Heine, Heinrich. *Selected Poems*. Oxford, 1965. $7.

Hesse, Hermann. *Poems*. Farrar, 1970. $5.

Lessing, Gotthold. *Lacocoon and Other Writings*. Dutton. $4.

Mann, Thomas. *Essays of Three Decades*. Knopf, 1947. $9.

———. *Last Essays*. Knopf, 1959. $6.

Rilke, Rainer. *Poems*. Oxford, 1965. $2.

Robertson, John G. *History of German Literature*. 6th ed. Brit. Bk. Center, 1971. $12.

Thomas, J. W. *German Verse from 12th to 20th Century*. AMS, 1963. $10.

839   SCANDINAVIAN LITERATURE

Ibsen, Henrik. *Eleven Plays*. Mod. Library. $5.

Strindberg, August. *Six Plays*. Doubleday, 1955. paper, $3.

840   FRENCH LITERATURE

Anouilh, Jean. *Seven Plays*. Hill, 1967. paper, $3.

Baudelaire, Charles P. *Flowers of Evil*. New Directions, 1962. $9.

Bentley, Eric R. *Classic Theater, Vol. 4: Six French Plays*. Doubleday. paper, $3.

Bree, Germaine. *Camus*. rev. ed. Rutgers, 1972. $8.

Camus, Albert. *Caligula and Three Other Plays*. Knopf, 1958. $6.

———. *Myth of Sisyphus and Other Essays*. Knopf, 1955. $6.

———. *Resistance, Rebellion and Death*. Mod. Library, 1963, $3.

Cazamian, Louis F. *History of French Literature*. Oxford, 1955. $12.

Corneille, Pierre. *Chief Plays of Corneille*. Princeton, 1957. $9.

Flores, Angel. *Anthology of French Poetry*. Peter Smith. $5.

Fowlie, Wallace. *Guide to Contemporary French Literature*. Peter Smith. $6.

Gibson, Robert D. *Modern French Poets on Poetry*. Cambridge, 1961. $14.

Giraudoux, Jean. *Four Plays*. Hill, 1958. paper, $3.

———. *Three Plays*. Hill, 1964. $5.

Hartley, Anthony. *Penguin Book of French Verse: 19th Century, Vol. 3*. Penguin. paper, $2.

LaFontaine, Jean de. *Fables*. Viking, 1966. $4.

Maupassant, Guy de. *Portable Maupassant*. Viking, 1947. $6.

Molière, Jean B. *Comedies*. 2 vols. Dutton. each, $4.

Montaigne, Michele de. *Complete Essays*. Stanford, 1958. $10.

Nitze, William A. *History of French Literature*. 3rd ed. West, 1973. $25.

Peyre, Henri. *French Novelists of Today*. Oxford, 1967. $11.

Rimbaud, Arthur. *Selected Verse*. Peter Smith. $4.

Rostand, Edmund. *Cyrano de Bergerac*. Mod. Library, 1957. $3.

Sartre, Jean-Paul. *No Exit, and Three Other Plays*. Random. paper, $2.

Song of Roland. Michigan, 1959. $5.

Valery, Paul. *Selected Writings*. New Directions. paper, $3.

Voltaire, François M. *Portable Voltaire*. Viking, 1949. $5.

850   ITALIAN LITERATURE
Bentley, Eric R. *Classic Theater, Vol. 1: Six Italian Plays*. Doubleday.
    paper, $3.
Dante Alighieri. *Divine Comedy*. Dutton, 1933. $4.
_____. *Portable Dante*. Viking, 1969. $6.
Kay, George. *Penguin Book of Italian Verse*. Penguin, 1968. paper, $2.
Pacifici, Sergio. *Guide to Contemporary Italian Literature*. Peter Smith. $5.
_____. *Modern Italian Novel: from Capuana to Tozzi*. S. Illinois, 1973. $6.
_____. *Modern Italian Novel: from Manzoni to Svevo*. S. Illinois, 1967. $5.
Petrarch, Francesco. *Sonnets and Songs*. Grosset, 1968. $4.
Wilkins, Ernest. *History of Italian Literature*. Harvard, 1954, $14.

860   SPANISH AND PORTUGUESE LITERATURE
Anderson-Imbert, Enrique. *Spanish American Literature: a History*. 2nd
    rev. ed., 2 vols. Wayne. paper, each, $6.
Bentley, Eric R. *Classic Theater, Vol. 3: Six Spanish Plays*. Doubleday.
    paper, $3.
Brenan, Gerald. *Literature of the Spanish People*. Cambridge, 1953. $16.
Cervantes Saavedra, Miguel De. *Portable Cervantes*. Viking, 1951. $6.
Chandler, Richard E. *New History of Spanish Literature*. Louisiana State,
    1961. $12.
Fitzmaurice-Kelly, James. *Oxford Book of Spanish Verse, 13th Century to
    20th Century*. Oxford, 1940. $8.
Garcia Lorca, Federico. *Five Plays*. New Directions. $5.
_____. *Selected Poems*. New Directions. paper, $2.
Resnick, Seymour. *Anthology of Spanish Literature in English Translation*.
    2 vols. Ungar, 1958. set, $15.
Torres Rioseco, Arturo. *Epic of Latin American Literature*. Peter Smith,
    1957. $5.
Turnbull, Eleanor L. *Ten Centuries of Spanish Poetry*. Johns Hopkins,
    1969. $12.

870   LATIN LITERATURE
Cicero, Marcus T. *Basic Works*. Mod. Library, 1951. paper, $2.
Copley, Frank O. *Latin Literature*. Michigan, 1969. $13.
Davenport, Basil. *Portable Roman Reader*. Viking. $6.
Hadas, Moses. *History of Latin Literature*. Columbia, 1952. $11.
Hamilton, Edith. *Roman Way*. Norton, 1932. $7.
Highet, Gilbert. *Poets in a Landscape*. Knopf, 1957. $9.
Horace. *Odes and Epodes*. Harvard. $5.
_____. *Satires, Epistles, and Ars Poetica*. Harvard. $5.
Ovid. *Metamorphosis*. 2 vols. Harvard. each, $5.
Virgil. *Aeneid*. Dutton. $4.

———. *Aeneid of Virgil*. Scribner, 1951. $8.

Waddell, Helen J. *Medieval Latin Lyrics*. 5th ed. B&N, 1966. $6.

———. *Wandering Scholars*. 7th ed. B&N, 1968. $6.

880   GREEK LITERATURE

Aristotle. *Basic Works*. Random, 1941. $10.

Auden, W. H. *Portable Greek Reader*. Viking. $6.

Barnstone, Willis. *Greek Lyric Poetry*. Schocken, 1972. $9.

Cooper, Lane. *Fifteen Greek Plays*. Oxford, 1943. $9.

Finley, Moses I. *Portable Greek Historians*. Viking, 1959. $5.

Fitts, Dudley. *Greek Plays in Modern Translation*. Holt, 1947. $9.

———. *Poems from the Greek Anthology*. New Directions, 1956. $3.

Hadas, Moses. *Greek Drama*. Bantam, 1968. paper, $2.

———. *History of Greek Literature*. Columbia, 1950. $10.

Hamilton, Edith. *Greek Way*. 2nd ed. Norton, 1930. $7.

Homer. *Iliad*. Chicago, 1962. $7.

———. *Odyssey*. Oxford, 1956. paper, $2.

Murphy, Charles T. *Greek and Roman Classics in Translation*. McKay, 1947. $9.

Oates, Whitney J. *Complete Greek Drama*. 2 vols. Random, 1938. each, $9.

Plato. *Portable Plato*. Viking. $6.

Rose, Herbert J. *Handbook of Greek Literature*. rev. ed. Dutton. paper, $3.

890   AFRICAN AND ASIAN LITERATURE

Anderson, George L. *Masterpieces of the Orient*. Norton, 1965. paper, $4.

Birch, Cyril. *Anthology of Chinese Literature*. Grove, 1965/72. vol. 1, paper, $4; vol. 2, $10.

Bownas, Geoffrey. *Penguin Book of Japanese Verse*. Penguin, 1964. paper, $2.

Chai, Ch'U. *Treasury of Chinese Literature*. Hawthorn, 1965. $9.

Drachler, Jacob. *African Heritage*. Macmillan, 1963. $4.

Gibran, Kahlil. *Prophet*. Knopf, 1923. $5.

Hughes, Langston. *African Treasury*. Crown, 1960. $4.

———. *Poems from Black Africa*. Indiana, 1963. $6.

Keene, Donald. *Anthology of Japanese Literature*. Grove, 1956. paper, $3.

———. *Modern Japanese Literature*. Grove, 1956. $3.

Kgosistsile, Keorapetse. *Word is Here; Poetry from Modern Africa*. Doubleday, 1973. paper, $3.

Lin Yutang. *Wisdom of China and India*. Mod. Library. $5.

Liptzin, Solomon. *Flowering of Yiddish Literature*. B&N. $4.

Omar Khayam. *Rubaiyat*. Crowell. $5.

Rutherford, Peddy. *African Voices*. Grossset, 1970. paper, $3.

Waley, Arthur. *Translations from the Chinese*. Random, 1971. paper, $2.

891   RUSSIAN LITERATURE

Chekov, Anton. *Portable Chekov*. Viking, 1947. $7.

Guerney, Bernard G. *Portable Russian Reader*. Viking. $6.

———. *Treasury of Russian Literature*. Vanguard. $10.

Magarshack, David. *Storm, and Other Russian Plays*. Hill, 1960. paper, $2.

Mirsky, Dmitry S. *History of Russian Literature to 1900*. Random, 1949. paper, $2.

Nabokov, Vladimir. *Portable Nabokov*. Viking, 1971. $6.

Noyes, George. *Masterpieces of Russian Drama*. 2 vols. Peter Smith, 1933. set, $6.

Pasternak, Boris. *Poems*. Kent, 1963. $6.

Pushkin, Aleksandr S. *Poems, Prose, and Plays*. Mod. Library. $5.

Slonim, Marc L. *Epic of Russian Literature*. Oxford, 1964. paper, $4.

———. *Outline of Russian Literature*. Oxford, 1958. $7.

———. *Soviet Russian Literature*. Oxford, 1964. $9.

Solzhenitzyn, Aleksandr I. *Gulag Archipelago*. Harper, 1974. $13.

———. *Stories and Prose Poems*. Farrar, 1971. $8.

Tolstoy, Leo. *Selections*. Oxford, 1959. $4.

Yarmolinsky, Avrahm. *Treasury of Great Russian Short Stories*. Macmillan, 1944. $10.

———. *Treasury of Russian Verse*. Bks for Libs, 1949. $15.

Yevtushenko, Yevgeny. *Poems*. Hill, 1971. $4.

900

GEOGRAPHY, BIOGRAPHY, HISTORY

900 GENERAL AND WORLD HISTORY

Brinton, Crane. *Ideas and Men*. 2nd ed. Prentice, 1963. $12.

Carr, Edward H. *What Is History?* Knopf, 1962. $5.

Chambers, Frank P. *This Age of Conflict*. 3rd ed. Harcourt, 1962. $11.

Colton, Joel G. *Twentieth Century*. Time, 1968. $6.

Davies, Herbert A. *Outline History of the World*. 5th ed. Oxford, 1968. $4.

Durant, Will. *Lessons of History*. S&S, 1968. $5.

———. *Story of Civilization*. 10 vols. S&S, 1935/65. set, $113.

Garraty, John A. *Columbia History of the World*. Harper, 1972. $20.

Gay, Peter. *Historians at Work*. 2 vols. Harper, 1972. set, $30.

Heilbroner, Robert L. *Future as History*. Harper, 1960. $5.

Kirchner, Walther. *Western Civilization*. 2 vols. B&N, 1960/66. set, $5.

Langer, William L. *Encyclopedia of World History*. 5th ed. Houghton, 1972. $18.

McNeill, William H. *Rise of the West*. Chicago, 1963. $10.

Marwick, Arthur. *Nature of History*. Knopf, 1971. $9.

Mazlish, Bruce. *Riddle of History*. Harper, 1966. $11.

Morris, Richard B. *Harper Encyclopedia of Modern World History*. Harper, 1970. $18.

Muller, Herbert J. *Uses of the Past*. Oxford, 1952. $8.

Mydans, Carl. *Violent Peace*. Atheneum, 1968. $13.

Piel, Gerard. *Acceleration of History*. Knopf, 1964. $4.

Potter, Elmer B. *Sea Power*. Prentice, 1960. $15.

Robertson, Archibald. *How to Read History*. Ungar, 1954. $5.

Smith, Page. *Historian and History*. Knopf, 1964. $4.

Spengler, Oswald. *Decline of the West*. Mod. Library, 1945. $5.

Stavrianos, L. S. *Epic of Modern Man*. 2nd ed. Prentice, 1971. $6.

Toynbee, Arnold J. *Study of History*. 12 vols. Oxford, 1935/61. set, $145.

_____. *Surviving the Future*. Oxford, 1971. $6.

Ward, Barbara. *Five Ideas that Changed the World*. Norton, 1959. $5.

Wells, H. G. *Outline of History*. rev. ed. Doubleday, 1971. $10.

White, Morton. *Foundations of Historical Knowledge*. Harper, 1965. paper, $3.

910 GEOGRAPHY, DISCOVERY

Dana, Richard H. *Two Years before the Mast*. Dutton, 1946. $4.

Graham, Robin L. *Dove*. Harper, 1972. $8.

Heyerdahl, Thor. *Kon-Tiki*. Rand, 1950. $9.

_____. *RA Expeditions*. Doubleday, 1971. $10.

Hoyt, Joseph B. *Man and Earth*. 3rd ed. Prentice, 1973. $13.

Lord, Walter, *Night to Remember*. Harper, 1955. $6.

912 ATLASES

Goode's World Atlas. 13th ed. Rand, 1971. $12.

Rand McNally Road Atlas. rev. ed. Rand, 1973. paper, $3.

Rand McNally World Atlas. family ed. Rand, 1973. $10.

913 ARCHAEOLOGY

Ceram, C. W. *Gods, Graves, and Scholars*. rev. ed. Knopf, 1967. $9.

DeCamp, L. Sprague. *Great Cities of the Ancient World*. Doubleday, 1972. $13.

Hawkins, Gerald S. *Stonehenge Decoded*. Doubleday, 1965. $7.

Magnusson, Magnus. *Introducing Archaeology*. Walck, 1973. $9.

Meyer, Karl E. *Pleasures of Archaeology*. Atheneum, 1971. $13.

Muller, Artur. *Seven Wonders of the World*. McGraw, 1969. $15.

Quennell, Charles H. *Everyday Life in Prehistoric Times*. rev. ed. Putnam, 1959. $5.

914– TRAVEL
919

There are many series of travel books which are frequently revised. Latest edition should be specified on orders. Each series notation here gives publisher, average price, and sometimes an author. Choose those most appropriate to your budget and clientele.

American Heritage. *Historic Houses*. McGraw, 1971. $7.

American Heritage. *Natural Wonders of America*. McGraw, 1972. $7.

Area Handbook of . . . for most countries. U.S. Govt. Printing Office.

Bracken, Peg. *But I Wouldn't Have Missed It for the World*. Harcourt, 1973. $7.

Clarke, Sydney A. *All the Best in* . . . . (for *Europe, the Mediterraneum,* etc.) Dodd, varied. $5–$13.

Clery, Val. *Canada in Colour*. Haunslow, 1973. $7.

Cross, Wilbur. *Guide to Unusual Vacations*. Hart, 1973. paper, $4.

Doubleday, Nelson. *Encyclopedia of World Travel*. 2nd rev. ed., 2 vols. Doubleday, 1973. set, $13.

Ehrlich, Arnold. *Beautiful Country: Maine to Hawaii*. Viking, 1970. $17.

Fielding, Temple. *Fielding's Guides*. Fielding. $9 each.

Fodor, Eugene. Fodor guides to individual countries, continents, and cities. McKay. $8–$12.

Ford, Norman. Various paperback guides to traveling the U.S. Harian Publ. $2–$4.

Frommer, Arthur. . . . . *on $5 and/or $10 a Day*. Frommer. paper, $4.

Kane, Robert. . . . . *A to Z*. Doubleday, $8.

MacLennan, Hugh. *Colour of Canada*. rev. ed. Little, 1972. $7.

Mobil Travel Guide to sections of the U.S. S&S, published annually. paper, $3.

National Geographic Soc. Several titles on travel. National Geographic. $5–$12.

Pan American World Airways. Guides. S&S. paper, $2.

Rand McNally. Guides and road atlases. Rand. $4.

Robinson, Jeffrey. *All of Europe at Low Cost*. 8th rev. ed. Harian, 1973. paper, $4.

Sterling. *Europe—with Pictures*. Sterling, 1973. $14.

Sunset Magazine, eds. Travel guides to states, areas, countries. $10; paper, $3.

Time-Life Books. Titles on various countries and sections of the U.S. May also be considered as history. Time. $7.

Waldo, Myra. Travel guides. Macmillan. $8.

920   COLLECTIVE BIOGRAPHY

Adams, Russell. *Great Negroes, Past and Present*. 3rd rev. ed. Afro-Am, 1969. $8.

Associated Press, eds. *Sports Immortals*. Prentice, 1972. $13.

Attwater, Donald. *Penguin Dictionary of Saints*. Peter Smith. $4.

Aubrey, John. *Aubrey's Brief Lives*. Michigan, 1957. $6.

Barzman, Sol. *First Ladies*. Regnery, 1970. $9.

Bell, Eric. *Men of Mathematics*. S&S, 1961. $8.

Bolton, Sarah K. *Famous Men of Science*. 4th ed. Crowell, 1960. $4.

Brockway, Wallace. *Men of Music*. S&S, 1950. $9.

Canby, Henry S. *Classic Americans*. Russell, 1959. $13.

David, Jay. *Growing up Black*. Morrow, 1968. $7.

———. *Living Black in White America*. Morrow, 1972. $7.

Davies, Hunter. *Beatles: Authorized Biography*. McGraw, 1972. $8.

DeKruif, Paul. *Men against Death*. Harcourt, 1932. $7.

_____. *Microbe Hunters*. Harcourt, 1932. $7.

Drotning, Philip T. *Black Heroes in Our Nation's History*. Regnery, 1969. $7.

Flexner, James. *Doctors on Horseback*. Peter Smith. $5.

Freidel, Frank B. *Our Country's Presidents*. National Geographic, 1966. $5.

Goldman, David J. *Presidential Losers*. Lerner, 1970. $4.

Haskins, James. *Piece of the Power: Four Black Mayors*. Dial, 1972. $5.

_____. *Profiles in Black Power*. Doubleday, 1972. $4.

Highet, Gilbert. *Poets in a Landscape*. Knopf, 1957. $9.

Holbrook, Stewart H. *Age of the Moguls*. Doubleday, 1953. $7.

Kennedy, John F. *Profiles in Courage*. Harper, 1964. $8.

Malvern, Gladys. *Six Wives of Henry VIII*. Vanguard, 1969. $5.

Manchester, William A. *Rockefeller Family Portrait*. Little, 1959. $6.

Maurois, André. *Titans*. Greenwood, 1971. $21.

Morgan, James. *Our Presidents*. 2nd ed. Macmillan, 1969. $9.

Nash, J. Robert. *Bloodletters and Badmen*. Evans, 1973. $17.

Pleasants, Henry. *Great Singers*. S&S, 1966. $8.

Plutarch. *Lives*. Mod. Library. $5.

Richardson, Ben. *Great American Negroes*. rev. ed. Crowell, 1956. $5.

Roosevelt, Elliot. *Untold Story: the Roosevelts of Hyde Park*. Putnam, 1973. $9.

Schonberg, Harold C. *Great Conductors*. S&S, 1967. $8.

_____. *Great Pianists*. S&S, 1966. $8.

_____. *Lives of Great Composers*. Norton, 1970. $13.

Smith, Bradford. *Men of Peace*. Lippincott, 1964. $7.

Stacton, David. *Bonapartes*. S&S, 1966. $8.

Stone, Irving. *They Also Ran*. rev. ed. Doubleday, 1965. $6.

Strachey, Lytton. *Eminent Victorians*. Peter Smith. $4.

Tharp, Louise H. *Peabody Sisters of Salem*. Little, 1950. $7.

Untermeyer, Louis. *Lives of the Poets*. S&S, 1960. $8.

_____. *Makers of the Modern World*. S&S, 1962. $8.

Vasari, Giorgio. *Lives of the Painters, Sculptors, and Architects*. 4 vols. Dutton. each, $4.

Williams, Roger. *The Bonds*. Atheneum, 1971. $10.

INDIVIDUAL BIOGRAPHY

The following section lists books about persons of general interest. Some titles are included because they are interesting examples of the genre. Individual libraries are urged to add materials about persons of local or topical interest as needed.

AARON, HENRY
   Aaron, Henry. *Bad Henry*. Chilton, 1974. $7.
ABRAHAMS, PETER
   Abrahams, Peter. *Tell Freedom*. Knopf, 1954. $6.
ADAMS, HENRY
   Adams, Henry. *Education of Henry Adams*. Houghton, 1973. $10.
ADAMS, JOHN
   Bowen, Catherine. *John Adams and the American Revolution*. Little, 1950. $10.
ADAMSON, GEORGE
   Adamson, George. *Lifetime with Lions*. Doubleday, 1968. $7.
ADDAMS, JANE
   Addams, Jane. *20 Years at Hull House*. Macmillan, 1966. $7.
ALCINDOR, LEW *see* Jabbar, Kareem Abdul
ALEXANDRA (ROMANOV) *see* Nicholas
ALFRED THE GREAT
   Helm, Peter J. *Alfred the Great*. Crowell, 1965. $5.
ALSOP, STEWART
   Alsop, Stewart. *Stay of Execution*. Lippincott, 1973. $7.
ANDERSON, MARION
   Anderson, Marion. *My Lord, What a Morning*. Viking, 1956. $6.
ANGELOU, MAYA
   Angelou, Maya. *I Know Why the Caged Bird Sings*. Random, 1970. $6.
ASHTON-WARNER, SYLVIA
   Ashton-Warner, Sylvia. *Myself*. S&S, 1967. $5.
AUGUSTINE
   Augustine. *Confessions*. Dutton, 1950. $4.
AUGUSTUS
   Buchan, John. *Augustus*. Verry, 1947. $4.
AUSTEN, JANE
   Hodge, Jane A. *Only a Novel*. Coward, 1972. $7.
BACON, FRANCIS
   Bowen, Catherine. *Francis Bacon*. Atlantic, 1963. $8.
BAEZ, JOAN
   Baez, Joan. *Daybreak*. Dial, 1968. $4.
BAILEY, F. LEE
   Bailey, F. Lee. *Defense Never Rests*. Stein, 1972. $8.

BAILEY, PEARL
  Bailey, Pearl. *Raw Pearl*. Harcourt, 1968. $6.
BALDWIN, JAMES
  Baldwin, James. *Nobody Knows My Name*. Dial, 1961. $6.
BALZAC, HONORE DE
  Maurois, Andre. *Prometheus*. Harper, 1966. $10.
BARNUM, P. T.
  Wallace, Irving. *Fabulous Showman*. Knopf, 1959. $7.
BARTON, CLARA
  Ross, Ishbel. *Angel of the Battlefield*. Harper, 1956. $6.
BARUCH, BERNARD M.
  Baruch, Bernard M. *Baruch: My Own Story*. Holt, 1957. $7.
BEERS, CLIFFORD
  Beers, Clifford. *Mind that Found Itself*. Doubleday, 1948. $8.
BEETHOVEN, LUDWIG VON
  Sullivan, John W. *Beethoven*. Knopf, 1960. $5.
BEHAN, BRENDAN
  Behan, Dominic. *My Brother Brendan*. S&S, 1966. $5.
BEN-GURION, DAVID
  St. John, Robert. *Ben-Gurion*. Doubleday, 1971. $7.
BERNHARDT, SARAH
  Skinner, Cornelia. *Madame Sarah*. Houghton, 1967. $7.
BERNSTEIN, LEONARD
  Gruen, John. *Private World of Leonard Bernstein*. Viking, 1968. $13.
BOURKE-WHITE, MARGARET
  Bourke-White, Margaret. *Portrait of Myself*. S&S, 1963. $7.
BRAITHWAITE, EDWARD
  Braithwaite, Edward. *To Sir with Love*. Holt, 1960. $6.
BRONTË, CHARLOTTE
  Gaskell, Elizabeth. *Life of Charlotte Brontë*. Dutton, 1919, $4.
BROWN, CLAUDE
  Brown, Claude. *Manchild in the Promised Land*. Macmillan, 1965. $7.
BROWNING
  Winwar, Francis S. *Immortal Lovers*. Harper, 1950. $8.
BRYAN, WILLIAM JENNINGS
  Levine, Lawrence W. *Defender of the Faith*. Oxford, 1965. $8.
BUCK, PEARL S.
  Buck, Pearl S. *Bridge for Passing*. John Day, 1962. $8.
  _____. *My Several Worlds*. John Day, 1954. $10.
BURR, AARON
  Chidsey, Donald. *Great Conspiracy*. Crown, 1967. $5.
BYRD, RICHARD E.
  Byrd, Richard E. *Alone*. Putnam, 1938. $7.
BYRON, GEORGE NOEL GORDON
  Maurois, André. *Byron*. Ungar, 1964. $11.

CAESAR, JULIUS
  Duggan, Alfred. *Julius Caesar*. Knopf, 1955. $4.
CAPONE, AL
  Kobler, John. *Capone*. Putnam, 1971. $9.
CARSON, KIT
  Vestal, Stanley. *Kit Carson*. Houghton, 1928. $6.
CARVER, GEORGE WASHINGTON
  Holt, Rackham. *George Washington Carver*. Doubleday, 1963. $6.
CASTRO, FIDEL
  Matthews, Herbert L. *Fidel Castro*. S&S, 1969. $7.
CATHERINE OF ARAGON
  Mattingly, Garrett. *Catherine of Aragon*. Peter Smith. $5.
CATHERINE II
  Oldenbourg, Zoe. *Catherine the Great*. Pantheon, 1965. $9.
CELLINI, BENVENUTO
  Cellini, Benvenuto. *Life of Benvenuto Cellini*. Liveright. $7.
CHAPLIN, CHARLES
  Chaplin, Charles. *My Autobiography*. S&S, 1964. $7.
CHARLEMAGNE
  Lamb, Harold. *Charlemagne*. Doubleday, 1954. $5.
CHAUCER, GEOFFREY
  Chute, Marchette. *Geoffrey Chaucer of England*. Dutton, 1951. $8.
CHISHOLM, SHIRLEY
  Chisholm, Shirley. *Unbought and Unbossed*. Houghton, 1970. $5.
CHRISTINA (QUEEN OF SWEDEN)
  Masson, Georgina. *Queen Christina*. Farrar, 1969. $9.
CHURCHILL, LADY RANDOLPH
  Martin, Ralph. *Jennie: the Life of Lady Randolph Churchill; Romantic Years, 1854-1895*. Prentice, 1968. $9.
  Martin, Ralph. *Jennie: the Life of Lady Randolph Churchill; Dramatic Years, 1895-1921*. Prentice, 1971. $9.
CHURCHILL, WINSTON
  Bonham-Carter, Violet. *Winston Churchill: an Intimate Portrait*. Harcourt, 1965. $9.
CLAY, CASSIUS *see* Muhammed Ali
CLAY, HENRY
  Eaton, Clement. *Henry Clay and the Art of American Politics*. Little, 1957. $5.
CLEAVER, ELDRIDGE
  Cleaver, Eldridge. *Soul on Ice*. McGraw, 1968. $7.
CLEMENS, SAMUEL
  Kaplan, Justin. *Mr. Clemens and Mark Twain*. S&S, 1966. $8.
COLUMBUS, CHRISTOPHER
  Morrison, Samuel E. *Admiral of the Ocean Sea*. Little, 1966. $8.
CROMWELL, OLIVER
  Fraser, Antonia. *Cromwell*. Knopf, 1973. $13.

CUSTER, GEORGE
  Kinsley, D. A. *Favor the Bold*. 2 vols. Holt, 1967. each, $7.
CYRUS THE GREAT
  Lamb, Harold. *Cyrus the Great*. Doubleday, 1960. $6.
DALEY, RICHARD
  Royko, Mike. *Boss*. Dutton, 1971. $7.
DARROW, CLARENCE
  Stone, Irving. *Clarence Darrow for the Defense*. Doubleday, 1949. $7.
DARWIN, CHARLES
  Moorehead, Alan. *Darwin and the Beagle*. Harper, 1969. $15.
DAVIS, SAMMY
  Davis, Sammy. *Yes I Can*. Farrar, 1965. $8.
DICKENS, CHARLES
  Johnson, Edgar. *Charles Dickens*. Little, 1965. $20
DICKINSON, EMILY
  Johnson, Thomas. *Emily Dickinson*. Harvard, 1955. $8.
DISRAELI, BENJAMIN
  Blake, Robert. *Disraeli*. St. Martin, 1967. $13.
DOOLEY, THOMAS A.
  Dooley, Thomas A. *Dr. Tom Dooley's Three Great Books*. Farrar, 1960. $8.
DOSTOYEVSKY, FEDOR
  Payne, Robert. *Dostoyevsky*. Knopf, 1961. $9.
DOUGLASS, FREDERICK
  Douglass, Frederick. *Narratives of the Life of an American Slave*. Harvard, 1960.
    $5.
DOYLE, SIR ARTHUR CONAN
  Carr, John. *Life of Sir Arthur Conan Doyle*. Harper, 1949. $8.
DREISER, THEODORE
  Swanberg, W. A. *Dreiser*. Scribner, 1965. $13.
DULLES, JOHN FOSTER
  Hoopes, Townsend. *Devil and John Foster Dulles*. Little, 1973. $13.
DUMAS, ALEXANDER
  See Maurois, André in Collective Biography.
DUNCAN, ISADORA
  Seroff, Victor. *Real Isadora*. Dial, 1971. $10.
EARHART, AMELIA
  Goerner, Fred. *Search for Amelia Earhart*. Doubleday, 1966. $8.
EDWARD VII
  Magnus, Philip. *King Edward VII*. Dutton, 1964. $13.
EISENHOWER, DWIGHT DAVID
  Eisenhower, Dwight D. *White House Years*. 2 vols. Doubleday. each, $8.
ELEANOR OF AQUITAINE
  Kelly, Amy. *Eleanor of Aquitaine and the Four Kings*. Harvard, 1950. $10.
ELIZABETH I
  Jenkins, Elizabeth. *Elizabeth the Great*. Coward, 1959. $9.

EVERS, MEDGAR
  Evers, Mrs. Medgar. *For Us, the Living*. Doubleday, 1967. $7.
ESPOSITOS, THE
  Esposito, Phil. *Brothers Esposito*. Hawthorn, 1971. $6.
FERMI, ENRICO
  Fermi, Laura. *Atoms in the Family*. Chicago, 1954. $5.
FITZGERALD, F. SCOTT
  Mizener, Arthur. *Far Side of Paradise*. Houghton, 1965. paper, $3.
  Turnbull, Andrew. *Scott Fitzgerald*. Scribner, 1962. paper, $3.
FITZGERALD, ZELDA
  Mitford, Nancy. *Zelda*. Harper, 1970. $10.
FORD, HENRY
  Burlingame, Roger. *Henry Ford*. Knopf, 1955. $4.
FRANK, ANNE
  Frank, Anne. *Diary of a Young Girl*. Watts, 1961. $9.
FRANKLIN, BENJAMIN
  Franklin, Benjamin. *Autobiography*. Dodd, 1963. $6.
  Fleming, Thomas J. *Man Who Dared the Lightning*. Morrow, 1971. $10.
FREUD, SIGMUND
  Jones, Ernest. *Life and Work of Sigmund Freud*. abr. ed. Basic, 1961. $11.
GANDHI, INDIRA
  Mohan, Anand. *Indira Gandhi*. Hawthorn, 1967. $7.
GANDHI, MAHATMA
  Sheean, Vincent. *Mahatma Gandhi*. Knopf, 1955. $4.
GEORGE III
  Ayling, Stanley. *George the Third*. Knopf, 1972. $13.
GERONIMO
  Adams, Alexander B. *Geronimo*. Putnam, 1971. $9.
GERSHWIN, GEORGE
  Ewen, David. *Story of George Gershwin*. Holt, 1957. $4.
GILBRETHS, THE
  Gilbreth, Frank B. *Cheaper by the Dozen*. Crowell, 1963. $5.
GIOVANNI, NIKKI
  Giovanni, Nikki. *Gemini*. Bobbs, 1972. $6.
GOGH, VINCENT VAN
  Lubin, Albert J. *Stranger on the Earth*. Holt, 1972. $9.
GOGOL, NIKOLAI
  Troyat, Henri. *Divided Soul*. Doubleday, 1973. $13.
GRANT, ULYSSES S.
  Catton, Bruce. *U.S. Grant and the American Military Tradition*. Little, 1954. $5.
GREGORY, DICK
  Gregory, Dick. *nigger*. Dutton, 1964. $6.
GUNTHER, JOHN
  Gunther, John. *Death Be Not Proud*. Mod. Library, 1953. $3.

HAMILTON, ALEXANDER
 Mitchell, Broadus. *Alexander Hamilton*. Crowell, 1970. $10.
HAMMARSKJOLD, DAG
 Kelen, Emery. *Hammarskjold*. Putnam, 1966. $6.
HAN, SUYIN
 Han, Suyin. *Many-Splendored Thing*. Little, 1952. $6.
HART, MOSS
 Hart, Moss. *Act One*. Random, 1959. $8.
HARTE, BRET
 O'Connor, Richard. *Bret Harte*. Little, 1966. $8.
HEARST, WILLIAM RANDOLPH
 Swanberg, W. A. *Citizen Hearst*. Scribner, 1961. $13.
HELLMAN, LILLIAN
 Hellman, Lillian. *Pentimento*. Little, 1973. $8.
 _____. *Unfinished Woman*. Little, 1969. $8.
HEMINGWAY, ERNEST
 Baker, Carlos. *Ernest Hemingway*. Scribner, 1969. $13.
 Hemingway, Ernest. *Moveable Feast*. Scribner, 1964. $6.
HENRY VIII
 Scarisbrick, J. J. *Henry VIII*. California, 1968. $11.
HERBERT, ANTHONY
 Herbert, Anthony. *Soldier*. Holt, 1973. $11.
HERRIOT, JAMES
 Herriot, James. *All Creatures Great and Small*. St. Martin, 1972. $8.
 _____. *All Things Bright and Beautiful*. St. Martin, 1974. $9.
HITLER, ADOLPH
 Bullock, Alan. *Hitler: a Study in Tyranny*. Harper, 1964. $10.
 Hitler, Adolf. *Mein Kampf*. Houghton, 1943, $10
 Langer, Walter C. *Mind of Adolf Hitler*. Basic, 1972. $10.
HO CHI MINH
 Halberstam, David. *Ho*. Random, 1971. $5.
HOFFER, ERIC
 Tomkins, Calvin. *Eric Hoffer: an American Odyssey*. Dutton, 1968. $6.
HOMER, WINSLOW
 Beam, Philip C. *Winslow Homer at Prout's Neck*. Little, 1966. $8.
HOUDINI, HARRY
 Gresham, William L. *Houdini*. Holt, 1959. $6.
JABBAR, KAREEM ABDUL
 Haskins, James. *Lew Alcindor*. Lothrop, 1972. $4.
JACKSON, ANDREW
 James, Marquis. *Andrew Jackson*. Peter Smith. $5.
JACKSON, THOMAS (STONEWALL)
 Davis, Burke. *They Called Him Stonewall*. Holt, 1954. $7.
JAMESES, THE
 Matthiessen, Francis O. *James Family*. Knopf, 1947. $10.

JEFFERSON, THOMAS
  Brodie, Fawn M. *Thomas Jefferson*. Norton, 1974. $13.
  Malone, Dumas. *Jefferson and the Ordeal of Liberty*. Little, 1969. $10.
  Malone, Dumas. *Jefferson and the Rights of Man*. Little, 1951. $10.
  Malone, Dumas. *Jefferson the President*. Little, 1970. $10.
  _____. *Jefferson the President: Second Term*. Little, 1974. $13.
  _____. *Jefferson the Virginian*. Little, 1948. $13.
JOHNSON, LYNDON BAINES
  Goldman, Eric F. *Tragedy of Lyndon*. Knopf, 1969. $9.
  Sherrill, Robert. *Accidental President*. Grossman, 1967. $5.
JOLSON, AL
  Sieben, Pearl. *Immortal Jolson*. Fell, 1962. $6.
JOPLIN, JANIS
  Friedman, Myra. *Buried Alive*. Morrow, 1973. $8.
JOYCE, JAMES
  Ellman, Richard. *James Joyce*. Oxford, 1959. $18.
KELLER, HELEN
  Keller, Helen. *Story of My Life*. Doubleday, 1954. $7.
KENNEDY, EDWARD
  Hersh, Burton. *Education of Edward Kennedy*. Morrow, 1972. $11.
KENNEDY, JOHN F.
  Manchester, William. *Death of a President*. Harper, 1967. $10.
  Sorenson, Theodore. *Kennedy*. Harper, 1965. $10.
KENNEDY, ROBERT F.
  Halberstam, David. *Unfinished Odyssey*. Random, 1969. $5.
  Newfield, Jack. *Robert Kennedy, a Memoir*. Dutton, 1969. $8.
KENNEDY, ROSE
  Cameron, Gail. *Rose*. Putnam, 1971. $7.
  Kennedy, Rose. *Times to Remember*. Doubleday, 1974. $13.
KHRUSHCHEV, NIKITA
  Crankshaw, Edward. *Khrushchev*. Viking, 1966. $8.
KING, MARTIN LUTHER, JR.
  Bennett, Lerone. *What Manner of Man*. Johnson, 1964. $6.
  King, Coretta. *My Life with Martin Luther King*. Holt, 1970. $6.
KRENTS, HAROLD
  Krents, Harold. *To Race the Wind*. Putnam, 1972. $7.
KRUPP
  Manchester, William. *Arms of Krupp*. Little, 1968. $13.
LANDON, MARGARET
  Landon, Margaret. *Anna and the King of Siam*. Day, 1944. $8.
LENIN, VLADIMIR
  Payne, Robert. *Life and Death of Lenin*. S&S, 1964. $9.
LEVENSON, SAM
  Levenson, Sam. *Everything but Money*. S&S, 1966. $5.
  _____. *In One Era and out the Other*. S&S, 1973. $7.

LIBERACE
  Liberace. *Liberace*. Putnam, 1973. $8.
LINCOLN, ABRAHAM
  Bishop, James. *Day Lincoln Was Shot*. Harper, 1955. $7.
  Thomas, Benjamin. *Abraham Lincoln*. Mod. Library, 1968. $5.
LINCOLN, MARY TODD
  Turner, Justin G. *Mary Todd Lincoln*. Knopf, 1972. $15.
LINDBERG, ANNE MORROW
  Lindberg, Anne M. *Bring Me a Unicorn*. Harcourt, 1972. $7.
  _____. *Hour of Gold, Hour of Lead*. Harcourt, 1973. $8.
LINDBERGH, CHARLES A.
  Lindbergh, Charles A. *Spirit of St. Louis*. Scribner, 1953. $10.
LITTLE, MALCOLM *see* Malcolm X
LOMBARDI, VINCE
  Dowling, Tom. *Coach*. Norton, 1970. $8.
LONDON, JACK
  Stone, Irving. *Sailor on Horseback*. Doubleday, 1947. $7.
LOUIS XIV (KING OF FRANCE)
  Mitford, Nancy. *Sun King*. Harper, 1966. $15.
  Wolf, John B. *Louis XIV*. Norton, 1968. $13.
LUCE, HENRY
  Swanberg, W. A. *Luce and His Empire*. Scribner, 1972. $13.
LUTHER, MARTIN
  Bainton, Roland. *Here I Stand*. Abingdon, 1951. $7.
MAC ARTHUR, DOUGLAS
  MacArthur, Douglas. *Reminiscences*. McGraw, 1964. $9.
McCARTHY, MARY
  McCarthy, Mary. *Memories of a Catholic Girlhood*. Harcourt, 1957. $5.
MALCOLM X
  Little, Malcolm. *Autobiography of Malcolm X*. Grove, 1965. $8.
MAO TSE TUNG
  Schram, Stuart R. *Mao Tse Tung*. S&S, 1967. $8.
MARSHALL, GEORGE C.
  Pogue, Forrest. *Education of a General*. Viking, 1963. $8.
  Pogue, Forrest. *Ordeal and Hope*. Viking, 1966. $13.
MARX, KARL
  Payne, Robert. *Marx*. S&S, 1968. $10.
MARY STUART
  Fraser, Antonia. *Mary Queen of Scots*. Delacorte, 1969. $10.
  Morrison, Brysson N. *Mary, Queen of Scots*. Vanguard, 1960. $6.
MARY TUDOR
  Prescott, Hilda. *Mary Tudor*. rev. ed. Macmillan, 1962. $6.
MAYO
  Clapesattle, Helen B. *Doctors Mayo*. 2nd ed. Minnesota, 1954. $10.

MAYS, WILLIE
  Mays, Willie. *My Life in and out of Baseball*. rev. ed. Dutton, 1972. $7.
MEAD, MARGARET
  Mead, Margaret. *Blackberry Winter*. Morrow, 1972. $9.
MEIR, GOLDA
  Mann, Peggy. *Golda*. Coward, 1971. $6.
MILLAY, EDNA ST. VINCENT
  Gurko, Miriam. *Restless Spirit*. Crowell, 1962. $5.
MUHAMMED ALI
  Torres, Jose. *Sting like a Bee*. Abelard, 1971. $7.
MUSSOLINI, BENITO
  Fermi, Laura. *Mussolini*. Chicago, 1961. $7.
NABOKOV, VLADIMIR
  Nabokov, Vladimir. *Speak, Memory*. Putnam, 1966. $8.
NAPOLEON I
  Guerard, Albert L. *Napoleon I*. Knopf, 1956. $5.
NAPOLEON III
  Guerard, Albert L. *Napoleon III*. Knopf, 1955. $5.
NEFERTITI
  Wells, Evelyn. *Nefertiti*. Doubleday, 1964. $6.
NICHOLAS (ROMANOV)
  Massie, Robert. *Nicholas and Alexandra*. Atheneum, 1967. $13.
NIVEN, DAVID
  Niven, David. *Moon's a Balloon*. Putnam, 1972. $8.
OLMSTED, FREDERIC LAW
  Mitchell, Broadus. *Critic of the Old South*. Russell, 1968. $8.
O'NEILL, EUGENE
  Gelb, Barbara. *O'Neill*. rev. ed. Harper, 1974. $18.
  Sheaffer, Louis. *O'Neill: Son and Artist*. Little, 1973. $15.
PARKS, GORDON
  Parks, Gordon. *Choice of Weapons*. Harper, 1966. $7.
PASTEUR, LOUIS
  Vallery-Radot, René. *Louis Pasteur*. Knopf, 1958. $4.
PATTON, GEORGE S.
  Ayer, Fred. *Before the Colors Fade*. Houghton, 1971. $10.
PEPYS, SAMUEL
  Pepys, Samuel. *Diary*. 2 vols. Random, 1946. set, $15.
PICCOLO, BRIAN
  Morris, Jeannie. *Short Season*. Rand, 1961. $6.
POE, EDGAR ALLAN
  Wagenknecht, Edward. *Poe*. Oxford, 1963. $8.
PRESLEY, ELVIS
  Hopkins, Jerry. *Elvis*. S&S, 1971. $8.

PRITCHETT, VICTOR S.
   Pritchett, Victor S. *Cab at the Door*. Random, 1968. $8.
   _____. *Midnight Oil*. Random, 1972. $7.
PROUST, MARCEL
   Painter, George. *Early Years*. Little, 1959. $9.
   _____. *Later Years*. Little, 1965. $9.
RASPUTIN, GRIGORII
   Wilson, Colin. *Rasputin and the Fall of the Romanovs*. Citadel, 1967. paper, $3.
RENOIR, PIERRE AUGUSTE
   Renoir, Jean. *Renoir, My Father*. Little, 1962. $10.
REVERE, PAUL
   Forbes, Esther. *Paul Revere and the World He Lived in*. Houghton, 1942. $10.
RICHARD III
   Kendall, Paul. *Richard III*. Norton, 1956. $11.
RICKENBACKER, EDDIE
   Rickenbacker, Eddie. *Rickenbacker*. Prentice, 1967. $9.
ROCKEFELLER, JOHN D.
   Nevins, Allan. *John D. Rockefeller*. abr. ed. Scribner, 1959. $10.
   See also Manchester, William A., in Collective Biography.
ROMMEL, ERWIN
   Young, Desmond. *Rommel, the Desert Fox*. Harper, 1951. $8.
ROOSEVELT, ELEANOR & FRANKLIN
   Burns, James. *Roosevelt*. 2 vols. Harcourt, 1970. set, $20.
   Lash, Joseph. *Eleanor and Franklin*. Norton, 1971. $13.
   _____. *Eleanor: the Years Alone*. Norton, 1972. $10.
   Roosevelt, Eleanor. *Autobiography*. Harper, 1961. $9.
   See also Roosevelt, Elliot, in Collective Biography.
ROTHSCHILDS, THE
   Morton, Frederick. *Rothschilds*. Atheneum, 1962. $7.
ROUSSEAU, JEAN-JACQUES
   Rousseau, Jean-Jacques. *Confessions*. 2 vols. Dutton, 1945. set, $7.
RUSSELL, BERTRAND
   Russell, Bertrand. *Autobiography*. Little, 1967. $8.
RUSSELL, ROBERT
   Russell, Robert. *To Catch an Angel*. Vanguard, 1962. $6.
RUTH, BABE
   Creamer, Robert. *Babe: Legend Comes to Life*. S&S, 1974. $10.
   Smith, Robert. *Babe*. Crowell, 1974. $10.
SANDBERG, CARL
   Sandberg, Carl. *Always the Young Strangers*. Harcourt, 1970. $9.
SAYERS, GALE
   Sayers, Gale. *I Am Third*. Viking, 1970. $7.
SCHLIEMANN, HEINRICH & SOPHIA
   Poole, Lynn. *One Passion, Two Loves*. Crowell, 1966. $7.

SCHWEITZER, ALBERT
  Schweitzer, Albert. *Out of My Life and Thought*. Holt, 1949. $5.
SERPICO, FRANK
  Maas, Peter. *Serpico*. Viking, 1973. $8.
SITWELL, DAME EDITH
  Sitwell, Edith. *Taken Care Of*. Atheneum, 1965. $6.
SMITH, JOHN
  Smith, Bradford. *Captain John Smith*. Lippincott, 1953. $5.
STALIN, JOSEF
  Hyde, H. Montgomery. *Stalin*. Farrar, 1971. $13.
STEFFENS, LINCOLN
  Steffens, Lincoln. *Autobiography*. Harcourt, 1968. $12.
STEIN, GERTRUDE
  Stein, Gertrude. *Autobiography of Alice B. Toklas*. Peter Smith, 1933. $4.
STEVENSON, ADLAI
  Muller, Herbert J. *Adlai Stevenson*. Harper, 1967. $7.
STUART, JESSE
  Gray, Martin. *For Those I Loved*. Little, 1972. $9.
SULLIVAN, LOUIS
  Wright, Frank Lloyd. *Genius and the Mobocracy*. Horizon, 1971. $20.
TEILHARD DE CHARDIN, PIERRE
  Teilhard, de Chardin, Pierre. *Making of a Mind*. Harper, 1965. $5.
THOMAS, PIRI
  Thomas, Piri. *Down These Mean Streets*. Knopf, 1967. $8.
TOLSTOY, LEO
  Troyat, Henri. *Tolstoy*. Doubleday, 1967. $8.
TRAPP
  Trapp, Maria A. *Maria*. Creation House. $6.
  _____. *Trapp Family Singers*. Lippincott, 1949. $8.
TROTSKY, LEON
  Deutsche, Issac. *Prophet Armed*. Oxford, 1954. $13.
  _____. *Prophet Outcast*. Oxford, 1963. $13.
  _____. *Prophet Unarmed*. Oxford, 1959. $13.
TRUMAN, HARRY S.
  Miller, Merle. *Plain Speaking*. Putnam, 1974. $9.
  Truman, Harry S. *Memoirs*. 2 vols. Doubleday, 1958. set, $9.
  Truman, Margaret. *Harry S. Truman*. Morrow, 1973. $11.
VICTORIA, QUEEN OF ENGLAND
  Longford, Elizabeth. *Queen Victoria*. Harper, 1965. $10.
  Strachey, Lytton. *Queen Victoria*. Harcourt, 1949. $3.
WASHINGTON, BOOKER T.
  Washington, Booker T. *Up from Slavery*. Doubleday, 1933. $6.
WASHINGTON, GEORGE
  Cunliffe, Marcus. *George Washington*. Little, 1958. $7.

WEIZMANN, CHAIM
  Weizmann, Chaim. *Trial and Error*. Greenwood, 1949. $18.
WHITMAN, WALT
  Allen, Gay W. *Solitary Singer*. NYU, 1967. $12.
WILDE, OSCAR
  Croft-Cooke, Rupert. *Unrecorded Life of Oscar Wilde*. McKay, 1972. $7.
WILLIAMS, WILLIAM CARLOS
  Williams, William C. *Autobiography*. New Directions, 1951. $7.
WILSON, WOODROW
  Smith, Gene. *When the Cheering Stopped*. Morrow, 1971. $7.
WINTHROP, JOHN
  Morgan, Edmund. *Puritan Dilemma*. Little, 1958. $5.
WOLFE, THOMAS
  Turnbull, Andrew. *Thomas Wolfe*. S&S, 1970. paper, $3.
WOLLSTONCRAFT, MARY
  Flexner, Eleanor. *Mary Wollstoncraft*. Coward, 1972. $9.
WOLSEY, CARDINAL
  Ferguson, Charles. *Naked to Mine Enemies*. Little, 1958. $9.
WOOLF, VIRGINIA
  Bell, Quentin. *Virginia Woolf*. Harcourt, 1972. $13.
WRIGHT, RICHARD
  Webb, Constance. *Richard Wright*. Putnam, 1968. $10.
  Wright, Richard. *Black Boy*. Harper, 1969. $7.

929   NAMES, GENEALOGY, HERALDRY
  Barraclough, E. M. *Flags of the World*. rev. ed. Warne, 1969. $15.
  Brooke-Little, J. P. *Boutell's Heraldry*. rev. ed. Warne, 1973. $20.
  Doane, Gilbert. *Searching for Your Ancestors*. 3rd ed. Minnesota, 1960. $5.
  Jacobus, Donald L. *Genealogy as Pastime and Profession*. 2nd ed. Genealogical, 1971. $8.
  Kirkham, Kay E. *Simplified Genealogy for Americans*. Deseret. $4.
  Latham, Edward. *Dictionary of Names, Nicknames, and Surnames*. Gale, 1966. $10.
  Pedersen, Christian F. *International Flag Book in Color*. Morrow, 1971. $6.
  Pine, Leslie G. *Story of Surnames*. Tuttle, 1966. $5.
  Smith, Elsdon C. *American Surnames*. Chilton, 1969. $10.
  _____. *Naming Your Baby*. 2nd rev. ed. Chilton, 1970. $4.
  Smith, Whitney. *Flag Book of the United States*. Morrow, 1970. $13.
  Wells, Evelyn. *What to Name the Baby*. Doubleday, 1953. $5.
  Wells, Jane. *Name for Your Baby*. Westover, 1972. paper, $2.

930 ANCIENT WORLD

Avery, Catherine B. *New Century Classical Handbook*. Appleton, 1962. $19.

Bibby, Geoffrey. *Four Thousand Years Ago*. Knopf, 1961. $9.

Bouquet, Alan C. *Everyday Life in New Testament Times*. Scribner, 1953. $9.

Casson, Lionel. *Ancient Egypt*. Time, 1965. $6.

Ceram, C. W. *Secret of the Hittites*. Knopf, 1956. $9.

Contenau, Georges. *Everyday Life in Babylon and Assyria*. St. Martin, 1954. $12.

Cottrell, Leonard. *Bull of Minos*. Holt, 1958. $5.

_____. *Life under the Pharaohs*. Holt, 1960. $5.

DeCoulanges, Fustel. *Ancient City*. Peter Smith, 1959. $5.

Hawkes, Jacquetta. *First Great Civilizations*. Knopf, 1973. $13.

_____. *World of the Past*. 2 vols. Knopf, 1963. set, $25.

Murray, Margaret A. *Splendor That Was Egypt*. rev. ed. Praeger, 1969. $10.

Palmer, Leonard. *Mycenaeans and Minoans*. rev. ed. Knopf, 1965. $8.

Schreiber, Hermann. *Vanished Cities*. Knopf, 1957. $8.

Silverberg, Robert. *Lost Cities and Vanished Civilizations*. Chilton, 1962. $4.

Starr, Chester G. *History of the Ancient World*. Oxford, 1965. $10.

Steindorff, George. *When Egypt Ruled the East*. rev. ed. Chicago, 1957. $8.

Taylour, William. *Mycenaeans*. Praeger, 1964. $9.

White, Jon M. *Everyday Life in Ancient Egypt*. Putnam, 1964. $5.

937 ANCIENT ROME

Boak, Arthur E. *History of Rome to A.D. 565*. 5th ed. Macmillan, 1965. $11.

Cowell, Frank R. *Everyday Life in Ancient Rome*. Putnam, 1961. $5.

Gibbon, Edward. *Decline and Fall of the Roman Empire*. abr. ed. Harcourt, 1960. $10.

Grant, Michael. *World of Rome*. new ed. Praeger, 1970. $10.

Hadas, Moses. *Imperial Rome*. Time, 1965. $7.

Huergon, Jacques. *Daily Life of the Etruscans*. Macmillan, 1964. $7.

Petrie, Alexander. *An Introduction to Roman History, Literature and Antiquities*. 3rd ed. Oxford, 1963. $3.

Quennell, Marjorie. *Everyday life in Roman and Anglo-Saxon Times*. rev. ed. Putnam, 1960. $5.

Richardson, Emeline. *Etruscans: their Art and Civilization*. Chicago, 1964. $8.

Stobart, John C. *Grandeur That Was Rome*. 4th ed. Praeger, 1969. $12.

Suetonius. *Twelve Caesars*. Penguin. paper, $2.

938   ANCIENT GREECE

Andrewes, Antony. *Greeks*. Knopf, 1967. $8.

Bowersock, Glen W. *Augustus and the Greek World*. Oxford, 1965. $6.

Bowra, Cecil M. *Greek Experience*. Praeger, 1970. $10.

Bowra, Maurice. *Classical Greece*. Time, 1965. $6.

Bury, John B. *History of Greece*. 3rd ed. Mod. Library. $5.

Grant, Michael. *Ancient Historians*. Scribner, 1970. paper, $5.

Hale, William H. *Ancient Greece*. abr. ed. McGraw, 1970. $7.

Hamilton, Edith. *Greek Way*. Norton, 1930. $7.

Mireaux, Emile. *Daily Life in the Time of Homer*. Macmillan, 1959. $6.

Robinson, Charles A., Jr. *Athens in the Age of Pericles*. Oklahoma, 1971.
$4.

Robinson, Cyril E. *Everyday Life in Ancient Greece*. Oxford, 1933. $3.

Stobart, John C. *Glory That Was Greece*. 4th ed. Praeger, 1969. $12.

Toynbee, Arnold. *Hellenism*. Oxford, 1959. $6.

Vermeule, Emily. *Greece in the Bronze Age*. Chicago, 1964. $10.

940   EUROPE–GENERAL HISTORY

Albrecht-Carrie, René. *Diplomatic History of Europe since the Congress of
Vienna*. rev. ed. Harper, 1973. $7.

Blum, Jerome. *European World: a History*. 2nd ed. Little, 1970. $6.

Breach, R. W. *Documents and Descriptions in European History, 1815–
1939*. Oxford, 1964. $3.

Childe, V. Gordon. *Dawn of European Civilization*. 6th rev. ed. Knopf,
1958. $10.

Clark, Kenneth. *Civilisation*. Harper, 1969. $15.

Ferguson, Wallace K. *Europe in Transition: 1300–1520*. Houghton, 1963.
$10.

Stearns, Raymond P. *Pageant of Europe*. rev. ed. Harcourt. $7.

940.1   EUROPE: 476–1453

Artz, Fredericka B. *Mind of the Middle Ages*. 3rd ed. Knopf, 1958. $9.

Bishop, Morris. *Middle Ages*. rev. abr. ed. McGraw, 1970. $7.

Burckhardt, Jacob. *Civilization of the Renaissance in Italy*. 2 vols. Peter
Smith, 1965. set, $9.

Cheyney, Edward P. *Dawn of a New Era*. Harper, 1936. $10.

Coulton, George G. *Medieval Scene*. Peter Smith. $5.

Davis, William S. *Life on a Medieval Barony*. Harper, 1928. $5.

Duggan, Alfred. *Story of the Crusades*. Pantheon, 1964. $7.

Ferguson, Wallace K. *Renaissance*. Peter Smith. $5.

Gies, Joseph. *Life in a Medieval City*. Crowell, 1969. $7.

Huizinga, Johan. *Waning of the Middle Ages*. St. Martin, 1924. $10.

Lucas, Henry S. *Renaissance and the Reformation*. 2nd ed. Harper, 1960.
$14.

Pirene, Henri. *Medieval Cities*. Princeton. $9.

Power, Eileen. *Medieval People*. 10th ed. B&N, 1963. $5.

Previte-Orton, Charles W. *Shorter Cambridge Medieval History*. 2 vols. Cambridge, 1952. set, $29.

Taylor, Henry O. *Medieval Mind*. 4th ed., 2 vols. Harvard, 1959. set, $19.

Treece, Hency. *Crusades*. Random, 1963. $8

940.2   EUROPE: 1453-1914

Albrecht-Carrie, René. *Concert of Europe*. Walker, 1968. $13.

Artz, Frederick B. *Reaction and Revolution: 1814-1832*. Harper, 1935. $8.

Barzun, Jacques. *Darwin, Marx, Wagner: Critique of a Heritage*. 2nd ed. Peter Smith. $5.

Bruun, Geoffrey. *Enlightened Despots*. Peter Smith. $4.

Cronin, Vincent. *Flowering of the Renaissance*. Dutton, 1969. $9.

Friedrich, Carl J. *Age of the Baroque*. Harper, 1952. $13.

Gershoy, Leo. *From Despotism to Revolution*. Harper, 1952. $13.

Gilmore, Myron P. *World of Humanism: 1453-1517*. Harper, 1952. $8.

Grimm, Harold J. *Reformation Era*. rev. ed. Macmillan, 1965. $10.

Hale, John R. *Renaissance*. Time, 1966. $6.

Howarth, David. *Waterloo*. Atheneum, 1968. $8.

Mahan, Alfred T. *Influence of Sea Power upon History, 1660-1783*. Peter Smith. $5.

May, Arthur. *Age of Metternich*. rev. ed. Peter Smith. $5.

Mosse, George L. *Reformation*. 3rd ed. Peter Smith. $5.

Nussbaum, Frederick L. *Triumph of Science and Reason*. Harper, 1953. $8.

Palmer, Robert R. *Age of the Democratic Revolution*. 2 vols. Princeton, 1969/70. paper, each, $3.

Parry, John H. *European Reconnaissance*. Walker, 1968. $13.

Routh, Charles R. *They Saw It Happen in Europe: 1453-1600*. B&N, 1966. $7.

Schmeller, Kurt E. *Course of Europe since Waterloo*. 5th ed., 2 vols. Appleton, 1968. paper, set, $11.

Setton, Kenneth M. *Renaissance: Maker of Modern Man*. National Geographic, 1970. $12.

Stoye, John. *Europe Unfolding*. Harper, 1970. $8.

Taylor, Alan J. *Struggle for Mastery in Europe, 1848-1918*. Oxford, 1954. $15.

Wedgwood, C. V. *Thirty Years' War*. Peter Smith. $6.

Weller, Jack. *Wellington at Waterloo*. Crowell, 1967. $7.

940.3   EUROPE: WORLD WAR I

American Heritage. *World War I*. McGraw, 1964. $17.

Benns, F. Lee. *Europe since 1914*. 8th ed. Appleton, 1954. $11.

Falls, Cyril. *Great War*. Putnam, 1961. paper, $4.

Gregory, Ross. *Origins of American Intervention in the First World War*. Norton, 1972. paper, $3.

Horne, Alistair. *Price of Glory: Verdun 1916*. St. Martin, 1962. $6.

Lawrence, T. E. *Seven Pillars of Wisdom*. rev. ed. Doubleday, 1947. $10.

May, Ernest R. *World War and American Isolation*. Harvard, 1959. $19.

Parkinson, Roger. *Origins of World War One*. Putnam, 1970. $6.

Reynolds, Quentin. *They Fought for the Sky*. Holt, 1957. $6.

Stallings, Laurence. *Doughboys*. Harper, 1963. $10.

Tuchman, Barbara W. *Guns of August*. Macmillan, 1962. $9.

———. *Proud Tower*. Macmillan, 1966. $8.

940.5   EUROPE: 1918 TO THE PRESENT; WORLD WAR II

Blumenson, Martin. *Duel for France, 1944*. Houghton, 1963. $8.

Churchill, Winston. *Second World War*. 6 vols. Houghton, 1948/53. set, $50.

Conrat, Raisie. *Executive Order 9066, Interment of 110,000 Japanese Americans*. MIT, 1971. $13.

Czernin, Ferdinand. *Versailles, 1919*. Putnam, 1964. $7.

Donovan, Robert J. *PT 109*. McGraw, 1961. $8.

Farago, Ladislas. *Game of the Foxes*. McKay, 1971. $12.

Feis, Herbert. *Churchill, Roosevelt, Stalin*. 2nd ed. Princeton, 1967. $15.

———. *Road to Pearl Harbor*. Princeton, 1950. $13.

Fenno, Richard F. *Yalta Conference*. Heath, 1972. paper, $3.

Forester, Cecil S. *Last Nine Days of the Bismarck*. Little, 1959. $6.

Hersey, John R. *Hiroshima*. Mod. Library. $3.

———. *Into the Valley*. Knopf, 1943. $4.

Hoyle, Martha B. *World in Flames: History of World War II*. Atheneum, 1970. $10.

Hughes, H. Stuart. *Contemporary Europe*. 3rd ed. Prentice, 1971. $12.

Lord, Walter. *Day of Infamy*. Holt, 1957. $6.

Michener, James A. *Bridge at Andau*. Random, 1957. $7.

Morrison, Samuel E. *Two-Ocean War*. Little, 1963. $15.

Parkinson, Roger. *Origins of World War II*. Putnam, 1970. $6.

Ryan, Cornelius. *Longest Day: June 6, 1944*. S&S, 1959. $8.

Salisbury, Harrison E. *900 Days: Siege of Leningrad*. Harper, 1969. $10.

Seton-Watson, Hugh. *Eastern Europe between the Wars: 1918–1941*. Harper, 1967. paper, $4.

Snyder, Louis L. *War: a Concise History, 1939–1945*. S&S, 1959. $8.

Stearns, Peter N. *European Society in Upheaval*. Macmillan, 1967. $8.

Steiner, Jean F. *Treblinka*. S&S, 1967. $6.

Sulzberger, C. L. *Picture History of World War II*. S&S, 1966. $20.

———. *World War II*. rev. ed. McGraw, 1970. $7.

Toland, John. *Battle: Story of the Bulge*. Random, 1959. $9.

White, Theodore. *Fire in the Ashes*. Apollo, 1968. paper, $3.

941   IRELAND

Coogan, Timothy P. *I. R. A.* Praeger, 1970. $9.

Curtis, Edmund. *History of Ireland.* 6th rev. ed. B&N, 1968. paper, $4.

Hahn, Emily. *Fractured Emerald.* Doubleday, 1971. $8.

Hastins, Mac. *Barricades in Belfast.* Taplinger, 1970. $6.

London Sunday Times Insight Team. *Northern Ireland: a Report on the Conflict.* Random, 1972. $8.

McCarthy, Joe. *Ireland.* rev. ed. Time, 1964. $6.

O'Connor, Richard. *Irish: Portrait of a People.* Putnam, 1971. $8.

942   GREAT BRITAIN

Arnold, Ralph. *Social History of England: 55 B.C.–A.D. 1215.* B&N, 1967. $11.

Ashley, Maurice P. *Great Britain to 1688.* Michigan, 1961. $8.

Bagley, John J. *Life in Medieval England.* Putnam, 1960. $5.

Briggs, Asa. *Victorian People.* new ed. Chicago, 1970. $8.

Churchill, Winston. *History of the English Speaking People.* 4 vols. Dodd. set, $25.

Clark, Sir George N. *English History: a Survey.* Oxford, 1971. $10.

Costain, Thomas B. *Conquering Family.* Doubleday, 1949. $7.

_____. *Last Plantagenets.* Doubleday, 1962. $7.

_____. *Three Edwards.* Doubleday, 1958. $8.

Derry, Thomas K. *Making of Modern Britain.* new ed. Transatlantic, 1971. $5.

Garmonsway, G. N. *Anglo-Saxon Chronicle,* Dutton, 1934. $4.

Green, John R. *Short History of English People.* 2 vols. Dutton. set, $7.

Halliday, Frank E. *Concise History of England.* Viking, 1965. $8.

_____. *Illustrated Cultural History of England.* Viking, 1967. $9.

Harrison, John F. *Society and Politics in England: 1780–1960.* Harper, 1965. paper, $6.

Kronenberger, Louis. *Kings and Desperate Men: Life in 18th Century England.* Peter Smith. $5.

Lloyd, Alan. *Making of the King: 1066.* Holt, 1966. $6.

Luke, Mary M. *Crown for Elizabeth.* Coward, 1970. $10.

Mattingly, Garrett. *Armada.* Houghton, 1959. $8.

Mowat, Charles L. *Britain between the Wars: 1918–1940.* Chicago, 1955. $9.

Notestein, Wallace. *English People on the Eve of Colonization.* Harper, 1954. $9.

Pocock, Tom. *Nelson and His World.* Viking, 1968. $7.

Poole, Austin. *From Doomsday Book to Magna Carta.* 2nd ed. Oxford, 1955. $10.

Rowse, Alfred F. *England of Elizabeth.* Macmillan, 1961. paper, $3.

Smith, Goldwin A. *England, a Short History.* Scribner, 1971. paper, $6.

Taylor, Alan J. *English History: 1919–1945*. Oxford, 1965. $13.
Tomkeieff, O. G. *Life in Norman England*. Putnam, 1966. $5.
Trevelyan, George M. *English Revolution: 1688*. Oxford, 1938. $4.
_____. *Illustrated English Social History*. 4 vols. McKay, 1949/52. each,
    $12.
White, R. J. *Horizon Concise History of England*. Macmillan, 1972. $9.
Williams, E. Neville. *Life in Georgian England*. Putnam, 1962. $5.
Woodham-Smith, Cecil. *Reason Why*. McGraw, 1971. $8.

943   GERMANY
Crankshaw, Edward. *Hapsburgs*. Viking, 1971. $17.
Dill, Marshall. *Germany*. rev. ed Michigan, 1970. $10.
Flenley, Ralph. *Modern German History*. rev. ed. Dutton, 1969. $10.
Gallo, Max. *Night of Long Knives*. Harper, 1972. $9.
Grunberger, Richard. *12-Year Reich*. Holt, 1971. $10.
Shirer, William L. *Rise and Fall of the Third Reich*. S&S, 1960. $13.
Speer, Albert. *Inside the Third Reich*. Macmillan, 1970. $13.
Taylor, Alan J. *Course of German History*. Putnam, 1962. paper, $3.
Waite, Robert G. *Hitler and Nazi Germany*. Peter Smith. $5.

944   FRANCE
Artz, Frederick B. *France under the Bourbon Restoration*. Russell, 1963.
    $11.
Behrens, Catherine B. *Ancient Regime*. Harcourt, 1967. $6.
Brinton, Crane. *Decade of Revolution*. Harper, 1935. $8.
Brogan, Denis W. *French Nation from Napoleon to Petain*. Gannon, 1970.
    $5.
Burke, Edmund. *Reflections on the Revolution in France*. Bobbs, 1955. $5.
Collins, Larry. *Is Paris Burning?* S&S, 1965. $7.
Davidson, Marshall B. *Horizon Concise History of France*. new ed. McGraw,
    1972. $9.
Furet, Francois. *French Revolution*. Macmillan, 1970. $10.
Guerard, Albert L. *France: a Modern History*. rev. ed. Michigan, 1969. $9.
Herold, J. Christopher. *Age of Napoleon*. Harper, 1963. $8.
Holtman, Robert B. *Napoleonic Revolution*. Lippincott, 1967. $5.
Knapton, Ernest J. *France: an Interpretative History*. Scribner, 1971. $15.
Lamb, Harold. *Charlemagne*. Doubleday, 1954. $5.
Osgood, Samuel M. *Fall of France, 1940*. 2nd ed. Heath, 1972. paper, $3.
Padover, Saul K. *Life and Death of Louis XVI*. Taplinger, 1963. $8.
Shirer, William L. *Collapse of the Third Republic*. S&S, 1969. $13.
Voltaire, Francois M. *Age of Louis XIV*. Dutton. $4.

945   ITALY
Barzini, Luigi G. *Italians*. Atheneum, 1964. $7.
Deakin, Frederick W. *Brutal Friendship*. Harper, 1963. $15.

Holt, Edgar. *Making of Italy, 1815-1870*. Atheneum, 1971. $8.
Llewellyn, Peter. *Rome in the Dark Ages*. Praeger, 1971. $10.

946 SPAIN

Brenan, Gerald. *Spanish Labyrinth*. 2nd ed. Cambridge, 1960. $14.
Carr, Raymond. *Spain 1808-1939*. Oxford, 1966. $15.
DeMadariaga, Salvador. *Spain: a Modern History*. Praeger, 1958. $30.
Elliott, John H. *Imperial Spain: 1469-1716*. St. Martin, 1963. $8.
Hills, George. *Spain*. Praeger, 1970. $10.
Michener, James. *Iberia*. Random, 1968. $13.
Payne, Stanley G. *Franco's Spain*. Crowell, 1967. $5.
Thomas, Hugh. *Spanish Civil War*. Harper, 1961. $13.

947 RUSSIA

Bauer, Raymond. *Nine Soviet Portraits*. MIT, 1955. $8.
Conquest, Robert. *Great Terror: Stalin's Purge*. rev. ed. Macmillan, 1973. $9.
Deutscher, Isaac. *Unfinished Revolution*. Oxford, 1967. $4.
Florinsky, Michael. *Russia: a Short History*. 2nd ed. Macmillan, 1969. $12.
Harcave, Sidney. *Russia*. 6th ed. Lippincott, 1968. $11.
Hill, Christopher. *Lenin and the Russian Revolution*. Verry, 1947. $5.
Mazour, Anatole. *Russia: Tsarist and Communist*. Van Nostrand, 1962. $13.
Moorehead, Alan. *Russian Revolution*. Harper, 1958. $8.
Moscow, Henry. *Russia under the Czars*. Harper, 1962. $6.
Parkes, Bernard. *History of Russia*. Knopf, 1953. $13.
Reed, John. *Ten Days That Shook the World*. International, 1967. $8.
Salisbury, Harrison. *Soviet Union: the 50 Years*. Harcourt, 1967. $10.
Spector, Ivar. *Introduction to Russian History and Culture*. 5th ed. Van Nostrand, 1969. $11.
Thayer, Charles. *Russia*. Time, 1965. $6.
Varnadsky, George. *History of Russia*. rev. ed. Yale, 1961. $13.
Van Laue, Theodore H. *Why Lenin, Why Stalin*. Lippincott, 1964. $4.
Von Rauch, Georg. *History of Soviet Russia*. 6th rev. ed. Praeger, 1972. $12.
Walsh, Warren B. *Russia and the Soviet Union*. rev. ed. Michigan, 1968. $10.

948 SCANDINAVIA

Anderson, Robert T. *Denmark*. Schenkman, 1973. $9.
Bradley, David. *Lion among Roses*. Holt, 1965. $6.
Butler, Ewan. *Horizon Concise History of Scandinavia*. Macmillan, 1973. $9.
Donovan, Frank. *Vikings*. Harper, 1964. $6.
Larsen, Karen. *History of Norway*. Princeton, 1948. $18.

National Geographic Soc. *Vikings*. National Geographic, 1972. $5.
Oakley, Stewart. *Short History of Sweden*. Praeger, 1966. $9.
Wuoringen, John H. *History of Finland*. Columbia, 1965. $15.

949   OTHER EUROPEAN COUNTRIES

Bonjour, Edgar. *Short History of Switzerland*. Oxford, 1952. $9.
Byron, Robert. *Byzantine Achievement*. Russell, 1964. $11.
Chapman, Colin. *August 21: the Rape of Czechoslovakia*. Lippincott, 1968. $4.
Clissold, Stephen. *Short History of Yugoslavia*. Cambridge, 1968. $10.
De Meeus, Adrien. *History of the Belgians*. Praeger, 1962. $9.
Diehl, Charles. *Byzantium: Greatness and Decline*. Rutgers, 1957. $9.
Eliot, A. *Horizon Concise History of Greece*. Macmillan, 1973. $9.
Palmer, Alan W. *Lands Between*. Macmillan, 1970. $10.
Papandreou, Andreas. *Democracy at Gunpoint*. Doubleday, 1970. $8.
Roberts, Henry L. *Eastern Europe*. Knopf, 1970. $7.
Runciman, Steven. *Byzantine Civilization*. St. Martin, 1933. $9.
Seton-Watson, Robert. *History of the Roumanians*. Shoestring, 1963. $12.
Szulc, Tad. *Czechoslovakia since World War II*. Viking, 1971. $14.
Wolff, Robert L. *Balkans in Our Time*. Harvard, 1956. $13.

950   ASIA

Cressey, George. *Asia's Land and People*. 3rd ed. McGraw, 1963. $15.
Latourette, Kenneth S. *Short History of the Far East*. 4th ed. Macmillan, 1964. $11.
Nakamura, Hajime. *Ways of Thinking of Eastern Peoples*. rev. ed. Hawaii, 1964. $13.
Peffer, Nathaniel. *Far East*. rev. ed. Michigan, 1968. $9.
Prawdin, Michael. *Mongol Empire*. 2nd ed. B&N, 1961. $9.
Welty, Paul T. *Asians: Their Heritage and Their Destiny*. 3rd rev. ed. Lippincott, 1970. $7.

951   CHINA

Barnstone, Willis. *New Faces of China*. Indiana, 1973. $9.
Bloodworth, Dennis. *Chinese Looking Glass*. Farrar, 1967. $8.
Cheng, Peter. *Chronology of the People's Republic of China from October 1, 1949*. Rowman, 1972. $9.
Clubb, Oliver E. *20th Century China*. rev. ed. Columbia, 1972. $12.
Cohen, Arthur A. *Communism of Mao Tse Tung*. Chicago, 1964. $7.
Fairbank, John K. *United States and China*. 3rd ed. Harvard, 1971. $10.
Houn, Franklin W. *Short History of Chinese Communism*. Prentice, 1973. $7.
Isaacs, Harold R. *Tragedy of the Chinese Revolution*. 2nd rev. ed. Stanford, 1971. $10.

Latourette, Kenneth. *Chinese*. 4th rev. ed. Macmillan, 1964. $13.
McAleavy, Henry. *Modern History of China*. Praeger, 1967. $9.
Polo, Marco. *Travels of Marco Polo*. Dutton, 1954. $4.
Seeger, Elizabeth. *Pageant of Chinese History*. 4th ed. McKay, 1962. $7.
Wilson, Dick. *Long March, 1935*. Viking, 1972. $9.

951.9 KOREA

Chung, Kyung C. *Korea; the Third Republic*. Macmillan, 1971. $7.
McGovern, James. *To the Yalu*. Morrow, 1972. $7.

952 JAPAN

Buck, Pearl S. *People of Japan*. S&S, 1966. $8.
Busch. *Horizon Concise History of Japan*. Macmillan, 1973. $9.
Craig, William. *Fall of Japan*. Dial, 1967. $8.
Hall, John W. *Japan*. Delacorte, 1970. $10.
Langer, P. F. *Japan*. Holt, 1966. $5.
Latourette, Kenneth. *History of Japan*. rev. ed. Macmillan, 1957. $7.
Reischauer, Edwin O. *Japan*. rev. ed. Knopf, 1970. $7.
Toland, John. *Rising Sun, 1936–1945*. Random, 1970. $13.

954 INDIA, PAKISTAN, CEYLON, IRAN

Armajani, Yahya. *Iran*. Prentice, 1972. $7.
Brown, W. Norman. *India, Pakistan, and Ceylon*. rev. ed. Pennsylvania, 1964. $10.
De Bary, William T. *Sources of Indian Tradition*. 2 vols. Columbia, 1958. paper, set, $7.
Griffiths, Percival. *Modern India*. 4th rev. ed. Praeger, 1965. $8.
Lord, John. *Maharajahs*. Random, 1971. $8.
Smith, Vincent A. *Oxford History of India*. 3rd ed. Oxford, 1967. $12.
Spear, Percival. *India*. rev. ed. Michigan, 1972. $10.
Tariq, Ali. *Pakistan: Military Rule or People's Power*. Morrow, 1971. $8.
Williams, Laurence R. *East Pakistan Tragedy*. new ed. Drake, 1972. $6.
Zinkin, Taya. *India*. Walker, 1966. $9.

955 NEAR EAST

Ben Gurion, David. *Israel's Years of Challenge*. Holt, 1963. $5.
Burdett, Winston. *Encounter with the Middle East*. Atheneum, 1969. $10.
Collins, Larry. *O Jerusalem!* S&S, 1972. $10.
Coon, Carleton S. *Caravan*. rev. ed. Holt, 1958. $10.
Fisher, Sydney N. *Middle East*. Knopf, 1968. $11.
Glubb, Sir John. *Short History of the Arab Peoples*. Stein, 1970. paper, $3.
Harris, George L. *Iraq*. HRAFP, 1958. $10.
Hitti, Philip K. *History of the Arabs*. 10th ed. St. Martin, 1970. $13.
Kimche, Jon. *Second Arab Awakening*. Holt, 1972. paper, $3.

Legg, Stuart. *Heartland*. Farrar, 1970. $9.
Lewis, Bernard. *Emergence of Modern Turkey*. 2nd ed. Oxford, 1968.
  paper, $4.
Yale, William. *Near East*. rev. ed. Michigan, 1968. $9.

959   SOUTHEAST ASIA
Busch, Noel F. *Thailand*. 2nd ed. Van Nostrand, 1964. $5.
Cady, John F. *Southeast Asia*. McGraw, 1964. $13.
Draper, Theodore. *Abuse of Power*. Viking, 1967. $5.
Fall, Bernard B. *Hell in a Very Small Place*. Lippincott, 1966. $10.
——. *Street without Joy*. rev. ed. Stackpole, 1967. $8.
——. *Two Viet Nams*. 2nd rev. ed. Praeger, 1967. $10.
Fisher, Charles A. *South-East Asia*. 2nd ed. B&N, 1966. $21.
FitzGerald, Frances. *Fire in the Lake*. Little, 1972. $13.
Glasser, Ronald J. *365 Days*. Braziller, 1971. $7.
Halberstam, David. *Making of a Quagmire*. Random, 1965. $8.
Hammer, Ellen J. *Struggle for Indochina: 1940–1955*. Stanford, 1955. $10.
Hersh, Seymour M. *My Lai 4*. Random, 1970. $6.
Parrish, John A. *12, 20, and 5: a Doctor's Year in Vietnam*. Dutton, 1972.
  $8.
West, Francis J. *Village*. Harper, 1972. $8.

960   AFRICA
Boahen, J. Desmond. *Horizon History of Africa*. American Heritage, 1971.
  $25.
Cary, Joyce. *Case for African Freedom*. Texas, 1962. $8.
Davidson, Basil. *African Kingdoms*. Time, 1966. $7.
——. *African Past*. Little, 1964. $9.
——. *Black Mother*. Little, 1961. $9.
Dinesen, Isak. *Out of Africa*. Random, 1970. $8.
Lumumba, Patrice. *Congo, My Country*. Praeger, 1962. $7.
Luthuli, Albert J. *Let My People Go*. McGraw, 1962. $6.
Marquand, Leo. *Peoples and Policies of South Africa*. 4th ed. Oxford, 1969.
  paper, $2.
Mboya, Tom. *Freedom and After*. Little, 1963. $7.
Moorehead, Alan. *Blue Nile*. new ed. Harper, 1972. $15.
——. *White Nile*. Harper, 1971. $15.
Morris, Donald R. *Washing of the Spears*. S&S, 1965. $12.
Nickerson, Jane S. *Short History of North Africa*. rev. ed. Devin, 1961.
  $7.
Nkrumah, Kwame. *Africa Must Unite*. International, 1970. $7.
Oliver, Roland A. *Africa since 1800*. 2nd ed. Cambridge, 1972. $12.
——. *Short History of Africa*. NYU, 1963. $9.
Paton, Alan. *Land and People of South Africa*. rev. ed. Lippincott, 1972.
  $5.

Perham, Margery. *African Discovery*. Northwestern, 1963. $9.
West, Richard. *Back to Africa*. Holt, 1971. $7.
Wills, Alfred J. *Introduction to the History of Central Africa*. 2nd ed.
  Oxford, 1967. $10.

970 **INDIANS OF NORTH AMERICA**
American Heritage. *Indians*. McGraw, 1961. $18.
Balikei, Asen. *Netsilik Eskimo*. Natural History, 1971. $9.
Briggs, Jean L. *Never in Anger: Portrait of an Eskimo Family*. Harvard,
  1970. $16.
Brown, Dee. *Bury My Heart at Wounded Knee*. Holt, 1971. $11.
Capps, Benjamin. *Indians*. Time, 1973. $10.
Ceram, C. W. *First American*. Harcourt, 1971. $10.
Deloria, Vine. *Custer Died for Your Sins*. Macmillan, 1969. $6.
Dennis, Henry C. *American Indian 1492-1970*. Oceana, 1971. $5.
Driver, Harold E. *Indians of North America*. 2nd rev. ed. Chicago, 1969.
  $13.
Hagan, William T. *American Indians*. Chicago, 1961. $6.
Hamilton, Henry W. *Sioux of the Rosebud*. Oklahoma, 1972. $13.
Jacobs, Wilbur R. *Dispossessing the American Indian*. Scribner, 1972. $8.
Josephy, Alvin M. *Indian Heritage of America*. Knopf, 1968. $10.
____. *Red Power*. McGraw, 1971. $7.
Leacock, Eleanor. *North American Indians in Historical Perspective*.
  Random, 1971. $11.
Leonard, Jonathan. *Ancient America*. Time, 1967. $6.
Levitan, Sar A. *Big Brother's Indian Program: with Reservations*. McGraw,
  1971. $9.
Locke, Raymond F. *American Indian*. Hawthorn, 1971. $6.
McLuhan, T. C. *Touch the Earth*. Outerbridge, 1971. $7.
Mails, Thomas E. *Dog Soldiers, Bear Men and Buffalo Women*. Prentice,
  1973. $20.
____. *Mystic Warriors of the Plains*. Doubleday, 1972. $25.
Oswalt, Wendell H. *This Land Was Theirs*. 2nd ed. Wiley, 1973. $13.
Silverburg, Robert. *Mound Builders of Ancient America*. NYGS, 1968. $10.
Swanton, John R. *Indian Tribes of North America*. Scholarly, 1968. $15.
Tunis, Edwin. *Indians*. World, 1959. $7.
Van Every, Dale. *Disinherited*. Morrow, 1971. $9.
Washburn, Wilcomb E. *Red Man's Land/White Man's Law*. Scribner, 1971.
  $8.
Williams, Jeanne. *Trails of Tears*. Putnam, 1972. $5.
Wissler, Clark. *Indians of the United States*. Doubleday, 1966. $8.

971 **CANADA**
Brebner, J. B. *Canada*. rev. ed. Michigan, 1970. $10.
Costain, Thomas B. *White and the Gold*. Doubleday, 1954. $6.

Creighton, Donald G. *Canada's First Century*. St. Martin, 1970. $10.
Lamb, William K. *History of Canada*. American Heritage, 1972. $18.
Moore, Brian. *Canada*. Time, 1968. $6.
Morison, Samuel E. *Parkman Reader*. Little, 1955. $9.

972   MEXICO, CENTRAL AMERICA, CARIBBEAN
Alba, Victor. *Horizon Concise History of Mexico*. Macmillan, 1973. $9.
_____. *Mexicans: Making of a Nation*. Praeger, 1967. $7.
Caso, Alfonso. *Aztecs, People of the Sun*. Oklahoma, 1970. $9.
Coy, Harold. *Mexicans*. Little, 1970. $6.
Draper, Theodore. *Castro's Revolution*. Praeger, 1962. $7.
Lavine, Harold. *Central America*. Time, 1968. $6.
Lopez, Alfredo. *Puerto Rican Papers: Notes on the Re-emergence of a Nation*. Bobbs. $9.
Maldonado-Denis, Manuel. *Puerto Rico*. Random, 1972. $9.
Parker, Franklin D. *Central American Republics*. Oxford, 1964. $8.
Rotberg, Robert I. *Haiti: the Politics of Squalor*. Houghton, 1971. $10.
Thomas, Hugh. *Cuba; the Pursuit of Freedom*. Harper, 1971. $20.
Wagenheim, Kal. *Puerto Ricans*. Praeger, 1973. $13.

973   UNITED STATES–GENERAL
Abernethy, Robert G. *Introduction to Tomorrow: the U.S. and the Wider World*. Harcourt, 1966. $7.
Alden, John R. *Pioneer America*. Knopf, 1966. $8.
American Heritage Publ. Co. *American Album*. McGraw, 1968. $18.
Bailey, Thomas A. *American Spirit*. 3rd ed., 2 vols. Heath, 1973. each, $6.
Baumer, William H. *Little Wars of the United States*. Hawthorn, 1969. $8.
Beard, Charles A. *New Basic History of the United States*. rev. ed. Doubleday, 1968. $8.
Billington, Ray A. *Westward Expansion*. 3rd ed. Macmillan, 1967. $12.
Boorstin, Daniel. *Americans: the Colonial Experience*. Random, 1958. $13.
_____. *Americans: the Democratic Experience*. Random, 1973. $13.
_____. *Americans: the National Experience*. Random, 1965. $13.
Bradley, Harold W. *United States 1492-1877*. Scribner, 1972. $13.
Brogan, Denis W. *American Character*. Peter Smith. $4.
Butterfield, Roger. *American Past*. 2nd rev. ed. S&S, 1966. $10.
Carruth, Gorton V. *Encyclopedia of American Facts and Dates*. 6th ed. Crowell, 1972. $9.
Commager, Henry. *Documents of American History*. 8th ed. Appleton, 1969. each, $7.
Cooke, Alistair. *America*. Knopf, 1973. $15.
David, Jay. *Black Soldier*. Morrow, 1972. $7.
Dos Passos, John. *Shackles of Power*. Doubleday. $8.
Drimmer, Melvin. *Black History: a Reappraisal*. Doubleday, 1968. $8.

Foner, Eric. *America's Black Past.* Harper, 1970. $13.
Furnas, Joseph C. *Americans.* Putnam, 1969. $13.
Garraty, John A. *American Nation.* Harper, 1968. $16.
Handlin, Oscar. *Harvard Guide to American History.* Harvard, 1954. $15.
Hicks, John D. *Federal Union.* 5th ed. Houghton, 1970. $12.
Kirkland, Edward C. *History of American Economic Life.* 4th ed. Appleton, 1969. $11.
Kraus, Michael. *United States to 1865.* rev. ed. Michigan, 1969. $9.
Morison, Samuel E. *Growth of the American Republic.* 6th ed., 2 vols. Oxford, 1969. each, $10.
_____. *Oxford History of the American People.* Oxford, 1965. $11.
Morris, Richard. *Encyclopedia of American History.* rev. ed. Harper, 1970. $13.
Nevins, Allan. *Short History of the United States.* rev. ed. Knopf, 1966. $10.
Perkins, Dexter. *History of the Monroe Doctrine.* rev. ed. Little, 1963. $8.
_____. *United States of America.* 2nd ed., 2 vols. Macmillan, 1968. each, $10.
Schlesinger, Arthur M. *Nothing Stands Still.* Harvard, 1969. $7.
Turner, Frederick. *Frontier in American History.* Peter Smith. $8.
Weisberger, Bernard A. *American Heritage History of the American People.* McGraw, 1971. $20.

973.1   UNITED STATES: TO 1607
Ashe, Geoffrey. *Quest for America.* Praeger, 1972. $15.
Cumming, William P. *Discovery of North America.* McGraw, 1972. $25.
Morison, Samuel E. *European Discovery of America.* Oxford, 1971. $15.
Pohl, Frederick. *Viking Settlements of North America.* Potter, 1972. $7.

973.2   UNITED STATES: 1607-1775
Acheson, Patricia C. *America's Colonial Heritage.* Dodd, 1957. $5.
Earle, Alice M. *Home and Child Life in Colonial Days.* abr. ed. Macmillan, 1969. $7.
Edmonds, Walter D. *Musket and the Cross.* Little, 1968. $11.
Keller, Allan. *Colonial America.* Hawthorn, 1971. $8.
Morison, Samuel. *Builders of the Bay Colony.* rev. ed. Houghton, 1963. $7.
Peckham, Howard H. *Colonial Wars.* Chicago, 1964. $7.
Tunis, Edwin. *Colonial Living.* World, 1957. $7.
Van Every, Dale. *Forth to the Wilderness.* Morrow, 1961. $6.
Wright, Louis B. *Cultural Life of the American Colonies.* Harper, 1957. $9.

973.3   UNITED STATES: 1775-1789
Alden, John R. *American Revolution.* Harper, 1954. $8.
_____. *History of the American Revolution.* Knopf, 1969. $10.

Becker, Carl L. *Declaration of Independence.* Knopf, 1942. $6.

Dupuy, Richard E. *Compact History of the Revolutionary War.* Hawthorn, 1963. $9.

Gipson, Lawrence H. *Coming of the Revolution.* Harper, 1954. $8.

Kitman, Marvin. *George Washington's Expense Account.* S&S, 1970. $6.

Leckie, Robert. *World Turned Upside Down.* new ed. Putnam, 1973. $6.

Maier, Pauline. *From Resistance to Revolution.* Knopf, 1972. $10.

Morgan, Edmund S. *Birth of the Republic.* Chicago, 1956. $5.

Morris, Richard B. *American Revolution.* South Carolina, 1971. $8.

———. *American Revolution Reconsidered.* Harper, 1967. $5.

Nye, Russell B. *Cultural Life of the New Nation.* Harper, 1960. $8.

Pearson, Michael. *Those Damned Rebels: American Revolution as Seen through British Eyes.* Putnam, 1972. $9.

Smelser, Marshall. *Winning of Independence.* Watts, 1971. $4.

Wheeler, Richard. *Voices of 1776.* Crowell, 1972. $10.

Wright, Esmond. *Fabric of Freedom.* Hill, 1961. $5.

973.4   UNITED STATES: 1789–1809

Bowers, Claude G. *Jefferson and Hamilton.* Houghton, 1967. $9.

Chidsey, Donald B. *Wars in Barbary.* Crown, 1971. $5.

Cunliffe, Marcus. *Nation Takes Shape.* Chicago, 1959. $5.

Eaton, Clement. *Growth of Southern Civilization.* Harper, 1961. $8.

Lewis, Meriwether, and William Clark. *Journals of Lewis and Clark.* Houghton, 1953. $8.

Miller, John C. *Federalist Era.* Harper, 1960. $8.

Smelser, Marshall. *Democratic Republic.* Harper, 1968. $8.

Van Every, Dale. *Final Challenge.* Morrow, 1964. $6.

973.5   UNITED STATES: 1809–1845

Alden, John R. *Pioneer America.* Knopf, 1966. $8.

Billington, Ray A. *Far Western Frontier.* Harper, 1956. $8.

Carter, Samuel. *Blaze of Glory: Fight for New Orleans.* St. Martin, 1971. $10.

Clark, Thomas D. *Frontier America.* 2nd ed. Scribner, 1969. $15.

Coit, Margaret. *Fight for Union.* Houghton, 1961. $4.

Coles, Harry L. *War of 1812.* Chicago, 1965. $7.

De Tocqueville, Alexis. *Democracy in America.* 2 vols. Knopf, 1944. set, $15.

Filler, Louis. *Crusade against Slavery.* Harper, 1960. $8.

Horsman, Reginald. *War of 1812.* Knopf, 1969. $7.

Schlesinger, Arthur M. *Age of Jackson.* Little, 1945. $9.

Stone, Irving. *Men to Match My Mountains.* Doubleday, 1956. $9.

Tunis, Edwin. *Frontier Living.* World, 1961. $7.

Van Deusen, Glyndon G. *Jacksonian Era.* Harper, 1959. $8.

Wiltse, Charles M. *New Nation 1800–1845.* Hill, 1961. paper, $2.

973.6 UNITED STATES: 1845–1861

Chidsey, Donald B. *War with Mexico.* Crown, 1968. $5.

Connor, Seymour V. *North America Divided: the Mexican War.* Oxford, 1971. $9.

Craven, Avery. *Coming of the Civil War.* 2nd ed. Chicago, 1957. $8.

DeVoto, Bernard. *Year of Decision.* Houghton, 1950. $8.

Singletary, Otis A. *Mexican War.* Chicago, 1960. $6.

Stampp, Kenneth M. *Causes of the Civil War.* rev. ed. Peter Smith, 1965. $5.

973.7 UNITED STATES: 1861–1865

Boatner, Mark M. *Civil War Dictionary.* McKay, 1959. $15.

Catton, Bruce. *Civil War.* McGraw, 1971. $7.

――――. *Never Call Retreat.* Doubleday, 1965. $10.

――――. *Stillness at Appomatox.* Doubleday, 1953. $7.

Commager, Henry S. *Blue and the Gray.* Bobbs, 1950. $12.

Davis, Burke. *To Appomattox.* Holt, 1959. $9.

Dubois, William E. B. *Black Reconstruction in America.* Atheneum, 1969. $5.

Dupuy, R. E. *Compact History of the Civil War.* Hawthorn, 1960. $9.

Nash, Howard P. *Naval History of the Civil War.* B&N, 1972. $10.

National Geographic Soc. *Civil War.* National Geographic, 1969. $5.

Nevins, Allan. *Ordeal of the Union.* Scribner, 1973. $13.

Nichols, Roy F. *Battles and Leaders of the Civil War.* 4 vols. B&N, 1957. set, $50.

Randall, James G. *Civil War and Reconstruction.* 2nd rev. ed. Heath, 1969. $12.

Stampp, Kenneth M. *And the War Came.* Louisiana, 1950. $9.

973.8 UNITED STATES: 1865–1901

Andrews, Sidney. *South since the War.* Houghton, 1971. $10.

Buck, Paul H. *Road to Reunion.* Peter Smith, 1959. $4.

Craven, Avery O. *Reconstruction.* Holt, 1969. paper, $5.

Franklin, John H. *Reconstruction.* Chicago, 1961. $5.

Freidel, Frank. *Splendid Little War.* Little, 1958. $13.

Garraty, John A. *New Commonwealth.* Harper, 1968. $9.

Hacker, Louis M. *World of Andrew Carnegie.* Lippincott, 1968. $9.

Holbrook, Stewart H. *Age of the Moguls.* Doubleday, 1953. $7.

Josephson, Matthew. *Politics.* Harcourt, 1963. paper, $5.

――――. *Robber Barons.* Harcourt, 1934. paper, $3.

Keller, Morton. *Art and Politics of Thomas Nast.* Oxford, 1968. $13.

Leech, Margaret K. *In the Days of McKinley.* Harper, 1959. $14.

Stampp, Kenneth. *Era of Reconstruction.* Knopf, 1965. $6.

Woodward, C. Vann. *Reunion and Reaction.* rev. ed. Little, 1966. $6.

――――. *Strange Career of Jim Crow.* 2nd rev. ed. Oxford, 1966. $7.

973.9   UNITED STATES: 1901 TO THE PRESENT

Acheson, Dean. *Present at the Creation: My Years in the State Department.* Norton, 1969. $13.

Allen, Frederick. *Big Change.* Harper, 1952. $7.

_____. *Only Yesterday.* Harper, 1957. $7.

American Heritage Publ. Co. *History of the 20's and 30's.* McGraw, 1970. $20.

Bailey, Thomas A. *Woodrow Wilson and the Lost Peace.* Peter Smith. $5.

Barck, Oscar T. *Since 1900.* 4th ed. Macmillan, 1965. $12.

Boardman, Fon Wyman. *Thirties* Walck, 1967. $6.

Buchannan, A. Russell. *United States and World War II.* 2 vols. Harper, 1964. each, $8.

Carr, Edward H. *Twenty Years' Crisis.* 2nd ed. St. Martin, 1946. $9.

Commager, Henry S. *American Mind.* Yale, 1950. $13.

Cook, Fred J. *Nightmare Decade.* Random, 1971. $10.

Degler, Carl N. *New Deal.* Watts, 1970. $7.

Dos Passos, John. *Mister Wilson's War.* Doubleday, 1962. $8.

Goldman, Eric. *Crucial Decade.* Knopf, 1956. $7.

Halberstam, David. *Best and the Brightest.* Random, 1972. $10.

Heren, Louis. *No Hail, No Farewell.* Harper, 1970. $7.

Hicks, John D. *Republican Ascendancy.* Harper, 1960. $8.

Hollon, W. Eugene. *Southwest: Old and New.* Knopf, 1961. $9.

Horan, James D. *Desperate Years.* Crown, 1962. $8.

Johnson, Lyndon B. *Vantage Point.* Holt, 1971. $15.

Josephson, Matthew. *President Makers.* Ungar, 1964. $13.

Koenig, Louis W. *Truman Administration.* NYU, 1956. $10.

Krock, Arthur. *Consent of the Governed, and Other Deceits.* Little, 1971. $9.

Leuchtenberg, William E. *Franklin D. Roosevelt and the New Deal.* Harper, 1963. $8.

_____. *Perils of Prosperity.* Chicago, 1958. $5.

Link, Arthur, S. *Woodrow Wilson and the Progressive Era.* Harper, 1954. $8.

Lord, Walter. *Good Years.* Harper, 1960. $7.

McGill, Ralph. *South and the Southerner.* Little, 1963. $8.

Phillips, Cabell. *From the Crash to the Blitz.* Macmillan, 1969. $13.

Schlesinger, Arthur M. *Age of Roosevelt.* 3 vols. Houghton, 1957/60. each, $10.

_____. *Thousand Days.* Houghton, 1965. $9.

Schoener, Allan. *Harlem on My Mind 1900–1968.* Random, 1969. $13.

Shannon, David A. *Great Depression.* Peter Smith, 1960. $5.

Time-Life Books. *This Fabulous Century.* 8 vols. Time, 1969/71. each, $8.

Warren, Harris G. *Herbert Hoover and the Great Depression.* Oxford, 1959. $10.

West, J. B. *Upstairs at the White House.* Coward, 1973. $9.

White, Theodore H. *Making of the President 1960.* Atheneum, 1961. $10.

_____. *Making of the President 1964.* Atheneum, 1965. $10.

_____. *Making of the President 1968.* Atheneum, 1969. $10.

_____. *Making of the President 1972.* Atheneum, 1973. $10.

Wish, Harvey. *Contemporary America.* 4th ed. Harper, 1966. $12.

Woodward, C. Vann. *Burden of Southern History.* Louisiana State, 1968. $6.

Woodward, Robert. *All the President's Men.* S&S, 1974. $9.

974-979 UNITED STATES–REGIONAL AREAS

Individual libraries should be attentive to the historical development of their own locality and should purchase a good selection of materials to back up that history. Subject and area bibliographies should be consulted and regional publishers contacted to keep collection up to date.

980 SOUTH AMERICA

Arciniegas, German. *Latin America, a Cultural History.* Knopf, 1967. $8.

Baudin, Louis. *Daily Life in Peru under the Last Incas.* Macmillan, 1962. $6.

Bishop, Elizabeth. *Brazil.* Time, 1971. $7.

Brundage, Burr C. *Lords of Cuzco.* Oklahoma, 1967. $10.

Crow, John A. *Epic of Latin America.* rev. ed. Doubleday, 1971. $13.

Fehrenback, T. R. *Fire and Blood.* Macmillan, 1973. $13.

Freyre, Gilberto. *Masters and the Slaves.* Knopf, 1964. $13.

Galdames, Luis. *History of Chile.* Russell, 1964. $15.

Herring, Hubert. *History of Latin America.* 3rd rev. ed. Knopf, 1968. $11.

Holt, Pat M. *Colombia Today and Tomorrow.* Praeger, 1964. $6.

Ivanoff, Pierre. *Mayan Enigma.* Delacorte, 1971. $6.

Katz, Friedrich. *Ancient American Civilizations.* Praeger, 1972. $15.

Lieuwen, Edwin. *Venezuela.* 2nd ed. Oxford, 1965. $5.

Linke, Lilo. *Ecuador.* 3rd ed. Oxford, 1960. $5.

Moron, Guillermo. *History of Venezuela.* International, 1964. $8.

Osborne, Harold. *Bolivia.* 3rd ed. Oxford, 1964. $5.

Owens, Ronald. *Peru.* Oxford, 1963. $5.

Scobie, James R. *Argentina.* 2nd ed. Oxford, 1971. $8.

Whitaker, Arthur. *Argentina.* Prentice, 1964. $6.

Worcester, Donald E. *Growth and Culture of Latin America.* 2nd ed., 2 vols. Oxford, 1971. set, $20.

990 OTHER PARTS OF THE WORLD

Aitken, Johnathan. *Land of Fortune.* Atheneum, 1971. $9.

Cameron, Roderick. *Australia.* Columbia, 1971. $15.

_____. *New Zealand.* Prentice, 1965. $6.

Daws, Gavan. *Shoal of Time.* Macmillan, 1968. $10.
Grant, Bruce. *Indonesia.* 2nd ed. Cambridge, 1966. $6.
Grattan, C. Hartley. *Southwest Pacific.* 2 vols. Michigan, 1963. set, $18.
Howard & Copley. *Australia in the 20th Century.* Soccer, 1968. $7.
Kuykendall, Ralph S. *Hawaii: a History.* 2nd ed. Prentice, 1961. $9.
Moorhead, Alan. *Fatal Impact.* Harper, 1966. $7.
Scott, Ernest. *Short History of Australia.* 7th ed. Oxford, 1947. $7.

INDEX

ABCs of Lasers and Masers. Lytel, A., 52

Aaron, Henry. Bad Henry, 97

Aaron, James E. First Aid and Emergency Care, 48

Aaronson, Joseph. Encyclopedia of Furniture, 69

Abell, George. Exploration of the Universe: Brief Updated Edition, 37

Abernethy, Robert G. Introduction to Tomorrow: the U.S. and the Wider World, 120

Abortion. Mace, D., 8

Abortion: Law, Choice and Morality. Callahan, D., 8

About Epilepsy. Scott, D., 50

Abraham, George. Green Thumb Book of Fruit and Vegetable Gardening, 56

———. Green Thumb Book of Indoor Gardening, 65

———. Green Thumb Garden Handbook, 65

Abraham, Lincoln. Thomas, B., 104

Abrahams, Peter. Tell Freedom, 97

Abrams, Meyer H. Norton Anthology of English Literature, 85

Abramson, Doris E. Negro Playwrights in the American Theatre, 81

Absorbent Mind. Montessori, M., 7

Absurd Convictions, Modest Hopes. Berrigan, D., 11

Abuse of Power. Draper, T., 118

Abyss. Idyll, C., 39

Acceleration of History. Piel, G., 93

Accidental President. Sherrill, R., 103

Acheson, Dean. Present at the Creation: My Years in the State Department, 124

Acheson, Patricia C. America's Colonial Heritage, 121

Acne and Related Disorders of Complexion and Scalp. Bobroff, A., 49

Acoustical Foundations of Music. Backus, J., 38

Acrylic and Other Water-Base Paints. Torche, J., 71

Act of Creation. Koestler, A., 6

Act One. Hart, M., 102

Acting. Theatre Student Series, 75

Acupuncture. Duke, M., 49

Adams, Alexander B. Geronimo, 101

Adams, Ansel. Artificial Light Photography, 71

———. Camera and Lens, 71

———. Natural Light Photography, 71

———. Negative, 71

———. Print, 71

Adams, Evangeline. Astrology for Everyone, 5

———. Astrology: Your Place Among the Stars, 5

———. Astrology: Your Place in the Sun, 5

Adams, George F. Landforms, 39

Adams, Henry. Education of Henry Adams, 97

Adams, Jeanette. Complete Woodworking Handbook, 62

Adams, Joey. Encyclopedia of Humor, 85

Adams, Joseph Q. Chief Pre-Shakespearean Drama, 87

Adams, Russell. Great Negroes, Past and Present, 95

Adamson, George. Lifetime with Lions, 97

Adamson, Joy. Born Free, 45

———. Forever Free, 45

———. Living Free, 46

Adapting American Antiques. Warner, D., 70

Addams, Jane. 20 Years at Hull House, 97

Adlai Stevenson. Muller, H., 107

Adler, Henry. Introduction to Probability and Statistics, 35

Adler, Irving. New Look at Geometry, 36

———. New Mathematics, 36

———. Probability and Statistics for Everyman, 36

———. Thinking Machines, 36

Adler, Mortimer. Time of our Lives: Ethics of Common Sense, 8

———. How to Read a Book, 4

Administration of the Small Public Library. Sinclair, D., 2

Admiral of the Ocean Sea. Morrison, S., 99

Adoff, Arnold. Poetry of Black America, 83

Advanced Woodwork and Furniture Making. Feirer, J., 62

Adventures in Crocheting. Aytes, B., 67

Advertising Fundamentals. Burton, P., 60

Advertising Procedure. Kleppner, O., 61

Aeneid of Virgil. Virgil, 91

Affluent Society. Galbraith, J., 22

Africa Must Unite. Nkrumah, K., 118

Africa Since 1800. Oliver, R., 118

African Art. Willett, F., 65

African Beginnings. Vlahos, O., 41

African Discovery. Perham, M., 119

African Genesis. Ardrey, R., 40

African Heritage. Drachler, J., 91

African Kingdoms. Davidson, B., 118

African Past. Davidson, B., 118

African Treasury. Hughes, L., 91

African Voices. Rutherford, Peddy, 91

African Wildlife. Roedelberger, F., 46

After the Assassination. Sparrow, J., 26

After the Genteel Tradition. Cowley, M., 82

Afzelius, Bjorn. Anatomy of the Cell, 42

Age of Discontinuity. Drucker, P., 16

Age of Giant Mammals. Cohen, D., 40

Age of Jackson. Schlesinger, A., 122

Age of Keynes. Lekachman, R., 23

Age of Louis XIV. Voltaire, F., 114

Age of Metternich. May, A., 111

Age of Napoleon. Herold, J., 114

Age of Roosevelt. Schlesinger, A., 124

Age of the Baroque. Friedrich, C., 111

Age of the Democratic Revolution. Palmer, R., 111

Age of the Moguls. Holbrook, S., 96, 123

Aging with Honor and Dignity. Field, M., 19

Ahnstrom, D. N. Complete Book of Helicopters, 54

Aiken, Conrad P. Twentieth Century American Poetry, 83

Aitken, Johnathan. Land of Fortune, 125

Alba, Victor. Horizon Concise History of Mexico, 120

———. Mexicans: Making of a Nation, 120

Albee, Edward. Death of Bessie Smith, 83

———. Sandbox, 83

———. Who's Afraid of Virginia Woolf?, 83

———. Zoo Story, 83

Albrecht-Carrie, René. Concert of Europe, 111

———. Diplomatic History of Europe since the Congress of Vienna, 110

Alcindor, Lew see Jabbar, Kareem Abdul

Alcohol: Drink or Drug? Hyde, M., 49

Alcoholism. Bloch, M., 49

Alden, John R. American Revolution, 121

———. History of the American Revolution, 121

———. Pioneer America, 120, 122

Aldridge, Alan. Beatles Illustrated Lyrics, 73

Alexander, Taylor R. Botany, 42

Alexander Hamilton. Mitchell, B., 102

Alexandra (Romanov) see Nicholas

Alfred the Great. Helm, P., 97

Alkers, Susan G. Simple Library Cataloging, 1

All About Antiquing and Restoring Furniture. Berger, R., 62

All about Meetings. Long, F., 21

All about Repairing Small Appliances. Squeglia, M., 59

All About Upholstering. Bergen, J., 62

All About Words. Nurnberg, M., 33

All Creatures Great and Small. Herriot, J., 102

All of Europe at Low Cost. Robinson, J., 95

All the Best in . . . (for Europe, the Mediterraneum, etc.). Clarke, S., 94

All the President's Men. Woodward, R. and Bernstein, C., 125

All the World's a Stage. Swortzell, L., 81

All Things Bright and Beautiful. Herriot, James, 102

Allah, the God of Islam. Fitch, F., 15

Allen, Donald M. New American Poetry 1945–1960, 83
Allen, Frederick. Big Change, 124
———. Only Yesterday, 124
Allen, Gay W. American Poetry, 83
———. American Prosody, 82
———. Solitary Singer, 108
Allen, Walter E. English Novel, 88
———. Modern Novel, 88
———. Writers on Writing, 80
Allendoerfer, Carl B. Fundamentals of College Algebra, 36
———. Fundamentals of Freshman Mathematics, 36
Almanac of American Politics. Barone, M., 22
Alone. Byrd, R., 98
Alsop, Stewart. Stay of Execution, 97
Alter, Dinsmore. Practical Astronomy, 37
———. Pictorial Guide to the Moon, 37
Alternative: Communal Life. Hedgepeth, W., 24
Althouse, Andrew D. Modern Welding, 61
Alvarez, A. Savage God, 16
Alvarez, Walter C. Live at Peace with Your Nerves, 50
Always the Young Strangers. Sandberg, C., 106
Amacher, Richard E. Edward Albee, 84
Amateur Magician's Handbook. Hay, H., 75
Amateur Photographer's Handbook. Sussman, A., 72
Amateur Taxidermist. Labrie, J., 42
Amaya, Maris. Pop Art and After, 64
Ambassador's Journal. Galbraith, J., 21
America. Cooke, A., 120
America, the Raped. Marine, G., 24
American Album. American Heritage Publ. Co., 120
American Architecture and Urbanism. Scully, V., 67
American Architecture since 1780. Whiffen, M., 67
American Automobile Assn. Sportsmanlike Driving, 54
American Badges and Insignia. Kerrigan, E., 27
American Book of Days. Douglas, G., 30
American Catholicism. Ellis, J., 13
American Challenge. Servan-Schreiber, J., 21
American Character. Brogan, D., 120
American Constitution. Kelly, A., 25
American Democracy. Magrath, C., 20
American Dramatic Literature. Miller, J., 84

American Economic History. Faulkner, H., 22
American Fiction. Quinn, A., 84
American Folklore. Dorson, R., 31
American Government Today. Caldwell, G., 26
American Heritage. American Album, 120
———. Historic Houses, 94
———. Indians, 119
———. Great Days of the Circus, 75
———. History of the 20's and 30's, 124
———. Natural Wonders of America, 94
———. Shakespeare: His Life, His Times, His Works, 87
———. World War I, 111
American Heritage Dictionary of the English Language, 32
American Heritage Guide to Antiques. Durant, M., 70
American Heritage History of the American People. Weisberger, B., 121
American Houses. Hoag, E., 66
American Humorist. Yates, N., 85
American Indian. Locke, R., 119
American Indian Ceremonial Dances. Collier, J., 30
American Indian 1492–1970. Dennis, H., 119
American Indian Mythology. Marriott, A., 15
American Indian Poetry. Cronyn, G., 83
American Indian Religions. Hurdy, J., 15
American Indians. Hagan, W., 119
American Journalism. Mott, F., 4
American Kennel Club. Complete Dog Book, 57
American Labor Unions. Peterson, F., 23
American Landscape. Nairn, I., 65
American Language. Mencken, H., 33
American Library Association. Minimum Standards for Public Library Systems, 1
———. Reference Books for Small and Medium-sized Libraries, 1
American Melodrama: Presidential Campaign of 1968. Chester, L., 22
American Mind. Commager, H., 124
American Music. Nanry, C., 73
American Nation. Garraty, J., 121
American Negro Poetry. Bontemps, A., 83
American Novel, 1789–1939. Van Doren, C., 84
American Painting. Time-Life Books, 71
American Past. Butterfield, R., 120
American Poetry. Allen, G., 83
American Poetry. Shapiro, K., 83
American Poetry and Prose. Foerster, N., 82

American Poetry in the Twentieth Century. Rexroth, K., 83

American Poets. Waggoner, H., 83

American Plays and Playwrights of the Contemporary Theater. Lewis, A., 84

American Political Dictionary. Plano, J., 22

American Political Parties. Binkley, W., 22

American Political Parties. Wynar, L., 22

American Popular Songs from the Revolutionary War to the Present. Ewen, D., 73

American Presidency. Rossiter, C., 27

American Prosody. Allen, G., 82

American Protestantism. Hudson, W., 13

American Public Addresses. Baird, A., 82

American Radio Relay League. Radio Amateur's Handbook, 52

American Red Cross. First Aid Textbook, 48

American Renaissance. Matthiessen, F., 82

American Revolution. Alden, J., 121

American Revolution. Morris, R., 122

American Revolution Reconsidered. Morris, R., 122

American Roulette: History and Dilemma of the Vice Presidency. Young, D., 27

American Spirit. Bailey, T., 120

American Surnames. Smith, E., 108

American University. Barzun, J., 28

American War Medals and Decorations. Kerrigan, E., 27

American Way of Death. Mitford, J., 30

Americans. Furnas, J., 121

Americans: the Colonial Experience. Boorstin, D., 120

Americans: the Democratic Experience. Boorstin, D., 120

Americans: the National Experience. Boorstin, D., 120

America's Black Past. Foner, E., 121

America's Colonial Heritage. Acheson, P., 121

America's Crochet Book. Taylor, G., 69

America's Greatest Depression. Chandler, L., 22

America's Handyman Book, Family Handyman, 63

America's Knitting Book. Taylor, G., 69

America's Music. Chase, G., 72

Amish Society. Hostetler, J., 13

Amlick, Barbara A. Dried Flower Craft, 67

Ammer, Christine. Harper's Dictionary of Music, 72

Amy Vanderbilt's Etiquette. Vanderbilt, A., 30

Analytical Psychology. Jung, C., 6

Anatomy and Physiology. Kimber, D., 48

Anatomy of Human Destructiveness. Fromm, E., 6

Anatomy of Liberty. Douglas, W., 25

Anatomy of the Cell. Afzelius, B., 42

Ancient America. Leonard, J., 119

Ancient American Civilizations. Katz, F., 125

Ancient City, DeCoulanges, F., 109

Ancient Egypt. Casson, L., 109

Ancient Greece. Hale, W., 110

Ancient Historians. Grant, M., 110

Ancient Regime. Behrens, C., 114

And the War Came. Stampp, K., 123

Andersen, Paul G. Organ Building and Design, 74

Andersen, Yvonne. Make Your Own Animated Movies, 72

Anderson, Edwin P. Audel's Home Appliance Servicing, 59

———. Electric Motors, 52

———. Home Refrigeration and Air Conditioning Guide, 59

Anderson, George L. Masterpieces of the Orient, 91

Anderson, Marion. My Lord, What a Morning, 97

Anderson, Robert T. Denmark, 115

Anderson-Imbert, Enrique. Spanish American Literature: a History, 90

Andrew Jackson. James, M., 102

Andrewes, Antony. Greeks, 110

Andrewes, Christopher H. Natural History of Viruses, 42

Andrews, Matthew. Parent's Guide to Drugs, 49

Andrews, Sidney. South since the War, 123

Anesaki, Masaharu. History of Japanese Religion, 14

Angel, Juvenal L. Why and How to Prepare an Effective Job Resume, 60

Angel of the Battlefield. Ross, I., 98

Angelou, Maya. I Know Why the Caged Bird Sings, 97

Angier, Bradford. Feasting Free on Wild Edibles, 58

———. Home in Your Pack, 76

Anglo-Saxon Chronicle. Garmonsway, G., 113

Angoff, Allan. Psychic Force, 5

Animal Agents and Vectors of Human Disease. Faust, E., 49

Animal Atlas of the World. Jordan, E., 46

Animal Traps and Trapping. Bateman, J., 57, 78

Animals and Men. Dembeck, H., 43

Animals Nobody Loves: Varmint Ecology. Rood, R., 46

Animals of the Antarctic. Stonehouse, B., 46

Animals of the Artic. Stonehouse, B., 46

Animals without Backbones. Buchsbaum, R., 43

Animals without Parents. Jenkins, M., 46

Anna and the King of Siam. Landon, M., 103

Anniversaries and Holidays. Hazeltine, M., 30

Anouilh, Jean. Seven Plays, 89

Anthology. Whitehead, A., 9

Anthology of Chinese Literature. Birch, C., 91

Anthology of French Poetry. Flores, A., 89

Anthology of Japanese Literature. Keene, D., 91

Anthology of Old English Poetry. Kennedy, C., 86

Anthology of Spanish Literature in English Translation. Resnick, S., 90

Anthology of World Poetry. Van Doren, M., 81

Anthropology. Hoebel, E., 41

Antiques' Guide to Decorative Arts in America, 1600–1875. Stillinger, E., 70

Antiques Past and Present. McClinton, K., 70

Antiques You Can Decorate With. Grotz, G., 70

Antreasian, Garo Z. Tamarind Book of Lithography, 71

Anybody's Bike Book. Cuthbertson, T., 56

Ape People. Bourne, G., 46

Appalachians. Brooks, M., 39

Applied Genetics. Paterson, D., 42

Arbuthnot, May H. Children's Reading in the Home, 4

Archer, Jules. Treason in America, 26

Archery. Barrett, J., 78

Archery for All. Roberts, D., 78

Architectural Drawing and Planning. Goodban, W., 66

Architectural Rendering. Halse, A., 66

Architecture. Spence, W., 67

Architecture: Drafting and Design. Hepler, D., 66

Architecture through the Ages. Hamlin, T., 66

Arciniegas, German. Latin America, a Cultural History, 125

Arco Publ. Co. Civil Service Arithmetic and Vocabulary, 26

———. Federal Service Entrance Examinations, 26

———. High School Equivalency Diploma Tests, 28

———. Practice for the Armed Forces Tests, 27

———. U.S. Service Academy Admission Tests, 27

Arctander, Erik. New Book of Motorcycles, 54

Ardrey, Robert. African Genesis, 40

Are Parents Bad for Children. Blaine, G., 18

Are You Running with Me, Jesus? Boyd, M., 12

Area Handbooks, 94

Arena of Life. Milne, L., 41

Arendt, Hannah. Origins of Totalitarianism, 20

Argentina. Scobie, J., 125

Argentina. Whitaker, A., 125

Argumentation and Debate. McBurney, J., 82

Arisian, Khoren. New Wedding, 30

Aristotle. Basic Works, 91

———. Poetics; Rhetoric, 80

———. Politics, 22

Armada. Mattingly, G., 113

Armajani, Yahya. Iran, 117

Armor, Reginald C. Magic of Love, 11

Arms of Krupp. Manchester, W., 103

Armstrong, James W. Elements of Mathematics, 36

Arnold, Matthew. Portable Matthew Arnold, 88

Arnold, Ralph. Social History of England: 55 B.C.–A.D. 1215, 113

Arnold, Robert R. Modern Data Processing, 60

Art and Career Guide. Holden, H., 64

Art and Life in America. Larkin, O., 64

Art and Politics of Thomas Nast. Keller, M., 123

Art and the Young Child. Jameson, K., 64

Art and Times of the Guitar. Grunefeld, F., 74

Art as Therapy with Children. Kramer, E., 64

Art Books: a Basic Bibliography on the Fine Arts. Lucas, E., 64

Art of Acting. Dolman, J., 74

Art of Clear Thinking. Flesch, R., 6

Art of Contemplation. Watts, A., 14

Art of Loving. Fromm, E., 6

Art of Making Good Candies at Home. Herrmann, M., 58

Art of Papier Mache. Kenny, C., 68

Art of Pictorial Composition. Wolchonok, L., 67

Art of Play Production. Dolman, J., 74

Art of the Essay. Fielder, L., 88

Art of Theatrical Makeup for Stage and Screen. Westmore, M., 75

Artificial Light Photography. Adams, A., 71

Artist's Guide to His Market. Chamberlain, B., 64

Artists' Handbook of Materials and Techniques. Mayer, R., 71

Arts and Their Interrelations. Munro, T., 64

Artz, Frederick B. France under the Bourbon Restoration, 114

———. Mind of the Middle Ages, 110

———. Reaction and Revolution, 111

Ashabranner, Brent. Moment in History, 24

Ashe, Geoffrey. Quest for America, 121

Ashley, Maurice P. Great Britain to 1688, 113

Ashton, Thomas S. Industrial Revolution, 22

Ashton-Warner, Sylvia. Myself, 97

Asians, Their Heritage and Their Destiny. Welty, P., 116

Asia's Land and People. Cressey, G., 116

Asimov, Isaac. Genetic Code, 41

———. Human Body, 47

———. Solar System and Back, 37

———. Stars in their Courses, 37

———. Universe, 37

Ask the Doctor. Fishbein, M., 50

Aspects of the Novel. Forster, E., 81

Associated Press. Century of Sports, 76

———. Sports Immortals, 95

Astrology. MacNiece, L., 6

Astrology for Everyone. Adams, E., 5

Astrology for Everyone. Lynde, E., 6

Astrology: Your Place Among the Stars. Adams, E., 5

Astrology: Your Place in the Sun. Adams, E., 5

Astronomy. Baker, R., 37

Astronomy. Jastrow, R., 37

Astronomy. Menzel, D., 37

At Wit's End. Bombeck, E., 85

Athens in the Age of Pericles. Robinson, C., Jr., 110

Atkins, Jim. Filming TV News and Documentaries, 72

Atkins, Kenneth R. Physics, 38

Atkinson, Bruce W. Weather Business, 39

Atkinson, Robert E. Complete Book of Groundcovers, 65

Atlantic Shore. Hay, J., 39

Atlas of Animal Migration. Jarman, C., 43

Atlas of Human Anatomy. Frohse, F., 48

Atlas of Wildlife. Nayman, J., 44

Atomic Submarines. Polmar, N., 53

Atoms in the Family. Fermi, L., 101

Auto Service and Repair. Stockel, M., 56

Atwater, Constance. Baton Twirling, 73

Attwater, Donald. Penguin Dictionary of Saints, 95

Aubrey, John. Aubrey's Brief Lives, 95

Aubrey's Brief Lives. Aubrey, J., 95

Auchincloss, Louis. Pioneers and Caretakers, 84

Audel & Co. Builders Encyclopedia, 62

Audel's Home Appliance Servicing. Anderson, E., 59

Auden, Wystan H. Poets of the English Language, 86

———. Portable Greek Reader, 91

Audubon, John J. Birds of America, 45

Audubon Water Bird Guide. Pough, R., 45

August 21: the Rape of Czechoslovakia. Chapman, C., 116

Augustine, Saint. City of God, 11

———. Confessions, 97

Augustus. Buchan, J., 97

Augustus and the Greek World. Bowersock, G., 110

Aurbach, Joseph. Transformational Grammar, 32

Auslander, Joseph. Winged Horse, 80

Austell, Jan. What's in a Play?, 74

Austin, William. Music in the 20th Century, 72

Australia. Cameron, R., 125

Australia in the 20th Century. Howard & Copley, 126

Ausubel, Nathan. Treasury of Jewish Folklore, 31

Authentic Child. Button, A., 7

Autistic Children. Wing, L., 8

Auto Body Repairing and Repainting. Toboldt, W., 56

Auto Engine Tune-Up. Roeing, R., 55

Auto Mechanics Fundamentals. Stockel, M., 55

Auto Repairs You Can Make. Weissler, P., 56

Auto Service and Repair. Stockel, M., 55

Autobiography. Franklin, B., 101

Autobiography. Roosevelt, E., 106

Autobiography. Russell, B., 106

Autobiography. Steffens, L., 107

Autobiography. Williams, W., 108
Autobiography of Alice B. Toklas. Stein, G., 107
Autobiography of an Ex-Coloured Man. Johnson, J., 19
Autobiography of Malcolm X. Little, M., 104
Automechanics. Glenn, H., 55
Automobile Engine Rebuilding and Maintenance. Glenn, H., 55
Automobile Sheet Metal Repair. Sargent, R., 55
Automotive Chassis and Body. Crouse, W., 55
Automotive Collision Work. Spicer, E., 55
Automotive Electric Equipment. Crouse, W., 55
Automotive Emission Control. Crouse, W., 55
Automotive Engines. Crouse, W., 55
Automotive Transmissions and Power Trains. Crouse, W., 55
Autumn across America. Teale, E., 40
Avery, Catherine B. New Century Classical Handbook, 109
Axel's Castle. Wilson, E., 79
Axelrod, Herbert R. Color Guide to Tropical Fish, 44
_____. Encyclopedia of Tropical Fish, 44
_____. Tropical Fish as a Hobby, 44
_____. Tropical Fish in Your Home, 44
Ayer, Fred. Before the Colors Fade, 105
Ayling, Stanley. George the Third, 101
Aymar, Brandt. Pictorial History of the World's Great Trials, 25
Aytes, Barbara. Adventures in Crocheting, 67
_____. Knitting Made Easy, 67
Aztecs, People of the Sun. Caso, A., 120

Babbitt, Harold E. Plumbing, 62
Babe. Smith, R., 106
Babe: Legend Comes to Life. Creamer, R., 106
Baby and Child Care. Spock, B., 60
Bach, Marcus. Major Religions of the World, 13
_____. Strangers at the Door, 14
Bachman, Aberto. Encyclopedia of the Violin, 74
Back to Africa. West, R., 119
Backus, John. Acoustical Foundations of Music, 38
Bacon, Edmond N. Design of Cities, 65
Bacon, Francis, Essays, 88
Bacon, Margaret H. Quiet Rebels, 13

Bad Henry. Aaron, H., 97
Baddeley, W. Hugh. Technique of Documentary Film Production, 72
Badminton. Sports Illustrated, 77
Baer, Adela S. Central Concepts of Biology, 41
Baez, Joan. Daybreak, 97
Bagley, John J. Life in Medieval England, 113
Baigell, Matthew. History of American Painting, 70
Bailey, Albert E. Gospel in Hymns, 11
Bailey, F. Lee. Defense Never Rests, 97
Bailey, Pearl. Raw Pearl, 98
Bailey, Thomas A. American Spirit, 120
_____. Woodrow Wilson and the Lost Peace, 124
Bain, Carolyn. It's Easy to Become a Citizen, 20
Bainton, Roland H. Early Christianity, 13
_____. Here I Stand, 104
Baird, A. Craig. American Public Addresses, 82
_____. Essentials of General Speech Communication, 82
Baker, Carlos. Ernest Hemingway, 102
Baker, Herbert G. Plants and Civilization, 42
Baker, Jeffrey. Truth about Contact Lenses, 51
Baker, Robert H. Astronomy, 37
Baldry, P. E. Battle against Bacteria, 49
_____. Battle against Heart Disease, 49
Baldwin, James. Nobody Knows My Name, 98
_____. Notes of a Native Son, 19
Balikei, Asen. Netsilik Eskimo, 119
Balkans in Our Time. Wolff, R., 116
Ballet Companion. Terry, W., 75
Baltzell, E. Digby. Protestant Establishment, 17
Banco, Charriere, H., 27
Banister, Manly. Lithographic Prints from Stone and Plate, 71
_____. Prints—from Linoblocks and Woodcuts, 71
Banned Books. Haight, A., 4
Barber, Bernard. Sociology of Science, 35
Barbour, Roger W. Bats of America, 45
Barck, Oscar T. Since 1900, 124
Bardach, John. Harvest of the Sea, 39
Barker, Elizabeth. Cold War, 20
Barker, Will. Familiar Animals of America, 46

_____. Familiar Reptiles and Amphibians of America, 45

Barlow, Joseph W. Basic Elements of Spanish, 34

Barlow's Tables of Squares, Cubes, Square Roots, and Reciprocals. Comrie, L., 36

Barnes, R. A. Fundamentals of Music, 72

Barnes, Robert D. Invertebrate Zoology, 43

Barnett, Lincoln. Universe and Dr. Einstein, 38

Barnett, Samuel A. Instinct and Intelligence, 40

Barnstone, Willis. Greek Lyric Poetry, 91

_____. New Faces of China, 116

Baron, Robert A. Tyranny of Noise, 53

Barone, Michael. Almanac of American Politics, 22

Barraclough, E. M. Flags of the World, 108

Barrett, Jean A. Archery, 78

Barrett, William E. Red Laquered Gate, 12

Barricades in Belfast. Hastins, M., 113

Barrie, James M. Plays, 87

Barron, Jerome A. Freedom of the Press for Whom?, 4

Barron's Guide to the Two-Year Colleges, 28

Barron's How to Prepare for College Entrance Examinations, 28

Bartee, Thomas C. Digital Computer Fundamentals, 60

Bartlett, Eric G. Judo and Self Defense, 76

Barton, Mary N. Reference Books: A Brief Guide, 1

Baruch, Bernard M. Baruch: My Own Story, 98

Baruch: My Own Story. Baruch, B., 98

Barzini, Luigi G. Italians, 114

Barzman, Sol. First Ladies, 95

Barzun, Jacques. American University, 28

_____. Darwin, Marx, Wagner: Critique of a Heritage, 111

_____. Modern Researcher, 3

Baseball. Sports Illustrated, 77

Basic Auditing Principles. Holmes, A., 61

Basic Beliefs. Fairchild, J., 14

Basic Color Photography. Feininger, A., 72

Basic Concepts in Sociology. Weber, M., 16

Basic Electricity. Marcus, A., 52

Basic Electricity Training Manual. Pipe, T., 53

Basic Electronics. Grob, B., 52

Basic Electronics. Marcus, A., 52

Basic Elements of Spanish. Barlow, J., 34

Basic Gardening Illustrated. Sunset Magazine, eds., 66

Basic Japanese Conversation. Martin, S., 34

Basic Judaism. Steinberg, M., 14

Basic Mathematics. Lang, S., 36

Basic Mathematics for Electricity and Electronics. Singer, E., 37

Basic Mathematics for Electronics. Cooke, N., 36

Basic Principles of Data Processing. Saxon, J., 4

Basic Principles of Music Theory. Brye, J., 72

Basic Teachings of the Great Philosophers. Frost, S., 8

Basic Works. Aristotle, 91

Basic Works. Cicero, M., 90

Basic Writings. Freud, S., 6

Basic Writings. Russell, B., 9

Basketball. Cousy, R., 76

Basketball. Sports Illustrated, 77

Bast, Herbert. New Essentials of Modern Upholstery, 62

Bateman, James A. Animal Traps and Trapping, 57, 78

Bates, Marston. Forest and the Sea, 39

_____. Natural History of Mosquitoes, 44

Bateson, Frederick W. English Poetry: A Critical Introduction, 86

Baton Twirling. Atwater, C., 73

Bats of America. Barbour, R., 45

Battered Child. Helfer, R., 18

Battle: Story of the Bulge. Toland, J., 112

Battle against Bacteria. Baldry, P., 49

Battle against Heart Disease. Baldry, P., 49

Battle for Stock Market Profits. Loeb, G., 23

Battles and Leaders of the Civil War. Nichols, R., 123

Baudelaire, Charles P. Flowers of Evil, 89

Baudin, Louis. Daily Life in Peru under the Last Incas, 125

Bauer, Raymond. Nine Soviet Portraits, 115

Baugh, Albert C. Literary History of England, 85

Baumer, William H. Little Wars of the United States, 120

Baumgart, Fritz. History of Architectural Styles, 66

Bazin, Andre. What Is Cinema?, 74

Beadle, Muriel. Child's Mind, 7

Beals, Ralph L. Introduction to Anthropology, 40

Beam, Philip C. Winslow Homer at Prout's Neck, 102

Beard, Charles A. Economic Interpretation of the Constitution of the United States, 25

———. New Basic History of the United States, 120

Beard, James. Menus for Entertaining, 58

Beat Generation. Cook, B., 16

Beatles: Authorized Biography. Davies, H., 95

Beatles Illustrated Lyrics. Aldridge, A., 73

Beautiful Country: Maine to Hawaii. Ehrlich, A., 95

Beauty of America in Great American Art. Country Beautiful, eds., 70

Beaver, William C. General Biology, 41

Becker, Carl L. Declaration of Independence, 122

Beckwith, Lillian. Rope-In Case, 88

———. Sea for Breakfast, 88

Becoming Partners. Rogers, C., 19

Bedau, Hugh A. Death Penalty in America, 25

Beddoes, Richard. Hockey!, 76

Beedell, Suzanne. Restoring Junk, 70

Beerbower, James R. Search for the Past, 40

Beers, Clifford. Mind that Found Itself, 98

Beethoven. Sullivan, J., 98

Before and After Socrates. Conford, F., 8

Before the Colors Fade. Ayer, F., 105

Begeman, Myron L. Manufacturing Processes, 61

Beginner's Book of Magic. Rigney, F., 76

Beginner's Guide to Botany. Duddington, C., 42

Beginning French, a Cultural Approach. Hendrix, W., 33

Beginning Russian. Cornyn, W., 34

Behan, Dominic. My Brother Brendan, 98

Behr, Merlyn J. Fundamentals of Elementary Mathematics: Number Systems and Algebra, 36

Behrens, Catherine B. Ancient Regime, 114

Behrman, Abraham S. Water Is Everybody's Business, 53

Beiser, Germaine. Story of Cosmic Rays, 38

Beitler, Ethel J. Hooked and Knotted Rugs, 68

Bekker, Paul. Orchestra, 73

Bell, Eric. Men of Mathematics, 36, 95

Bell, Quentin. Virginia Woolf, 108

Bellairs, Angus. World of Reptiles, 45

Belt, Forest H. Easi-Guide to Color TV, 59

Belz, Carl. Story of Rock, 73

Ben Gurion, David. Israel's Years of Challenge, 117

Ben-Gurion. St. John, R., 98

Benchley, Robert. Benchley Roundup, 85

Benchley Roundup. Benchley, R., 85

Benedict, Ruth. Patterns of Culture, 40

Benet, William R. Reader's Encyclopedia, 79

Benford, Jay. Practical Ferro-Cement Boatbuilding, 53

Benice, Daniel D. Introduction to Computers and Data Processing, 4

Benjamin, Bry. In Case of Emergency, What to Do until the Doctor Arrives, 48

Bennett, Alan. Crystals: Perfect and Imperfect, 38

Bennett, Lerone. What Manner of Man, 103

Benns, F. Lee. Europe since 1914, 111

Benson, Dennis C. Now Generation, 12

Benson, Sidney W. Chemical Calculations, 38

Bentley, Eric. Classic Theatre, 81

———. Classic Theater, Vol. 1: Six Italian Plays, 90

———. Classic Theater, Vol. 2: Five German Plays, 88

———. Classic Theater, Vol. 3: Six Spanish Plays, 90

———. Classic Theater, Vol. 4: Six French Plays, 89

———. Life of the Drama, 81

———. Modern Theater, 81

Berelson, Bernard. Human Behavior, 16

Bergen, John. All about Upholstering, 62

Berger, Robert. All about Antiquing and Restoring Furniture, 62

Berland, Theodore. Living with Your Ulcer, 49

———. Your Children's Teeth, 51

Bernal, J. D. Extension of Man: History of Physics before the Modern Age, 38

———. Science in History, 35

Berne, Eric. Games People Play, 17

———. Layman's Guide to Psychiatry and Psychoanalysis, 50

Bernstein, Leonard. Infinite Variety of Music, 72

Berrigan, Daniel. Absurd Convictions, Modest Hopes, 11

———. False Gods, Real Men, 11

Berstein, Martin. Introduction to Music, 72

Berstein, Peter L. Primer on Money, Banking and Gold, 23

Berton, Pierre. Comfortable Pew, 12

Best American Plays, 1939–1945. Gassner, J., 84

Best American Plays, 1945–1951. Gassner, J., 84

Best American Plays, 1951–1957. Gassner, J., 84

Best American Plays, 1957–1963. Gassner, J., 84

Best American Plays, 1963–1967. Gassner, J., 84

Best American Plays, 1918–1958 Suppl. Vol. Gassner, J., 84

Best and the Brightest. Halberstam, D., 124

Best Loved Poems of the American People. Felleman, H., 83

Best Mystery and Suspense Plays of the Modern Theatre. Richards, S., 81

Best Plays of 19–, 81

Best Plays of the Early American Theater (to 1916). Gassner, J., 84

Best Plays of the Modern American Theater. Gassner, J., 84

Best Plays of the Sixties. Richards, S., 81

Bestic, Alan. Praise the Lord and Pass the Contribution, 12

Bettelheim, Bruno. Children of the Dream, 17

_____. Love Is Not Enough, 7

_____Social Change and Prejudice, 16

Better Boating. Sports Illustrated, eds., 78

Better Homes & Gardens, eds. Better Homes & Gardens House Plants, 65

_____. Casserole Cook Book, 58

_____. Creative Decorating on a Budget, 69

_____. Creative Table Settings, 58

_____. Decorating Ideas under $100, 69

_____. Flower Arranging, 65

_____. Handyman's Book, 62

_____. Hundreds of Ideas, 69

_____. New Cook Book, 58

_____. Stitchery and Crafts, 68

Better Homes & Gardens House Plants. Better Homes & Gardens, eds., 65

Betty Crocker's Cook Book. Crocker, B., 58

Betty Crocker's Cooky Book. Crocker, B., 58

Betty Crocker's Parties for Children. Freeman, L., 75

Between Parent and Child. Ginott, H., 60

Between Parent and Teenager. Ginott, H., 60

Beyond Freedom and Dignity. Skinner, B., 7

Beyond Ourselves. Marshall, C., 12

Beyond Racism. Young, W., 20

Beyond Science. Burland, C., 5

Beyond the Melting Pot. Glazer, N., 21

Bibby, Geoffrey. Four Thousand Years Ago, 109

Bible and Archaeology. Thompson, J., 11

Bible and the Common Reader. Chase, M., 10

Big Bands. Simon G., 74

Big Brother's Indian Program: with Reservations. Levitan, S., 119

Big Change. Allen, F., 124

Bike Book, McIntyre, B., 56

Bikeways. Frankel, L., 56

Billingsley, Andrew. Black Families in White America, 19

Billington, Ray A. Far Western Frontier, 122

_____. Westward Expansion, 120

Binkley, Wilfred E. American Political Parties, 22

Biological Science. Keeton, W., 41

Biology. Curtis, H., 41

Biology of Flowering. Salisbury, F., 43

Bionics. Marteka, V., 3

Birch, Cyril. Anthology of Chinese Literature, 91

Bird, Caroline. Born Female, 17

Birds of America. Audubon, J., 45

Birkner, Heinrich. Screen Printing, 71

Birren, Faber. History of Color in Painting, 70

Birth of the Republic. Morgan, E., 122

Bishop, Edna B. Super Sewing, 60

Bishop, Elizabeth. Brazil, 125

Bishop, Jim. Day Christ Died, 11

_____. Day Christ Was Born, 11

_____. Day Lincoln Was Shot, 104

Bishop, Morris. Middle Ages, 110

Bitchell, Jethro. Modern German Literature, 88

Black, Charles L., Jr. Impeachment: A Handbook, 26

Black, Henry C. Black's Law Dictionary, 25

Black, Perry. Machinist's Library, 52

_____. Pumps, 51

Black American: A Documentary History. Fishel, L., 21

Black Boy. Wright, R., 108

Black English. Dillard, J., 33

Black Expressions. Gayle, A., 82

Black Families in White America. Billingsley, A., 19

Black Heroes in Our Nation's History. Drotning, P., 96

Black History: A Reappraisal. Drimmer, M., 120

Black Like Me. Griffin, J., 19

Black Mother. Davidson, B., 118

Black Rage. Grier, W., 6

Black Reconstruction in America. Dubois, W., 123

Black Skins, White Masks. Fanon, F., 21

Black Soldier. David, J., 120

Black Song. Lovell, J., Jr., 73

Blackberry Winter. Mead, M., 105

Black's Law Dictionary. Black, H., 25

Blaine, Graham B. Are Parents Bad for Children?, 18

Blake, Claire. Greenhouse Gardening for Fun, 56

Blake, Eugene C. Church in the Next Decade, 12

Blake, Robert. Disraeli, 100

Blake, William. Portable Blake, 88

Blakiston's New Gould Medical Dictionary, 47

Blaming the Victim. Ryan, W., 19

Blaze of Glory: Fight for New Orleans. Carter, S., 122

Blender Way to Better Cooking. Sullivan, B., 59

Bloch, Marvin A. Alcoholism, 49

Bloodletters and Badmen. Nash, J., 96

Bloodworth, Dennis. Chinese Looking Glass, 116

Bloom, Murray. Trouble with Lawyers, 24

Bloomquist, E. R. Marijuana, 49

Bloomstein, Morris J. Verdict: The Jury System, 24

Blue and the Gray. Commager, H., 123

Blue Nile. Moorehead, A., 118

Blum, Daniel. New Pictorial History of the Talkies, 74

Blum, Jerome. European World: A History, 110

Blumberg, Robert S. Fine Wines of California, 61

Blumenson, Martin. Duel for France, 1944, 112

Boahen, J. Desmond. Horizon History of Africa, 118

Boak, Arthur E. History of Rome to A.D. 565, 109

Boardman, Fon Wyman. Thirties, 124

Boating from Bow to Stern. Kenealy, J., 77

Boatner, Mark M. Civil War Dictionary, 123

Bob Dylan Song Book, Dylan, B., 73

Bobroff, Arthur. Acne and Related Disorders of Complexion and Scalp, 49

Body, The. Nourse, A., 48

Body and Antibody. Wilson, D., 50

Body Harmony. Zorn, W., 8

Body Language. Fast, J., 6

Body Time: Physiological Rhythms and Social Stress. Luce, G., 6

Boettcher, Helmuth M. Wonder Drugs: A History of Antibiotics, 49

Bogert, L. Jean. Nutrition and Physical Fitness, 48

Bolivia. Osborne, H., 125

Bolton, Sarah K. Famous Men of Science, 95

Bombeck, Erma. At Wit's End, 85

———. Just Wait Till You Have Children of Your Own, 85

Bonapartes. Stacton, D., 96

Bond, Guy L. Teaching the Child to Read, 28

Bonds, The. Williams, R., 96

Bone, Robert A. Negro Novel in America, 84

Bonham-Carter, Violet. Winston Churchill: An Intimate Portrait, 99

Bonhoeffer, Dietrich. Letters and Papers from Prison, 11

Bonjour, Edgar. Short History of Switzerland, 116

Bonnie Prudden's Fitness Book. Prudden, B., 77

Bonsai. Sunset Magazine, eds., 66

Bontemps, Arna. American Negro Poetry, 83

Book for Brides. Greer, R., 30

Book of Changes. I. Ching, 8

Book of Common Prayer, 12

Book of Festivals. Spicer, D., 30

Book of Good Grooming for Men. Esquire, eds., 30

Book of Health. Clark, R., 49

Book of Interior Design. Pahlman, W., 69

Book of Mormon, 13

Book of Negro Folklore. Hughes, L., 31

Book of Religious Holidays and Celebrations. Ickis, M., 30

Books and the Teenage Reader. Carlsen, R., 4

Books, Children and Men. Hazard, P., 4

Books in Print, 1

Boorstin, Daniel. Americans: The Colonial Experience, 120

———. Americans: The Democratic Experience, 120

———. Americans: The National Experience, 120

Borek, Ernest. Code of Life, 41

Borgeson, Lillian. Skin and Scuba Diver, 77

Born Black. Parks, G., 19

Born Female, Bird, C., 17

Born Free. Adamson, J., 45

Boss. Royko, M., 100

Boston Children's Medical Center. Pregnancy, Birth and the Newborn Baby, 51

Boston Women's Health Book Collective. Our Bodies, Ourselves, 17

Botany. Alexander, T., 42

Botany. Muller, W., 43

Botany. Sinnott, E., 43

Botany. Wilson, C., 43
Boulay, Roger. Make Your Own Elegant
  Jewelry, 68
Boundaries of the Soul. Singer, J., 7
Bouquet, Alan C. Everyday Life in New
  Testament Times, 109
Bourke-White, Margaret. Portrait of Myself,
  98
Bourne, Geoffrey H. Ape People, 46
Boutell's Heraldry. Brooke-Little, J., 108
Bova, Ben. Fourth State of Matter, 38
Bowen, Angela J. Diabetic Gourmet, 58
Bowen, Catherine. Francis Bacon, 97
_____. John Adams and the American
  Revolution, 97
_____. Miracle at Philadelphia, 25
Bowers, Claude G. Jefferson and Hamilton,
  122
Bowers, Melvyn K. Easy Bulletin Boards, 68
Bowersock, Glen W. Augustus and the
  Greek World, 110
Bowie, Walter R. Story of the Church, 13
Bowling. Burton, N., 76
Bowman, Henry D. Marriage for Moderns, 18
Bownas, Geoffrey. Penguin Book of Japanese
  Verse, 91
Bowra, Cecil M. Greek Experience, 110
Bowra, Maurice. Classical Greece, 110
Bowring, Jean. New Cake Decorating Book,
  58
Boyd, Malcolm. Are Your Running with Me,
  Jesus?, 12
_____. Human Like Me, Jesus, 12
Boyd, Waldo T. World of Cyrogenics, 52
Boyer, Carl T. History of Mathematics, 36
Boylan, Brian R. New Heart, 49
_____. Legal Rights of Women, 24
Boynton, Lewis D. 20th Century Bookkeep-
  ing and Accounting, 60
Boys and Sex. Pemeroy, W., 48
Bracken, Peg. But I Wouldn't Have Missed
  It for the World, 94
Bradley, Andrew C. Shakespearean Tragedy,
  87
Bradley, David. Lion among Roses, 115
Bradley, Harold W. United States 1492-1877,
  120
Bradley, Van Allen. New Gold in Your Attic,
  3
Brady, George S. Materials Handbook, 51
Braithwaite, Edward. To Sir with Love, 98
Brams, William A. Managing Your Coronary,
  49

Brandon, S. G. Dictionary of Comparative
  Religion, 13
Brasch, R. Judaic Heritage, 14
Brasch, Rudolph. How Did Sports Begin?, 76
Brauer, Earle W. Your Skin and Hair, 59
Brazil. Bishop, E., 125
Breach, R. W. Documents and Descriptions
  in European History, 110
Break-Up: The Core of Modern Art. Kuh, K.,
  64
Breaking into Print. Weeks, E., 80
Breath of Life. Carr, D., 53
Brebner, J. B. Canada, 119
Brecher, Edward M. Licit and Illicit Drugs, 49
Brecht, Bertolt. Seven Plays, 88
Bree, Germaine. Camus, 89
Brenan, Gerald. Literature of the Spanish
  People, 90
_____. Spanish Labyrinth, 115
Brennan, Joseph. Meaning of Philosophy, 5
Bressard, M. J. Creating with Burlap, 68
Bret Harte. O'Connor, R., 102
Bride's Book of Etiquette. Bride's Magazine,
  eds., 30
Bride's Magazine, eds. Bride's Book of
  Etiquette, 30
Bridge at Andau. Michener, J., 112
Bridge for Passing. Buck, P., 98
Bridges, Canals, and Tunnels. Jacobs, D., 29
Briggs, Asa. Victorian People, 113
Briggs, Jean L. Never in Anger: Portrait of an
  Eskimo Family, 119
Brill, Mordecai L. Write Your Own Wedding,
  30
Brimer, John B. Homeowner's Complete
  Outdoor Building Book, 62
Bring Me a Unicorn. Lindbergh, A., 104
Brinnin, John M. Modern Poets, 80
Brinton, Crane. Decade of Revolution, 114
_____. Ideas and Men, 93
Britain between the Wars: 1918-1940.
  Mowat, C., 113
British Drama, Nicoll, A., 87
British Empiricists: Locke, Berkeley, Hume.
  Collins, J., 8
British Literature. Spencer, H., 86
Broadribb, Violet. Modern Parent's Guide
  to Baby and Child Care, 60
Brockman, C. Frank. Trees of North America,
  42
Brockway, Wallace. Men of Music, 95
Brodie, Fawn M., Thomas Jefferson, 103
Broehl, Wayne G. Molly Maguires, 23

Brogan, Denis W. American Character, 120
_____. French Nation from Napoleon to
Petain, 114
Brooke-Little, J. P. Boutell's Heraldry, 108
Brookes, Vincent J. Poisons, 49
Brooks, Cleanth. Fundamentals of Good
Writing, 80
_____. Understanding Fiction, 81
_____. Understanding Poetry, 80
Brooks, Leonard. Painter's Workshop, 70
Brooks, Maurice. Appalachians, 39
Brooks, Stewart M. V. D. Story, 49
_____. Integrated Basic Science, 35
Brooks, Thomas R. Toil and Trouble, 23
Brothers and Sisters All Over This Land.
Lawson, D., 24
Brothers Esposito. Esposito, P., 101
Brothers, Joyce. Brothers' System for
Liberated Love and Marriage, 18
Brothers' System for Liberated Love and
Marriage. Brothers, J. 18
Brotherton, Manfred. Masers and Lasers, 52
Brower, David. Only a Little Planet, 25
Brown, Claude. Manchild in the Promised
Land, 98
Brown, Dee. Bury My Heart at Wounded
Knee, 119
Brown, Les. Television, 29
Brown, Leslie. Life of the African Plains, 43
Brown, Lloyd A. Map Making, 38
Brown, Ronald. Lasers, 52
_____. Telecommunications: Booming
Technology, 52
Brown, Sam. Cooking Creatively with
Natural Foods, 58
Brown, W. Norman. India, Pakistan, and
Ceylon, 117
Brown, Wenzell. How to Tell Fortunes with
Cards, 5
Browning, Elizabeth B. Complete Poetical
Works, 86
Browning, Elizabeth L. With Love and Elbow
Grease, 70
Browning, Robert. Poems and Plays, 86
Brumfel, Charles F. Principles of Arithmetic,
36
Brundage, Burr C. Lords of Cuzco, 125
Bruner, Jerome S. Process of Education, 28
Bruner, Wally. Wally's Workshop, 62
Brustein, Robert S. Theatre of Revolt, 81
Brutal Friendship. Deakin, F., 114
Bruun, Geoffrey. Enlightened Despots, 111
Bryant, Flora F. It's Your Wedding, 30

Bryant, William C. Poetical Works, 83
Brye, Joseph C. Basic Principles of Music
Theory, 72
Bryer, Jackson R. Sixteen Modern American
Authors, 82
Buban, Peter. Understanding Electricity and
Electronics, 52
Buber, Martin. I and Thou, 14
Buchan, John. Augustus, 97
Buchannan, A. Russell. United States and
World War II, 124
Bucher, Jo. Complete Guide to Embroidery
Stitches and Crewel, 68
Buchman, Herman. Stage Makeup, 74
Buchsbaum, Ralph. Animals without
Backbones, 43
Buchsbaum, Walter H. Color TV Servicing, 52
Buck, Paul H. Road to Reunion, 123
Buck, Pearl S. Bridge for Passing, 98
_____. My Several Worlds, 98
_____. People of Japan, 117
Buckley, Joseph C. Retirement Handbook, 19
Buddha, Guatama. Teachings of the Compas-
sionate Buddha, 14
Buddhism, the Light of Asia. Ch'en, K., 14
Budker, Paul. Life of Sharks, 44
Builders Encyclopedia. Audel & Co., 62
Builders of the Bay Colony. Morison, S., 121
Building and Flying Model Airplanes.
Musciano, W., 54
Building and Flying Scale Model Aircraft.
Musciano, W., 54
Building Blocks of Life. Vishniac, R., 41
Building Construction Handbook. Merritt, F.,
63
Building Your Own Home. Hasenau, J., 63
Bulfinch, Thomas. Bulfinch's Mythology, 14
Bulfinch's Mythology. Bulfinch, T., 14
Bull of Minos. Cottrell, L., 109
Bullock, Alan. Hitler: A Study in Tyranny,
102
Bulman, A. D. Model Making for Physicists, 38
Burach, A. S. Writer's Handbook, 80
Burckhardt, Jacob. Civilization of the
Renaissance in Italy, 110
Burdett, Winston. Encounter with the
Middle East, 117
Buried Alive. Friedman, M., 103
Burke, Carl F. God Is for Real, Man, 10
Burke, Edmund. Reflections on the
Revolution in France, 114
Burland, Cottie A. Beyond Science, 5
Burlingame, Roger. Henry Ford, 101

Burnham, Robert W. Color, 38
Burns, James. Roosevelt, 106
Burns, James M. Government by the
  People: National, State and Local
  Edition, 26
Burns, Robert. Complete Poetical Works, 86
Burrill, Bob. Who's Who in Boxing, 76
Burrows, Millar. Dead Sea Scrolls, 10
―――. More Light on the Dead Sea Scrolls,
  10
Burt, William H. Field Guide to the
  Mammals, 46
Burton, Nelson. Bowling, 76
Burton, Philip W. Advertising Fundamentals,
  60
Bury, John B. History of Greece, 110
Bury My Heart at Wounded Knee. Brown,
  D., 119
Busch. Horizon Concise History of Japan,
  117
Busch, Noel F. Thailand, 118
Business, Legal and Ethical Phases of
  Engineering. Canfield, D., 51
Business Management Handbook. Lasser, J.,
  61
But I Wouldn't Have Missed It for the
  World. Bracken, P., 94
Butler, Anne. Embroidery Stitches, 68
Butler, David F. New Archery, 78
Butler, Ewan. Horizon Concise History of
  Scandinavia, 115
Butterfield, Roger. American Past, 120
Button, Alan D. Authentic Child, 7
Buying and Renovating a House in the
  City. Stanforth, D., 63
Byrd, E. How Things Work, 47
Byrd, Richard E. Alone, 98
Byron. Maurois, A., 98
Byron, Robert. Byzantine Achievement, 116
Byzantine Achievement. Byron, R., 116
Byzantine Civilization. Runciman, S., 116
Byzantium: Greatness and Decline. Diehl, C.,
  116

Cab at the Door. Pritchett, V., 106
Cabeen, Richard M. Standard Handbook of
  Stamp Collecting, 75
Cacti and Succulents. Haage, W., 65
Cady, John F. Southeast Asia, 118
Cahill, Kevin M. Medical Advice for the
  Traveler, 48
Caidin, Martin. Destination Mars, 56
Cain, Arthur H. Young People and
  Religion, 12

Calder, Nigel. Restless Earth, 39
―――. Unless Peace Comes, 25
Calder, Ritchie. Evolution of the Machine,
  51
Caldwallader, Sharon. Whole Earth Cook
  Book, 58
Caldwell, Gaylon L. American Government
  Today, 26
Caligula and Three Other Plays. Camus, A.,
  89
Callahan, Daniel. Abortion: Law, Choice
  and Morality, 8
Callahan, Parnell. Your Complete Guide to
  Estate Planning, 25
Callahan, Sidney C. Working Mother, 18
Cambridge History of American Literature,
  82
Camera and Lens. Adams, A., 71
Cameron, Gail. Rose, 103
Cameron, Roderick. Austrialia, 125
―――. New Zealand, 125
Campbell, Don G. Handbook of Real Estate
  Investment, 24
Campbell, Hugh G. Introduction to
  Matrices, Vectors and Linear Programming,
  36
Campbell, Oscar J. Reader's Encyclopedia
  of Shakespeare, 87
Camper's Bible. Riviere, W., 77
Camus, Albert. Caligula and Three Other
  Plays, 89
―――. Myth of Sisyphus and Other Essays, 89
―――. Rebel, 8
―――. Resistance, Rebellion and Death, 89
Camus. Bree, G., 89
Canada. Brebner, J., 119
Canada. Moore, B., 120
Canada in Colour. Clery, V., 95
Canada's First Century, Creighton, D., 120
Canady, John E. Keys to Art, 64
Canby, Henry S. Classic Americans, 82, 95
Candlemaking. Carey, M., 68
Canfield, D. T. Business, Legal, and Ethical
  Phases of Engineering, 51
Canterbury Tales. Chaucer, G., 86
Capital Punishment. McCafferty, J., 25
Capital Punishment. Sellin, T., 26
Capital Punishment, U.S.A. Horwitz, E., 25
Capone. Kobler, J., 99
Capote, Truman. In Cold Blood, 27
Capps, Benjamin. Indians, 119
Captain John Smith. Smith, B., 107
Car Owner's Handbook. Stapley, R., 55
Caravan. Coon, C., 117

Care and Breeding of Laboratory Animals. Farris, E., 41

Care and Feeding of Your Diabetic Child. Vanderpoel, Sally, 60

Careless Atom. Novick, S., 52

Carey, Mary. Candlemaking, 68

Caring for Your Cat. Thatcher, W., 58

Carl Rogers on Encounter Groups. Rogers, C., 7

Carlsen Robert G. Books and the Teenage Reader, 4

Carlson, Bernice W. Party Book for Boys and Girls, 75

Carlson, Elof A. Modern Biology, 41

Carlyle, Thomas. Selected Works, 88

Carnegie, Dale. Quick and Easy Way to Effective Speaking, 82

Carpenter, Philip L. Microbiology, 42

Carr, Archie. Handbook of Turtles, 44

Carr, Donald E. Breath of Life, 53

——. Death of the Sweet Waters, 54

Carr, Edward H. Twenty Years' Crisis, 124

——. What is History?, 93

Carr, John. Life of Sir Arthur Conan Doyle, 100

Carr, Raymond. Spain 1808-1939, 115

Carrell, Al. Super Handyman's Encyclopedia of Home Repairs Hints, 62

Carroll, John M. Story of the Laser, 52

Carruth, Gorton V. Encyclopedia of American Facts and Dates, 120

Carruth, Hayden. The Voice that is Great within Us, 83

Carson, Rachel. Edge of the Sea, 54

——. Sea Around Us, 54

——. Silent Spring, 54

Carter, Samuel. Blaze of Glory: Fight for New Orleans, 122

Cary, Joyce. Case for African Freedom, 118

Case for African Freedom, Cary, J., 118

Case for the Working Mother. Cotton, D., 18

Case of the Midwife Toad. Koestler, A., 42

Caso, Alfonso. Aztecs, People of the Sun, 120

Cass, James. Comparative Guide to American Colleges, 28

Cassels, Louis. Reality of God, 11

Cassell's New Compact French Dictionary, 33

Cassell's New Compact German Dictionary, 33

Cassell's New Compact Latin Dictionary, 34

Cassell's New Compact Spanish Dictionary, 34

Casserole Cook Book. Better Homes & Gardens, eds., 58

Casson, Lionel. Ancient Egypt, 109

Caste and Class in a Southern Town. Dollard, J., 17

Castellini, John. Rudiments of Music, 72

Castro's Revolution. Draper, T., 120

Catalogue of the World's Most Popular Coins. Reinfeld, F., 75

Catherine of Aragon. Mattingly, G., 99

Catherine the Great. Oldenbourg, Z., 99

Cattell, Psyche. Raising Children with Love and Limits, 60

Catton, Bruce. Civil War, 123

——. Never Call Retreat, 123

——. Stillness at Appomatox, 123

——. U.S. Grant and the American Military Tradition, 101

Causes of the Civil War. Stampp, K., 123

Cavalcade of the American Novel. Wagenknecht, E., 84

Cavalcade of the English Novel. Wagenknecht, E., 88

Cazamian, Louis F. History of French Literature, 89

Cell. Swanson, C., 42

Cellini, Benvenuto. Life of Benvenuto Cellini, 99

Censorship. Ernst, M., 20

Censorship in the United States. McClellan, G., 20

Central America. Lavine, H., 120

Central American Republics. Parker, F., 120

Central Concepts of Biology. Baer, A., 41

Century of Sports. Associated Press, 76

Century of Struggle. Flexner, E., 17

Century Readings in the English Essay. Wann, L., 88

Ceram, C. W. First American, 119

——. Gods, Graves, and Scholars, 94

——. Secret of the Hittites, 109

Ceramic Glazes. Harman & Parmelee, 67

Ceramics. Nelson, G., 67

Ceramics. Sunset Magazine, 67

Ceramics and How to Decorate Them. Priolo, J., 67

Cerebral Palsy. Cruikshank, W., 49

Cerf, Bennett A. 24 Favorite One-Act Plays, 81

Cervantes Saavedra, Miguel De. Portable Cervantes, 90

Chai, Ch'U. Treasury of Chinese Literature, 91

Challenge of Climate. Silverberg, R., 40

Chalmers, David M. Hooded Americanism, 22

Chamberlain, Betty. Artist's Guide to His Market, 64

Chamberlain, John. Enterprising Americans, 22

Chambers, Edmund K. Short Life of Shakespeare, 87

Chambers, Frank P. This Age of Conflict, 93

Chambers, Whittaker. Witness, 26

Chambers, William N. Democratic Party in American Politics, 22

Chandler, Lester V. America's Greatest Depression, 22

Chandler, Richard E. New History of Spanish Literature, 90

Chaney, Margaret S. Nutrition, 48

Changing Years: Menopause without Fear. Gray, M., 48

Chapel, Charles E. Complete Book of Gun Collecting, 53

——. Complete Guide to Gunsmithing, Gun Care, and Repair, 53

——. Gun Collector's Handbook of Values, 53

Chaplin, Charles. My Autobiography, 99

Chapman, Charles F. Piloting, Seamanship and Small Boat Handling, 53

Chapman, Colin. August 21: The Rape of Czechoslovakia, 116

Characters of Shakespeare's Plays. Hazlitt, W., 87

Chariots of the Gods: Unsolved Mysteries of the Past. Von Daniken, E., 41

Charlemagne. Lamb, H., 99, 114

Charles, Anton, J. Machinery of the Body, 47

Charles Dickens. Johnson, E., 100

Charriere, Henri. Banco, 27

——. Papillon, 27

Chase, Gilbert. America's Music, 72

Chase, Mary E. Bible and the Common Reader, 10

——. Psalms for the Common Reader, 10

Chase, Stuart. Guides to Straight Thinking, 8

——. Power of Words, 32

——. Proper Study of Mankind, 16

Chaucer, Geoffrey. Canterbury Tales, 86

——. Modern Reader's Chaucer, 86

——. Portable Chaucer, 86

Cheaper by the Dozen. Gilbreth, F., 101

Chedd, Graham. New Biology, 41

Ch'en, Kenneth K. Buddhism, the Light of Asia, 14

Chekov, Anton. Portable Chekov, 92

Chemical Calculations. Benson, S., 38

Chemical Principles. Masterson, W., 38

Chemistry. Mortimer, C., 38

Chemistry. Sienko, M., 39

Chemistry for the Million. Smith, R., 39

Chemistry of Life. Patton, A., 41

Cheney, Frances N. Fundamental Reference Sources, 3

Cheney, Sheldon. Sculpture of the World, 67

Cheng, Peter. Chronology of the People's Republic of China from October 1, 1949, 116

Cherepov, George. Discovering Oil Painting, 70

Chernik, Vladimir P. Consumer's Guide to Insurance Buying, 28

Chess for Young People. Reinfeld, F., 75

Chess in a Nutshell. Reinfeld, F., 76

Chester, Laura. Rising Tides; 20th Century American Women Poets, 83

Chester, Lewis. American Melodrama: Presidential Campaign of 1968, 22

Cheyney, Edward P. Dawn of a New Era, 110

Chicano Manifest. Rendon, A., 19

Chicanos. Meier, M., 19

Chidsey, Donald. Great Conspiracy, 98

——. Wars in Barbary, 122

——. War with Mexico, 123

Chief Contemporary Dramatists. Dickinson, T., 81

Chief Executive. Koenig, L., 27

Chief Plays of Corneille. Corneille, P., 89

Chief Pre-Shakespearean Drama. Adams, J., 87

Chief Works. Spinoza, B., 9

Child, Francis J. English and Scottish Popular Ballads, 86

Child, Julia. Mastering the Art of French Cooking, 58

Child Growth and Development. Hurlock, E., 60

Child Study Assn. of America. What to Tell Your Children about Sex, 47

Child Under Six. Humes, J., Jr., 60

Childbirth without Fear. Dick-Read, G., 51

Childe, V. Gordon. Dawn of European Civilization, 110

Children and Dance and Music. Maynards, O., 75

Children and Parents. Sheen, F., 19

Children of Sanchez. Lewis, O., 19

Children of the Dream. Bettelheim, B., 17

Children of the Uprooted. Handlin, O., 21

Children's Reading in the Home. Arbuthnot, M., 4

Children's Rooms and Play Yards. Sunset Magazine, eds., 70
Child's Mind. Beadle, M., 7
Chilton's Auto Repair Manual, 54
Chilton's Import Car Repair Manual, 54
Chilton's Motorcycle Carburetion Systems. Ritch O., 55
Chilton's Motorcycle Electrical Systems. Ritch, O., 55
Chilton's Motorcycle Repair Manual, 54
Chilton's Repair and Tune-Up Guide for Snowmobiles, 54
Chilton's Repair and Tune-up Guide for the Volkswagen, 54
Chilton's Truck Manual, 55
Chinese. Latourette, K., 117
Chinese Art of Healing. Palos, S., 50
Chinese Language for Beginners. Cooper, L., 34
Chinese Looking Glass. Bloodworth, D., 116
Chinese Thought from Confucious to Mao Tse-Tung. Creel, H., 8
Ching, I. Book of Changes, 8
Chipp, Herschel B. Theories of Modern Art, 64
Chisholm, Shirley. Unbought and Unbossed, 99
Choate, Sharr. Creative Casting, 68
Choice of Weapons. Parks, G., 105
Choral Music of the Church. Wienandt, E., 73
Christ and the Fine Arts. Maus, C., 11
Christensen, Clyde M. Molds and Man, 42
Christian Agnostic. Weatherhead, L., 11
Christian Freedom in a Permissive Society. Robinson, J., 12
Christian Way of Death. Hunt, G., 12
Christmas Customs around the World. Wernecke, H., 30
Christopher, Milbourne. ESP, Seers and Psychics, 5
Chronology of the People's Republic of China from October 1, 1949. Cheng, P., 116
Chuks-Orji, Ogonna. Names from Africa: Their Origin, Meaning, and Pronunciation, 34
Chung, Kyung C. Korea: The Third Republic, 117
Church in the Next Decade. Blake, E., 12
Churchill, Roosevelt, Stalin. Feis, H., 112
Churchill, Winston. History of the English Speaking People, 113

_____. Second World War, 112
Chute, Marchette. Geoffrey Chaucer of England, 99
_____. Introduction to Shakespeare, 87
_____. Shakespeare of London, 87
_____. Stories from Shakespeare, 87
Ciardi, John. How Does a Poem Mean?, 80
_____. Mid-Century American Poetry, 83
Cicero, Marcus T. Basic Works, 90
Citadel: Story of the U.S. Senate. White, W., 27
Citizen Hearst. Swanberg, W., 102
City in Crisis. Isenberg, I., 20
City in History. Mumford, L., 21
City of God. Augustine, Saint, 11
Civil Disobedience. Cohen, C., 20
Civil Rights. McClellan, G., 20
Civil Service Arithmetic and Vocabulary. Arco Publ. Co., 26
Civil War. Catton, B., 123
Civil War. National Geographic Soc., 123
Civil War and Reconstruction. Randall, J., 123
Civil War Dictionary. Boatner, M., 123
Civilisation. Clark, K., 110
Civilization of the Renaissance in Italy. Burckhardt, J., 110
Claiborne, Craig. New York Times International Cook Book, 58
Clapesattle, Helen B. Doctors Mayo, 104
Clapper, Edna N. Pack-O-Fun Treasury of Crafts, Gifts, and Toys, 68
Clare, Patricia. Struggle for the Great Barrier Reef, 39
Clarence Darrow for the Defense. Stone, I., 100
Clark, Barrett H. World Drama, 81
Clark, Elmer T. Small Sects in America, 13
Clark, Kenneth. Civilisation, 110
_____. Dark Ghetto, 19
Clark, Ramsey. Crime in America, 25
Clark, Randolph L. Book of Health, 49
Clark, Sir George N. English History: a Survey, 113
Clark, Sydney A. All the Best in . . . . (for Europe, the Mediterraneum, etc.), 94
Clark, Thomas D. Frontier America, 122
Clarke, Arthur C. Man and Space, 56
_____. Promise of Space, 56
Classic American Philosophers. Fisch, M., 8
Classic Americans. Canby, H., 82, 95
Classic Guitar Instruction. Sloane, I., 74

Classic Theatre. Bentley, E., 81

Classic Theater, Vol. 1: Six Italian Plays. Bentley, E., 90

Classic Theater, Vol. 2: Five German Plays. Bentley, E., 88

Classic Theater, Vol. 3: Six Spanish Plays. Bentley, E., 90

Classic Theater, Vol. 4, Six French Plays. Bentley, E., 89

Classical Greece. Bowra, M., 110

Classical Tradition. Highet, G., 79

Classics and Commercials. Wilson, E., 79

Clay, Cassuis *see* Muhammed Ali

Clear, Val. Common Cagebirds in America, 57

Cleary, Malachy. Woman's Guide to Fixing the Car, 55

Cleaver, Eldridge. Soul on Ice, 99

Clerical Office Typing. Lessenberry, D., 61

Clery, Val. Canada in Colour, 95

Clissold, Stephen. Short History of Yugoslavia, 116

Closing Circle. Commoner, B., 16

Club Handybook. Stern, R., 28

Clubb, Oliver E. 20th Century China, 116

Clurman, Harold. Seven Plays of the Modern Theatre, 81

Coach. Dowling, T., 104

Coats, Peter. Great Gardens of the Western World, 65

Cobb, Boughton. Field Guide to the Ferns, 42

Cochran, Willard W. World Food Problem, 24

Code of Life. Borek, E., 41

Coh, Nik. Rock, from the Beginning, 73

Cohen, Arthur A. Communism of Mao Tse Tung, 116

Cohen, Carl. Civil Disobedience, 20

——. Communism, Fascism and Democracy, 20

Cohen, Daniel. Age of Giant Mammals, 40

——. ESP, 5

Cohen, Robert. Color of Man, 40

Cohen, Ruby. Twentieth Century Drama, 87

Cohen, Sanford. Labor in the United States, 23

Cohen, Sidney. Drug Dilemma, 49

Coil of Life. Moore, R., 41

Coit, Margaret. Fight for Union, 122

Cokesbury Game Book. Depew, A., 75

Cokesbury Marriage Manual. Leach, W., 30

Cokesbury Party Book. Depew, A., 75

Colbert, Edwin H. Dinosaurs, 40

——. Evolution of the Vertebrates, 41

Colby, Carroll B. Today's Camping, 76

Colby, Edward E. Everything You Always Wanted to Know about the Law, but Couldn't Afford to Ask, 25

Cold against Disease. Kavaler, L., 50

Cold War. Barker, E., 20

Cole, Ann K. Golden Guide to American Antiques, 70

Cole, Larry. Our Children's Keepers, 18

Cole Porter Song Book. Porter, C., 74

Coleman, James A. Relativity for the Layman, 38

Coleridge, Samuel. Portable Coleridge, 86

Coles, Harry L. War of 1812, 122

Coles, Robert. Still Hungry in America, 24

Collapse of the Third Republic. Shirer, W., 114

Collected Essays. Huxley, A., 88

Collected Plays. Hellman, L., 84

Collected Plays. Miller, A., 84

Collected Poems. Cummings, E., 83

Collected Poems. Houseman, A., 86

Collected Poems. Service, R., 83

Collected Poems. Thomas, D., 86

Collecting Tomorrow's Antiques Today, Flayderman, N., 70

Collector's Encyclopedia of Antiques. Phillips, P., 70

Collector's Encyclopedia of Rocks and Minerals. Deeson, A., 39

College Chemistry. Pauling, L., 39

Collier, James L. Practical Music Theory, 72

Collier, John. American Indian Ceremonial Dances, 30

Collins, A. Fredrick. Radio Amateur's Handbook, 52

Collins, James D. British Empiricists: Locke, Berkeley, Hume, 8

Collins, Larry. Is Paris Burning?, 114

——. O Jerusalem!, 117

Collins, Thomas. Complete Guide to Retirement, 19

Colombia Today and Tomorrow. Holt, P., 125

Colonial America. Keller, A., 121

Colonial Living. Tunis, E., 121

Colonial Wars. Peckham, H., 121

Color. Burnham, R., 38

Color: a Complete Guide for Artists. Fabri, R., 71

Color Guide to Tropical Fish. Axelrod, H., 44

Color in Oil Painting. DiValentin, M., 70

Color in Your Garden. Sunset Magazine, eds., 66

Color of Man. Cohen, R., 40
Color TV Servicing. Buchsbaum, W., 52
Colorful Mineral Identifier. Tennissen, A., 40
Colour of Canada. MacLennan, H., 95
Colton, Joel G. Twentieth Century, 93
Columbia History of the World. Garraty, J., 93
Comedies. Molière, J., 89
Comfortable Pew. Berton, P., 12
Coming Age of Solar Energy. Halacy, D., Jr., 52
Coming of Age in Samoa. Mead, M., 41
Coming of the Civil War. Craven, A., 123
Coming of the Revolution. Gipson, L., 122
Coming Water Famine. Wright, J., 54
Comins, Jeremy. Getting Started in African Crafts, 68
Commager, Henry S. American Mind, 124
——. Blue and the Gray, 123
——. Documents of American History, 120
Committee: the Extraordinary Career of the House Committee on Un-American Activities. Goodman, W., 26
Common Cagebirds in America. Clear, V., 57
Common Sense and Other Political Writings. Paine, T., 22
Common Sense in Child Rearing. Wright, E., 60
Commoner, Barry. Science and Survival, 35
——. Closing Circle, 16
Commonsense Grammar and Style. Morsberger, R., 33
Commonwealth vs. Sacco and Vanzetti. Weeks, R., 26
Communications in Space. Dunlap, O., 29
Communism, Fascism and Democracy. Cohen, C., 20
Communism of Mao Tse Tung. Cohen, A., 116
Communist Manifesto. Marx, K., 24
Community Activist's Handbook. Huenefeld, J., 17
Community Groups and You. Swift, H., 16
Compact History of the Civil War. Dupuy, R., 123
Compact History of the Revolutionary War. Dupuy, R., 122
Comparative Guide to American Colleges. Cass, J., 28
Comparative Vertebrate Anatomy. Hyman, L., 43
Complete Allergy Guide. Rapaport, H., 50
Complete Aquarium. Vogt, D., 45

Complete Art of Printing and Enlarging. Croy, D., 72
Complete Beginner's Guide to Water Skiing. Tyll, A., 78
Complete Bicycle Book-Buyer's Guide, 56
Complete Book of Boating. Zadig, E., 78
Complete Book of Cat Care. Whitney, L., 58
Complete Book of Decoupage. Wing, F., 69
Complete Book of Dog Training and Care. McCoy, J., 57
Complete Book of Drawing and Painting. Laidman, H., 71
Complete Book of Engagement and Wedding Etiquette. Wilson, B., 30
Complete Book of Entertaining. Lee, N., 58
Complete Book of Groundcovers. Atkinson, R., 65
Complete Book of Gun Collecting. Chapel, C., 53
Complete Book of Helicopters. Ahnstrom, D., 54
Complete Book of Home Freezing. Meyer, H., 59
Complete Book of Home Improvement. Huff, D., 63
Complete Book of Home Remodeling, Improvement, and Repair. Watkins, A., 63
Complete Book of Home Repairs and Maintenance. Hand, J., 63
Complete Book of Houseplants. Fitch, C., 65
Complete Book of Hunting. Ormond, C., 78
Complete Book of Judo. Tegner, B., 77
Complete Book of Karate. Tegner, B., 77
Complete Book of Karting. Day, D., 55
Complete Book of Mobil Home Living. Engel, L., 58
Complete Book of Model Railroading. Hertz, L., 29
Complete Book of Motor Camping. Engel, L., 76
Complete Book of Progressive Knitting. Duncan, I., 68
Complete Book of Trailering. Engel, L., 76
Complete Book of Water Sports. Liebers, A., 78
Complete Book of Winter Sports. Liebers, A., 76
Complete Cat Encyclopedia. Pond, G., 57
Complete Chessplayer. Reinfeld, F., 76
Complete Dog Book. American Kennel Club, 57
Complete Encyclopedia of Antiques. Connoisseur, 70

Complete Encyclopedia of Motor Cars: 1885–1968. Georgano, G., 55

Complete Essays. Montaigne, M. de, 89

Complete Essays. Twain, M., 85

Complete Greek Drama. Oates, W., 91

Complete Guide to Beekeeping. Morse, R., 57

Complete Guide to Canoeing and Canoe-Camping. Malo, J., 78

Complete Guide to Cross Country Skiing and Touring. Tokle, A., 77

Complete Guide to Embroidery Stitches and Crewel. Bucher, J., 68

Complete Guide to Everyday Law. Kling, S., 25

Complete Guide to Fishing. Evanoff, V., 78

Complete Guide to Gunsmithing, Gun Care, and Repair. Chapel, C., 53

Complete Guide to House Boating. Malo, J., 78

Complete Guide to Interior Decoration. House & Garden, 69

Complete Guide to Retirement. Collins, T., 19

Complete Guide to the Tarot. Gray, E., 5

Complete Guide to Watercolor Painting. Whitney, E., 71

Complete Home Medical Encyclopedia. Hyman, H., 50

Complete Homeowner. Schwartz, R., 63

Complete Humorous Sketches and Tales. Twain, M., 85

Complete Nonsense Book. Lear, E., 86

Complete Pelican Shakespeare, 87

Complete Photographer. Feininger, A., 72

Complete Poems. Dickinson, E., 83

Complete Poems and Plays. Eliot, T. S., 83

Complete Poetical Works. Browning, E., 86

Complete Poetical Works. Burns, R., 86

Complete Poetical Works. Longfellow, H., 83

Complete Poetical Works. Lowell, J., 83

Complete Poetical Works. Shelley, P., 86

Complete Poetry. Frost, R., 83

Complete Prophecies. Nostradamus, 6

Complete Shower Party Book. Gleeson, M., 75

Complete Stories and Poems. Poe, E., 85

Complete Walker. Fletcher, C., 76

Complete Woodworking Handbook. Adams, J., 62

Complete Works of Shakespeare. Shakespeare, W., 87

Comprehensive High School. Conant, J., 28

Compton, Joan. House Plants, 65

Computer and Music. Lincoln, H., 74

Computer Dictionary and Handbook. Sippl, C., 4

Computers. Davidson, C., 4

Computers: a Self-teaching Introduction. Farina, M., 4

Comrie, Leslie J. Barlow's Tables of Squares, Cubes, Square Roots, and Reciprocals, 36

Comstock, Helen. Concise Encyclopedia of American Antiques, 70

———. 100 Most Beautiful Rooms in America, 69

Conant, James B. Comprehensive High School, 28

Conant, Roger. Field Guide to Reptiles and Amphibians, 45

Conception, Birth and Contraception. Demarest, R., 51

Concert of Europe, Albrecht-Carrie, R., 111

Concise Cambridge History of English Literature. Sampson, G., 86

Concise Color Encyclopedia of Nature. Dempsey, M., 43

Concise Encyclopedia of American Antiques. Comstock, H., 70

Concise History of Costume and Fashion. Laver, J., 30

Concise History of England. Halliday, F., 113

Concise History of English Painting. Gaunt, W., 71

Concise History of Modern Sculpture. Read, H., 67

Concise History of Russian Art. Rice, T., 65

Concise History of Watercolors. Reynolds, G., 71

Confessions. Augustine, 97

Confessions. Rousseau, J., 106

Conford, Francis M. Before and After Socrates, 8

Congo, My Country. Lumumba, P., 118

Congress. Griffith, E., 26

Congress and the Legislative Process. Harris, J., 26

Congress and the Presidency. Polsby, N., 27

Congressional Committees. Morrow, W., 27

Connoisseur. Complete Encyclopedia of Antiques, 70

Connor, Seymour V. North America Divided: the Mexican War, 123

Conot, Robert E. Rivers of Blood, Years of Darkness, 20

Conquering Family. Costain, T., 113

Conquest, Robert. Great Terror: Stalin's Purge, 115

Conquest of Tuberculosis. Waksman, S., 50

Conrad, James. Portable Conrad, 88

Conrat, Raisie. Executive Order 9066, Interment of 110,000 Japanese Americans, 112

Consent of the Governed, and Other Deceits. Krock, A., 124

Conservatism in America. Rossiter, C., 20

Conspiracy Against Childhood. LeShan, E., 29

Constitution in Crisis Times. Murphy, P., 25

Construction and Maintenance for Farm and Home. Foss, E., 56

Consumer's Guide to Insurance Buying. Chernik, V., 28

Consuming Public. McClellan, G., 24

Contact Lenses. McDonald, L., 51

Contemporaries. Kazin, A., 82

Contemporary America. Wish, H., 125

Contemporary Europe. Huges, H., 112

Contenau, Georges. Everyday Life in Babylon and Assyria, 109

Continental Drift. Tarling, D., 40

Control of Pain. Prescott, F., 50

Conversational Brazilian-Portuguese. Cortina Method Language Series, 34

Conversational Chinese for Beginners. Swadesh, M., 34

Conversational Japanese. Cortina Method Language Series, 34

Coogan, Timothy P. I. R. A., 113

Cook, Bruce. Beat Generation, 16

Cook, Fred J. FBI Nobody Knows, 26

_____. Nightmare Decade, 124

Cooke, Alistair. America, 120

Cooke, Joanne. New Women, 17

Cooke, Nelson M. Basic Mathematics for Electronics, 36

Cooking Creatively with Natural Foods. Brown, S., 58

Cooking with Wholegrains. Orton, M., 59

Cooley, Hollis R. Introduction to Mathematics, 36

Coon. Carleton S. Caravan, 117

Cooper, Kenneth H. New Aerobics, 48

Cooper, Lane. Fifteen Greek Plays, 91

Cooper, Lee. Chinese Language for Beginners, 34

Cooper, M. J. What the Computer Can Do: a Guide for the Plain Man, 4

Copeland, Lewis. World's Greatest Speeches, 82

Copi, Irving M. Introduction to Logic, 8

Coplan, Kate. Poster Ideas and Bulletin Board Techniques, 68

Copley, Frank O. Latin Literature, 90

Corneille, Pierre. Chief Plays of Corneille, 89

Cornyn, William S. Beginning Russian, 34

Cortina Method Language Series. Conversational Brazilian-Portuguese, 34

_____. Conversational Japanese, 34

Corwin, Edward S. President: Office and Powers, 26

Cost Accounting and Financial Control System. Dearden, J., 60

Costain, Thomas B. Conquering Family, 113

Costain, Thomas B. Last Plantagenets, 113

_____. Three Edwards, 113

_____. White and the Gold, 119

Costume Through the Ages. Evans, M., 30

Costumes for Children. Snook, B., 30

Costuming. Theatre Student Series, 75

Cotter, Charles H. Physical Geography of the Oceans, 39

Cotton, Dorothy W. Case for the Working Mother, 18

Cottrell, Leonard. Bull of Minos, 109

_____. Life under the Pharaohs, 109

Cougar Doesn't Live Here Anymore. Milne, L., 46

Coulter, Merle C. Story of the Plant Kingdom, 42

Coulton, George G. Medieval Scene, 110

Country Beautiful, eds. Beauty of America in Great American Art, 70

Courant, Richard. What is Mathematics?, 36

Course of Europe Since Waterloo. Schmeller, K., 111

Course of German History. Taylor, A., 114

Cousteau, Jacques Y. Life and Death in a Coral Sea, 39

_____. Octopus and Squid, 44

_____. Shark, 44

_____. Silent World, 39

_____. Whale, 46

Cousy, Robert. Basketball, 76

Cowell, Frank R. Everyday Life in Ancient Rome, 109

Cowley, Malcolm. After the Genteel Tradition, 82

_____. Lesson of the Masters, 81

Cox, Harvey. The Secular City, 12

Coxeter, H. S. M. Introduction to Geometry, 36

Coy, Harold. Mexicans, 120

Craft of Intelligence. Dulles, A., 26

Crafts for Children. Sunset Magazine, eds., 69

Crafts for Fun and Profit. Van Zandt, E., 69

Crafts You Can Make. Sunset Magazine, eds., 69

Craig, Marjorie. 21-Day Shape-up Program for Men and Women, 48

Craig, William. Fall of Japan, 117

Crankshaw, Edward. Hapsburgs, 114

_____. Khrushchev, 103

Crash Go the Chariots; an Alternative to Chariots of the Gods. Wilson, C., 41

Craven, Avery. Coming of the Civil War, 123

_____. Reconstruction, 123

Crawford, William P. Mariner's Notebook: a Guide to Boating Fundamentals, 53

Creamer, Robert. Babe: Legend Comes to Life, 106

Creating Art from Anything. Meilach, D., 68

Creating with Beads. LaCroix, G., 68

Creating with Burlap. Bressard, M., 68

Creating with Paper. Johnson, P., 68

Creative Casting. Choate, S., 68

Creative Claywork. Isenstein, H., 67

Creative Decorating on a Budget. Better Homes & Gardens, eds., 69

Creative Film Making. Smallman, K., 72

Creative Table Settings. Better Homes & Gardens, eds., 58

Creative 35mm Techniques. Woolley, A., 72

Creative Wood Design. Rottger, E., 69

Creekmore, Hubert. Little Treasury of World Poetry, 80

Creel, Herrlee G. Chinese Thought from Confucious to Mao Tse-Tung, 8

Creighton, Donald G. Canada's First Century, 120

Cressey, George. Asia's Land and People, 116

Crime and its Prevention. Lewin, S., 27

Crime in America. Clark, R., 25

Crime of Punishment. Menninger, K., 28

Crisis in Black and White. Silberman, C., 20

Crisis in the Classroom. Silberman, C., 29

Crisis of Confidence. Schlesinger, A., 16

Crisis of Psychoanalysis. Fromm, E., 50

Crispin, Frederic S. Dictionary of Technical Terms, 47

Critic of the Old South. Mitchell, B., 105

Critical Approaches to Literature. Daiches, D., 79

Critical History of English Literature. Daiches, D., 85

Critical History of Old English Literature. Greenfield, S., 85

Critics Choice. Gaver, J., 84

Crocker, Betty. Betty Crocker's Cook Book, 58

Crockett, James U. Landscape Gardening, 65

Croft-Cooke, Rupert. Unrecorded Life of Oscar Wilde, 108

Cromwell. Fraser, A., 99

Cronin, Vincent. Flowering of the Renaissance, 111

Cronyn, George W. American Indian Poetry, 83

Cross, Wilbur. Guide to Unusual Vacations, 95

Cross and the Switchblade. Wilkerson, D., 12

Crouse, William H. Automotive Chassis and Body, 55

_____. Automotive Electric Equipment, 55

_____. Automotive Emission Control, 55

_____. Automotive Engines, 55

_____. Automotive Transmissions and Power Trains, 55

_____. Small Engines, 52

Crow, John A. Epic of Latin America, 125

Crowhurst, Norman H. Servicing Modern Hi-Fi-Stereo Systems, 52

Crown for Elizabeth. Luke, M., 113

Crowning Years. May, S., 19

Croy, D. R. Complete Art of Printing and Enlarging, 72

Crucial Decade. Goldman, E., 124

Cruden, Alexander. Cruden's Concordance, 10

Cruden's Concordance. Cruden, A., 10

Cruikshank, William M. Cerebral Palsy, 49

_____. Education of Exceptional Children and Youth, 28

Crusade Against Slavery. Filler, L., 122

Crusades. Treece, H., 111

Cruso, Thalassa. Making Things Grow Outdoors, 65

Crustaceans. Schmitt, W., 44

Crystals: Perfect and Imperfect. Bennett, A., 38

Crystals-Crystal Growing. Holden, A., 38

Cuba: the Pursuit of Freedom. Thomas, H., 120

Culpeper, Nicholas. Culpeper's Complete Herbal, 65

Culpeper's Complete Herbal. Culpeper, N., 65

Cultural Life of the American Colonies. Wright, L., 121

Cultural Life of the New Nation. Nye, R., 122

Culture and Commitment. Mead, M., 18

Cumming, William P. Discovery of North America, 121

Cummings, E. E. Collected Poems, 83

Cunliffe, Marcus. George Washington, 107
——. Nation Takes Shape, 122

Cunningham, Gladys. Singer Sewing Book, 60

Curme, George O. Grammar of the German Language, 33

Curry-Lindahl, Kai. Let Them Live, 46

Curtin, Sharon. Nobody Ever Died of Old Age, 19

Curtis, Edmund. History of Ireland, 113

Curtis, Helene. Biology, 41

Curves and Automation: the Scientist's Plot. Dilson, J., 35

Cushman, Robert E. Leading Constitutional Decisions, 25

Custer Died for Your Sins. Deloria, V., 119

Cuthbertson, Tom. Anybody's Bike Book, 56

Cybernetic Revolution. Rothman, M., 3

Cybernetics for the Modern Mind. Fuchs, W., 3

Cyrano de Bergerac. Rostand, E., 89

Cyrus the Great. Lamb, H., 100

Czechoslovakia since World War II. Szulc, T., 116

Czernin, Ferdinand. Versailles, 1919, 112

Dacey, Norman F. How to Avoid Probate, 23

Daiches, David. Critical Approaches to Literature, 79
——. Critical History of English Literature, 85
——. Novel and the Modern World, 81
——. Study of Literature for Readers and Critics, 79

Daily Life in Peru under the Last Incas. Baudin, L., 125

Daily Life in the Time of Homer. Mireaux, E., 110

Daily Life of the Etruscans. Huergon, J., 109

Daily Needs and Interests of Older People. Hoffman, A., 19

Dalzell, J. Ralph. Simplified Concrete Masonry Planning and Building, 63

Dana, Richard H. Two Years before the Mast, 94

Dance Awhile: Handbook of Folk, Square, and Social Dance. Harris, J., 75

Dangerfield, Stanley. International Encyclopedia of Dogs, 57

Daniels, Farrington. Direct Use of the Sun's Energy, 52

Daniels, George. How to Use Hand and Power Tools, 63
——. Science in American Society, 35

Daniels, Robert V. Nature of Communism, 24

Danowski, T. S. Diabetes as a Way of Life, 49

Dante Alighieri. Divine Comedy, 90
——. Portable Dante, 90

Dantzig, Tobias. Number, the Language of Science, 36

Dark Ghetto. Clark, K., 19

Darkening Land. Longgood, W., 17

Darwin, Charles. Origin of the Species; and Descent of Man, 42

Darwin, Marx, Wagner: Critique of a Heritage. Barzun, J., 111

Darwin and the Beagle. Moorehead, A., 100

Darwin's Century. Eiseley, L., 42

Das Kapital. Marx, K., 24

Dasmann, Raymond F. Environmental Conservation, 24

Davenport, Basil. Portable Roman Reader, 90

David, Jay. Black Soldier, 120
——. Growing up Black, 95
——. Living Black in White America, 95

Davidson, Basil. African Kingdoms, 118
——. African Past, 118
——. Black Mother, 118

Davidson, Charles H. Computers, 4

Davidson, Henry A. Handbook of Parliamentary Procedure, 21

Davidson, Marshall B. Horizon Concise History of France, 114

Davies, Herbert A. Outline History of the World, 93

Davies, Hunter. Beatles: Authorized Biography, 95

Davis, Adelle. Let's Eat Right to Keep Fit, 58

Davis, Burke. They Called Him Stonewall, 102
——. To Appomattox, 123

Davis, George E. Radiation and Life, 38

Davis, Henry P. New Dog Encyclopedia, 57

Davis, Kenneth S. Paradox of Poverty in America, 27

Davis, Philip J. 3.1414 and All That, 36

Davis, Sammy. Yes I Can, 100

Davis, William S. Life on a Medieval Barony, 110

Dawn of a New Era. Cheyney, E., 110

Dawn of European Civilization. Childe, V., 110

Dawn of Man. Megaw, V., 41

Dawn of Zoology. Ley, W., 43

Daws, Gavan. Shoal of Time, 126

Day, Dick. Complete Book of Karting, 55

———. How to Service and Repair Your Own Car, 55

Day, John A. Science of Weather, 39

Day, Richard. Electrical Repairs and Projects for the Handyman, 52

———. Remodeling Rooms, 63

Day Christ Died. Bishop, J., 11

Day Christ Was Born. Bishop, J., 11

Day Lincoln Was Shot. Bishop, J., 104

Day of Infamy. Lord, W., 112

Day of the Dinosaur. DeCamp, L., 40

Daybreak. Baez, J., 97

Dead Sea Scrolls. Burrows, M., 10

Deafness. Wright, D., 51

Deakin, Frederick W. Brutal Friendship, 114

Dearden, John. Cost Accounting and Financial Control System, 60

Death and Life of Great American Cities. Jacobs, J., 65

Death at an Early Age. Kozol, J., 29

Death Be Not Proud. Gunther, J., 101

Death Is a Noun. Langone, J., 8

Death of a President. Manchester, W., 103

Death of Bessie Smith. Albee, E., 83

Death of the Sweet Waters. Carr, D., 54

Death Penalty in America. Bedau, H., 25

De Bary, William T. Sources of Indian Tradition, 117

DeBeauvoir, Simone. Second Sex, 17

Decade of Revolution. Brinton, C., 114

DeCamp. L. S. Day of the Dinosaur, 40

———. Great Cities of the Ancient World, 94

DeChardin, Pierre T. Hymn of the Universe, 10

Declaration of Independence. Becker, C., 122

Decline and Fall of the Roman Empire. Gibbon, E., 109

Decline of the West. Spengler, O., 93

Decorating Ideas under $100. Better Homes & Gardens, eds., 69

Decorative Stitchery. Sunset Magazine, eds., 69

DeCoulanges, Fustel. Ancient City, 109

Decoupage. Nimocks, P., 69

DeCourcy, Peter. Silent Tragedy, 18

DeCrow, Karen. Young Woman's Guide to Liberation, 17

Dedek, John F. Human Life, 8

Deeson, A. F. L. Collector's Encyclopedia of Rocks and Minerals, 39

Defender of the Faith. Levine, L., 98

Defense Never Rests. Bailey, F., 97

Degler, Carl N. New Deal, 124

DeKruif, Paul. Men Against Death, 95

———. Microbe Hunters, 96

Deloria, Vine. Custer Died for Your Sins, 119

DeMadariaga, Salvador. Spain: A Modern History, 115

Demarest, Robert J. Conception, Birth and Contraception, 51

Dembeck, Hermann. Animals and Men, 43

De Meeus, Adrien. History of the Belgians, 116

DeMille, Agnes. To a Young Dancer, 74

Democracy and Education. Dewey, J., 28

Democracy at Gunpoint. Papandreou, A., 116

Democracy in America. De Tocqueville, A., 20, 122

Democratic Party in American Politics. Chambers, W., 22

Democratic Republic. Smelser, M., 122

Dempsey, Michael. Concise Color Encyclopedia of Nature, 43

Denatured Novel. Van Nostrand, A., 81

Denby, Edwin. Looking at the Dance, 74

Dendel, Esther W. Needleweaving: Easy as Embroidery, 68

Denis, Paul. Opportunities in Dancing, 74

Denmark. Anderson, R., 115

Dennis, Henry C. American Indian 1492–1970, 119

Depew, Arthur M. Cokesbury Game Book, 75

———. Cokesbury Party Book, 75

Depuy, Charles H. Introduction to Organic Chemistry, 38

Derry, T. K. Short History of Technology from the Earliest Times to A.D. 1900, 47

———. Making of Modern Britain, 113

Desalination: Water for the World's Future. Popkin, R., 54

Desautels, Paul E. Mineral Kingdom, 39

Desert Gardening. Sunset Magazine, eds., 66

Design for the Real World. Papanek, V., 69

Design of Cities. Bacon, E., 65

Designer Furniture Anyone Can Make. Schremp, W., 62

Designing and Making Mosaics. Timmons, V., 69

Designs for Fund Raising. Seymour, H., 28

DeSimone, Daniel V. Metric America: A Decision Whose Time Has Come, 29

Desperate Years. Horan, J., 124

Destination Mars. Caidin, M., 56

De Tocqueville, Alexis. Democracy in America, 20, 122

Deutsch, Babette. Poetry Handbook, 80

Deutsch, Morton. Theories in Social Psychology, 16

Deutsche, Issac. Prophet Armed, 107

———. Prophet Outcast, 107

———. Prophet Unarmed, 107

Deutscher, Issac, Unfinished Revolution, 115

Devil and John Foster Dulles. Hoopes, T., 100

Devotional Programs for Every Month. Ikerman, R., 12

DeVoto, Bernard. Year of Decision, 123

Dewey, John. Democracy and Education, 28

———. How We Think, 6

———. On Education, 28

Dewey Decimal Classification and Relative Index, 1

Diabetes as a Way of Life. Danowski, T., 49

Diabetes for Diabetics. Schmitt, G., 50

Diabetic Gourmet. Bowen, A., 58

Diagrams for Living. Fox, E., 10

Diary. Pepys, S., 105

Diary of a Young Girl. Frank, A., 101

Diary of Prayer. Goudge, E., 12

Dible, Donald M. Up Your Own Organization, 61

Dickinson, Emily. Complete Poems, 83

Dickinson, Thomas H. Chief Contemporary Dramatists, 81

Dickinson, Thorold. Discovery of Cinema, 74

Dick-Read, Grantly. Childbirth without Fear, 51

Dictionary of Antiques. Savage, G., 70

Dictionary of Classical Mythology. Zimmerman, J., 14

Dictionary of Comparative Religion. Brandon, S., 13

Dictionary of Modern Usage. Fowler, H., 33

Dictionary of Names, Nicknames, and Surnames. Latham, E., 108

Dictionary of Technical Terms. Crispin, F., 47

Dictionary of the Bible. Hastings, J., 10

Dictionary of the Bible. McKenzie, J., 11

Dictionary of the Biological Sciences. Gray, P., 41

Diebold, John. Man and the Computer, 4

Diehl, Charles. Byzantium: Greatness and Decline, 116

Diehl, Harold S. Healthful Living, 48

———. Tobacco and Your Health, 49

Digital Computer Fundamentals. Bartee, T., 60

Dill, Marshall. Germany, 114

Dillard, Joey L. Black English, 33

Dilson, Jesse. Curves and Automation: The Scientist's Plot, 35

Dimont, Max. Jews, God and History, 14

Dines, Arthur. Honeybees from Close Up, 44

Dinesen, Isak. Out of Africa, 118

Dinosaurs. Colbert, E., 40

Dipboye, Jessie J. Trailer Owners Handbook, 55

Diplomatic History of Europe since the Congress of Vienna. Albrecht-Carrie, R., 110

Direct Use of the Sun's Energy. Daniels, F., 52

Directing. Theatre Student Series, 75

Directory of American Silver, Pewter, and Silver Plate. Kovel, R., 70

Discovering Freedom. Hoffmann, H., 11

Discovering Oil Painting. Cherepov, G., 70

Discovering Ourselves. Strecker, E., 7

Discovering Plants. Klein, R., 43

Discovery of Cinema. Dickinson, T., 74

Discovery of North America. Cumming, W., 121

Discovery of our Galaxy. Whitney, C., 37

Discovery of the Elements. Weeks, M., 39

Disinherited. Van Every, D., 119

Dispossessing the American Indian. Jacobs, W., 119

Disraeli. Blake, R., 100

Ditmars, Raymond L. Reptiles of North America, 45

DiValentin, Maria M. Color in Oil Painting, 70

———. Practical Encyclopedia of Crafts, 68

———. Sculpture for Beginners, 67

Divided Self. Laing, R., 51

Divided Soul. Troyat, H., 101

Divine Comedy. Dante Alighieri, 90

Diving. Sports Illustrated, eds., 78

Dixon, Robert L. Executive's Accounting Primer, 61

Djilas, Milovan. New Class, 24

Do-it-all-Yourself Needlepoint. Scobey, J., 69

Doane, Gilbert. Searching for Your Ancestors, 108

Dr. Tom Dooley's Three Great Books. Dooley, T., 100

Doctor's Case against the Pill. Seaman, B., 51

Doctors on Horseback. Flexner, J., 96

Doctors Mayo. Clapesattle, H., 104

Documentary Explorations. Levin, G., 74

Documents and Descriptions in European History. Breach, R., 110

Documents of American History. Commager, H., 120

Dodson, Firtzhugh. How to Parent, 60

Doerr, Catherine M. Smart Sewing, 60

Dog Soldiers, Bear Man and Buffalo Women. Mails, T., 119

Dog Training. Sports Illustrated, 57

Dolan, Robert E. Music in Modern Media, 74

Dolger, Henry. How to Live with Diabetes, 49

Dollard, John. Caste and Class in a Southern Town, 17

Dollars and Sense. Watkins, A., 23

Dolman, John. Art of Acting, 74

———. Art of Play Production, 74

Domestic Rabbit Production. Templeton, G., 58

Donoghue, Dennis. Third Voice, 87

Donovan, Frank. Prepare Now for a Metric Future, 29

———. Vikings, 115

Donovan, Robert J. PT 109, 112

Don't Shoot—We Are Your Children. Lukas, J., 18

Doole, Louise E. Herb Magic & Garden Craft, 65

Dooley, Thomas A. Dr. Tom Dooley's Three Great Books, 100

Dorland, William A. N. Dorland's Illustrated Medical Dictionary, 47

Dorland's Illustrated Medical Dictionary. Dorland, W., 47

Dorson, Richard. American Folklore, 31

Dorst, Jean. Field Guide to Larger Mammals of Africa, 46

Dos Passos, John. Mister Wilson's War, 124

———. Shackles of Power, 120

Dostoyevsky. Payne, R., 100

Double Helix. Watson, J., 42

Double-Speak in America. Pei, M., 33

Doubleday, Nelson. Encyclopedia of World Travel, 95

Doughboys. Stallings, L., 112

Douglas, Bob. Wrestling, 76

Douglas, George W. American Book of Days, 30

Douglas, William O. Anatomy of Liberty, 25

Douglass, Frederick. Narratives of the Life of an American Slave, 100

Dove. Graham, R., 94

Dowdell, Dorothy. Tree Farms, 56

Dowling, Tom. Coach, 104

Down These Mean Streets. Thomas, P., 107

Downs, Robert B. First Freedom, 20

———. How to Do Library Research, 3

Downtown. Liston, R., 20

Doyle, Robert V. Your Career in Interior Design, 69

Drachler, Jacob. African Heritage, 91

Drama from Ibsen to Brecht. Williams, R., 81

Draper, Dorothy. 365 Shortcuts to Home Decorating, 69

Draper, Theodore. Abuse of Power, 118

———. Castro's Revolution, 120

Drawing from Nature. Gollwitzer, G., 67

Dreiser. Swanberg, W., 100

Dressmaking Book. Margolis, A., 60

Drew, Elizabeth A. Poetry, 80

Drew, Ellen. Novel, 81

Dried Flower Craft. Amlick, B., 67

Drimmer, Melvin. Black History: A Reappraisal, 120

Driver, Harold E. Indians of North America, 119

Droscher, Vitus B. Friendly Beast, 46

Drotning, Philip T. Black Heros in Our Nation's History, 96

Drownproofing. Lanoue, F., 77

Drucker, Peter. Age of Discontinuity, 16

Drug Dilemma. Cohen, S., 49

Drugs. Modell, W., 49

Drugs and Youth. Harms, E., 49

Dryden, Ken. Face-off at the Summit, 76

Dublin, Louis I. Factbook on Man, 47

Dubois, William E. B. Black Reconstruction in in America, 123

———. Souls of Black Folk, 19

Dubos, René. Reason Awake: Science for Man, 35

———. So Human an Animal, 16

Duckert, Mary. Help! I'm a Sunday School Teacher, 12

Duddington, C. L. Beginner's Guide to Botany, 42

Duel for France, 1944. Blumenson, M., 112

Duggen, Alfred. Julius Caesar, 99

———. Story of the Crusades, 110

Duke, Mark. Acupuncture, 49

Dulcimer Book. Ritchie, J., 74

Dulles, Allen. Craft of Intelligence, 26

Dulles, Foster. Labor in America, 23

Dumas, Alexander *see* Maurois André, 96

Duncan, Delbert J. Modern Retailing Management, 61

Duncan, Ida R. Complete Book of Progressive Knitting, 68

Duncan, Molly. Spin, Dye, and Weave Your Own Wool, 68

Dunlap, Orrin E. Communications in Space, 29

Dupuy, R. E. Compact History of the Civil War, 123

――. Compact History of the Revolutionary War, 122

Durant, Mary B. American Hertiage Guide to Antiques, 70

Durant, Will. Lessons of History, 93

――. Story of Civilization, 93

――. Story of Philosophy, 5

Durkheim, Emile. Suicide, 16

Dylan, Bob. Bob Dylan Song Book, 73

Dynamic Symmetry. Herter, C., 67

Earle, Alice M. Home and Child Life in Colonial Days, 121

Earliest English Poetry. Kennedy, C., 86

Early American Rooms. Kettell, R., 70

Early Christianity. Bainton, R., 13

Early English Christian Poetry. Kennedy, C., 86

Early Years. Painter, G., 106

Earth beneath the Sea. Sheperd, F., 40

Earth beneath Us. Mather, K., 40

Earth Medicine—Earth Food. Weiner, M., 49

Earth We Live On. Moore, R., 40

Easi-Guide to Color TV. Belt, F., 59

Easiest Way to Learn Chess. Reinfeld, F., 76

East, Sara T. Law in American Society, 25

East Pakistan Tragedy. Williams, L., 117

Eastern Europe. Roberts, H., 116

Eastern Europe between the Wars: 1918–1941. Seton-Watson, H., 112

Eastern Religions in the Electric Age. Garabedian, J., 14

Eastman, Max. Enjoyment of Poetry, 80

Eastman, Nicholas J. Expectant Motherhood, 51

Eastman Kodak Co. Home Movies Made Easy 72

Easy Bulletin Boards. Bowers, M., 68

Easy Expert in Collecting and Restoring American Antiques. Marsh, M., 70

Eat Well and Stay Well. Keys, A., 58

Eaton, Clement. Growth of Southern Civilization, 122

――. Henry Clay and the Art of American Politics, 99

Ebenstein, William. Today's Isms, 24

Economic Interpretation of the Constitution of the United States. Beard, C., 25

Economic Problem. Heilbroner, R., 22

Economics. Samuelson, P., 23

Economics of Crisis. Janeway, E., 23

Ecuador. Linke, L., 125

Eddings, Claire N. Secretary's Complete Model Letter Handbook, 61

Eddy, Mary B. Science and Health with Key to the Scriptures, 13

Edgar Cayce, the Sleeping Prophet. Stearn, J., 6

Edge of the Sea. Carson, R., 54

Edmonds, I. G. Minibikes and Minicycles for Beginners, 76

――. Motorcycling for Beginners, 76

Edmonds, Walter D. Musket and the Cross, 121

Education of a General. Pogue, F., 104

Education of Edward Kennedy. Hersh, B., 103

Education of Exceptional Children and Youth. Cruickshank, W., 28

Education of Henry Adams. Adams, H., 97

Educational Psychology in the Classroom. Lindgren, H., 29

Edward Albee. Amacher, R., 84

Egg, Maria. When a Child Is Different, 7

Ehrlich, Arnold. Beautiful Country: Maine to Hawaii, 95

Ehrlich, Eugene H. How to Study Better and Get Higher Marks, 28

Ehrlich, Paul R. Population Bomb, 17

――. Process of Evolution, 42

Eichelberger, Clark M. U.N.: The First 25 Years, 25

8mm/16mm Movie Making. Provisor, H., 72

Einstein, Albert. Meaning of Relativity, 38

Einstein, Alfred. Short History of Music, 73

Einstein Theory of Relativity. Lieber, L., 38

Eiseley, Loren. Darwin's Century, 42

――. Invisible Pyramid, 35

――. Night Country, 40

Eisenhower, Dwight D. White House Years, 100

Eisenstaedt, Alfred. Eye of Eisenstaedt, 72

Eisinger, Chester E. Fiction of the Forties, 84

Eleanor: The Years Alone. Lash, J., 106

Eleanor and Franklin. Lash, I., 106

Eleanor of Aquitaine and the Four Kings. Kelly, A., 100

Electric Generating Systems. Mages, L., 52

Electric Motors. Anderson, E., 52

Electrical Repairs and Projects for the Handyman. Day, R., 52

Electronic Mathematics. Nunz, G. 36

Electronic Music and Musique Concrete. Judd, F., 74

Electronics in Our World. Nunz, G., 52

Elementary Concepts of Mathematics. Jones, B., 36

Elements of Cartography. Robinson, A., 38

Elements of Computer Programming. Swallow, K., 4

Elements of Entymology. Oldroyd, H., 44

Elements of General Linguistics. Martinet, A., 32

Elements of Mathematics. Armstrong, J., 36

Elements of Style. Strunk, W., 80

Eleven Plays. Ibsen, H., 89

El-Hi Textbooks in Print, 1

Eliel, Lambert. Trailer Owner's Manual, 55

Eliot, A. Horizon Concise History of Greece, 116

Eliot, T. S. Complete Poems and Plays, 83

———. Essays, 79

Elizabeth the Great. Jenkins, E., 100

Elizabethan Playwrights. Schelling, F., 87

Elkins, Stanley, M. Slavery, 21

Elliott, Alfred M. Zoology, 43

Elliott, John H. Imperial Spain: 1469–1716, 115

Ellis, Hamilton. Pictorial Encyclopedia of Railways, 29

Ellis, John T. American Catholicism, 13

Ellman, Richard. James Joyce, 103

———. Norton Anthology of Modern Poetry, 80

Ellwood, Robert S. Religious and Spiritual Groups in Modern America, 13

Elmstown's Youth. Hollingshead, A., 17

Elvis. Hopkins, J., 105

Embroidery Stitches. Butler, A., 68

"Emergence of Man" series. Time-Life Books, 41

Emergence of Modern Turkey. Lewis. B., 118

Emergency Medical Guide. Henderson, J., 48

Emerging Personality. Gardner, G., 7

Emerson, Ralph W. Essays, 85

———. Portable Emerson, 85

Emily Dickinson. Johnson, T., 100

Eminent Victorians. Strachey, L., 96

Emphysema. Obley, F., 50

Encounter with the Middle East. Burdett, W., 117

Encyclopedia of American Facts and Dates. Carruth, G., 120

Encyclopedia of American History. Morris, R., 121

Encyclopedia of Art. Munro, E., 64

Encyclopedia of Birds. Hanzak, J., 45

Encyclopedia of English. Zeiger, A., 80

Encyclopedia of Furniture. Aaronson, J., 69

Encyclopedia of Gardening. Taylor, N., 66

Encyclopedia of Humor. Adams, J., 85

Encyclopedia of Jazz. Feather, L., 73

Encyclopedia of Jazz in the Sixties. Feather, L., 73

Encyclopedia of Knots and Fancy Rope Work. Graumont, R., 53

Encyclopedia of Oceanography. Fairbridge, R., 39

Encyclopedia of Painting. Myers, B., 71

Encyclopedia of Pleasure Boating. Liebers, A., 78

Encyclopedia of the Violin. Bachman, A., 74

Encyclopedia of Tropical Fish. Axelrod, H., 44

Encyclopedia of World History. Langer, W., 93

Encyclopedia of World Travel. Doubleday, N., 95

End of the Roaring Twenties: Prohibition and Repeal. Severn, W., 8

Endore, Guy. Synanon, 49

Engel, L. Words with Music, 73

Engel, Louis. How to Buy Stocks, 23

Engel, Lyle K. Indianapolis 500, 76

———. Complete Book of Mobil Home Living, 58

———. Complete Book of Motor Camping, 76

———. Complete Book of Trailering, 76

Energy into Power. Sterland, E., 38

Engineer and His Profession. Kemper, J., 51

Engineering Encyclopedia. Jones, F., 51

Engineering in History. Kirby, R., 51

Engineering Manual. Perry, R., 52

England, a Short History. Smith, G., 113

England of Elizabeth. Rowse, A., 113

Engle, Paul. On Creative Writing, 80

English and Scotish Popular Ballads. Child, F., 86

English History: A Survey. Clark, G., 113

English History: 1919–1945. Taylor, A., 114

English Miracle Plays, Moralities, and Interludes. Pollard, A., 87

English Novel. Allen, W., 88

English Novel from Dickens to Lawrence. Williams, R., 88

English People on the Eve of Colonization. Notestein, W., 113

English Poetry: A Critical Introduction Bateson, F., 86

English Revolution: 1688. Trevelyan, G., 114

Enjoyment of Poetry. Eastman, M., 80

Enlarging. Jacobson, C., 72

Enlightened Despots. Bruun, G., 111

Enterprising Americans. Chamberlain, J., 22

Enthusiasm Makes the Difference. Peale, N., 12

Environmental Conservation. Dasmann, R., 24

Environmental Man. Kuhns, W., 13

Enzymes: Agents of Life. Locke, D., 48

Epic of Latin America. Crow, J., 125

Epic of Latin American Literature. Torres Rioseco, A., 90

Epic of Russian Literature. Slonim, M., 92

Epstein, Edward J. Inquest, 27

Epstein, Jason, Great Conspiracy Trial, 20

Era of Reconstruction. Stampp, K., 123

Eric Hoffer: An American Odyssey. Tomkins, C., 102

Erickson, Erik H. Identity: Youth and Crisis, 7

Ernest Hemingway. Baker, C., 102

Ernst, Morris L. Censorship, 20

Escape from Loneliness. Tournier, P., 7

Esdaile, Arundell. Esdaile's Manual of Bibliography, 1

Esdaile's Manual of Bibliography. Esdaile, A., 1

Eshelman, Philip V. Tractors and Crawlers, 55

Eskanazi, Gerald. Thinking Man's Guide to Pro Hockey, 76

ESP. Cohen, D., 5

ESP, Seers and Psychics. Christopher, M., 5

ESP Curriculum Guide. McConnell, R., 6

Esposito, John C. Vanishing Air, 54

Esposito, Phil. Brothers Esposito, 101

Esquire, eds. Book of Good Grooming for Men, 30

———.Esquire's Guide to Modern Etiquette, 30

Esquire's Guide to Modern Etiquette. Esquire, eds., 30

Essays. Bacon, F., 88

Essays. Elliot, T., 79

Essays. Emerson, R., 85

Essays of Three Decades. Mann, T., 89

Essays on Faith and Morals. James, W., 5

Essential Wisdom of George Santayana. Munson, T., 9

Essentials of Electricity. Timbie, W., 53

Essentials of General Speech Communication. Baird, A., 82

Essentials of Zen Buddhism. Suzuki, D., 14

Esslin, Martin. Theatre of the Absurd, 81

Eternal Bliss Machine. Seligson, M., 19

Etiquette. Post, E., 30

Etruscans: Their Art and Civilization. Richardson, E., 109

Europe in Transition: 1300–1520. Ferguson, W., 110

Europe since 1914. Benns, F., 111

Europe Unfolding. Stoye, J., 111

Europe–with Pictures. Sterling, 95

European Discovery of America. Morison, S., 121

European Folk Dances. Lawson, J., 75

European Reconnaissance. Parry, J., 111

European Society in Upheaval. Stearns, P., 112

European World: A History. Blum, J., 110

Evanoff, Vlad. Complete Guide to Fishing, 78

Evans, Howard. Life on a Little Known Planet, 44

———. Freshwater Fisherman's Bible, 78

Ever-Present Past. Hamilton, E., 79

Evers, Mrs. Medgar. For Us, the Living, 101

Every Boy's Judo. Harrington, A., 76

Everyday Life in Ancient Egypt. White, J., 109

Everyday Life in Ancient Greece. Robinson, C. 110

Everyday Life in Ancient Rome. Cowell, F., 109

Everyday Life in Babylon and Assyria. Contenau, G., 109

Everyday Life in New Testament Times. Bouquet, A., 109

Everyday Life in Prehistoric Times. Quennell, C., 94

Everyday Life in Roman and Anglo-Saxon Times. Quennell, M., 109

Everyman's United Nations, 25

Everything but Money. Levenson, S., 103

Everything You Always Wanted to Know about the Law, but Couldn't Afford to Ask. Colby, E., 25

Everything You Want to Know about Hockey. McFarlane, B., 77

Everything's Green . . . But My Thumb. Karolevitz, R., 56

Eves, Howard. Introduction to the History of Mathematics, 36

Evolution of Chemistry. Farber, E., 38

Evolution of the Machine. Calder, R., 51

Evolution of the Vertebrates. Colbert, E., 41

Evans, Mary. Costume through the Ages, 30

Ewan, Joseph. Short History of Botany in the United States, 43

Ewen, David. American Popular Songs from the Revolutionary War to the Present, 73

———. New Encyclopedia of the Opera, 73

———. Story of George Gershwin, 101

Ewers, William. Sincere's Air Conditioning Service, 52

———. Sincere's Bicycle Service Book, 56

———. Sincere's Lawn Mower Service Book, 56

———. Sincere's Mini Bike Service, 55

———. Sincere's Sewing Machine Service Book, 59

———. Sincere's Vacuum Cleaner and Small Appliance Service Manual, 59

Executive Order 9066, Interment of 110,000 Japanese Americans. Conrat, R., 112

Executive's Accounting Primer. Dixon, R., 61

Exhaustive Concordance of the Bible. Strong, J., 11

Exhibit Methods. Warren, J., 2

Exotic Aquarium Fish. Innes, W., 44

Exotic Zoology. Ley, W., 43

Expanding Liberties. Konvitz, M., 20

Expectant Motherhood. Eastman, N., 51

Expert Obedience Training for Dogs. Strickland, W., 57

Explaining Death to Children. Grollman, E., 7

Exploration of the Universe: Brief Updated Edition. Abell, G., 37

Exploring the Universe. Young, L., 37

Express Yourself in Drawing. Gollwitzer, G., 67

Eye of Eisenstaedt. Eisenstaedt, A., 72

Fables. LaFontaine, J., de, 89

Fabre, J. Henri. Life of the Spider, 44

Fabri, Ralph. Color: a Complete Guide for Artists, 71

Fabric of Freedom. Wright, E., 122

Fabulous Showman. Wallace, I., 98

Face of North America. Farb, P., 35

Face-off at the Summit. Dryden, K., 76

Factbook on Man. Dublin, L., 47

Fader, Daniel N. Hooked on Books, 4

Fairbank, John K. United States and China, 116

Fairbridge, Rhodes W. Encyclopedia of Oceanography, 39

Fairbrother, Nan. New Lives, New Landscapes: Planning for the 21st Century, 65

Fairchild, Johnson E. Basic Beliefs, 14

Faith, Hope and Hillarity. Van Dyke, D., 85

Faiths of Mankind. Parrinder, G., 14

Fall, Bernard B. Hell in a Very Small Place, 118

———. Street without Joy, 118

———. Two Viet Nams, 118

Fall of France. Osgood, S., 114

Fall of Japan. Craig, W., 117

Falls, Cyril. Great War, 111

Falls, Harold B. Foundations of Conditioning, 48

False Gods, Real Men. Berrigan, D., 11

Familiar Animals of America. Barker, W., 46

Familiar Reptiles and Amphibians of America. Barker, W., 45

Family. Nye, F., 18

Family Book of Crafts. Hellegers, L., 68

Family Games America Plays. Gibson, W., 75

Family Handyman. America's Handyman Book, 63

Famous Men of Science. Bolton, S., 95

Fannie Farmer Cookbook. Farmer, F., 58

Fanon, Frantz. Black Skins, White Masks, 21

Far East. Peffer, N., 116

Far Side of Paradise. Mizener, A., 101

Far Western Frontier. Billington, R., 122

Farago, Ladislas. Game of the Foxes, 112

Farago, Peter. Life in Action: Biochemistry Explained, 41

Farb, Peter. Face of North America, 35

Farber, Eduard. Evolution of Chemistry, 38

Farina, Mario V. Computers: a Self-teaching Introduction, 4

Farm Journal, eds. Freezing and Canning Cookbook, 58

———. Homemade Bread, 58

———. How to Make Your Home More Convenient, 69

Farm Machinery and Equipment. Smith, H., 57

Farm Management Handbook. Mortenson, W., 57

Farmer, Fannie M. Fannie Farmer Cookbook, 58

Farmer, Robert. How to Adopt a Child, 25

———. How to Avoid Problems with Your Will, 25

Farris, Edmond J. Care and Breeding of Laboratory Animals, 41

Fast, Julius. Body Language, 6

———. You and Your Feet, 49

Fat and Sodium Control Cookbook. Payne, A., 59

Fatal Impact. Moorhead, A., 126
Faulkner, Harold U. American Economic History, 22
Faulkner, Ray N. Inside Today's Home, 69
Faulkner, William. Portable Faulkner, 84
Faust, Ernest C. Animal Agents and Vectors of Human Disease, 49
Faust. Goethe, J., 88
Favor the Bold. Kinsley, D., 100
Favorite Poems Old and New. Ferris, H., 80
FBI and the Berrigans. Nelson, J., 26
FBI Nobody Knows. Cook, F., 26
FBI's Most Famous Cases. Tully, A., 26
Feast on a Diabetic Diet. Gibbons, J., 48
Feasting Free on Wild Edibles. Angier, B., 58
Feather, Leonard. Encyclopedia of Jazz, 73
_____. Encyclopedia of Jazz in the Sixties, 73
Feature Writer's Handbook. Harral, S., 80
Federal Service Entrance Examinations. Arco Publ. Co., 26
Federal Union. Hicks, J., 121
Federalist. Hamilton, A., 22
Federalist Era. Miller, J., 122
Feeling Alive After 65. Taylor, R., 19
Fehrenback, T. R. Fire and Blood, 125
Feininger, Andreas. Basic Color Photography, 72
_____. Complete Photographer, 72
Feirer, John L. Advanced Woodwork and Furniture Making, 62
_____. General Metals, 61
Feis, Herbert. Churchill, Roosevelt, Stalin, 112
_____. Road to Pearl Harbor, 112
Feldzaman, A. N. Intelligent Man's Easy Guide to Computers, 4
Felleman, Hazel. Best Loved Poems of the American People, 83
Fellows, Donald K. Mosaic of America's Ethnic Minorities, 21
Fell's Guide to Commercial Art. Nelson, R., 67
Fell's Guide to Mobile Home Living. Oaks, M., 59
Female Eunuch. Greer, G., 18
Feminine Fix-it Handbook. Ward, K., 59
Feminine Mystique. Friedan, B., 18
Fenner, Terrence W. Inventor's Handbook, 47
Fenno, Richard F. Yalta Conference, 112
Fenton, Carroll L. Fossil Book, 40
_____. Rock Book, 39
_____. Tales Told by Fossils, 40
Ferguson, Charles. Naked to Mine Enemies, 108

Ferguson, Robert. How to Make Movies, 72
Ferguson, Wallace K. Europe in Transition: 1300–1520, 110
_____. Renaissance, 110
Fergusson, Francis. Idea of a Theater, 81
Fermi, Laura. Atoms in the Family, 101
_____. Illustrious Immigrants, 21
_____. Mussolini, 105
Ferris, Helen. Favorite Poems Old and New, 80
Festivals of the Jewish Year. Gaster, T., 30
Festive Decorations the Year 'Round. Waugh, D., 30
Ficarotta, Phyllis. Sewing without a Pattern, 60
Fiction of the Forties. Eisinger, C., 84
Fidel Castro. Matthews, H., 99
Field, Minna. Aging with Honor and Dignity, 19
Field Book of American Trees and Shrubs. Mathews, F., 43
Field Book of American Wild Flowers. Mathews, F., 43
Field Book of Common Mushrooms. Thomas, W., 43
Field Book of Common Rocks and Minerals. Loomis, F., 39
Field Book of Insects. Lutz, F., 44
Field Book of Snakes of U.S. and Canada. Schmidt, K., 45
Field Book of the Skies. Olcott, W., 37
Field Guide to Animal Tracks. Murie, O., 44
Field Guide to Larger Mammals of Africa. Dorst, J., 46
Field Guide to Reptiles and Amphibians. Conant, R., 45
Field Guide to Rocks and Minerals. Pough, F., 40
Field Guide to the Birds. Peterson, R., 45
Field Guide to the Butterflies. Klots, A., 44
Field Guide to the Ferns. Cobb, B., 42
Field Guide to the Mammals. Burt, W., 46
Field Guide to the Shells of Our Atlantic and Gulf Coasts. Morris, P., 44
Field Guide to the Shells of the Pacific Coast and Hawaii. Morris, P., 44
Field Guide to the Stars and Planets. Menzel, D., 37
Field Guide to the Western Reptiles and Amphibians. Stebbins, R., 45
Field Guide to Trees and Shrubs. Petrides, G., 43
Field Guide to Western Birds. Peterson, R., 45

Fielder, Leslie. Art of the Essay, 88
Fielding, Temple. Fielding's Guides, 95
Fielding's Guides. Fielding, T., 95
Fifteen Greek Plays. Cooper, L., 91
Fifty Best Plays of the American Theater. Gassner, J., 84
Fight for Union. Coit, M., 122
Filing and Records Management. Weeks, R., 61
Filler, Louis. Crusade Against Slavery, 122
Film Making. Theatre Student Series, 75
Filming TV News and Documentaries. Atkins, J., 72
Final Challenge. Van Every, D., 122
Fine, Benjamin. Underachievers, 28
Fine Wines of California. Blumberg, R., 61
Finley, Moses I. Portable Greek Historians, 91
Fire and Blood. Fehrenback, T., 125
Fire in the Ashes. White, T., 112
Fire in the Lake. FitzGerald, F., 118
First Aid and Emergency Care. Aaron, J., 48
First Aid for Pets. Whitney, L., 58
First Aid Textbook. American Red Cross, 48
First American. Ceram, C., 119
First Fifty Years. National Football League, 77
First Freedom. Downs, R., 20
First Great Civilizations. Hawkes, J., 109
First Horse. Hapgood, R., 57
First Ladies. Barzman, S., 95
First Principle of Verse. Hillyer, R., 80
Fisch, Max H. Classic American Philosophers, 8
Fishbein, Morris. Ask the Doctor, 50
_____. Handy Home Medical Adviser and Concise Medical Encyclopedia, 50
_____. Modern Family Health Guide, 50
Fishel, Leslie. Black American: a Documentary History, 21
Fisher, Charles A. South-East Asia, 118
Fisher, James. Zoos of the World, 43
Fisher, P. J. Science of Gems, 39
Fisher, Roger D. International Conflict for Beginners, 21
Fisher, Sydney N. Middle East, 117
Fisherman's Almanac. Morris, D., 78
Fisherman's Handbook. Power, J., 78
Fishes of North America. Herlad, E., 44
Fitch, Charles M. Complete Book of Houseplants, 65
Fitch, Florence M. Allah, the God of Islam, 15
Fitter, Richard. Vanishing Wild Animals of the World, 46

Fitts, Dudley. Greek Plays in Modern Translation, 91
_____. Poems from the Creek Anthology, 91
Fitzgerald, F. Scott. Fitzgerald Reader, 85
FitzGerald, Frances. Fire in the Lake, 118
Fitzgerald Reader. Fitzgerald, F., 85
Fitzmaurice-Kelly, James. Oxford Book of Spanish Verse, 90
Five C's of Cinematography. Mascelli, J., 72
Five Centuries of American Costume. Wilcox, E., 30
Five Ideas that Changed the World. Ward, B., 94
Five Plays. Garcia Lorca, F., 90
Fix Your Chevrolet. Toboldt, W., 56
Fix Your Ford. Toboldt, W., 56
Fix Your Volkswagen. Johnson, L., 55
Flags of the World. Barraclough, E., 108
Flayderman, Norman. Collecting Tomorrow's Antiques Today, 70
Fleck, Henrietta. Introduction to Nutrition, 48
Fleming, Alice. Psychiatry, 50
Fleming, Thomas J. Man Who Dared the Lightning, 101
Flenley, Ralph. Modern German History, 114
Flesch, Rudolf, F. Art of Clear Thinking, 6
Fletcher, Colin. Complete Walker, 76
Fletcher, Edward. Pebble Collecting and Polishing, 39
Fletcher, Grace N. What's Right with our Young People?, 18
Flexner, Eleanor. Century of Struggle, 17
_____. Mary Wollstoncraft, 108
Flexner, James. Doctors on Horseback, 96
Flores, Angel. Anthology of French Poetry, 89
Florinsky, Michael. Russia: a Short History, 115
Flower Arranging. Better Homes & Gardens, eds., 65
Flowering of the Renaissance. Cronin, V., 111
Flowering of Yiddish Literature. Liptzin, S., 91
Flowers of Evil. Baudelaire, C., 89
Fodor, Eugene. Fodor Guides, 95
Fodor Guides. Fodor, E., 95
Foerster, Norman. American Poetry and Prose, 82
_____. Writing and Thinking, 80
Foldes, Joe. Large-Format Camera Practice, 72
Folk and Traditional Music on the Western Continents. Nettl, B., 73

Folk Dancing. Kraus, R., 74
Folksingers and Folksongs in America. Lawless, R., 73
Foner, Eric. America's Black Past, 121
Fontana, V. J. Maltreated Child, 18
Food and Nutrition. Haggerty, J., 48
Food for Fifty. Fowler, S., 58
Foolproof Birth Control. Lader, L., 51
Football. Sports Illustrated, 77
For Instance. Kauffman, D., 12
For Those I Loved. Gray, M., 107
For Us, the Living. Evers, Mrs. M., 101
Forbes, Esther. Paul Revere and the World He Lived in, 106
Ford Arthur A. Life Beyond Death, 5
Ford, Leighton. One Way to Change the World, 10
Ford, Norman. Travel Guides, 95
Forest and the Sea. Bates, M., 39
Forester, Cecil S. Last Nine Days of the Bismarck, 112
Forever Free. Adamson, J., 45
Forging of Our Continent. Ogburn, C., Jr., 40
Form and Fable in American Fiction. Hoffman, D., 84
Forms of Poetry. Untermeyer, L., 80
Formulas for Painters. Massey, R., 71
Forster, E. M. Aspects of the Novel, 81
Fort, Joel. Pleasure Seekers, 49
Forth to the Wilderness. Van Every, D., 121
Fortran Programming. Stuart, F., 37
Foss, E. W. Construction and Maintenance for Farm and Home, 56
Fossil Book. Fenton, C., 40
Fossils for Amateurs. MacFall, R., 40
Foster, Robert F. Foster's Complete Hoyle, 75
Foster's Complete Hoyle. Foster, R., 75
Foundations of Conditioning. Falls, H., 48
Foundations of Historical Knowledge. White, M., 94
Four Ages of Music. Wiora, W., 73
Four D Time Lock. Fuller, B., 8
Four Plays. Giraudoux, J., 89
Four Plays. Inge, W., 84
Four Religions of Asia. Stroup, H., 10
Four Thousand Years Ago. Bibby, G., 109
Fourth Dimension Simply Explained. Manning, H., 38
Fourth State of Matter. Bova, B., 38
Fowler, Henry W. Dictionary of Modern Usage, 33
Fowler, Sina F. Food for Fifty, 58
Fowlie, Wallace. Guide to Contemporary French Literature, 89

Fox, Emmett. Diagrams for Living, 10
Fox, Helen M. Gardening with Herbs, 65
Foxe, John. Foxe Book of Martyrs, 13
Foxe Book of Martyrs. Foxe, J., 13
Foxfire Book. Wigginton, B., 57
Foxfire Two. Wigginton, B., 57
Fractured Emerald. Hahn, E., 113
Fraenkel, Osmond K. Rights We Have, 20
France: a Modern History. Guerard, A., 114
France: an Interpretative History. Knapton, E., 114
France under the Bourbon Restoration. Artz, F., 114
Francis Bacon. Bowen, C., 97
Franco's Spain. Payne, S., 115
Frank, Anne. Diary of a Young Girl, 101
Frankel, Charles. Golden Age of American Philosophy, 8
Frankel, Lillian. Bikeways, 56
Franklin, Benjamin. Autobiography, 101
Franklin, John H. Fram Slavery to Freedom, 21
——. Reconstruction, 123
Franklin D. Roosevelt and the New Deal. Leuchtenberg, W., 124
Fraser, Antonia. Cromwell, 99
——. Mary Queen of Scots, 104
Frazer, James G. Golden Bough, 14
Frazier, E. Franklin. Negro Family in the United States, 19
——. Negro in the United States, 21
Free, Anne R. Social Usage, 30
Free, James L. Training Your Retriever, 57
Free, Montague. Plant Propagation in Pictures, 56
Free and Female. Seaman, B., 18
Freedland, Nat. Occult Explosion, 5
Freedom and After. Mboya, T., 118
Freedom of the Press for Whom? Barron, J., 4
Freehand Lettering. Richardson, H., 67
Freeman, Louis M. Betty Crocker's Parties for Children, 75
Freeman, Mitchell. Practical and Industrial Formulary, 47
Freeman, Orville L. World Without Hunger, 24
Freezing and Canning Cookbook. Farm Journal, eds., 58
Freezing Point. Kavaler, L., 38
Freidel, Frank B. Our Country's Presidents, 96
Freidel, Frank. Splendid Little War, 123
French, Scott R. New Earth Catalog, 3

French, Thomas E. Fundamentals of Engineering Drawing, 63
———. Mechanical Drawing, 63
French Nation from Napoleon to Petain. Brogan, D., 114
French Novelists of Today. Peyre, H., 89
French Revolution. Furet, F., 114
Freshwater Fisherman's Bible. Evanoff, V., 78
Freud, Sigmund. Basic Writings, 6
———. General Introduction to Psychoanalysis, 6
———. Interpretation of Dreams, 6
Freyre, Gilberto. Masters and the Slaves, 125
Friedan, Betty. Feminine Mystique, 18
Friedberg, Robert. Paper Money of the United States, 22
Friedman, Myra. Buried Alive, 103
Friedrich, Carl J. Age of the Baroque, 111
Friendly Beast. Droscher, V., 46
Frisch, Otto. Nature of Matter, 38
Frohse, Franz. Atlas of Human Anatomy, 48
From Ape to Adam. Wendt, H., 42
From Childhood to Adolescence. Montessori, M., 7
From Conception to Birth, Rugh, R., 51
From Despotism to Revolution. Gershoy, L., 111
From Doomsday Book to Magna Carta. Poole, A., 113
From Gunk to Glow. Grotz, G., 62
From Resistance to Revolution. Maier, P., 122
From Slavery to Freedom. Franklin, J., 21
From the Crash to the Blitz. Phillips, C., 124
Fromm, Erich. Anatomy of Human Destructiveness, 6
———. Art of Loving, 6
———. Crisis of Psychoanalysis, 50
———. Psychoanalysis and Religion, 6
———. Zen Buddhism and Psychoanalysis, 14
Frommer, Arthur. . . . . on $5 and/or $10 a Day, 95
Frontier America. Clark, T., 122
Frontier in American History. Turner, F., 121
Frontier Living. Tunis, E., 122
Frost, Robert. Complete Poetry, 83
Frost, S. E. Basic Teachings of the Great Philosophers, 8
Fuchs, Walter R. Cybernetics for the Modern Mind, 3
Fuller, Buckminster. Four D Time Lock, 8
———. Ideas and Integrities, 8

Fun Encyclopedia. Harbin, E., 75
Fun with Fabric Printing. Monk, K., 71
Fundamental Reference Sources. Cheney, F., 3
Fundamentals of College Algebra. Allendoerfer, C., 36
Fundamentals of Ecology. Odum, E., 54
Fundamentals of Electronics. Mandl, M., 52
Fundamentals of Elementary Mathematics: Number Systems and Algebra. Behr, M., 36
Fundamentals of Engineering Drawing. French, T., 63
Fundamentals of Freshman Mathematics. Allendoerfer, C., 36
Fundamentals of Good Writing. Brooks, C., 80
Fundamentals of Mathematics. Stein, E., 37
Fundamentals of Music. Barnes, R., 72
Fundamentals of Photography. Neblette, C., 72
Fundamentals of Surveying. Rayner, W., 38
Fundamentals of Tennis. Plagenhoef, S., 77
Funk, Peter V. It Pays to Increase Your Word Power, 33
Funk & Wagnalls. Standard College Dictionary, 32
Furet, Francois. French Revolution, 114
Furfey, Paul H. Morality Gap, 12
Furnas, Joseph C. Americans, 121
Furniture Finishing and Refinishing. Sunset Magazine, eds., 62
Furniture Upholstery and Repair. Sunset Magazine, eds., 62
Future as History. Heilbroner, R., 93
Future of Religions. Tillich, P., 11
Future Shock. Toffler, A., 17

Gablehouse, Charles. Helicopters and Autogyros, 54
Gaer, Joseph. What the Great Religions Believe, 14
Gage, Nicholas. Mafia is Not an Equal Opportunity Employer, 27
Galaxies. Shapley, H., 37
Galbraith, John K. Affluent Society, 22
———. Ambassador's Journal, 21
———. Great Crash, 22
Galdames, Luis. History of Chile, 125
Galin, Saul. Reference Books: How to Select and Use Them, 1
Gallo, Max. Night of Long Knives, 114
Galton, Lawrence. Outdoorsman's Fitness and Medical Guide, 48
Game of the Foxes. Farago, L., 112

Games People Play. Berne, E., 17

Gamow, George. Moon, 37

———. One, Two, Three-Infinity, 36

Gans, Herbert J. Levittowners, 17

Garabedian, John H. Eastern Religions in the Electric Age, 14

Garcia Lorca, Federico. Five Plays, 90

———. Selected Poems, 90

Garden and Patio Building Book. Sunset Magazine, eds., 66

Garden Pools, Fountains and Waterfalls. Sunset Magazine, eds., 66

Gardener's Basic Book of Trees and Shrubs. Schuler, S., 66

Gardener's Bug Book. Westcott, C., 57

Gardening and Home Landscaping. Kramer, J., 65

Gardening in Containers. Sunset Magazine, eds., 66

Gardening Indoors Under Lights. Kranz, F., 65

Gardening with Herbs. Fox, H., 65

Gardner, Archibald W. New Essential First Aid, 48

Gardner, George E. Emerging Personality, 7

Gardner, John W. Self-Renewal, 16

Gardner, Martin. New Mathematical Diversions, 36

———. Relativity for the Millions, 38

Gardner, Richard A. Understanding Children, 7

Garmonsway, G. N. Anglo-Saxon Chronicle, 113

Garner, Robert J. Grafter's Handbook, 56

Garraty, John A. American Nation, 121

———. Columbia History of the World, 93

———. New Commonwealth, 123

———. Quarrels That Have Shaped the Constitution, 25

Garrett, Henry E. Great Experiments in Psychology, 6

Gaskell, Elizabeth. Life of Charlotte Brontë, 98

Gassner, John. Best American Plays, 1918–1958 Suppl. Vol., 84

———. Best American Plays, 1939–1945, 84

———. Best American Plays, 1945–1951, 84

———. Best American Plays, 1951–1957, 84

———. Best American Plays, 1957–1963, 84

———. Best American Plays, 1963–1967, 84

———. Best Plays of the Early American Theater (to 1916), 84

———Best Plays of the Modern American Theater, 84

———. Fifty Best Plays of the American Theater, 84

———. Introducing the Drama, 81

———. Masters of the Drama, 81

———. Medieval and Tudor Drama, 87

———. Treasury of the Theatre, 81

———. Twenty-five Plays of the Modern Theater, 84

Gaster, Theodor H. Festivals of the Jewish Year, 30

Gaston, E. Thayer. Music in Therapy, 73

Gaunt, William. Concise History of English Painting, 71

Gaver, Jack. Critics Choice, 84

Gavin, Ruth E. Reference Manual for Stenographers and Typists, 61

Gay, Peter. Historians at Work, 93

Gayle, Addison. Black Expressions, 82

Geisinger, Marion. Plays, Players, and Playwrights: an Illustrated History of the Theatre, 74

Gelb, Barbara. O'Neill, 105

Gemini. Giovanni, N., 101

Gems and Gem Materials. Kraus, E., 39

Genealogy as Pastime and Profession. Jacobus, D., 108

General and Applied Entomology. Little, V., 44

General Biology. Beaver, W., 41

General Biology. Taylor, W., 41

General Introduction to Psychoanalysis. Freud, S., 6

General Metals. Feirer, J., 61

General Theory of Employment, Interest and Money. Keynes, J., 23

General Zoology. Storer, T., 44

Genetic Code. Asimov, I., 41

Genetics. Winchester, A., 42

Genius and the Mobocracy. Wright, F., 107

Geoffrey Chaucer of England. Chute, M., 99

Geographical Ecology. MacArthur, R., 43

Geography of Life. Neill, W., 41

Georgano, G. N. Complete Encyclopedia of Motor Cars: 1885–1968, 55

George and Ira Gershwin Songbook. Gershwin, G., 73

George the Third. Ayling, S., 101

George Washington. Cunliffe, M., 107

George Washington Carver. Holt, R., 99

George Washington's Expense Account. Kitman, M., 122

German Painting: Old Masters. Werner, A., 71

German Verse from 12th to 20th Century. Thomas, J., 89

Germany. Dill, M., 114

Geronimo. Adams, A., 101

Gerould, Gordon H. Patterns in English, 32

Gershoy, Leo. From Despotism to Revolution, 111

Gershwin, George. George and Ira Gershwin Songbook, 73

Gessell, Arnold. The Infant and Child in the Culture of Today, 7

Gettens, Rutherford J. Painting Materials, 71

Getting Along in Italian. Pei, M., 33

Getting Back Together. Houriet, R., 24

Getting Older and Staying Young. Stonecypher, D., Jr., 19

Getting Started in African Crafts. Comins, J., 68

Giachino, J. W. Welding Technology, 61

Gibbon, Edward. Decline and Fall of the Roman Empire, 109

Gibbons, Euell. Stalking the Wild Asparagus, 43

Gibbons, Joe. Feast on a Diabetic Diet, 48

Gibbs, Hamilton A. Mohammedanism, 15

Gibbs, Tony. Practical Sailing, 53

Gibran, Kahlil. Prophet, 91

Gibson, Robert D. Modern French Poets on Poetry, 89

Gibson, Ulric P. Water Well Manual, 53

Gibson, Walter, B. Family Games America Plays, 75

_____. Hoyle's Simplified Guide to the Popular Card Games, 75

Gies, Joseph. Life in a Medieval City, 110

Giesecke, Frederick E. Technical Drawing, 63

Gieseking, Walter. Piano Technique, 74

Gifford-Jones, W. On Being a Woman, 51

Gift of Prophecy. Montgomery, R., 6

Gil, David. Violence Against Children, 18

Gilbert, Pia. Music for the Modern Dance, 74

Gilbert, Rod. Playing Hockey the Professional Way, 76

Gilbert, Thomas F. Thinking Metrics, 30

Gilbreth, Frank B. Cheaper by the Dozen, 101

Gillespie, Paul. No-Fault, 28

Gillie, Oliver. Living Cell, 42

Gilluly, James. Principles of Geology, 39

Gilmore, J. Herbert. When Love Prevails, 12

Gilmore, Myron P. World of Humanism, 111

Gilmore, Theopolis L. Swahili Phrase Book, 34

Ginott, Haim G. Between Parent and Child, 60

_____. Between Parent and Teenager, 60

_____. Teacher and Child, 28

Giovanni, Nikki. Gemini, 101

Gipson, Lawrence H. Coming of the Revolution, 122

Giraudoux, Jean. Four Plays, 89

_____. Three Plays, 89

Girls and Sex. Pomeroy, W., 48

Gladstone, Bernard. New York Times Complete Manual of Home Repair, 63

Glamour Magazine. Glamour Beauty and Health Book, 59

Glamour Beauty and Health Book. Glamour Magazine, 59

Glanville, Brian. Soccer, 76

Glass: a Guide for Collectors. Gros-Galliner, G., 70

Glass House. Wadsworth, J., 25

Glasser, Ronald J. 365 Days, 118

Glazer, Nathan. Beyond the Melting Pot, 21

Gleeson, Margaret. Complete Shower Party Book, 75

Glemser, Bernard. Man against Cancer, 50

Glenn, Harold T. Automechanics, 55

_____. Automobile Engine Rebuilding and Maintenance, 55

Glessing, Robert J. Underground Press in America, 4

Glory That Was Greece. Stobart, J., 110

Gloster, Hugh M. Negro Voice in American Fiction, 84

Glubb, Sir John. Short History of the Arab Peoples, 117

Go Ask Alice. 50

Go for Broke. Palmer, A., 77

God is for Real, Man. Burke, C., 10

Gods from Outer Space. Von Daniken, E., 41

Gods, Graves, and Scholars. Ceram, C., 94

God's Trombones. Johnson, J., 83

Godson, John. Unsafe at Any Height, 54

Godwin, John. Occult America, 5

Goerner, Fred. Search for Amelia Earhart, 100

Goethe, Johann W. Faust, 88

Goin, Coleman J. Introduction to Herpetology, 45

Gold. . . ABC's of Panning. LeGaye, E., 53

Golda. Mann, P., 105

Golden Age of American Philosophy. Frankel, C., 8

Golden Bough. Frazer, J., 14

Golden Guide to American Antiques. Cole, A., 70

Golden Hands Handicrafts, 68
Golden Treasury. Palgrave, F., 86
Goldman, David J. Presidential Losers, 96
Goldman, Eric. Crucial Decade, 124
———. Tragedy of Lyndon, 103
Goldman, Richard F. Harmony in Western Music, 73
Goldsby, Richard A. Race and Races, 40
Goldstein, Richard. Poetry of Rock, 73
Golf. Sports Illustrated, 77
Golf My Way. Nicklaus, J., 77
Gollwitzer, Gerhard. Drawing from Nature, 67
———. Express Yourself in Drawing, 67
Gombrich, Ernst H. Story of Art, 64
Good, Carter V. Methods of Research, 3
Good, Harry G. History of American Education, 28
Good Housekeeping New Complete Book of Needlecraft. Guild, V., 68
Good Years. Lord, W., 124
Goodall, Daphne M. Horses of the World, 57
Goodban, W. T. Architectural Drawing and Planning, 66
Goode's World Atlas, 94
Goodman, Linda. Sun Signs, 5
Goodman, Walter. Committee: the Extraordinary Career of the House Committee on Un-American Activities, 26
Goodspeed, Edgar J. Life of Jesus, 11
———. The Twelve, 10
———. Story of the Apocrypha, 10
Gordon, Thomas. Parent Effectiveness Training, 60
Goren, Charles, H. Goren's New Contract Bridge in a Nutshell, 75
———. Modern Backgammon, 75
Goren's New Contract Bridge in a Nutshell. Goren C., 75
Gorrell, Robert M. Modern English Handbook, 82
Gorsline, Douglas. What People Wore, 30
Gospel in Hymns. Bailey, A., 11
Gottlieb, Milton. Seven States of Matter, 38
Gottshall, Franklin H. How to Make Colonial Furniture, 62
———. Reproducing Antique Furniture, 62
Goudge, Elizabeth. Diary of Prayer, 12
Government by the People: National, State and Local Edition. Burns, J., 26
Grafter's Handbook. Garner, R., 56
Graham, Benjamin. Intelligent Investor, 23
Graham, Billy. Jesus Generation, 13
———. World Aflame, 12

Graham, Frank, Jr. Since Silent Spring, 54
Graham, Frank D. Truck and Tractor Guide, 55
Graham, Kennard C. Interior Electric Wiring: Residential, 52
Graham, Robin L. Dove, 94
Grammar of Present-Day English. Pence, R., 33
Grammar of the German Language. Curme, G., 33
Grandeur That Was Rome. Stobart, J., 109
Grant, Bruce. Indonesia, 126
Grant, Michael. Ancient Historians, 110
———. World of Rome, 109
Grantz, Gerald J. Home Book of Taxidermy and Tanning, 42
Grattan, C. Hartley. Southwest Pacific, 126
Graumont, Raoul. Encyclopedia of Knots and Fancy Rope Work, 53
Graves, John. Water Hustlers, 54
Gray, Eden. Complete Guide to the Tarot, 5
Gray, Madeline. Changing Years: Menopause without Fear, 48
Gray, Martin. For Those I Loved, 107
Gray, Peter. Dictionary of the Biological Sciences, 41
———. Student Dictionary of Biology, 41
Gray, Robert. Great Apes, 46
Great Age of Sail. Jobe, J., 53
Great American Forest. Platt, R., 57
Great American Negroes. Richardson, B., 96
Great Apes. Gray, R., 46
Great Britain to 1688. Ashley, M., 113
Great Chain of Life. Krutch, J., 42
Great Cities of the Ancient World. DeCamp, L., 94
Great Conductors. Schonberg, H., 96
Great Conspiracy. Chidsey, D., 98
Great Conspriacy Trial. Epstein, J., 20
Great Crash. Galbraith, J., 22
Great Critics. Smith, J., 79
Great Days of the Circus. American Heritage, 75
Great Depression. Shannon, D., 124
Great Experiments in Psychology. Garrett, H., 6
Great Gardens of the Western World. Coats, P., 65
Great Land. Herndon, B., 53
Great Negroes, Past and Present. Adams, R., 95
Great Philosophers. Jaspers, K., 5
Great Pianists. Schonberg, H., 96

Great Psychologists: From Aristotle to Freud. Watson, R., 7

Great Religions of the World. Smith, H., 14

Great Singers. Pleasants, H., 96

Great Terror: Stalin's Purge. Conquest, R., 115

Great War. Falls, C., 111

Greatest Book Ever Written. Oursler, F., 11

Greatest Story Ever Told. Oursler, F., 11

Greece in the Bronze Age. Vermeule, E., 110

Greek and Roman Classics in Translation. Murphy, C., 91

Greek Drama. Hadas, M., 91

Greek Experience, Bowra, C., 110

Greek Grammar. Smyth, H., 34

Greek Lyric Poetry. Barnstone, W., 91

Greek Plays in Modern Translation. Fitts, D., 91

Greek Way. Hamilton, E., 91, 110

Greeks. Andrewes, A., 110

Green, John R. Short History of English People, 113

Green, Stanley. World of Musical Comedy, 73

Green, Sylvia. Patchwork for Beginners, 68

Green Thumb Book of Fruit and Vegetable Gardening. Abraham, G., 56

Green Thumb Book of Indoor Gardening. Abraham, G., 65

Green Thumb Garden Handbook. Abraham, G., 65

Greenberg, Selig. Quality of Mercy, 27

Greene, Graham. Portable Graham Greene, 88

Greenfield, Stanley B. Critical History of Old English Literature, 85

Greenhood, David. Mapping, 38

Greenhouse Gardening for Fun. Blake, C., 56

Greening of America. Reich, C., 17

Greer, Germaine. Female Eunuch, 18

Greer, Rebecca. Book for Brides, 30

Gregg, Elizabeth M. What to Do When "There's Nothing to Do," 75

Gregg Notehand. Leslie, L., 61

Gregg Shorthand Functional Method. Leslie, L., 61

Gregg Typing. Rowe, J., 61

Gregory, Dick. nigger, 101

Gregory, Ross. Origins of American Intervention in the First World War, 112

Gresham, William L. Houdini, 102

Grier, William. Black Rage, 6

Griffin, Al. Motorcycles, 76

———. So You Want to Buy a House, 24

———. So You Want to Buy a Mobile Home, 24

Griffin, John H. Black Like Me, 19

Griffith, Anna N. Guide to Rock Garden Plants, 65

Griffith, Ernest S. Congress, 26

Griffiths, Percival. Modern India, 117

Grimm, Harold J. Reformation Era, 111

Grinspoon, Lester. Marijuana Reconsidered, 49

Griswold, Lester E. New Handicraft; Processes and Projects, 68

Grob, Bernard, Basic Electronics, 52

Grollman, Earl A. Explaining Death to Children, 7

Gros-Galliner, Gabriella. Glass: a Guide for Collectors, 70

Gross, Chaim. Technique of Wood Sculpture, 67

Grotz, George. Antiques You Can Decorate With, 70

———. From Gunk to Glow, 62

———. New Antiques, 70

Grout, Donald J. History of Western Music, 73

Grover, John W. V. D.: the ABC's, 50

Growing up Black. David, J., 95

Growing up in New Guinea. Mead, M., 41

Growth. Tanner, J., 48

Growth and Culture of Latin America. Worcester, D., 125

Growth of Southern Civilization. Eaton, C., 122

Growth of the American Republic. Morsion, S., 121

Gruber, Elmar. Metal and Wire Sculpture, 67

Gruen, John. Private World of Leonard Bernstein, 98

Gruenberg, Sidonie M. New Encyclopedia of Child Care and Guidance, 60

Grunberger, Richard. 12-Year Reich, 114

Grunfeld, Frederick V. Art and Times of the Guitar, 74

Guerard, Albert L. France: a Modern History, 114

———. Napoleon I, 105

———. Napoleon III, 105

Guerney, Bernard G. Portable Russian Reader, 92

———. Treasury of Russian Literature, 92

Guerny, Gene. Pilot's Handbook of Weather, 54

Guggisberg, C. A. Man and Wildlife, 43

Guide to American English. Myers, L., 32

Guide to Aquarium Fishes and Plants. Schiotz, A., 45

Guide to Better Bowling. Pezzano, C., 77
Guide to Contemporary French Literature. Fowlie, W., 89
Guide to Contemporary Italian Literature. Pacifici, S., 90
Guide to Garden Shrubs and Trees. Taylor, N., 66
Guide to Gymnastics. Musker, F., 77
Guide to Home Remodeling. Harmon, A., 63
Guide to Modern World Literature. Seymour-Smith, M., 79
Guide to Reference Books. Winchell, C., 2
Guide to Rock Garden Plants. Griffith, A., 65
Guide to Summer Camps and Summer Schools, 29
Guide to the Care and Collecting of Original Prints. Zigrosser, C., 71
Guide to Unusual Vacations. Cross, W., 95
Guides to Educational Media. Rufsvold, M., 3
Guides to Straight Thinking. Chase, S., 8
Guild, Vera P. Good Housekeeping New Complete Book of Needlecraft, 68
Guiness Book of World Records. McWhirter, N., 3
Guiness Sports Record Book. McWhirter, N., 77
Gulag Archipelago. Solzhenitzyn, A., 92
Gun Collector's Handobok of Values. Chapel, C., 53
Guns of August. Tuchman, B., 112
Gunther, John. Death Be Not Proud, 101
Gunther, Max. Writing the Modern Magazine Article, 80
Gurko, Miriam. Restless Spirit, 105
Guthrie, Esther L. Home Book of Animal Care, 57
Gymnastics. Loken, N., 76
Gypsies. Yoors, J., 16

Haage, Walter. Cacti and Succulents, 65
Haas, Emmy. Pride's Progress, 46
Habitation of Dragons. Miller, K., 12
Hacker, Louis M. World of Andrew Carnegie, 123
Hadas, Moses. Greek Drama, 91
_____. History of Latin Literature, 90
_____. Imperial Rome, 109
Hagan, William T. American Indians, 119
Haggerty, James J. Food and Nutrition, 48
Hague, William E. Your Vacation Home, 66
Hahn, Emily. Fractured Emerald, 113
_____. On the Side of the Apes, 46
Haight, Anne L. Banned Books, 4
Haight, Gordon S. Portable Victorian Reader, 85

Haines, Helen E. Living with Books, 4
_____. What's in a Novel, 81
Haiti: the Politics of Squalor. Rotberg, R., 120
Halacy, D. S., Jr. Coming Age of Solar Energy, 52
Halberstam, David. Best and the Brightest, 124
_____. Ho, 102
_____. Making of a Quagmire, 118
_____. Unfinished Odyssey, 103
Hale, John R. Renaissance, 111
Hale, William H. Ancient Greece, 110
Hall, John W. Japan, 117
Hall, Vernon. Short History of Literary Criticism, 79
Halliday, F. E. Shakespeare Companion, 87
_____. Concise History of England, 113
_____. Illustrated Cultural History of England, 113
Halse, Albert O. Architectural Rendering, 66
Hamilton, Alexander. Federalist, 22
Hamilton, Edith. Ever-Present Past, 79
_____. Greek Way, 91, 110
_____. Mythology, 14
_____. Roman Way, 90
Hamilton, Henry W. Sioux of the Rosebud, 119
Hamlin, Talbot. Architecture through the Ages, 66
Hammarskjold. Kelen, E., 102
Hammer, Ellen J. Struggle for Indochina: 1940–1955, 118
Hammond, James J. Woodworking Technology, 62
Han, Suyin. Many-Splendored Thing, 102
Hand, Jackson. Complete Book of Home Repairs and Maintenance, 63
_____. How to Do Your Own Wood Finishing, 62
Handbook for Vegetable Growers. Knott, J., 56
Handbook of Christian Feasts and Customs. Weiser, F., 13
Handbook of Denominations in the United States. Mead, F., 13
Handbook of Everyday Law. Ross, M., 26
Handbook of Greek Literature. Rose, H., 91
Handbook of Lawn Mower Repair. Peterson, F., 57
Handbook of Model Rocketry. Stine, G., 54
Handbook of Parliamentary Procedure. Davidson, H., 21

Handbook of Real Estate Investment. Campbell, D., 24

Handbook of Turtles. Carr, A., 44

Handbook on the Care of Paintings. Keck, C., 71

Handbook to Literature. Holman, C., 79

Handlin, Oscar. Children of the Uprooted, 21

———. Harvard Guide to American History, 121

Handmade Rugs for Practically Anything. Laury, J., 68

Handwriting. Teltscher, H., 6

Handy Home Medical Adviser and Concise Medical Encyclopedia. Fishbein, M., 50

Handyman's Book. Better Homes & Gardens, eds., 62

Hanley, Reid M. Who's Who in Track and Field, 76

Hansen, Chadwick. Witchcraft at Salem, 5

Hanzak, Jan. Pictorial Encyclopedia of Birds, 45

Hapgood, Ruth. First Horse, 57

Hapsburgs. Crankshaw, E., 114

Harbage, Alfred. Shakespeare: the Tragedies, 87

Harbin, Elvin O. Fun Encyclopedia, 75

Harbrace College Handbook. Hodges, J., 80

Harcave, Sidney. Russia, 115

Hardin, Garrett. Stalking the Wild Taboo, 16

Harkness, Kenneth. Official Chess Handbook, 75

———. Official Chess Rulebook, 75

Harlem on My Mind 1900-1968. Schoener, A., 124

Harman & Parmelee. Ceramic Glazes, 67

Harmless People. Thomas, E., 41

Harmon, A. J. Guide to Home Remodeling, 63

Harmony in Western Music. Goldman, R., 73

Harms, Ernest. Drugs and Youth, 49

Harper Encyclopedia of Modern World History. Morris, R., 93

Harper's Bible Commentary. Neil, W., 11

Harper's Dictionary of Music. Ammer, C., 72

Harper's English Grammar. Opdycke, J., 32

Harral, Stewart. Feature Writer's Handbook. 80

Harrington, A. P. Every Boy's Judo, 76

Harrington, Michael. Other America: Poverty in the United States, 22

Harris, Charles O. Slide Rule Simplified, 36

Harris, George L. Iraq, 117

Harris, Jane A. Dance Awhile: Handbook of Folk, Square, and Social Dance, 75

Harris, Janet. Single Standard, 18

Harris, Joseph P. Congress and the Legislative Process, 26

Harris, Sara. Sisters, 13

Harris, Thomas A. I'm OK, You're OK, 50

Harrison, Hal H. World of the Snake, 45

Harrison, John F. Society and Politics in England: 1780-1960, 113

Harry S. Truman. Truman, M., 107

Hart, Harold. Population Control, 17

Hart, James D. Oxford Companion to American Literature, 82

Hart, Jane. Where's Hannah?, 29

Hart, Moss. Act One, 102

Hart Roger W. Witchcraft, 5

Hartkopf, Roy. Math Without Tears, 36

Hartley, Anthony. Penguin Book of French Verse: 19th Century, 89

Hartog, Jan de. Hospital, 47

Harvard Guide to American History. Handlin, O., 121

Harvest of the Sea. Bardach, J., 39

Harvey, Paul. Oxford Companion to English Literature, 86

Hasenau, J. James. Building Your Own Home, 63

Haskins, James. Lew Alcindor, 102

———. Piece of the Power: Four Black Mayors, 96

———. Profiles in Black Power, 96

Haskins, James. Religions, 14

Hastings, James. Dictionary of the Bible, 10

Hastins, Mac. Barricades in Belfast, 113

Hauser, Philip M. Population Dilemma, 17

Hawaii: a History. Kuykendall, R., 126

Hawkes, Jacquetta. First Great Civilizations, 109

———. World of the Past, 109

Hawkins, Gerald S. Stonehenge Decoded, 94

Hawthorne, Nathaniel. Portable Hawthorne, 84

Hay, Henry. Amateur Magician's Handbook, 75

Hay, John. Atlantic Shore, 39

Hayakawa, Samuel I. Language in Thought and Action, 32

———. Symbol, Status and Personality, 6

Haydn, Hiram H. Portable Elizabethan Reader, 86

Hayter, Stanley W. New Ways of Gravure, 71

Hazard, Paul. Books, Children, and Men, 4

Hazeltine, Mary E. Anniversaries and Holidays, 30

Hazlitt, William. Characters of Shakespeare's Plays, 87

Healing Factor, Vitamin C. Stone, I., 48
Healthful Living. Diehl, H., 48
Heartland. Legg, S., 118
Hechinger, Grace. Teenage Tyranny, 18
Hecksher, Gunnar. Study of Comparative Government and Politics, 20
Hedgepeth, William. Alternative: Communal Life, 24
Hegarty, Edward J. How to Run Better Meetings, 28
Heilbroner, Robert L. Economic Problem, 22
———. Future as History, 93
———. Primer on Government Spending, 22
———. Worldly Philosophers, 22
Heine, Heinrich. Selected Poems, 88
Heisenberg, Werner. Physics and Beyond, 38
Helen V. Wilson's African Violet Book. Wilson, H., 66
Helfer, Ray E. Battered Child, 18
Helicopters and Autogyros. Gablehouse, C., 54
Hell in a Very Small Place. Fall, B., 118
Hellegers, Louisa F. Family Book of Crafts, 68
Hellenism. Toynbee, A., 110
Hellman, Lillian. Collected Plays, 84
———. Pentimento, 102
———. Unfinished Woman, 102
Helm, Peter J. Alfred the Great, 97
Helmker, Judith A. Manual of Snowmobiling, 76
Help! I'm a Parent. Narramore, B., 60
Help! I'm a Sunday School Teacher. Duckert, M., 12
Helping the Battered Child and his Family. Kempe, C., 18
Hemingway, Ernest. Moveable Feast, 102
Henderson, John. Emergency Medical Guide, 48
Hendrix, William S. Beginning French, a Cultural Approach, 33
Henry Clay and the Art of American Politics. Eaton, C., 99
Henry VIII. Scarisbrick, J., 102
Henry Ford. Burlingame, R., 101
Hepler, Donald E. Architecture: Drafting and Design, 66
Herb Magic & Garden Craft. Doole, L., 65
Herbalist. Meyer, J., 66
Herbert, Anthony. Soldier, 102
Herbert Hoover and the Great Depression. Warren, H., 124
Herbs to Grow Indoors. Simmons, A., 66

Here I Stand. Bainton, R., 104
Here, Mr. Splitfoot. Somerlott, R., 6
Heren, Louis. No Hail, No Farewell, 124
Herford, R. Travers. Talmud and Apocrypha, 10
Herlad, Earl S. Fishes of North America, 44
Herndon, Booton. Great Land, 53
Herndon, James. Way it 'Spozed to Be, 29
Herold, J. Christopher. Age of Napoleon, 114
Herring, Hubert. History of Latin America, 125
Herriot, James. All Creatures Great and Small, 102
———. All Things Bright and Beautiful, 102
Herrmann, Martin K. Art of Making Good Candies at Home, 58
Hersey, John, R. Hiroshima, 112
———. Into the Valley, 112
Hersh, Burton. Education of Edward Kennedy, 103
Hersh, Seymour M. My Lai 4, 118
Hershey, Gerald L. Living Psychology, 6
Herter, Christine. Dynamic Symmetry, 67
Hertz, Louis H. Complete Book of Model Railroading, 29
Hertzberg, Arthur. Judaism, 14
Hertzberg, Robert. Repairing Small Electrical Appliances, 59
———. So You Want to be a Ham, 52
Hesse, Hermann. Poems, 89
Hesseltine, William B. Third Party Movements in the United States, 22
Hewitt, Jean. New York Times Natural Foods Cookbook, 58
Hey Preach, You're Comin' Through. Wilkerson, D., 12
Heyerdahl, Thor. Kon-Tiki, 94
———. RA Expeditions, 94
Hicks, John D. Federal Union, 121
———. Republican Ascendancy, 124
Hidden Persuaders. Packard, V., 61
High School Equivalency Diploma Tests. Arco, 28
Highet, Gilbert. Classical Tradition, 79
———. Man's Unconquerable Mind, 6
———. People, Places and Books, 79
———. Poets in a Landscape, 90, 96
———. Powers of Poetry, 80
Hilgard, Ernest. Introduction to Psychology, 6
Hill, Christopher. Lenin and the Russian Revolution, 115
Hillcourt, William. New Field Book of Nature Activities and Hobbies, 39

Hilliard, Robert L. Writing for TV and Radio, 80

Hills, George. Spain, 115

Hillyer, Robert. First Principle of Verse, 80

Hiroshima. Hersey, J., 112

Historian and History. Smith, P., 93

Historian's Approach to Religion. Toynbee, A., 14

Historians at Work. Gay, P., 93

Historic Houses. American Heritage, 94

History and Philosophy of the Metaphysical Movements in America. Judah, J., 13

History of American Art. Mendelowitz, D., 65

History of American Drama. Quinn, A., 84

History of American Economic Life. Kirkland, E., 121

History of American Education. Good, H., 28

History of American Painting. Baigell, M., 70

History of Architectural Styles. Baumgart, F., 66

History of Art. Janson, H., 64

History of Art and Music. Janson, H., 64

History of Canada. Lamb, W., 120

History of Chile. Galdames, L., 125

History of Christian Thoughts. Tillich, P., 11

History of Color in Painting. Birren, F., 70

History of English History. Leguois, E., 86

History of Far Eastern Art. Lee, S., 64

History of Finland. Wuoringen, J., 116

History of French Literature. Cazamian, L., 89

History of French Literature. Nitze, W., 89

History of German Literature. Robertson, J., 89

History of Greece. Bury, J., 110

History of Greek Literature. Hadas, M., 91

History of Ireland. Curtis, E., 113

History of Italian Literature. Wilkins, E., 90

History of Japan. Latourette, K., 117

History of Japanese Religion. Anesaki, M., 14

History of Latin America. Herring, H., 125

History of Latin Literature. Hadas, M., 90

History of Mathematics. Boyer, C., 36

History of Mechanical Inventions. Usher, A., 47

History of Modern Criticism. Wellek, R., 79

History of Musical Insturments. Sachs, C., 74

History of Norway. Larsen, K., 115

History of Photography. Newhall, B., 72

History of Physics before the Modern Age. Bernal, J., 38

History of Presidential Elections. Roseboom, E., 22

History of Rocketry and Space Travel. Von Braun, W., 56

History of Rome to A.D. 565. Boak, A., 109

History of Russia. Parkes, B., 115

History of Russia. Varnadksy, G., 115

History of Russian Literature to 1900. Mirsky, D., 92

History of Soviet Russia. Von Rauch, G., 115

History of the American Revolution. Alden, J., 121

History of the Ancient World. Starr, C., 109

History of the Arabs. Hitti, P., 117

History of the Belgians. De Meeus, A., 116

History of the English Speaking People. Churchill, W., 113

History of the Monroe Doctrine. Perkins, D., 121

History of the Roumanians. Seton-Watson, R., 116

History of the 20's and 30's. American Heritage, 124

History of the United States Army. Weigley, R., 27

History of Venezuela. Moron, G., 125

History of Western Music. Grout, D., 73

Hitler: a Study in Tyranny. Bullock, A., 102

Hitler, Adolf. Mein Kampf, 102

Hitler and Nazi Germany. Waite, R., 114

Hitti, Philip K. History of the Arabs, 117

Hittleman, Richard L. Yoga Way to Figure and Facial Beauty, 48

Ho. Halberstam, D., 102

Hoag, Edwin. American Houses, 66

Hockey! Beddoes, R., 76

Hodge, Jane A. Only a Novel, 97

Hodges, John. Harbrace College Handbook, 80

Hodnett, Edward. Poems to Read Aloud, 80

Hoebel, Edward A. Anthropology, 41

Hoffer, Eric. Ordeal of Change, 16

Hoffman, Adeline M. Daily Needs and Interests of Older People, 19

Hoffman, Daniel G. Form and Fable in American Fiction, 84

Hofmann, Hans. Discovering Freedom, 11

Hogben, Lancelot. Science for the Citizen, 35
——. Mathematics for the Millions, 36

Holbrook, Stewart H. Age of the Moguls, 96, 123

Holden, Alan. Crystals-Crystal Growing, 38

Holden, Honal. Art Career Guide, 64

Holland, Lawrence B. Who Designs America?, 65

Hollingshead, A. Elmstown's Youth, 17

Hollon, W. Eugene. Southwest: Old and New, 124

Holman, C. Hugh. Handbook to Literature, 79

Holmes, Arthur W. Basic Auditing Principles, 61

Holmes, Marjorie. I've Got to Talk to Somebody, God, 12

———. Who Am I, God?, 12

Holt, Edgar. Making of Italy, 1815-1870, 115

Holt, John. How Children Learn, 29

———. How Children Fail, 29

———. What Do I Do Monday?, 29

Holt, Pat M. Colombia Today and Tomorrow, 125

Holt, Rackham. George Washington Carver, 99

Holtman, Robert B. Napoleonic Revolution, 114

Holy Bibles, 11

Holzer, Hans, Power of Hypnosis, 5

Home and Building Maintenance. Woodin, J., 63

Home and Child Life in Colonial Days. Earle, A., 121

Home Bakebook of Natural Breads and Goodies. Sandler, S., 59

Home Book of Animal Care. Guthrie, E., 57

Home Book of Modern Verse. Stevenson, B., 80

Home Book of Smoke-Cooking Meat, Fish, and Game. Hull, R., 58

Home Book of Taxidermy and Tanning. Grantz, G., 42

Home Book of Verse. Stevenson, B., 80

Home in Your Pack. Angier, B., 76

Home Movies Made Easy. Eastman Kodak, 72

Home Refrigeration and Air Conditioning Guide. Anderson, E., 59

Homemade Bread. Farm Journal, eds., 58

Homeowner's Complete Outdoor Building Book. Brimer, J., 62

Homeowner's Survival Kit. Watkins, A., 63

Homer. Iliad, 91

———. Odyssey, 91

Homestudy Courses for Civil Service Jobs. Turner, D., 26

Honda, Isao. World of Origami, 68

Honeybees from Close Up. Dines, A., 44

Honor Thy Father. Talese, G., 28

Hooded Americanism. Chalmers, D., 22

Hooked and Knotted Rugs. Beitler, E., 68

Hooked on Books. Fader, D., 4

Hoopes, Townsend. Devil and John Foster Dulles, 100

Hopkins, Jerry. Elvis, 105

Hoppe, H. Whittling and Wood Carving, 67

Horace. Odes and Epodes, 90

———. Satires, Epistles, and Ars Poetica, 90

Horan, James D. Desparate Years, 124

Horizon Concise History of England. White, R., 114

Horizon Concise History of France. Davidson, M., 114

Horizon Concise History of Greece. Eliot, A., 116

Horizon Concise History of Japan. Busch, 117

Horizon Concise History of Mexico. Alba, V., 120

Horizon Concise History of Scandinavia. Butler, E., 115

Horizon History of Africa. Boahen, J., 118

Horne, Alistair. Price of Glory: Verdun 1916, 112

Horney, Karen. Our Inner Conflicts, 6

Horowitz, Elinor L. Mountain People, Mountain Crafts, 68

Horrocks, John E. Psychology of Adolescence, 7

Horseback Riding. Sports Illustrated, eds., 78

Horseman's Encyclopedia. Self, M., 57

Horses of the World. Goodall, D., 57

Horsman, Reginald. War of 1812, 122

Horwitz, Elinor L. Capital Punishment, U.S.A., 25

Hospital. Hartog, J., de, 47

Hostetler, John A. Amish Society, 13

Houdini. Gresham, W., 102

Houn, Franklin W. Short History of Chinese Communism, 116

Hour of Gold, Hour of Lead. Lindbergh, A., 104

Houriet, Robert. Getting Back Together, 24

Hours, Madeleine. Secrets of the Great Masters, 71

House & Garden. Complete Guide to Interior Decoration, 69

House Plants. Compton, J., 65

House Wiring. Palmquist, R., 53

Household Ecology. Percival, J., 59

Household Equipment. Peet, L., 59

Householder's Encyclopedia. Schuler, S., 63

Houseman, A. E. Collected Poems, 86

Houses of God. Mirsky, J., 66

How Black is the Gospel? Skinner, T., 10

How Children Fail. Holt, J., 29

How Children Learn. Holt, J., 29

How Did Sports Begin? Brasch, R., 76

How Does a Poem Mean? Ciardi, J., 80

How Things Work. Byrd, E., 47

How to Adopt a Child. Farmer, R., 25

How to Avoid Probate. Dacey, N., 23

How to Avoid Problems with Your Will. Farmer, R., 25

How to Avoid Social Diseases. Nicholas, L., 50

How to Be Fit. Kiphuth, R., 48

How to Be the Complete Professional Salesman. Shook, R., 61

How to Buy Stocks. Engel, L., 23

How to Clean Everything. Moore, A., 59

How to Control Plant Disease in Home and Garden. Shurtleff, M., 57

How to Debate. Summers, H., 82

How to Design and Build Flying Models. Laumer, K., 54

How to Do Library Research. Downs, R., 3

How to Do Your Own Wood Finishing. Hand, J., 62

How to Draw and Compose Pictures. Zaidenberg, A., 67

How to Drive Better and Avoid Accidents. Kearney, P., 55

How to Enjoy Mathematics with Your Child. Rosenberg, N., 37

How to Fix Almost Everything. Schuler, S., 63

How to Fix Up Old Cars. Smith, L., 55

How to Grow African Violets. Sunset Magazine, eds., 66

How to Grow and Use Annuals. Sunset Magazine, Eds., 66

How to Grow Bulbs. Sunset Magazine, eds., 66

How to Grow Herbs. Sunset Magazine, eds., 66

How to Grow House Plants. Sunset Magazine, eds., 66

How to Grow Roses. Sunset Magazine, eds., 66

How to Know the Grasses. Pohl, R., 43

How to Learn Languages and What Languages to Learn. Pei, M., 32

How to Lie with Statistics. Huff, D., 36

How to Live with a Heart Attack and How to Avoid One. Miller, R., 50

How to Live with Diabetes. Dolger, H., 49

How to Make a Telescope. Texereau, J., 37

How to Make Collages. Lynch, J., 68

How to Make Colonial Furniture. Gottshall, F., 62

How to Make Money in Real Estate. McMichael, S., 24

How to Make Movies. Ferguson, R., 72

How to Make Your Home More Convenient. Farm Journal, 69

How to Make Your Own Sewing Patterns. McCunn, D., 60

How to Organize and Operate a Small Business. Kelley, P., 61

How to Parent. Dodson F., 60

How to Plan and Plant Your Own Property. Ireys, A., 65

How to Read a Book. Adler, M., 4

How to Read Better and Faster. Lewis, N., 33

How to Read History. Robertson, A., 93

How to Repair Major Appliances. Tricomi, E., 59

How to Run a Small Business, Lasser, J., 61

How to Run Better Meetings. Hegarty, E., 28

How to Select, Buy, and Enjoy a Motor Home, Van, Camper, Tent-Top, or Tent. Hull, C., 55

How to Service and Repair Your Own Car. Day, D., 55

How to Start Your Own Small Business, 61

How to Study Better and Get Higher Marks. Ehrlich, E., 28

How to Talk to God When You Aren't Feeling Religious. Smith, C., 13

How to Teach Yourself and Your Family to Swim Well. Sava, C., 78

How to Tell Fortunes with Cards. Brown, W., 5

How to Use Hand and Power Tools. Daniels, G., 63

How to Write Reports, Papers, Theses, Articles. Riebel, J., 80

How to Write Successful Magazine Articles. Rose, C., 80

How We Got Our Denominations. Stuber, S., 13

How We Think. Dewey, J., 6

Howard, Jane. Please Touch, 16

Howard, Neale E. Telescope Handbook and Star Atlas, 37

Howard, Sylvia. Tin Can Crafting, 68

Howard & Copley. Australia in the 20th Century, 126

Howarth, David. Waterloo, 111

Hoyle, Fred. New Face of Science, 35

Hoyle, Martha B. World in Flames: History of World War II, 112

Hoyle's Simplified Guide to the Popular Card Games. Gibson, W., 75

Hoyt, Joseph B. Man and Earth, 94

Hubbard, Frank T. Three Centuries of Harpsichord Making, 74

Hudson, Winthrop S. American Protestantism, 13

Huenefeld, John. Community Activist's Handbook, 17

Huergon, Jacques. Daily Life of the Etruscans, 109

Huff, Darrell. Complete Book of Home Improvement, 63

———. How to Lie with Statistics, 36

Hughes, H. Stuart. Contemporary Europe, 112

Hughes, Langston. African Treasury, 91

———. Book of Negro Folklore, 31

———. New Negro Poets, 83

———. Poems from Black Africa, 91

Huizinga, Johan. Waning of the Middle Ages, 110

Hull, Clinton R. How to Select, Buy, and Enjoy a Motor Home, Van, Camper, Tent-Top, or Tent, 55

Hull, Raymond. Home Book of Smoke-Cooking Meat, Fish, and Game, 58

Human Aggression. Storr, A., 7

Human Behavior. Berelson, B., 16

Human Body. Asimov, I., 47

Human Life. Dedek, J., 8

Human Like Me, Jesus. Boyd, M., 12

Human Mind. Menninger, K., 7

Human Sexuality. McCary, J., 48

Human Zoo. Morris, D., 17

Hume, David. Philosophy of David Hume, 8

Hume, Robert E. World's Living Religions, 14

Humes, Jesild, Jr. Child Under Six, 60

Hundreds of Ideas. Better Homes & Gardens, eds., 69

Hungry Years. Paradis, A., 23

Hunt, Charles B. Physiography of the United States, 39

Hunt, Gladys, N. Christian Way of Death, 12

Hunt, Morton M. World of the Formerly Married, 18

Hunter, Beatrice T. Natural Foods Cookbook, 58

———. Natural Foods Primer, 58

Hunting in America. Waterman, C., 78

Hurd, Charles. Treasury of Great American Speeches, 82

Hurdy, John M. American Indian Religions, 15

Hurlbut, Cornelius S. Minerals and Man, 39

Hurlock, Elizabeth B. Child Growth and Development, 60

Hutchins, Robert M. Learning Society, 29

Hutchins, Ross E. Insects, 44

Hutchinson, Lois. Standard Handbook for Secretaries, 61

Hutchinson, Paul. Twenty Centuries of Christianity, 13

Huthmacher, J. Joseph. Nation of Newcomers, 21

Hutton, Helen. Practical Gemstone Craft, 68

Huxley, Aldous L. Collected Essays, 88

Hyde, H. Montgomery. Stalin, 107

Hyde, Margaret O. Alcohol: Drink or Drug?, 49

———. Mind Drugs, 49

Hyman, Harold T. Complete Home Medical Encyclopedia, 50

Hyman, Libbie H. Comparative Vertebrate Anatomy, 43

Hymn of the Universe. DeChardin, P., 10

Hynek, J. Allen. UFO Experience, 4

I. R. A. Coogan, T., 113

I Ain't Much, Baby-but I'm All I've Got. Lair, J., 12

I Am Third. Sayers, G., 106

I and Thou. Buber, M., 14

I Know Why the Caged Bird Sings. Angelou, M., 97

Ibarra, Francisco. Spanish Self-Taught, 34

Iberia. Michener, J., 115

Ibsen, Henrik. Eleven Plays, 89

Ice Hockey. Sports Illustrated, 77

Ichthyology. Lagler, K., 44

Ickis, Marguerite. Book of Religious Holidays and Celebrations, 30

Idea of a Theater. Fergusson, F., 81

Ideal Marriage. Van de Veld, T., 19

Ideas and Integrities. Fuller B., 8

Ideas and Men. Brinton, C., 93

Ideas for Landscaping. Sunset Magazine, eds., 66

Ideas for Recreation Rooms. Sunset Magazine, eds., 70

Ideas for Remodelling Your Home. Sunset Magazine, eds., 70

Ideas for Storage. Sunset Magazine, eds., 70

Identity: Youth and Crisis. Erickson, E., 7

Idyll, Clarence P. Abyss, 39

Ikerman, Ruth C. Devotional Programs for Every Month, 12

Iliad. Homer, 91

Illustrated Cultural History of England. Halliday. F., 113

Illustrated English Social History. Trevelyan, G., 114

Illustrated Hassle-Free Make Your Own Clothes Book. Rosenberg, S., 60

Illustrating Fashion. Sloane, E., 67

Illustrious Immigrants. Fermi, L., 21

I'm OK, You're OK. Harris, T., 50

Imitation of Christ. Kempis, S., 12

Immortal Jolson. Sieben, P., 103

Immortal Lovers. Winwar, F., 98

Impeachment: a Handbook. Black, C., Jr., 26

Imperial Presidency. Schlesinger, A., 27

Imperial Rome. Hadas, M., 109

Imperial Spain: 1469–1716. Elliot, J., 115

Implosion Conspiracy. Nizer, L., 26

Improve Your Bridge. Kelsey, H., 75

In Case of Emergency, What to Do until the Doctor Arrives. Benjamin, B., 48

In Cold Blood. Capote, T., 27

In Critical Condition. Kennedy, E., 27

In One Era and Out the Other. Levenson, S., 103

In Search of Ancient Gods. Von Daniken, E., 41

In the Days of McKinley. Leech, M., 123

Independent Filmmaking. Lipton, L., 72

India, Pakistan, and Ceylon. Brown, W., 117

India. Spear, P., 117

India. Zinkin, T., 117

Indian Heritage of America. Josephy, A., 119

Indian Tribes of North America. Swanton, J., 119

Indianapolis 500. Engel, L., 76

Indians. American Heritage, 119

Indians. Capps, B., 119

Indians of North America. Driver, H., 119

Indians of the United States. Wissler, C., 119

Indira Gandhi. Mohan, A., 101

Indonesia. Grant, B., 126

Indians. Tunis, E., 119

Industrial Revolution. Ashton, T., 22

The Infant and Child in the Culture of Today. Gesell, A., 7

Infinite Variety of Music. Bernstein, L., 72

Influence of Sea Power upon History. Mahan, A., 111

Information Systems. Vickery, B. 4

Inge, William M. Four Plays, 84

Inglis, Stuart J. Planets, Stars and Galaxies, 37

Innes, William T. Exotic Aquarium Fish, 44

Innocent Consumer vs. the Exploiters. Margolius, S., 58

Innocents Abroad. Twain, M., 85

Inorganic Chemistry. Sanderson, R., 39

Inquest. Epstein, E., 27

Insects. Hutchins, R., 44

Insects of North America. Klots, A., 44

Inside the Third Reich. Speer, A., 114

Inside Today's Home. Faulkner, R., 69

Insight and Outlook. Koestler, A., 8

Instant-Effect Decorating. Katz, M., 69

Instant Weather Forecasting. Watts, A., 53

Instinct and Intelligence. Barnett, S., 40

Integrated Basic Science. Brooks, S., 35

Intelligent Investor. Graham, B., 23

Intelligent Man's Easy Guide to Computers. Feldzaman, A. 4

Interior Electric Wiring: Residential. Graham, K., 52

International Conflict for Beginners. Fisher, R., 21

International Encyclopedia of Dogs. Dangerfield, S., 57

International Flag Book in Color. Pedersen, C., 108

International Relations Dictionary. Plano, J., 21

International Wine and Food Society's Encyclopedia of Wines. Simon, A., 62

Interpretation of Dreams. Freud, S., 6

Into the Valley. Hersey, J., 112

Introducing Archaeology. Magnusson, M., 94

Introducing the Drama. Gassner, J., 81

Introduction to American National Government. Ogg, F., 27

Introduction to Anthropology. Beals, R., 40

Introduction to Business. Jucius, M., 61

Introduction to Computers and Data Processing. Benice, D., 4

Introduction to Contemporary Music. Machlis, J., 73

Introduction to Geology. Stokes, W., 40

Introduction to Geometry. Coxeter, H., 36

Introduction to Herpetology. Goin, C., 45

Introduction to Logic. Copi, I., 8

Introduction to Mathematics. Cooley, H., 36

Introduction to Matrices, Vectors and Linear Programming. Campbell, H., 36

Introduction to Music. Bernstein, M., 72

Introduction to Music and Art in the Western World. Wold, M., 64

Introduction to Nutrition. Fleck, H., 48

Introduction to Organic Chemistry. Depuy, C., 38

Introduction to Probability and Statistics. Adler, H., 35

Introduction to Psychology. Hilgard, E., 6

Introduction to Psychology, Morgan, C., 7

An Introduction to Roman History, Literature and Antiquities. Petrie, A., 109

Introduction to Russian History and Culture. Spector, I., 115

Introduction to St. Thomas Aquinas. Thomas Aquinas, 11

Introduction to Shakespeare. Chute, M., 87

Introduction to Solid State Physics. Kittel, C., 38

Introduction to Textiles. Stout, E., 62

Introduction to the History of Central Africa. Wills, A., 119

Introduction to the History of Mathematics. Eves, H., 36

Introduction to the Theory of Numbers. Niven, I., 36

Introduction to Tomorrow: the U.S. and the Wider World. Abernethy, R., 120

Invention, Discovery and Creativity. Moore, A., 35

Inventor's Handbook. Fenner, T., 47

Inventor's Patent Handbook. Jones, S., 47

Invertebrate Zoology. Barnes, R., 43

Investigating the Unexplained. Sanderson, I., 4

Investing in Pottery and Porcelain. Morely-Fletcher, H., 67

Invisible Pyramid. Eiseley, L., 35

Invitation to French. Madrigal, M., 33

Invitation to German. Madrigal, M., 33

Invitation to Italian. Madrigal, M., 33

Invitation to Spanish. Madrigal, M., 34

Invitation to Geology. Matthews, W., III, 40

Invitation to the Talmud. Neusner, J., 14

Iran. Armajani, Y., 117

Iraq. Harris, G., 117

Ireland. McCarthy, J., 113

Ireys, Alice R. How to Plan and Plant Your Own Property, 65

Irion, Mary J. Yes, World, 12

Irish: Portrait of a People. O'Connor, R., 113

Irrigation. Zimmerman, J., 57

Irving, Washington. Sketch Book, 85

Irwin, Keith, G. Three Hundred Sixty-Five Days, 37

Is Paris Burning? Collins, L., 114

Isaacs, Harold R. Tragedy of the Chinese Revolution, 116

Isenstein, Harald. Creative Claywork, 67

Ishi in Two Worlds. Kroeber, T., 42

Israel's Years of Challenge. Ben Gurion, D., 117

It Pays to Increase Your Word Power. Funk, P., 33

Italian Grammar. Vittorini, D., 33

Italians. Barzini, L., 114

It's Easy to Become a Citizen. Bain, C., 20

It's Your Wedding. Bryant, F., 30

Ivanoff, Pierre. Mayan Enigma, 125

I've Got to Talk to Somebody, God. Holmes, M., 12

Ivey, Paul W. Successful Salesmanship, 61

JB. MacLeish, A., 84

Jackson, Joseph H. Pictorial Guide to the Planets, 37

Jackson, Sheila. Simple Stage Costumes and How to Make Them, 30

Jacksonian Era. Van Deusen, G., 122

Jacksonians. White, L., 27

Jacobs, Arthur. Opera, 73

Jacobs, David. Bridges, Canals, and Tunnels, 29

Jacobs, Harold R. Mathematics, 36

Jacobs, Jane. Death and Life of Great American Cities, 65

Jacobs, Wilbur R. Dispossessing the American Indian, 119

Jacobsen, Charles W. Oriental Rugs, 68

Jacobson, C. I. Enlarging, 72

Jacobus, Donald L. Genealogy as Pastime and Profession, 108

Jaeger, Edmund. North American Deserts, 39

Jaffe, Hans. 20,000 Years of World Painting, 71

James, Henry. Portable Henry James, 85

James, Marquis. Andrew Jackson, 102

James William. Essays on Faith and Morals, 5

——. Varieties of Religious Experience, 10

——. Writings, 9

James Family. Matthiessen, F., 102

James Joyce. Ellman, R., 103

Jameson, Kenneth. Art and the Young Child, 64

Janeway, Eliot. Economics of Crisis, 23

Janeway, Elizabeth. Man's World, Women's Place, 18

Janis, Jack H. New Standard Reference for Secretaries and Administrative Assistants, 61

Janson, Horst W. History of Art, 64
———. History of Art and Music, 64
Janus, Horst. Pond Life in the Aquarium, 44
Japan. Hall, J., 117
Japan. Langer, P., 117
Japan. Reischauer, E., 117
Jarman, Cathy. Atlas of Animal Migration, 43
Jaspers, Karl. Great Philosophers, 5
Jastrow, Robert. Astronomy, 37
———. Red Giants and White Dwarfs, 37
Jaxtheimer, Bodo W. Reinhold Drawing and
    Painting Book, 67
Jazz Dance. Stearns, M., 75
Jazz Improvisation. Mehegan, J., 74
Jefferson and Hamilton. Bowers, C., 122
Jefferson and the Ordeal of Liberty. Malone,
    D., 103
Jefferson and the Rights of Man. Malone,
    D., 103
Jefferson the President. Malone, D., 103
Jefferson the Virginian. Malone, D., 103
Jenkins, Elizabeth. Elizabeth the Great, 100
Jenkins, Marie M. Animals without Parents,
    46
Jennie: the Life of Lady Randolph Churchill;
    Dramatic Years, 1895–1921. Martin, R., 99
Jennie: the Life of Lady Randolph Churchill;
    Romantic Years, 1854–1895. Martin, R., 99
Jennings, Gary. Teenager's Realistic Guide to
    Astrology, 5
Jerusalem Bible 11
Jesus Generation. Graham, B., 13
Jesus Kids. Palmer, R., 12
Jewelry, Queen of Crafts. Sanford, W., 69
Jews, God and History. Dimont, M., 14
Jobe, Joseph. Great Age of Sail, 53
John Adams and the American Revolution.
    Bowen, C., 97
John D. Rockefeller. Nevins, A., 106
Johnson, Burgess. New Rhyming Dictionary
    and Poets' Handbook, 32
Johnson, Edgar. Charles Dickens, 100
Johnson, Eric W. Love and Sex in Plain
    Language, 48
———. Sex: Telling it Straight, 48
Johnson, James W. Autobiography of an
    Ex-Coloured Man, 19
———. God's Trombones, 83
Johnson, Larry. Fix Your Volkswagen, 55
Johnson, Lyndon B. Vantage Point, 124
Johnson, Mary. Sewing the Easy Way, 60
Johnson, Michael L. New Journalism, 4
Johnson, Pauline. Creating with Paper, 68

Johnson, Thomas. Emily Dickinson, 100
Johnstone, Kathleen Y. Sea Treasure, 44
Jonas, Paul. Manual of Darkroom Procedures
    and Techniques, 72
Jones, Burton W. Elementary Concepts of
    Mathematics, 36
Jones, Ernest. Life and Work of Sigmund
    Freud, 101
Jones, Franklin D. Engineering Encyclopedia,
    51
Jones, Louis C. Things That Go Bump in the
    Night, 6
Jones, Stacy V. Inventor's Patent Handbook,
    47
Jordan, Emil L. Animal Atlas of the World,
    46
Jordan, June M. Soulscript, 33
Josephson, Matthew. Politics, 123
———. President Makers, 124
———. Robber Barons, 123
Josephy, Alvin M. Indian Heritage of America,
    119
———. Red Power, 119
Journals of Lewis and Clark. Lewis, M., 122
Journey into Summer. Teale, E., 40
Joy of Cooking. Rombaur, I., 59
Joyce, James. Portable James Joyce, 88
Joys of Hunting Antiques. Salter, S., 70
Jucius, Michael J. Introduction to Business,
    61
Judah, J. Stillson. History and Philosophy of
    the Metaphysical Movements in America, 13
Judaic Hertiage. Brasch, R., 14
Judaism. Hertzberg, A., 14
Judd, F. C. Electronic Music and Musique
    Concrete, 74
Judo and Self Defense. Bartlett, E., 76
Jui-jitsu. Lowell, F., 77
Julius Caesar. Duggan, A., 99
Jung, Carl G. Analytical Psychology, 6
———. Portable Jung, 6
Junior Karate. Kozuki, R., 76
Just, Ward. Military Men, 27
Just Wait Till You Have Children of
    Own. Bombeck, E., 85
Justice in America. Lineberry, W., 25

Kalmus, H. 101 Simple Experiments with
    Insects, 44
Kaltenmark, Max. Lao Tzu and Taoism, 14
Kane, Robert . . . . A to Z, 95
Kannik, Preben. Military Uniforms of the
    World in Color, 27

Kanowitz, Leo. Women and the Law, 18

Kant, Immanual. Philosophy of Kant, 9

Kaplan, Abraham. New World Philosophy, 5

Kaplan, Justin. Mr. Clemens and Mark Twain, 99

Kaplan, Stuart R. Tarot Classic, 6

Karate. Tegner, B., 77

Karelitz, Samuel. When Your Child is Ill, 50

Karen. Killilea, M., 51

Kariher, Harry C. Who's Who in Hockey, 76

Karl, Frederick R. Reader's Guide to Great 20th Century English Novels, 88

Karolevitz, Robert F. Everything's Green . . . But My Thumb, 56

Karst, Gene. Who's Who in Professional Baseball, 76

Katz, Friedrich. Ancient American Civilizations, 125

Katz, Marjorie. Instant-Effect Decorating, 69

Kauffman, Donald T. For Instance, 12

Kauffmann, Edgar, Jr. Rise of an American Architecture, 66

Kaufman, John. Wings, Sun, and Stars, 45

Kaufman, Sherwin A. New Hope for the Childless Couple, 51

Kavaler, Lucy. Cold against Disease, 50

———. Freezing Point, 38

———. Mushrooms, Molds and Miracles, 43

Kavanaugh, James J. Modern Priest Looks at His Outdated Church, 11

Kay, George. Penquin Book of Italian Verse, 90

Kazin, Alfred. On Native Grounds, 82

———. Contemporaries, 82

Kearney, Paul W. How to Drive Better and Avoid Accidents, 55

Keck, Caroline K. Handbook on the Care of Paintings, 71

Kee, Howard C. Understanding the New Testament, 11

Keene, Donald. Anthology of Japanese Literature, 91

Keeslar, Oreon. National Catalog of Financial Aids for Higher Education, 29

Keeton, William. Biological Science, 41

Keith, Harold. Sports and Games, 76

Kelen, Emery. Hammarskjold, 102

Keller, Allan. Colonial America, 121

Keller, Helen. Story of My Life, 103

Keller, Morton. Art and Politics of Thomas Nast, 123

Kelley, Pearce C. How to Organize and Operate a Small Business, 61

Kelly, Alfred H. American Constitution, 25

Kelly, Amy. Eleanor of Aquitaine and the Four Kings, 100

Kelly, Gerald W. Metric System Simplified, 30

Kelsey, H. W. Improve Your Bridge, 75

Kempe, C. H. Helping the Battered Child and his Family, 18

Kemper, John D. Engineer and His Profession, 51

Kempis, Saint Thomas. Imitation of Christ, 12

Kendall, Paul. Richard III, 106

Kenealy, James P. Boating from Bow to Stern, 77

Kennan, George F. Russia and the West Under Lenin and Stalin, 21

Kennedy, Charles W. Anthology of Old English Poetry, 86

———. Earliest English Poetry, 86

———. Early English Christian Poetry, 86

Kennedy, Edward M. In Critical Condition, 27

Kennedy, Eugene C. New Sexuality: Myths, Fables and Hang-ups, 8

———. People are the Church, 13

Kennedy, John F. Profiles in Courage, 96

Kennedy, Rose. Times to Remember, 103

Kennedy. Sorenson, T., 103

Kenniston, Kenneth. Uncommitted, 18

———. Young Radicals, 18

Kenny, Carla. Art of Papier Mache, 68

Kent, Raymond P. Money and Banking, 23

Kerensky, Oleg. World of Ballet, 74

Kerr, Jean. Please Don't Eat the Daisies, 85

———. Snake Has All the Lines, 85

Kerrigan, Evans E. American Badges and Insignia, 27

———. American War Medals and Decorations, 27

Ketchum, Richard M. What is Communism?, 24

Kettell, Russell H. Early American Rooms, 70

Key, Vladimer O. Politics, Parties and Pressure Groups, 22

———. Public Opinion and American Democracy, 20

Key Monuments of the History of Architecture. Millon, H., 66

Key to Better Reading. Leedy, P., 33

Keyes, Frances P. Tongues of Fire, 13

Keynes, John M. General Theory of Employment, Interest and Money, 23

Keys, Ancel. Eat Well and Stay Well, 58

Keys to Art. Canady, J., 64

Kgosistsile, Keorapetse. Word is Here; Poetry from Modern Africa, 91

Khrushchev. Crankshaw, E., 103

Kierkegaard, Soren. Kierkegaard Anthology, 9

Kierzek, John M. Macmillan Handbook of English, 80

Killilea, Marie. Karen, 51

Kimber, Diana C. Anatomy and Physiology, 48

Kimche, Jon. Second Arab Awakening, 117

Kind and Usual Punishment. Mitford, J., 28

King, Coretta. My Life with Martin Luther King, 103

King, Lawrence J. Weeds of the World, 43

King, Martin Luther, Jr. Strength to Love, 12

King Edward VII. Magnus, P., 100

Kings and Desperate Men: Life in 18th Century England. Kronenberger, L., 113

Kinsley, D. A. Favor the Bold, 100

Kiphuth, Robert. How to be Fit, 48

Kirby, Richard S. Engineering in History, 51

Kirchner, Walther. Western Civilization, 93

Kirkham, Kay E. Simplified Genealogy for Americans, 108

Kirkland, Edward C. History of American Economic Life, 121

Kirkley, George W. Modern Weight Lifting, 76

———. Weight Lifting and Weight Training, 76

Kirkus, 1

Kit Carson. Vestal, S., 99

Kitchen Candlecrafting. Monroe, R., 69

Kitman, Marvin. George Washington's Expense Account, 122

Kittel, Charles. Introduction to Solid State Physics, 38

Klass, Philip J. UFOs Identified, 4

Klein, H. Arthur. Surf-Riding, 77

Klein, Richard M. Discovering Plants, 43

Kleppner, Otto. Advertising Procedure, 61

Kling, Samuel G. Complete Guide to Everyday Law, 25

Klots, Alexander. Field Guide to the Butterflies, 44

———. Insects of North America, 44

Klots, Elsie. New Field Book of Freshwater Life, 39

Knapton, Ernest J. France: an Interpretative History, 114

Knitting Made Easy. Aytes, B., 67

Knitting without Tears. Zimmerman, E., 69

Knott, James E. Handbook for Vegetable Growers, 56

Know Your Gerbils. Robinson, D., Jr., 57

Kobler, John. Capone, 99

Koedt, Anne. Radical Feminism, 18

Koenig, Louis W. Chief Executive, 27

———. Truman Administration, 124

Koestler, Arthur. Act of Creation, 6

———. Case of the Midwife Toad, 42

———. Insight and Outlook, 8

———. Sleepwalkers, 10

Kohl, Herbert. 36 Children, 29

Kohler, Foy D. Understanding the Russians, 21

Kohn, Bernice. Organic Living Book, 58

Kohn, Hans. Nationalism, 20

Koller, John M. Oriental Philosophies, 9

Kon-Tiki. Heyerdahl, T., 94

Konvitz, Milton. Expanding Liberties, 20

Koran. Rodwell, J., ed., 15

Korea: the Third Republic. Chung, K., 117

Kotler, Milton. Neighborhood Government, 27

Kovac, Steve. Learn to Bowl, 76

Kovel, Ralph M. Directory of American Silver, Pewter, and Silver Plate, 70

Kozol, Jonathan. Death at an Early Age, 29

Kozuki, Russell. Junior Karate, 76

Kramer, Edith. Art as Therapy with Children, 64

Kramer, Jack. Gardening and Home Landscaping, 65

———. 1000 Beautiful House Plants and How to Grow Them, 65

Kranz, Frederick H. Gardening Indoors Under Lights, 65

Kraus, Albert L. New York Times Guide to Business and Finance, 22

Kraus, Edward H. Gems and Gem Materials, 39

Kraus, Michael. United States to 1865, 121

Kraus, Philip E. Yesterday's Children, 29

Kraus, Richard G. Folk Dancing, 74

Krents, Harold. To Race the Wind, 103

Krieger, Louis C. Mushroom Handbook, 43

Krock, Arthur. Consent of the Governed, and Other Deceits, 124

Kroeber, Theodora. Ishi in Two Worlds, 42

Kronenberger, Louis. Kings and Desperate Men: Life in 18th Century England, 113

Kronenberger, Louis, ed. Portable Johnson and Boswell, 88

Krutch, Joseph W. Great Chain of Life, 42

Kuh, Katharine. Break-Up: the Core of Modern Art, 64

———. Open Eye: in Pursuit of Art, 64

Kuhns, William. Environmental Man, 13

Kulesza, Severyn R. Modern Riding, 78

Kuykendall, Ralph S. Hawaii: a History, 126

La Raza. Steiner, S., 20

Labor in America. Dulles, F., 23

Labor in the United States. Cohen, S., 23

Labor Wars. Lens, S., 23

Labrie, Jean. Amateur Taxidermist, 42

Lacocoon and Other Writings. Lessing, G., 89

Lacquer and Crackle. Nussbaumer, H., 69

LaCroix, Grethe. Creating with Beads, 68

Lacrosse. Morrill, W., 77

Lader, Lawrence. Foolproof Birth Control, 51

Ladies Home Journal Family Medical Guide. Nourse, A., 50

LaFontaine, Jean de. Fables, 89

Lagler, Karl. Ichthyology, 44

Laidman, Hugh. Complete Book of Drawing and Painting, 71

Laing, R. D. Divided Self, 51

———. Self and Others, 6

Lair, Jess. I Ain't Much, Baby-but I'm All I've Got, 12

Laird, Charlton. Language in America, 32

LaLonde, William S. Professional Engineer's Examination Questions and Answers, 51

Lamaze, Fernand. Painless Childbirth: LaMaze Method, 51

Lamb, Brian. Pocket Encyclopedia of Cacti and Succulents, 65

Lamb, Charles. Portable Charles Lamb, 88

———. Tales from Shakespeare, 87

Lamb, Harold. Charlemagne, 99, 114

———. Cyrus the Great, 100

Lamb, Lawrence E. Your Heart and How to Live with It, 50

Lamb, William K. History of Canada, 120

Lampert, Lincoln N. Modern Dairy Products, 57

Land and People of South Africa. Paton, A., 118

Land of Fortune. Aitken, J., 125

Landers, Chris. Learn to Ski, 76

Landforms. Adams, G., 39

Landis, Benson Y. World Religions, 14

Landis, Paul H. Making the Most of Marriage, 18

Landon, Margaret. Anna and the King of Siam, 103

Lands Between. Palmer, A., 116

Landsberg, Helmut E. Weather and Health, 39

Landscape Gardening. Crockett, J., 65

Landy, Euguene E. Underground Dictionary, 33

Lang, Paul H. Music in Western Civilization, 73

Lang, Serge. Basic Mathematics, 36

Langenscheidt Staff. New Pocket German Dictionary, 33

Langer, P. F. Japan, 117

Langer, Walter C. Mind of Adolf Hitler, 102

Langer, William L. Encyclopedia of World History, 93

Langley, Russell. Practical Statistics Simply Explained, 36

Langone, John. Death is a Noun, 8

Language in America. Laird, C., 32

Language in Thought and Action. Hayakawa, S., 32

Language Today. Pei, M., 32

Lanoue, Fred R. Drownproofing, 77

Lao Tzu and Taoism. Kaltenmark, M., 14

Lappin, Alvin R. Plastics-Projects and Techniques, 61

Lardner, Ring. Ring Lardner Reader, 85

Large-Format Camera Practice. Foldes, J., 72

Larkin, Oliver W. Art and Life in America, 64

Larsen, Karen. History of Norway, 115

Lasers. Brown, R., 52

Lash, Joseph. Eleanor and Franklin, 106

———. Eleanor: the Years Alone, 106

Lasser, Jacob K. Business Management Handbook, 61

———. How to Run a Small Business, 61

———. Managing Your Family Finances, 23

———. Your Income Tax, 23

Last Essays. Mann, T., 89

Last Nine Days of the Bismarck. Forester, C., 112

Last Plantagenets. Costain, T., 113

Last Rights. Mannes, M., 8

Last Years of the Church. Poling, D., 13

Late Great Planet Earth. Lindsey, H., 11

Latent Image. Newhall, B., 72

Later Years. Painter, G., 106

Latham, Edward. Dictionary of Names, Nicknames, and Surnames, 108

Latin: an Introductory Course. Wheelock F., 34

Latin America, a Cultural History. Arciniegas, G., 125

Latin Literature. Copley, F., 90

Latourette, Kenneth. Chinese, 117

———. History of Japan, 117

———. Short History of the Far East, 116

Laumer, Keith. How to Design and Build Flying Models, 54

Laury, Jean R. Handmade Rugs for Practically Anything, 68

Laver, James. Concise History of Costume and Fashion, 30

Lavine, Harold. Central America, 120

Law in American Society. East, S., 25

Law of Adoption. Leavy, M., 25

Lawless, Ray M. Folksingers and Folksongs in America, 73

Lawn Book. Schery, R., 66

Lawns and Ground Covers. Sunset Magazine, eds., 66

Lawrence, D. H. Portable D. H. Lawrence, 88

Lawrence, T. E. Seven Pillars of Wisdom, 112

Lawson, Donna. Brothers and Sisters All Over This Land, 24

Lawson, Joan. European Folk Dances, 75

Lawyers. Mayer, M., 25

Layman's Guide to Psychiatry and Psychoanalysis. Berne, E., 50

Leach, William H. Cokesbury Marriage Manual, 30

Leacock, Eleanor. North American Indians in Historical Perspective, 119

Leading Constitutional Decisions. Cushman, R., 25

Lear, Edward. Complete Nonsense Book, 86

Learn to Bowl. Kovac, S., 76

Learn to Ski. Landers, C., 76

Learning Society. Hutchins, R., 29

Learning to Live from the Acts. Price, E., 11

Learning to Read Music. Lilienfeld, R., 73

Leaves of Grass. Whitman, W., 83

Leavy Morton. L. Law of Adoption, 25

Leckie Robert. World Turned Upside Down, 122

Lederer, William J. Mirages of Marriage, 18

Lee, Nata. Complete Book of Entertaining, 58

Lee, Sherman E. History of Far Eastern Art, 64

Leech, Margaret K. In the Days of McKinley, 123

Leedy, Paul. Key to Better Reading, 33

Legal Rights of Women, The. Boylan, B., 24

LeGaye, E. S. Gold. . . ABC's of Panning, 53

Legg, Stuart. Heartland, 118

Leguois, Emile H. History of English History, 86

Leidy, W. Philip. Popular Guide to Government Publications, 3

Leitch, Addison H. Readers Introduction to the New Testament, 11

Lekachman, Robert. Age of Keynes, 23

Lemons, Wayne. Major Appliance Repair Manual, 59

———. Small Appliance Repair Guide, 59

Lenin and the Russian Revolution. Hill, C., 115

Lens, Sidney. Labor Wars, 23

———. Poverty: America's Enduring Paradox, 23

———. Radicalism in America, 17

Leonard, Jonathan. Ancient America, 119

Leopold, Aldo. Sand County Almanac, 39

LeShan, Eda J. Conspiracy Against Childhood, 29

Leslie, Louis A. Gregg Notehand, 61

———. Gregg Shorthand Functional Method, 61

Lessenberry, David D. Clerical Office Typing, 61

Lessing, Gotthold. Lacocoon and Other Writings, 89

Lesson of the Masters. Cowley, M., 81

Lessons of History. Durant, W., 93

Lester, Julius. Look Out Whitey! Black Power's Gon' Get Your Mama, 19

———. Revolutionary Notes, 20

———. Search for the New Land, 21

———. To Be a Slave, 21

Let My People Go. Luthuli, A., 118

Let Them Live. Curry-Lindahl, K., 46

Let's Eat Right to Keep Fit. Davis, A., 58

Letters and Papers from Prison. Bonhoeffer, D., 11

Letters to a Black Boy. Teague, B., 20

Leuchtenberg, William E. Franklin D. Roosevelt and the New Deal, 124

———. Perils of Prosperity, 124

Levarie, Seigmund. Tone, 73

Levenson, Sam. Everything but Money, 103

———. In One Era and Out the Other, 103

Levin, G. Roy. Documentary Explorations, 74

Levine, Alan. The Rights of Students, 25

Levine, Lawrence W. Defender of the Faith, 98

Levine, Nathan. Typing for Everyone, 61

Levitan, Sar A. Big Brother's Indian Program: with Reservations, 119

Leviton, Alan E. Reptiles and Amphibians of North America, 45

Levittowners. Gans, H., 17

Lew Alcindor. Haskins, J., 102
Lewin, Stephen. Crime and its Prevention, 27
Lewis, Allan. American Plays and Playwrights of the Contemporary Theater, 84
Lewis, Anthony. Portrait of a Decade, 20
Lewis, Bernard. Emergence of Modern Turkey, 118
Lewis, Clive S. Screwtape Letters, 12
Lewis, Howard, R. With Every Breath You Take, 54
Lewis, Meriwether, and William Clark. Journals of Lewis and Clark, 122
Lewis, Norman. How to Read Better and Faster, 33
———. Thirty Days to Better English, 33
———. Word Power Made Easy, 33
Lewis, Oscar. Children of Sanchez, 19
Ley, Willy. Dawn of Zoology, 43
———. Exotic Zoology, 43
———. Rockets, Missiles and Men in Space, 56
———. Watchers of the Skies, 37
Leyda, Jay. Portable Melville, 82
Liberace, 104
Library Journal, 1
Library of Astronomy. Page T., 37
Licit and Illicit Drugs. Brecher, E., 49
Lieber, Hugh. Mits, Wits and Logic, 8
Lieber, Lillian. Einstein Theory of Relativity, 38
Lieberman, E. James. Sex and Birth Control, 51
Liebers, Arthur. Complete Book of Water Sports, 78
———. Complete Book of Winter Sports, 76
———. Encyclopedia of Pleasure Boating, 78
Lieuwen, Edwin. Venezuela, 125
Life: an Introduction to Biology. Simpson, G., 41
Life and Death in a Coral Sea. Cousteau, J., 39
Life and Death of Lenin. Payne, R., 103
Life and Death of Louis XVI. Padover, S., 114
Life and Work of Sigmund Freud. Jones, E., 101
Life before Man. Spinar, Z., 41
Life Begins at Fifty. Pitkin, W., 19
Life Beyond Death. Ford, A., 5
Life in Action: Biochemistry Explained. Farago, P., 41
Life in Georgian England. Williams, E., 114
Life in a Medieval City. Gies, J., 110
Life in Medieval England. Bagley, J., 113

Life in Norman England. Tomkeieff, O., 114
Life in Photography. Steichen, E., 72
Life Nature Library. Time-Life Books, 35
Life of Benvenuto, Cellini. Celini, B., 99
Life of Charlotte Brontë. Gaskell, E., 98
Life of Fishes. Marshall, N., 45
Life of Insects. Wigglesworth, V., 44
Life of Jesus. Goodspeed, E., 11
Life of Sharks. Budker, P., 44
Life of Sir Arthur Conan Doyle. Carr, J., 100
Life of the African Plains. Brown, L., 43
Life of the Drama. Bentley, E., 81
Life of the Spider. Fabre, J., 44
Life of Vertebrates. Young, J., 44
Life on a Little Known Planet. Evans, H., 44
Life on a Medieval Barony. Davis, W., 110
Life on the Mississippi. Twain, M., 85
Life Science Library. Time-Life Books, 35
Life under the Pharaohs. Cottrell, L., 109
Lifetime with Lions. Adamson, G., 97
Light Horsekeeping. Mather, H., 57
Light on People. Petzold, P., 72
Liley, H. I. Modern Motherhood, 51
Lilienfeld, Robert. Learning to Read Music, 73
Lin Yutang. Wisdom of China and India, 91
Lincoln, Harry B. Computer and Music, 74
Lindbergh, Anne M. Bring Me a Unicorn, 104
———. Hour of Gold, Hour of Lead, 104
Lindbergh, Charles A. Spirit of St. Louis, 104
Lindgren, Henry C. Educational Psychology in the Classroom, 29
Lindsey, Hal. Late Great Planet Earth, 11
Lineberry, William P. Justice In America, 25
———. Mass Communications, 29
Link, Arthur, S. Woodrow Wilson and the Progressive Era, 124
Linke, Lilo. Ecuador, 125
Linton, George E. Modern Textile and Apparel Dictionary, 62
Lion Among Roses. Bradley, D., 115
Lippman, Walter. Public Opinion, 16
Lipton, Lenny. Independent Filmmaking, 72
Liptzin, Solomon. Flowering of Yiddish Literature, 91
Liston, Robert A. Downtown, 20
Literary Criticism in America. Van Nostrand, A., 79
Literary History of England. Baugh, A., 85
Literary History of the United States. Spiller, R., ed., 82
Literary Market Place, 1
Literature and Western Man. Priestly, J., 79

Literature of the American People. Quinn, A., 82

Literature of the Spanish People. Brenan, G., 90

Lithographic Prints from Stone and Plate. Banister, M., 71

Little, Malcolm. Autobiography of Malcolm X., 104

Little, Van Allen. General and Applied Entomology, 44

Little People. Wilkerson, D., 13

Little Treasury of American Poetry. Williams, O., 83

Little Treasury of Great Poetry. Williams, O., 81

Little Treasury of Modern Poetry. Williams, O., 81

Little Treasury of World Poetry. Creekmore, H., 80

Little Wars of the United States. Baumer, W., 120

Live at Peace with Your Nerves. Alvarez, W., 50

Lives. Plutarch, 96

Lives and Times of Archy and Mehitabel. Marquis, D., 85

Lives of Great Composers. Schonberg, H., 96

Lives of the Painters, Sculptors, and Architects. Vasari, G., 96

Lives of the Poets. Untermeyer, L., 96

Living Bible, 11

Living Black in White America. David, J., 95

Living Cell. Gillie, O., 42

Living Free, Adamson, J., 46

Living in Cities. Ridley, A., 17

Living Landscape. Sears, P., 40

Living Mammals of the World. Sanderson, I., 46

Living Novel, and Later Appreciations. Pritchett, V., 81

Living Psychology. Hershey, G., 6

Living with Books. Haines, H., 4

Living with your Ulcer. Berland, T., 49

Llewellyn, Peter. Rome in the Dark Ages, 115

Lloyd, Alan. Making of the King: 1066, 113

Lloyd, Alan C. Personal Typing, 61

Locke, David M. Enzymes: Agents of Life, 48

Locke, John. Two Treatises of Civil Government, 20

Locke, Raymond F. American Indian, 119

Loeb, Gerald M. Battle for Stock Market Profits, 23

Loken, Newton C. Gymnastics, 76

Lombardi, Vince. Run to Daylight, 77

London Sunday Times Insight Team. Northern Ireland: a Report on the Conflict, 113

Lonely Crowd. Riesman, D., 7

Long, Fern. All about Meetings, 21

Long March. Wilson, D., 117

Longfellow, Henry W. Complete Poetical Works, 83

Longford, Elizabeth. Queen Victoria, 107

Longest Day: June 6, 1944. Ryan, C., 112

Longgood, William. Darkening Land, 17

Longmore, Donald. Machines in Medicine, 47

——. Spare-Part Surgery, 50

Look Out Whitey! Black Power's Gon' Get Your Mama. Lester, J., 19

Looking at the Dance. Denby, E., 74

Loomis, Frederick B. Field Book of Common Rocks and Minerals, 39

Loomis, Roger. Medieval English Verse and Prose, 88

Lopez, Alfredo. Puerto Rican Papers: Notes on the Reemergence of a Nation, 120

Lorayne, Henry. Memory Book, 6

Lord, John. Maharajahs, 117

Lord, Walter. Day of Infamy, 112

——. Good Years, 124

——. Night to Remember, 94

Lords of Cuzco. Brundage, B., 125

Lost Cities and Vanished Civilizations. Silverberg, R., 109

Louria, Donald B. Overcoming Drugs, 49

Louis, XIV. Wolf, J., 104

Louis Pasteur. Vallery-Radot, R., 105

Love Against Hate. Menninger, K., 7

Love and Sex in Plain Language. Johnson, E., 48

Love and Will. May, R., 7

Love is Not Enough. Bettelheim, B., 7

Lovejoy, Clarence E. Lovejoy's Career and Vocational Guide, 23

——. Lovejoy's Career and Vocational School Guide, 29

——. Lovejoy's College Guide, 29

Lovejoy's Career and Vocational Guide. Lovejoy, C., 23

Lovejoy's Career and Vocational School Guide. Lovejoy, C., 29

Lovejoy's College Guide. Lovejoy, C., 29

Lovell, John, Jr. Black Song, 73

Low, Janet. Understanding the Stock Market, 23

Lowell, Frederick P. Jui-jitsu, 77

Lowell, James R. Complete Poetical Works, 83

Lowenfels, Walter. Poets of Today, 83

Low-Upkeep Book of Lawns and Landscape. McDonald, E., 66

Lozier, Herbert. Model Making, 68

Lubin, Albert J. Stranger on the Earth, 101

Lucas, E. Louise. Art Books: a Basic Bibliography on the Fine Arts, 64

Lucas, Henry S. Renaissance and the Reformation, 110

Luce, Gay. Body Time: Physiological Rhythms and Social Stress, 6

Luce and His Empire. Swanberg, W., 104

Lukas, J. Anthony. Don't Shoot—We are Your Children, 18

Luke, Mary M. Crown for Elizabeth, 113

Lumumba, Patrice. Congo, My Country, 118

Luna, Benjamin C. Upholstery, 62

Lund, Morten. Pleasures of Cross Country Skiing, 77

Luthuli, Albert J. Let My People Go, 118

Lutz, Frank E. Field Book of Insects, 44

Lynch, John. How to Make Collages, 68

Lynd, Robert. Middletown, 17

——. Middletown in Transition, 17

Lynde, Edward. Astrology for Everyone, 6

Lytel, Allan. ABC's of Lasers and Masers, 52

Maas, Peter. Serpico, 107

——. Valachi Papers, 28

McAleavy, Henry. Modern History of China, 117

MacArthur, Douglas. Reminiscences, 104

MacArthur, Robert H. Geographical Ecology, 43

McBurney, James R. Argumentation and Debate, 82

McCabe, Francis T. Mechanical Drafting Essentials, 63

McCafferty, James A. Capital Punishment, 25

McCalls' Garden Book, 65

McCall's Needlework Treasury, 68

McCall's Sewing Book, 60

McCart, Samuel W. Trial by Jury, 25

McCarthy, Joe. Ireland, 113

McCarthy, Mary. Memories of a Catholic Girlhood, 104

McCary, James L. Human Sexuality, 48

McCauley, William J. Vertebrate Physiology, 43

McClellan, Grant S. Censorship in the United States, 20

——. Civil Rights, 20

——. Consuming Public, 24

——. Protecting our Environment, 54

McClinton, Katherine M. Antiques Past and Present, 70

McConnell, Robert A. ESP Curriculum Guide, 6

McCormick, Harold. Shadows in the Sea, 45

McCoy, J. J. Complete Book of Dog Training and Care, 57

McCunn, Donald H. How to Make Your Own Sewing Patterns, 60

McDonagh, Don. Rise and Fall and Rise of Modern Dance, 75

McDonald, Elvin. Low-Upkeep Book of Lawns and Landscape, 66

McDonald, Linda. Contact Lenses, 51

Mace, David R. Abortion, 8

McEntee, Howard G. Model Aircraft Handbook, 54

MacFall, Russell P. Fossils for Amateurs, 40

McFarlane, Brian. Everything You Want to Know about Hockey, 77

McGill, Ralph. South and the Southerner, 124

MacGinitie, G. E. Natural History of Marine Animals, 39

McGinley, Phyllis. Saint Watching, 11

McGinniss, Joe. Selling of the President, 22

McGinnis, Tom. Your First Year of Marriage, 18

McGovern, James. To the Yalu, 117

McGuire, Thomas. Tooth Trip, 51

Machiavelli, Niccolo. Prince; and Discourses, 20

Machinery of the Body. Charles, A., 47

Machinery's Handbook. Oberg, E., 52

Machines in Medicine. Longmore, D., 47

Machinist's Library. Black, P., 52

Machlis, Joseph. Introduction to Contemporary Music, 73

McIntyre, Bibs. Bike Book, 56

McKay, Jim. My Wide World, 77

McKenzie, John L. Dictionary of the Bible, 11

MacKenzie, Norman. Secret Societies, 28

McLaughlin, Charles. Space Age Dictionary, 56

MacLeish, Archibald. JB, 84

MacLennan, Hugh. Colour of Canada, 95

McLuhan, T. C. Touch the Earth, 119

McMichael, Stanley L. How to Make Money in Real Estate, 24

Macmillan Handbook of English. Kierzek, J., 80

McNeill, William H. Rise of the West, 93

McNickle, L. S. Simplified Hydraulics, 51

MacNiece, Louis. Astrology, 6

Macrame. Sunset Magazine, eds., 69

McWhirter, Norriss. Guinness Book of World Records, 3

———. Guinness Sports Record Book, 77

Madame Sarah. Skinner, C., 98

Madrigal, Margarita. Invitation to French, 33

———. Invitation to German, 33

———. Invitation to Italian, 33

———. Invitation to Spanish, 34

Mafia is Not an Equal Opportunity Employer. Gage, N., 27

Magarshack, David. Storm, and Other Russian Plays, 92

Mages, Loren J. Electric Generating Systems, 52

Magic of Love. Armor, R., 11

Magill, Frank N. Masterpieces of World Philosophy in Summary Form, 5

Magnus, Philip. King Edward VII, 100

Magnusson, Magnus. Introducing Archaeology, 94

Magrath, C. Peter. American Democracy, 20

Mahan, Alfred T. Influence of Sea Power upon History, 111

Maharajahs. Lord, J., 117

Mahatma Gandhi. Sheean, V., 101

Maier, Pauline. From Resistance to Revolution, 122

Mails, Thomas E. Dog Soldiers, Bear Men and Buffalo Women, 119

———. Mystic Warriors of the Plains, 119

Main Currents in American Thought. Parrington, V., 82

Major Appliance Repair Manual. Lemons, W., 59

Major Religions of the World. Bach, M., 13

Major Writers of America. Miller, P., 82

Make Your Own Animated Movies. Andersen, 72

Make Your Own Elegant Jewelry. Boulay, R., 68

Make Your Own Mobiles. Schegger, T., 67

Make Your Own Sport Gear. Spielman, P., 62

Make Your Own TV Repairs. Margolis, A., 59

Makers of the Modern World. Untermeyer, L., 96

Makeup. Theatre Student Series, 75

Making Mobiles. Williams, G., 67

Making of a Counterculture. Roszak, T., 16

Making of a Mind. Teihard de Chardin, P., 107

Making of a Quagmire. Halberstam, D., 118

Making of a Surgeon. Nolen, W., 47

Making of Italy, 1815–1870. Holt, E., 115

Making of Modern Britain. Derry, T., 113

Making of the King; 1066. Lloyd, A., 113

Making of the President 1960. White, T., 125

Making of the President 1964. White, T., 125

Making of the President 1968. White, T., 125

Making of the President 1972. White, T., 125

Making the Media Revolution. Weiner, P., 72

Making the Most of Marriage. Landis, P., 18

Making Things Grow Outdoors. Cruso, T., 65

Maldonado-Denis, Manuel. Puerto Rico, 120

Malo, John. Complete Guide to Canoeing and Canoe-Camping, 78

———. Complete Guide to House Boating, 78

———. Snowmobiling, 77

Malone, Dumas. Jefferson and the Ordeal of Liberty, 103

———. Jefferson and the Rights of Man, 103

———. Jefferson the President, 103

———. Jefferson the Virginian, 103

Malthus, Thomas R. Population, 17

Maltreated Child. Fontana, V., 18

Malvern, Gladys. Six Wives of Henry VIII, 96

Mammals. Morris, D., 46

Man against Cancer. Glemser, B., 50

Man Against Himself. Menninger, K., 7

Man and Earth. Hoyt, J., 94

Man and Space. Clarke, A., 56

Man and the Computer. Diebold, J., 4

Man and Wildlife. Guggisberg, C., 43

Man, Time and Fossils. Moore, R., 41

Man Who Dared the Lightning. Fleming, T., 101

Managing your Coronary. Brams, W., 49

Managing Your Family Finances. Lasser, J., 23

Manchester, William. Arms of Krupp, 103

———. Death of a President, 103

———. Rockefeller Family Portrait, 96

Manchild in the Promised Land. Brown, C., 98

Mandl, Matthew. Fundamentals of Electronics, 52

Mann, Peggy. Golda, 105

Mann, Thomas. Essays of Three Decades, 89

———. Last Essays, 89

Mannes, Marya. Last Rights, 8

Manning, Henry. Fourth Dimension Simply Explained, 38

Man's Most Dangerous Myth: the Fallacy of Race. Montagu, A., 42

Man's Religions. Noss, J., 14

Man's Unconquerable Mind. Highet, G., 6

Man's World, Woman's Place. Janeway, E., 18

Manual for Writers of Term Papers, Theses, and Dissertations. Turabian, K., 3

Manual of Copyright Practice. Nicholson, M., 3

Manual of Darkroom Procedures and Techniques. Jonas, P., 72

Manual of Snowmobiling. Helmker, J., 76

Manufacturing Processes. Begeman, M., 61

Many Hues of English. Pei, M., 33

Many-Splendored Thing. Han, S., 102

Mao Tse Tung. Schram, S., 104

Map Making. Brown, L., 38

Maple, Eric. Superstition and the Superstitious, 31

Mapping. Greenhood, D., 38

Maps and Map-Makers. Tooley, R., 38

March of Science. Simak, C., 35

Marchwardt, Albert. Scribner Handbook of English, 80

Marcus, Abraham. Basic Electricity, 52

_____. Basic Electronics, 52

Marcuse, Herbert. Reason and Revolution, 16

Marden, Charles F. Minorities in American Society, 21

Margolis, Adele P. Dressmaking Book, 60

Margolis, Art. Make Your Own TV Repairs, 59

Margolis, Edward. Native Sons, 82

Margolius, Sidney. Innocent Consumer vs. the Exploiters, 58

Marijuana. Bloomquist, E., 49

Marijuana. Oursler, W., 49

Marijuana Reconsidered. Grinspoon, L., 49

Maria. Trapp, M., 107

Marin, Peter. Understanding Drug Use, 49

Marine, Gene. America, the Raped, 24

Mariner's Notebook: a Guide to Boating Fundamentals. Crawford, W., 53

Marketing: Principles and Methods. Phillips, C., 61

Marquand, Leo. Peoples and Policies of South Africa, 118

Marquis, Don. Lives and Times of Archy and Mehitabel, 85

Marriage for Moderns. Bowman, H., 18

Marriage in Black and White. Washington, J., 30

Marriott, Alice. American Indian Mythology, 15

Marsh, Moreton. Easy Expert in Collecting and Restoring American Antiques, 70

Marshall, Catherine. Beyond Ourselves, 12

Marshall, N. B. Life of Fishes, 45

Marshall, Peter. Mr. Jones, Meet the Master, 12

_____. Prayers of Peter Marshall, 13

Marteka, Vincent. Bionics, 3

Martin, Ralph. Jennie: the Life of Lady Randolph Churchill; Dramatic Years, 1895–1921, 99

Martin, Ralph. Jennie: the Life of Lady Randolph Churchill; Romantic Years, 1854–1895, 99

Martin, Samuel. Basic Japanese Conversation Dictionary, 34

Martinet, Andre. Elements of General Linguistics, 32

Marvels of Animal Behavior. National Geographic Society, 46

Marwick, Arthur. Nature of History, 93

Marx, Karl. Communist Manifesto, 24

_____. Das Kapital, 24

Marx. Payne, R., 104

Mary Queen of Scots. Fraser, A., 104

Mary, Queen of Scots. Morrison, B., 104

Mary Todd Lincoln. Turner, J., 104

Mary Tudor. Prescott, H., 104

Mary Wollstoncraft. Flexner, E., 108

Mascelli, Joseph V. Five C's of Cinematography, 72

Masefield, John. William Shakespeare, 87

Masers and Lasers. Brotherton, M., 52

Mass Communications. Lineberry, W., 29

Massey, Robert. Formulas for Painters, 71

Massie, Robert. Nicholas and Alexandra, 105

Masson, Georgina. Queen Christina, 99

Master Poems of the English Language. Williams, O., 81

Mastering the Art of French Cooking. Child, J., 58

Masterpieces of Russian Drama. Noyes, G., 92

Masterpieces of the Orient. Anderson, G., 91

Masterpieces of World Philosophy in Summary Form. Magill, F., 5

Masters, Edgar L. Spoon River Anthology, 83

Masters and the Slaves. Freyre, G., 125

Masters of the Drama. Gassner, J., 81

Masterson, William L. Chemical Principles, 38

Materials Handbook. Brady, G., 51

Math Without Tears. Hartkopf, R., 36
Mathematics. Jacobs, H., 36
Mathematics for the Millions. Hogben, L., 36
Mather, Helen. Light Horsekeeping, 57
Mather, Kirtley F. Earth beneath Us, 40
Mathews, F. Schuyler. Field Book of American Trees and Shrubs, 43
———. Field Book of American Wild Flowers, 43
Mathews, M. V. Technology of Computer Music, 74
Matter of Style. Namath, J., 77
Matthews, Herbert L. Fidel Castro, 99
Matthews, William H., III. Invitation to Geology, 40
Matthiessen, Francis O. American Renaissance, 82
———. James Family, 102
———. Oxford Book of American Verse, 83
Mattingly, Garrett. Armada, 113
———. Catherine of Aragon, 99
Mature Mind. Overstreet, H., 7
Maupassant, Guy de. Portable Maupassant, 89
Maurois, André. Byron, 98
———. Prometheus, 98
———. Titans, 96
Maus, Cynthie. Christ and the Fine Arts, 11
May, Arthur. Age of Metternich, 111
May, Ernest R. World War and American Isolation, 112
May, Rollo. Love and Will, 7
———. Meaning of Anxiety, 7
———. Power and Innocence: a Search for the Sources of Violence, 7
May, Siegmund H. Crowning Years, 19
Mayan Enigma. Ivanoff, P., 125
Mayer, Martin. Lawyers, 25
Mayer, Ralph. Artists' Handbook of Materials and Techniques, 71
Maynards, Olga. Children and Dance and Music, 75
Mays, Willie. My Life in and out of Baseball, 105
Mazlish, Bruce. Riddle of History, 93
Mazour, Anatole. Russia: Tsarist and Communist, 115
Mazzaro, Jerome. Modern American Poetry, 83
Mboya, Tom. Freedom and After, 118
Mead, Frank S. Handbook of Denominations in the United States, 13
Mead, Margaret. Blackberry Winter, 105
———. Coming of Age in Samoa, 41

———. Culture and Commitment, 18
———. Growing up in New Guinea, 41
Meaning of Anxiety. May, R., 7
Meaning of Philosophy. Brennan, J., 5
Meaning of Relativity. Einstein, A., 38
Mechanical Drafting Essentials. McCabe, F., 63
Mechanical Drawing. French, T., 63
Media. Sandman, P., 29
Medical Advice for the Traveler. Cahill, K., 48
Medical Aid Encyclopedia for the Home, 50
Medieval and Tudor Drama. Gassner, J., 87
Medieval Cities. Pirene, H., 111
Medieval Latin Lyrics. Waddell, H., 91
Medieval Mind. Taylor, H., 111
Medieval People. Power, E., 111
Medieval Scene. Coulton, G., 110
Medieval Verse and Prose. Loomis, R., 88
Megaw, Vincent. Dawn of Man, 41
Mehegan, John. Jazz Improvisation, 74
Meier, Matt S. Chicanos, 19
Meilach, Dona Z. Creating Art from Anything, 68
Mein Kampf. Hitler, A., 102
Meinhardt, Carl. So You Want to be an Architect, 66
Memoirs. Truman, H., 107
Memories of a Catholic Girlhood. McCarthy, M., 104
Memory Book. Lorayne, H., 6
Men Against Death. DeKruif, P., 95
Men and Pandas. Morris, R., 46
Men of Mathematics. Bell, E., 36, 95
Men of Music. Brockway, W., 95
Men of Peace. Smith, B., 96
Men to Match My Mountains. Stone, I., 122
Mencken, H. L. American Language, 33
———. Mencken Chrestomathy, 85
Mencken Chrestomathy. Mencken, H., 85
Mendell, Ronald. Who's Who in Basketball, 77
Mendelowitz, Daniel M. History of American Art, 65
Menninger, Karl. Crime of Punishment, 28
———. Human Mind, 7
———. Love Against Hate, 7
———. Man Against Himself, 7
Mental Illness. Stern, E., 51
Mentor Book of Major American Poets. Williams, O., 83
Mentor Book of Major British Poets. Williams, O., 86
Menus for Entertaining. Beard, J., 58
Menzel, Donald H. Astronomy, 37

_____. Field Guide to the Stars and Planets, 37

Merck Manual of Diagnosis and Therapy, 50

Merck Veterinary Manual, 57

Merrins, Eddie. Swing the Handle, Not the Clubhead, 77

Merritt, Frederick S. Building Construction Handbook, 63

Merton, Thomas. No Man is an Island, 12

Metal and Wire Sculpture. Gruber, E., 67

Metamorphosis. Ovid, 90

Methods of Research. Good, C., 3

Metric America: a Decision Whose Time Has Come. DeSimone, D., 29

Metric System Simplified. Kelly, G., 30

Mexican War. Singletary, O., 123

Mexicans. Coy, H., 120

Mexicans: Making of a Nation. Alba, V., 120

Meyer, Franks. What is Conservatism?, 20

Meyer, Hazel. Complete Book of Home Freezing, 59

Meyer, Joseph E. Herbalist, 66

Meyer, Karl E. Pleasures of Archaeology, 94

Meyers, Hans. 150 Techniques in Art, 64

Michener, James A. Bridge at Andau, 112

_____. Iberia, 115

Micks, Wilson. New Fundamental French, 33

Microbe Hunters. DeKruif, P., 96

Microbial World. Stanier, R., 42

Microbiology. Carpenter, P., 42

Microorganisms and Man. Wyss, O., 42

Microscope, a Practical Guide. Needham, G., 38

Mid-Century American Poetry. Ciardi, J., 83

Middle Ages. Bishop, M., 110

Middle East. Fisher, S., 117

Middleton, Robert G. Practical Electricity, 52

_____. Tape Recorder Servicing Guide, 52

Middletown. Lynd R., 17

Middletown in Transition. Lynd, R., 17

Midnight Oil. Pritchett, V., 106

Migraine. Sacks, O., 50

Milby, Robert V. Plastics Technology, 62

Military Men. Just, W., 27

Military Uniforms of the World in Color. Kannik, P., 27

Mill, John S. On Liberty, Representative Government, the Subjugation of Women, 18

Miller, Arthur. Collected Plays, 84

_____. Portable Arthur Miller, 84

Miller, Herman P. Rich Man, Poor Man, 24

Miller, John C. Federalist Era, 122

Miller, Jordan Y. American Dramatic Literature, 84

Miller, Keith. Habitation of Dragons, 12

Miller, Merle. Plain Speaking, 107

Miller, Perry. Major Writers of America, 82

Miller, Robert A. How to Live with a Heart Attack and How to Avoid One, 50

Millet, Kate. Sexual Politics, 18

Millon, Henry A. Key Monuments of the History of Architecture, 66

Mills, C. Wright. White Collar, 17, 20

Milne, Lorus. Arena of Life, 41

_____. Cougar Doesn't Live Here Anymore, 46

_____. Nature of Animals, 43

Milton, John. Portable Milton, 88

Mind. Wilson, J., 7

Mind Drugs. Hyde, M., 49

Mind of Adolf Hitler. Langer, W., 102

Mind of the Middle Ages. Artz, F., 110

Mind Over Matter. Rhine, L., 6

Mind that Found Itself. Beers, C., 98

Mineral Kingdom. Desautels, P., 39

Minerals and Man. Hurlbut, C., 39

Minibikes and Minicycles for Beginners. Edmonds, I., 76

Minimum Standards for Public Library Systems. American Library Association, 1

Minorities in American Society. Marden, C., 21

Minority Religions in America. Whalen, W., 13

Minton, Sherman, Venomous Reptiles, 45

Miracle at Philadelphia. Bowen, C., 25

Miracle Metals. Newcomb, E., 62

Mirages of Marriage. Lederer, W., 18

Mireaux, Emile. Daily Life in the Time of Homer, 110

Mirow, Gregory. Treasury of Designs for Artists and Craftsmen, 69

Mirsky, Dimitry S. History of Russian Literature to 1900, 92

Mirsky, Jeannette. Houses of God, 66

Missildene, W. Hugh. Your Inner Child of the Past, 7

Mr. Clemens and Mark Twain. Kaplan, J., 99

Mr. Jones, Meet the Master. Marshall, P., 12

Mister Wilson's War. Dos Passos, J., 124

Mitchell, Broadus. Alexander Hamilton, 102

_____. Critic of the Old South, 105

Mitford, Jessica. American Way of Death, 30

_____. Kind and Usual Punishment, 28

Mitford, Nancy. Sun King, 104

_____. Zelda, 101

Mits, Wits, and Logic. Lieber, H., 8

Mizener, Arthur. Far Side of Paradise, 101

Mobil Travel Guide, 95
Model Aircraft Handbook. McEntee, H., 54
Model Making. Lozier, H., 68
Model Making for Physicists. Bulman, A., 38
Modell, Walter. Drugs, 49
Modern ABC's of Family Camping. Wells, G., 77
Modern Airmanship. Van Sickle, N., 54
Modern American Poetry. Mazzaro, J., 83
Modern Backgammon. Goren, C., 75
Modern Biology. Carlson, E., 41
Modern Biology. Otto, J., 41
Modern British Drama. Popkin, H., 87
Modern Carpentry. Wagner, W., 63
Modern Criminal Investigation. Soderman, H., 26
Modern Dairy Products. Lampert, L., 57
Modern Data Processing. Arnold, R., 60
Modern Dictionary of Sociology. Theodorson, G., 16
Modern English Handbook. Gorrell, R., 82
Modern English Syntax. Onions, C., 33
Modern Family Health Guide. Fishbein, M., 50
Modern French Poets on Poetry. Gibson, R., 89
Modern German History. Flenley, R., 114
Modern German Literature. Bithell, J., 88
Modern Handbook of Humor. Woods, R., 85
Modern History of China. McAleavy, H., 117
Modern India. Griffiths, P., 117
Modern Italian Novel: from Capuana to Tozzi. Pacifici, S., 90
Modern Italian Novel: from Manzoni to Svevo. Pacifici, S., 90
Modern Metalworking. Walker, J., 62
Modern Motherhood. Liley, H., 51
Modern Newspaper Production. Woods, A., 4
Modern Novel. Allen, W., 88
Modern Parent's Guide to Baby and Child Care. Broadribb, V., 60
Modern Poets. Brinnin, J., 80
Modern Priest Looks at His Outdated Church. Kavanaugh, J., 11
Modern Reader's Chaucer. Chaucer, G., 86
Modern Researcher. Barzun, J., 3
Modern Retailing Management. Duncan, D., 61
Modern Riding. Kulesza, S., 78
Modern Textile and Apparel Dictionary. Linton, G., 62
Modern Theater. Bentley, E., 81
Modern Weight Lifting. Kirkley, G., 76

Modern Welding. Althouse, A., 61
Mohammedanism. Gibbs, H., 15
Mohan, Anand. Indira Gandhi, 101
Moholy-Nagy, Laszlo. Painting, Photography, Film, 72
Molds and Man. Christensen, C., 42
Molière, Jean B. Comedies, 89
Molly Maguires. Broehl, W., 23
Moment in History. Ashabranner, B., 24
Money and Banking. Kent, R., 23
Money Game. Smith, A., 23
Mongol Empire. Prawdin, M., 116
Monk, Kathleen. Fun with Fabric Printing, 71
Monroe, Ruth. Kitchen Candlecrafting, 69
Montagu, Ashley. Man's Most Dangerous Myth:, the Fallacy of Race, 42
_____. Natural Superiority of Women, 18
Montaigne, Michele de. Complete Essays, 89
Montessori, Maria. Absorbent Mind, 7
_____. From Childhood to Adolescence, 7
Montgomery, Ruth. Gift of Prophecy, 6
_____. World Beyond, 6
Moon. Gamow, G., 37
Moon's a Balloon. Niven, D., 105
Moore, A. D. Invention, Discovery and Creativity, 35
Moore, Alma C. How to Clean Everything, 59
Moore, Brian. Canada, 120
Moore, Patrick. New Guide to the Planets, 37
Moore, Ruth. Earth We Live On, 40
_____. Man, Time and Fossils, 41
_____. Coil of Life, 41
Moore, Truman E. Slaves We Rent, 23
Moorehead, Alan. Blue Nile, 118
_____. Darwin and the Beagle, 100
_____. Fatal Impact, 126
_____. Russian Revolution, 115
_____. White Nile, 118
Morality for Moderns. Oraison, M., 8
Morality Gap. Furfey, P., 12
More, Thomas. Utopia, 20
More About this Business of Music. Shemel, S., 73
More Houses for Good Living. Wills, R., 67
More Light on the Dead Sea Scrolls. Burrows, M., 10
More Than Skin Deep. Sternberg, T., 59
Morely-Fletcher, Hugo. Investing in Pottery and Porcelain, 67
Morgan, Clifford T. Introduction to Psychology, 7
Morgan, Edmund S. Birth of the Republic, 122

_____. Puritan Dilemma, 108
Morgan, James. Our Presidents, 96
Morgan, Robin. Sisterhood is Powerful, 18
Morison, Samuel E. Admiral of the Ocean Sea, 99
_____. Builders of the Bay Colony, 121
_____. European Discovery of America, 121
_____. Growth of the American Republic, 121
_____. Oxford History of the American People, 121
_____. Parkman Reader, 120
_____. Two-Ocean War, 112
Moron, Guillermo. History of Venezuela, 125
Morrill, William K. Lacrosse, 77
Morris, Dan. Fisherman's Almanac, 78
Morris, Desmond. Human Zoo, 17
_____. Mammals, 46
_____. Naked Ape, 41
Morris, Donald R. Washing of the Spears, 118
Morris, Jeannie. Short Season, 105
Morris, Percy A. Field Guide to the Shells of Our Atlantic and Gulf Coasts, 44
_____. Field Guide to the Shells of the Pacific Coast and Hawaii, 44
Morris, Ramona. Men and Pandas, 46
Morris, Richard B. American Reovlution, 122
_____. American Revolution Reconsidered, 122
_____. Encyclopedia of American History, 121
_____. Harper Encyclopedia of Modern World History, 93
Morrison, Brysson N. Mary, Queen of Scots, 104
Morrow, William L. Congressional Committees, 27
Morsberger, Robert E. Commonsense Grammar and Style, 33
Morse, Roger A. Complete Guide to Beekeeping, 57
Mortenson, William P. Farm Management Handbook, 57
Mortimer, Charles E. Chemistry, 38
Morton, Frederick. Rothschilds, 106
Mosaic of America's Ethnic Minorities. Fellows, D., 21
Moscow, Henry. Russia Under the Czars, 115
Mosse, George L. Reformation, 111
Mothers and Daughters. Neisser, E., 18
Motorcycles. Griffin, A., 76
Motorcycling for Beginners. Edmonds, I., 76
Motor's Auto Repair Manual, 55
Motor's Automobile Trouble Shooter, 55

Motor's Truck and Diesel Repair Manual, 55
Mott, Frank L. American Journalism, 4
Mound Builders of Ancient America. Silverburg, R., 119
Mountain People, The. Turnbull, C., 41
Mountain People, Mountain Crafts. Horowitz, E., 68
Moveable Feast. Hemingway, E., 102
Moving the Earth. Nichols, H., 53
Mowat, Charles L. Britain between the Wars: 1918-1940, 113
Moyer, John W. Practical Taxidermy, 42
Mulac, Margaret E. Party Fun, 75
Muller, Artur. Seven Wonders of the World, 94
Muller, Herbert J. Adlai Stevenson, 107
_____. Uses of the Past, 93
Muller, Walter H. Botany, 43
Mumford, Lewis. City in History, 21
Munro, Eleanor C. Encyclopedia of Art, 64
Munro, Thomas. Arts and Their Interrelations, 64
Munson, Thomas N. Essential Wisdom of George Santayana, 9
Murie, Olaus J. Field Guide to Animal Tracks, 44
Murphy, Charles T. Greek and Roman Classics in Translation, 91
Murphy, Paul L. Constitution in Crisis Times, 25
Murray, Margaret A. Splendor That Was Egypt, 109
Musciano, Walter A. Building and Flying Model Airplanes, 54
_____. Building and Flying Scale Model Aircraft, 54
Mushroom Handbook. Krieger, L., 43
Mushrooms, Molds and Miracles. Kavaler, L., 43
Music and Sound Effects. Theatre Student Series, 75
Music for the Modern Dance. Gilbert, P., 74
Music in Modern Media. Dolan, R., 74
Music in the 20th Century. Austin, W., 72
Music in Therapy. Gaston, E., 73
Music in Western Civilization. Lang, P., 73
Music of Black Americans: a History. Southern, E., 73
Music Therapy in Special Education. Nordoff, P., 73
Musicals. Theatre Student Series, 75
Musker, Frank F. Guide to Gymnastics, 77
Musket and the Cross. Edmonds, W., 121

Mussolini, Fermi, L., 105
My Autobiography. Chaplin, C., 99
My Brother Brendan. Behan, D., 98
My Favorite Things. Rodgers, D., 70
My Friends the Wild Chimpanzees.
    VanLawick-Goodall, J., 46
My Lai 4. Hersh, S., 118
My Life in and out of Baseball. Mays, W., 105
My Life in Court. Nizer, L., 26
My Life with Martin Luther King. King, C.,
    103
My Lord, What a Morning. Anderson, M., 97
My Several Worlds. Buck, P., 98
My Shadow Ran Fast. Sands, B., 28
My Wide World. McKay, J., 77
Mycenaeans. Taylour, W., 109
Mycenaeans and Minoans. Palmer, L., 109
Mydans, Carl. Violent Peace, 93
Myers, Bernard S. Encyclopedia of Painting,
    71
Myers, Louis M. Guide to American English,
    32
Myself. Ashton-Warner, S., 97
Mystic Warriors of the Plains. Mails, T., 119
Myth of Sisyphus and Other Essays. Camus,
    A., 89
Mythology. Hamilton, E., 14

NFPA Handbook of the National Electrical
    Code. National Fire Protection Assn., 52
Nabokov, Vladimir. Portable Nabokov, 92
——. Speak, Memory, 105
Nader, Ralph. Unsafe at Any Speed, 55
——. What to Do with Your Bad Car, 55
——. You and Your Pension, 19
Nahm, Milton C. Readings in the Philosophy
    of Art and Aesthetics, 64
Nairn, Ian. American Landscape, 65
Nakamura, Hajime. Ways of Thinking of
    Eastern Peoples, 116
Naked Ape. Morris, D., 41
Naked to Mine Enemies. Ferguson, Charles,
    108
Namath, Joe. Matter of Style, 77
Name for Your Baby. Wells, J., 108
Names from Africa: Their Origin, Meaning,
    and Pronunciation. Chuks-Orji, O., 34
Naming Your Baby. Smith, E., 108
Nanry, Charles. American Music, 73
Napoleon I. Guerard, A., 105
Napoleon III. Guerard, A., 105
Napoleonic Revolution. Holtman, R., 114

Narramore, Bruce. Help! I'm a Parent, 60
Narratives of the Life of an American Slave.
    Douglass, F., 100
Nash, Howard P. Naval History of the Civil
    War, 123
Nash, J. Robert. Bloodletters and Badmen, 96
Nation of Newcomers. Huthmacher, J., 21
Nation of Strangers. Packard, V., 17
Nation Takes Shape. Cunliffe, M., 122
National Anthems. Nettl, P., 74
National Catalog of Financial Aids for Higher
    Education. Keeslar, O., 29
National Fire Protection Assn. NFPA
    Handbook of the National Electrical Code,
    52
National Football League. First Fifty Years,
    77
National Geographic Soc. Civil War, 123
——. Marvels of Animal Behavior, 46
——. Those Inventive Americans, 51
——. Vikings, 116
——. Wild Animals of North America, 46
National Party Platforms. Porter, K., 22
Nationalism. Kohn, H., 20
Nationalism and Ideology. Ward, B., 20
Native Peoples of South America. Steward,
    J., 41
Native Sons. Margolis, E., 82
Natural Foods Cookbook. Hunter, B., 58
Natural Foods Primer. Hunter, B., 58
Natural History of Marine Animals.
    MacGinitie, G., 39
Natural History of Mosquitoes. Bates, M., 44
Natural History of Trees of Eastern and
    Central North America. Peattie, D., 43
Natural History of Viruses. Andrewes, C., 42
Natural History of Western Trees. Peattie, D.,
    43
Natural Light Photography. Adams, A., 71
Natural Superiority of Women. Montagu, A.,
    18
Natural Wonders of America. American
    Heritage, 94
Nature of Animals. Milne, L., 43
Nature of Communism. Daniels, R., 24
Nature of History. Marwick, A., 93
Nature of Matter. Frisch, O., 38
Nature of Metals. Rogers, B., 62
Naval History of the Civil War. Nash, H., 123
Nayman, Jacqueline. Atlas of Wildlife, 44
Near East. Yale, W., 118
Neblette, Carroll B. Fundamentals of
    Photography, 72

Needham, George H. Microscope, A Practical Guide, 38

Needleman, Jacob. New Religions, 14

Needlepoint. Sunset Magazine, eds., 69

Needleweaving: Easy as Embroidery. Dendel, E., 68

Neely, Henry M. Stars by Clock and Fist, 37

Nefertiti. Wells, E., 105

Negative. Adams, A., 71

Negro Family in the United States. Frazier, E., 19

Negro in the United States. Frazier, E., 21

Negro Novel in America. Bone, R., 84

Negro Playwrights in the American Theatre. Abramson, D., 81

Negro Voice in American Fiction. Gloster, H., 84

Neidle, Cecyle S. New Americans, 21

Neighborhood Government. Kotler, M., 27

Neil, William. Harper's Bible Commentary, 11

Neill, Alexander S. Summerhill, 29

Neill, Wilfred. Georgraphy of Life, 41

Neisser, Edith. Mothers and Daughters, 18

Nelson, Glenn C. Ceramics, 67

Nelson, Jack. FBI and the Berrigans, 26

Nelson, Roy P. Fell's Guide to Commercial Art, 67

Nelson and His World. Pocock, T., 113

Netsilik Eskimo. Balikei, A., 119

Nettl, Bruno. Folk and Traditional Music on the Western Continents, 73

Nettl, Paul. National Anthems, 74

Neusner, Jacob. Invitation to the Talmud, 14

Neustadt, Richard E. Presidential Power, 27

Never Call Retreat. Catton, B., 123

Never in Anger: Portrait of an Eskimo Family. Briggs, J., 119

Nevins, Allan. John D. Rockefeller, 106

———. Ordeal of the Union, 123

———. Short History of the United States, 121

New Aerobics. Cooper, K., 48

New American Poetry 1945-1960. Allen, D., 83

New Americans. Neidle, C., 21

New Antiques. Grotz, G., 70

New Archery. Butler, D., 78

New Basic History of the United States. Beard, C., 120

New Biology. Chedd, G., 41

New Book of Motorcycles. Arctander, E., 54

New Cake Decorating Book. Bowring, J., 58

New Century Classical Handbook. Avery, C., 109

New Class. Djilas, M., 24

New Commonwealth. Garraty, J., 123

New Communes, The. Roberts, R., 17

New Complete Book of Bicycling. Sloane, E., 77

New Concise Family Health and Medical Guide. Wagman, R., 49

New Cook Book. Better Homes & Gardens, eds., 58

New Deal. Degler, C., 124

New Directions in American Architecture. Stern, R., 67

New Dog Encyclopedia. Davis, H., 57

New Earth Catalog. French, S., 3

New Encyclopedia of Child Care and Guidance. Gruenberg, S., 60

New Encyclopedia of the Opera. Ewen, D., 73

New English Bible, 11

New Essential First Aid. Gardner, A., 48

New Essentials of Modern Upholstery. Bast, H., 62

New Face of Science. Hoyle, F., 35

New Faces of China. Barnstone, W., 116

New Field Book of Freshwater Life. Klots, E., 39

New Field Book of Nature Activities and Hobbies. Hillcourt, W., 39

New Fundamental French. Micks, W., 33

New Gold in Your Attic. Bradley, V., 3

New Guide to the Planets. Moore, P., 37

New Handicraft: Processes and Projects. Griswold, L., 68

New Heart. Boylan, B., 49

New History of Spanish Literature. Chandler, R., 90

New Hope for the Childless Couple. Kaufman, S., 51

New Journalism. Johnson, M., 4

New Lives, New Landscapes: Planning for the 21st Century. Fairbrother, N., 65

New Look at Geometry. Adler, I., 35

New Man for our Times. Trueblood, E., 12

New Materials in Sculpture. Percy, H., 67

New Mathematical Diversions. Gardner, M., 36

New Mathematics. Adler, I., 35

New Nation 1800-1845. Wiltse, C., 122

New Negro Poets. Hughes, L., 83

New Oxford Book of English Verse 1250-1950, 86

New Physics. Taylor, J., 38

New Pictorial History of the Talkies. Blum, D., 74

New Pocket German Dictionary. Langenscheidt, Staff, 33

New Pointers on Playwriting. Niggli, J., 80

New Religions. Needleman, J., 14

New Rhyming Dictionary and Poets' Handbook. Johnson, B., 32

New Sexuality: Myths, Fables and Hang-ups. Kennedy, E., 8

New Standard Reference for Secretaries and Administrative Assistants. Janis, J., 61

New Ways of Gravure. Hayter, S., 71

New Wedding. Arisian, K., 30

New Women. Cooke, J., 17

New World of Philosophy. Kaplan, A., 5

New York Times. New York Times Cookbook, 59

New York Times Book of Home Landscaping, 66

New York Times Complete Manual of Home Repair. Gladstone, B., 63

New York Times Cookbook. New York Times, 59

New York Times Guide to Business and Finance. Kraus, A., 22

New York Times Guide to Personal Finance. Nuccio, S., 23

New York Times International Cook Book. Claiborne, C., 58

New York Times Natural Foods Cookbook. Hewitt, J., 58

New Zealand. Cameron, R., 125

Newcomb, Ellsworth. Miracle Metals, 62

Newfield, Jack. Robert Kenedy, a Memoir, 103

Newhall, Beaumont. History of Photography, 72

_____. Latent Image, 72

Newlon, Clarke. 1001 Questions Asnwered About Space, 56

Newman, James R. World of Mathematics, 36

Newman, Thelma R. Plastics as an Art Form, 67

_____. Plastics as Design Form, 62

Nicholas, Leslie. How to Avoid Social Diseases, 50

Nicholas and Alexandra. Massie, R., 105

Nichols, Herbert. Moving the Earth, 53

Nichols, Roy F. Battles and Leaders of the Civil War, 123

Nicholson, Margaret. Manual of Copyright Practice, 3

Nickerson, Jane S. Short History of North Africa, 118

Nicklaus, Jack. Golf My Way, 77

_____. Take a Tip from Me, 77

Nicoll, Allardyce. British Drama, 87

_____. Studies in Shakespeare, 87

_____. World Drama, 81

Nidetch, Jean. Weight Watchers Program Cook Book, 59

Nietzsche, Friedrich W. Portable Nietzsche, 9

Nigg, Walter. Warriors of God, 13

nigger. Gregory, D., 101

Niggli, Josefina. New Pointers on Playwriting, 80

Night Country. Eisley, L., 40

Night of Long Knives. Gallo, M., 114

Night of the Grizzlies. Olsen, J., 46

Night to Remember. Lord, W., 94

Nightmare Decade. Cook, F., 124

Nimocks, Patricia. Decoupage, 69

900 Days: Siege of Leningrad. Salisbury, H., 112

Nine Planets. Nourse, A., 37

Nine Plays. O'Neill, E., 84

Nine Soviet Portraits. Bauer, R., 115

Nineteenth Century Plays. Rowell, G., 87

Nitze, William A. History of French Literature, 89

Niven, David. Moon's a Balloon, 105

Niven, Ivan. Introduction to the Theory of Numbers, 36

Nizer, Louis. Implosion Conspiracy, 26

_____. My Life in Court, 26

Nkrumah, Kwame. Africa Must Unite, 118

No Exit, and Three Other Plays. Sartre, J., 89

No-Fault. Gillespie, P., 28

No Hail, No Farewell. Heren, L., 124

No Man is an Island. Nerton, T., 12

Nobody Ever Died of Old Age. Curtin, S., 19

Nobody Knows My Name. Baldwin, J., 98

Nolen, William A. Making of a Surgeon, 47

Nordoff, Paul. Music Therapy in Special Education, 73

North America Divided: the Mexican War. Connor, S., 123

North American Deserts. Jaeger, E., 39

North American Indians in Historical Perspective. Leacock, 119

North with the Spring. Teale, E., 40

Northern Ireland: a Report on the Conflict. London Sunday Times Insight Team, 113

Norton Anthology of English Literature. Abrams, M., 85

Norton Anthology of Modern Poetry.
Ellman, R., 80
Norwick, Kenneth P. Your Legal Rights, 25
Noss, John, B. Man's Religions, 14
Nostradamus. Complete Prophecies, 6
Not So Rich as You Think. Stewart, G., 54
Notes of a Native Son. Baldwin, J., 19
Notestein, Wallace. English People on the
Eve of Colonization, 113
Nothing Stands Still. Schlesinger, A., 121
Nourse, Alan E. Ladies Home Journal
Family Medical Guide, 50
_____. Nine Planets, 37
_____. The Body, 48
Novak, F. A. Pictorial Encyclopedia of
Plants and Flowers, 43
Novel. Drew, E., 81
Novel and the Modern World. Daiches, D., 81
Novick, Sheldon. Careless Atom, 52
Now Generation. Benson, D., 12
Noyes, George. Masterpieces of Russian
Drama, 92
Nuccio, Sal. New York Times Guide to
Personal Finance, 23
Nueckel, Susan. Selected Guide to Make It,
Fix It, Do It Yourself Books, 1
Number, the Language of Science. Dantzig,
T., 36
Nunz, Gregory J. Electronics in our World, 52
_____. Electronics Mathematics, 36
Nurnberg, Maxwell. All About Words, 33
Nussbaum, Frederick L. Triumph of Science
and Reason, 111
Nussbaumer, Hanny. Lacquer and Crackle, 69
Nutrition. Chaney, M., 48
Nutrition and Physical Fitness. Bogert, L., 48
Nye, F. Ivan. Family, 18
Nye, Russell B. Cultural Life of the New
Nation, 122

O Jerusalem! Collins, L. 117
Oakely, Stewart. Short History of Sweden,
116
Oaks, Marian C. Fell's Guide to Mobile Home
Living, 59
Oates, Whitney J. Complete Greek Drama, 91
Oberg, Erik. Machinery's Handbook, 52
Obley, Fred A. Emphysema, 50
O'Brien, Patricia. The Woman Alone, 18
O'Casey, Sean. Selected Plays, 87
O'Connor, Richard. Bret Harte, 102
_____. Irish: Portrait of a People, 113
Occult. Wilson, C., 6

Occult America. Godwin, J., 5
Occult Explosion. Freedland, N., 5
Occupational Outlook Handbook. U.S.
Bureau of Labor Statistics, 23
Ochsner, Alton. Smoking, 49
Octopus and Squid. Cousteau, J., 44
Odes and Epodes. Horace, 90
Odum, Eugene P. Fundamentals of Ecology,
54
Odyssey. Homer, 91
Office Management Handbook. Wylie, H., 61
Official Chess Handbook. Harkness, K., 75
Official Chess Rulebook. Harkness, K., 75
Ogburn, Charlton, Jr. Forging of Our
Continent, 40
Ogburn, William F. Sociology, 16
Ogg, Frederic A. Introduction to American
National Government, 27
Ogg, Oscar. 26 Letters, 32
Oil Painting in Progress. Soyer, M., 71
Olcott, William T. Field Book of the Skies, 37
Oldenbourg, Zoe. Catherine the Great, 99
Oldroyd, Harold. Elements of Entymology,
44
Oliver, Paul. Story of the Blues, 73
Oliver, Roland A. Africa Since 1800, 118
_____. Short History of Africa, 118
Olney, Ross R. Simple Gasoline Engine
Repair, 52
Olsen, Jack. Night of the Grizzlies, 46
Olsen, John. Shooter's Bible, 53
Omar Khayam. Rubaiyat, 91
On Becoming a Person. Rogers, C., 7
On Being a Woman. Gifford-Jones, W., 51
On Creative Writing. Engle, P., 80
On Education. Dewey, J., 28
. . . . .on $5 and/or $10 a Day.
Frommer, A., 95
On Liberty, Representative Government, the
Subjugation of Women. Mill, J., 18
On Native Grounds. Kazin, A., 82
On the Poet and His Craft. Roethke, T., 80
On the Side of the Apes. Hahn, E., 46
One, Two, Three-Infinity. Gamow, G., 36
150 Techniques in Art. Meyers, H., 64
100 Most Beautiful Rooms in America.
Comstock, H., 69
101 Simple Experiments with Insects.
Kalmus, H., 44
One Man's Freedom. Williams, E., 25
One Passion, Two Loves. Poole, L., 106
1000 Beautiful House Plants and How to
Grow Them. Kramer, J., 65

1001 Questions Answered About Space. Newlon, C., 56

One Way to Change the World. Ford, L., 10

O'Neill, Eugene. Nine Plays, 84

O'Neill. Gelb, B., 105

O'Neill: Son and Artist. Sheaffer, L., 105

Onion Field. Wambaugh, J., 28

Onions, C. T. Modern English Syntax, 33

Only a Little Planet. Brower, D., 25

Only a Novel. Hodge, J., 97

Only One Earth. Ward, B., 17

Only Yesterday. Allen, F., 124

Opdycke, John B. Harper's English Grammar, 32

Open Eye: in Pursuit of Art. Kuh, K., 64

Opera. Jacobs, A., 73

Opportunities in Dancing. Denis, P., 74

Opposing Self. Trilling, L., 79

Optical Art: Theory and Practice. Pavola, R., 65

Oraison, Marc. Morality for Moderns, 8

Orchestra. Bekker, P., 73

Ordeal and Hope. Pogue, F., 104

Ordeal of Change. Hoffer, E., 16

Ordeal of the Union. Nevins, A., 123

Organ Building and Design. Andersen, P., 74

Organic Living Book. Kohn, B., 58

Oriental Philosophies. Koller, J., 9

Oriental Rugs. Jacobsen, C., 68

Origin of the Species; and Descent of Man. Darwin, C., 42

Origins of American Intervention in the First World War. Gregory, R., 112

Origins of Intelligence in Children. Piaget, J., 7

Origins of Totalitarianism. Arendt, H., 20

Origins of World War One. Parkinson, R., 112

Ormond, Clyde. Complete Book of Hunting, 78

———. Outdoorsman's Handbook, 78

———. Small Game Hunting, 78

Orr, William I. Radio Handbook, 53

Orton, Mildred E. Cooking with Wholegrains, 59

Osborne, Harold. Bolivia, 125

Osburn, Fairfield. Our Crowded Planet, 17

Osgood, Charles G. Voice of England, 86

Osgood, Samuel M. Fall of France, 114

Oswalt, Wendell H. This Land Was Theirs, 119

Other America: Poverty in the United States. Harrington, M., 22

Otto, James. Modern Biology, 41

Our Children's Keepers. Cole, L., 18

Our Country's Presidents. Freidel, F., 96

Our Crowded Planet. Osburn, F., 17

Our Inner Conflicts. Horney, K., 6

Our Presidents. Morgan, J., 96

Oursler, Fulton. Greatest Book Ever Written, 11

———. Greatest Story Ever Told, 11

Oursler, Will. Marijuana, 49

———. Religion: Out or Way Out, 13

Out of Africa. Dinesen, Isak, 118

Out of my Life and Thought. Schweitzer, A., 107

Outboard Motor Service Manual. Technical Publications, 53

Outdoorsman's Fitness and Medical Guide. Galton, L., 48

Outdoorsman's Handbook. Ormond, C., 78

Outline of European Architecture. Pevsner, N., 67

Outline of History. Wells, H., 94

Outline History of the World. Davies, H., 93

Outline of Russian Literature. Slonim, M., 92

Overcoming Drugs. Louria, D., 49

Overstreet, Harry A. Mature Mind, 7

Ovid. Metamorphosis, 90

Owens, Ronald. Peru, 125

Oxford Book of American Verse. Matthiessen, F., 83

Oxford Book of Ballads. Quiller-Couch, A., 86

Oxford Book of Modern Verse. Yeats, W., 81

Oxford Book of Spanish Verse. Fitzmaurice-Kelly, J., 90

Oxford Companion to American Literature. Hart, J., 82

Oxford Companion to English Literature. Harvey, P., 86

Oxford History of India. Smith, V., 117

Oxford History of the American People. Morison, S., 121

PT 109. Donovan, R., 112

Pacifici, Sergio. Guide to Contemporary Italian Literature, 90

———. Modern Italian Novel: from Capuana to Tozzi, 90

———. Modern Italian Novel: from Manzoni to Svevo, 90

Packard, Vance O. Hidden Persuaders, 61

———. Nation of Strangers, 7

———. Sexual Wilderness, 18

———. Status Seekers, 17

_____. Waste Makers, 24
Pack-O-Fun Treasury of Crafts, Gifts, and Toys. Clapper, E., 68
Padover, Saul K. Life and Death of Louis XVI, 114
Page, Thornton. Library of Astronomy, 37
Pageant of Chinese History. Seeger, E., 117
Pageant of Europe. Stearns, R., 110
Pahlman, William. Book of Interior Design, 69
Paine, Thomas. Common Sense and Other Political Writings, 22
Painless Childbirth: LaMaze Method. Lamaze, F., 51
Painter, George. Early Years, 106
Painter, George. Later Years, 106
Painter's Workshop. Brooks, L., 70
Painting, Photography, Film. Moholy-Nagy, L., 72
Painting in America, from 1502 to the Present. Richardson, E., 71
Painting Materials. Gettens, R., 71
Painting with Synthetic Media. Woody, R., 71
Pakistan: Military Rule or People's Power. Tariq, A., 117
Palgrave, Francis. Golden Treasury, 86
Palmer, Alan W. Lands Between, 116
Palmer, Arnold. Go for Broke, 77
Palmer, Leonard. Mycenaeans and Minoans, 109
Palmer, Robert R. Age of the Democratic Revolution, 111
Palmer, Roger C. Jesus Kids, 12
Palmquist, Roland E. House Wiring, 53
Palos, Stephan. Chinese Art of Healing, 50
Pan American World Airways. Guides, 95
Papandreou, Andreas. Democracy at Gunpoint, 116
Papanek, Victor. Design for the Real World, 69
Paper Money of the United States. Friedberg, R., 22
Paperbound Books in Print, 1
Papier Mache. Sunset Magazine, eds., 69
Papillon. Charriere, H., 27
Paradis, Adrian. Hungry Years, 23
Paradox of Poverty in America. Davis, K., 27
Parakeet Guide. Rogers, C., 57
Parent Effectiveness Training. Gordon, T., 60
Parent's Guide to Drugs. Andrews, M., 49
Parker, Franklin D. Central American Republics, 120
Parker, W. Oren. Scene Design and Stage Lighting, 75

Parkes, Bernard. History of Russia, 115
Parkinson, Roger. Origins of World War One, 112
_____. Origins of World War II, 112
Parkman Reader. Morison, S., 120
Parks, Gordon. Born Black, 19
_____. Choice of Weapons, 105
Parrinder, Geoffrey. Faiths of Mankind, 14
Parrington, Vernon L. Main Currents in American Thought, 82
Parrish, John A. 12, 20, and 5: a Doctor's Year in Vietnam, 118
Parry, John H. European Reconnaissance, 111
Parsegian, V. L. This Cybernetic World of Men, Machines and Earth, 3
Party Book for Boys and Girls. Carlson, B., 75
Party Fun. Mulac, M., 75
Pasternak, Boris. Poems, 92
Patchwork for Beginners. Green, S., 68
Paterson, David. Applied Genetics, 42
Paton, Alan. Land and People of South Africa, 118
Patterns in English. Gerould, G., 32
Patterns of Culture. Benedict, R., 40
Patton, A. Rae. Chemistry of Life, 41
Paul Revere and the World He Lived in. Forbes, E., 106
Pauling, Linus. College Chemistry, 39
_____. Vitamin C and the Common Cold, 48
Pavola, Rene. Optical Art: Theory and Practice, 65
Pax Americana. Steel, R., 21
Payne, Alma S. Fat and Sodium Control Cookbook, 59
Payne, Robert. Dostoyevsky, 100
_____. Life and Death of Lenin, 103
_____. Marx, 104
Payne, Stanley G. Franco's Spain, 115
Peabody Sisters of Salem. Tharp, L., 96
Peale, Norman V. Enthusiasm Makes the Difference, 12
_____. Power of Positive Thinking, 12
_____. Stay Alive All Your Life, 7
Pearson, Michael. Those Damned Rebels: American Revolution as Seen through British Eyes, 122
Peattie, Donald C. Natural History of Trees of Eastern and Central North America, 43
_____. Natural History of Western Trees, 43
Pebble Collecting and Polishing. Fletcher, E., 39

Peckham, Howard H. Colonial Wars, 121

Pedersen, Alwin. Polar Animals, 44

Pedersen, Christian F. International Flag Book in Color, 108

Peet, Louise J. Household Equipment, 59

Peffer, Nathaniel. Far East, 116

Pei, Mario. Double-Speak in America, 33

——. Getting Along in Italian, 33

——. How to Learn Languages and What Languages to Learn, 32

——. Language Today, 32

——. Many Hues of English, 33

——. Story of Language, 32

——. Story of the English Language, 32

Pence, Raymond W. Grammar of Present-Day English, 33

Penguin Book of French Verse: 19th Century. Hartley, A., 89

Penguin Book of Italian Verse. Kay, G., 90

Penguin Book of Japanese Verse. Bownas, G., 91

Penguin Dictionary of Saints. Attwater, D., 95

Pentimento. Hellman, L., 102

People are the Church. Kennedy, E., 13

People of Japan. Buck, P., 117

People, Places and Books. Highet, G., 79

Peoples and Policies of South Africa. Marquand, L., 118

Pepys, Samuel. Diary, 105

Percival, Julia. Household Ecology, 59

Percy, H. M. New Materials in Sculpture, 67

Perham, Margery. African Discovery, 119

Perils of Prosperity. Leuchtenberg, W., 124

Perkins, Dexter. History of the Monroe Doctrine, 121

——. United States of America, 121

Perry, Robert H. Engineering Manual, 52

Persichetti, Vincent. 20th Century Harmony, 73

Personal Typing. Lloyd, A., 61

Peru. Owens, R., 125

Pesticides and the Living Landscape. Rudd, R., 57

Peter, Laurence J. The Peter Principle, 61

Peter Principle, The. Peter, L., 61

Peterdi, Gabor. Printmaking, 71

Peters, Geoff. Woodturning, 62

Peterson, Florence. American Labor Unions, 23

Peterson, Franklynn. Handbook of Lawn Mower Repair, 57

Peterson, Roger T. Field Guide to the Birds, 45

——. Field Guide to Western Birds, 45

Petrarch, Francesco. Sonnets and Songs, 90

Petrides, George A. Field Guide to Trees and Shrubs, 43

Petrie, Alexander. An Introduction to Roman History, Literature and Antiquities, 109

Pets. Whitney, L., 58

Petzold, Paul. Light on People, 72

Pevsner, Nikolaus. Outline of European Architecture, 67

Peyre, Henri. French Novelists of Today, 89

Pezzano, Chuck. Guide to Better Bowling, 77

Phillips, Cabell. From the Crash to the Blitz, 124

Phillips, Charles F. Marketing: Principles and Methods, 61

Phillips, Mary W. Step-by-Step Macrame, 69

Phillips, Phoebe. Collector's Encyclopedia of Antiques, 70

Philosophy of David Hume. Hume, D., 8

Philosophy of Kant. Kant, I., 9

Photojournalism. Time-Life, 4

Phrase Book of Modern Greek, in English and Greek. Pring, J., 34

Physical Education Handbook. Seaton, D., 77

Physical Geography of the Oceans. Cotter, C., 39

Physics. Atkins, K., 38

Physics and Beyond. Heisenberg, W., 38

Physiography of the United States. Hunt, C., 39

Piaget, Jean. Origins of Intelligence in Children, 7

Piano Technique. Gieseking, W., 74

Pictorial Encyclopedia of Plants and Flowers. Novak, F., 43

Pictorial Encyclopedia of Railways. Ellis, H., 29

Pictorial Guide to the Mammals of North America. Rue, L., 46

Pictorial Guide to the Moon. Alter, D., 37

Pictorial Guide to the Planets. Jackson, J., 37

Pictorial History of the World's Great Trials. Aymar, B., 25

Picture History of World War II. Sulzberger, C., 112

Piece of the Power: Four Black Mayors. Haskins, J., 96

Piel, Gerard. Acceleration of History, 93

Pierce, Ruth I. Single and Pregnant, 19

Piloting, Seamanship and Small Boat Handling. Chapman, C., 53

Pilot's Handbook of Weather. Guerny, G., 54

Pine, Leslie G. Story of Surnames, 108

Pines, Maya. Revolution in Learning, 29

Pioneer America. Alden, J., 120, 122

Pioneers and Caretakers. Auchincloss, L., 84

Pipe, Ted. Basic Electricity Training Manual, 53

Pirene, Henri. Medieval Cities, 111

Pirone, Pascal P. Tree Maintenance, 57

Pitkin, Walter B. Life Begins at Fifty, 19

Piven, Frances F. Regulating the Poor, 27

Plagenhoef, Stanley. Fundamentals of Tennis, 77

Plain Speaking. Miller, M., 107

Planets, Stars and Galaxies. Inglis, S., 37

Planning and Remodeling Bathrooms. Sunset Magazine, eds., 70

Planning and Remodeling Kitchens. Sunset Magazine, eds., 70

Plano, Jack C. American Political Dictionary, 22

_____. International Relations Dictionary, 21

Plant Drugs that Changed the World. Taylor, N., 50

Plant Propagation in Pictures. Free, M., 56

Plants and Civilization. Baker, H., 42

Plastics as an Art Form. Newman, T., 67

Plastics as Design Form. Newman T., 62

Plastics-Projects and Techniques. Lappin, A., 61

Plastics Technology. Milby, R., 62

Plato. Portable Plato, 91

Platt, Rutherford H. Great American Forest, 57

Playing Hockey the Professional Way. Gilbert, R., 76

Plays. Barrie, J., 87

Plays, Players, and Playwrights: an Illustrated History of the Theatre. Geisinger, M., 74

Pleasants, Henry. Great Singers, 96

Please Don't Eat the Daisies. Kerr, J., 85

Please Touch. Howard, J., 16

Pleasure Seekers. Fort, J., 49

Pleasures of Archaeology. Meyer, K., 94

Pleasures of Cross Country Skiing. Lund, M., 77

Plumbing. Babbitt, H., 62

Plutarch. Lives, 96

Pocket Encyclopedia of Cacti and Succulents. Lamb, B., 65

Pocock, Tom. Nelson and His World, 113

Poe. Wagenknecht, E., 105

Poe, Edgar A. Complete Stories and Poems, 85

_____. Portable Poe, 85

Poems. Hesse, H., 89

Poems. Pasternak, B., 92

Poems. Rilke, R., 89

Poems. Yevtushenko, Y., 92

Poems and Plays. Browning, R., 86

Poems and Plays. Tennyson, A., 86

Poems for Pleasure. Ward, H., 83

Poems from Black Africa. Hughes, L., 91

Poems from the Greek Anthology. Fitts, D., 91

Poems, Prose, and Plays. Pushkin, A., 92

Poems to Read Aloud. Hodnett, E., 80

Poetical Works. Bryant, W., 83

Poetical Works. Wordsworth, W., 86

Poetics; Rhetoric. Aristotle, 80

Poetry. Drew, E., 80

Poetry Handbook. Deutsch, B., 80

Poetry of Black America. Adoff, A., 83

Poetry of Rock. Goldstein, R., 73

Poets in a Landscape. Highet, G., 90, 96

Poets of the English Language. Auden, W., 36

Poets of Today. Lowenfels, W., 83

Pogue, Forrest. Education of a General, 104

_____. Ordeal and Hope, 104

Pohl, Frederick. Viking Settlements of North America, 121

Pohl, Richard W. How to Know the Grasses, 43

Poisons. Brookes, V., 49

Polar Animals. Pedersen, A., 44

Police Administration. Wilson, O., 26

Police and the Public. Reiss, A., 26

Poling, David. Last Years of the Church, 13

Politics. Aristotle, 22

Politics. Josephson, M., 123

Politics, Parties and Pressure Groups. Key, V., 22

Pollard, Alfred W. English Miracle Plays, Moralities, and Interludes, 87

Polmar, Norman. Atomic Submarines, 53

Polo, Marco. Travels of Marco Polo, 117

Polsby, Nelson W. Congress and the Presidency, 27

Pomeroy, Wardell B. Boys and Sex, 48

_____. Girls and Sex, 48

_____. Your Child and Sex: A Guide for Parents, 48

Pond, Grace. Complete Cat Encyclopedia, 57

Pond Life. Reid, G., 40

Pond Life in the Aquarium. Janus, H., 44

Poole, Austin. From Doomsday Book to Magna Carta, 113

Poole, Lynn. One Passion, Two Loves, 106

Pop Art and After. Amaya, M., 64

Pop Art Redefined. Russell, J., 65

Popkin, Henry. Modern British Drama, 87

Popkin, Roy. Desalination: Water for the World's Future, 54

Popular Guide to Government Publications. Leidy, W., 3

Population. Malthus, T., 17

Population Bomb. Ehrlich, P., 17

Population Control. Hart, H., 17

Population Dilemma. Hauser, P., 17

Portable Arthur Miller. Miller, A., 84

Portable Blake. Blake, W., 88

Portable Cervantes. Cervantes Saavedra, M., De, 90

Portable Charles Lamb. Lamb, C., 88

Portable Chaucer. Chaucer, G., 86

Portable Chekov. Chekov, A., 92

Portable Coleridge. Coleridge, S., 86

Portable Conrad. Conrad, J., 88

Portable D. H. Lawrence. Lawrence, D. H., 88

Portable Dante. Dante Alighieri, 90

Portable Elizabethan Reader. Haydn, H., 86

Portable Emerson. Emerson, R., 85

Portable Faulkner. Faulkner, W., 84

Portable Graham Greene. Greene, G., 88

Portable Greek Historians. Finley, M., 91

Portable Greek Reader. Auden, W., 91

Portable Hawthorne. Hawthorne, N., 84

Portable Henry James. James, H., 85

Portable Irish Reader. Russell, D., 88

Portable James Joyce. Joyce, J., 88

Portable Johnson and Boswell. Kronenberger, L., 88

Portable Jung. Jung C., 6

Portable Mark Twain. Twain, M., 85

Portable Matthew Arnold. Arnold, M., 88

Portable Maupassant. Maupassant, G. de, 89

Portable Medieval Reader. Ross, J., 79

Portable Melville. Leyda, J., 82

Portable Milton. Milton, J., 88

Portable Nabokov. Nabokov, V., 92

Portable Nietzsche. Nietzsche, F., 9

Portable Oscar Wilde. Wilde, O., 86

Portable Plato. Plato, 91

Portable Poe. Poe, E., 85

Portable Renaissance Reader. Ross, J., 79

Portable Roman Reader. Davenport, Basil, 90

Portable Russian Reader. Guerney, B., 92

Portable Steinbeck. Steinbeck, J., 84

Porbatle Swift. Swift, J., 88

Portable Thoreau. Thoreau, H., 85

Portable Victorian Reader. Haight, G., 85

Portable Voltaire. Voltaire, F., 89

Portable Walt Whitman. Whitman, W., 83

Porter, Cole. Cole Porter Song Book, 74

Porter, George. World of the Frog and the Toad, 45

Porter, Kirk H. National Party Platforms, 22

Portrait of a Decade. Lewis, A., 20

Portrait of Myself. Bourke-White, M., 98

Post, Emily P. Etiquette, 30

Poster Ideas and Bulletin Board Techniques. Coplan, K., 68

Potter, Elmer B. Sea Power, 93

Pough, Frederick H. Field Guide to Rocks and Minerals, 40

Pough, Richard. Audubon Water Bird Guide, 45

Poverty: America's Enduring Paradox. Lens, S., 23

Power, Eileen. Medieval People, 111

Power, John. Fisherman's Handbook, 78

Power and Innocence: a Search for the Sources of Violence. May, R., 7

Power Elite. Mill, C., 20

Power of Calculus. Whipkey, K., 37

Power of Community School Education. Totten, W., 29

Power of Hypnosis. Holzer, H., 5

Power of Love. Sheen, F., 12

Power of Positive Thinking. Peale, N., 12

Power of Words. Chase, S., 32

Powers of Poetry. Highet, G., 80

Practical Administration of Public Libraries. Wheeler, J., 2

Practical and Industrial Formulary. Freeman, M., 47

Practical Applications in Mathematics. Stein, E., 37

Practical Astronomy. Alter, D., 37

Practical Electrical Wiring, Residential, Farm, and Industrial. Richter, H., 53

Practical Electricity. Middleton, R., 52

Practical Encyclopedia of Crafts. DiValentin, M., 68

Practical Ferro-Cement Boatbuilding. Benford, J., 53

Practical Gemstone Craft. Hutton, H., 68

Practical Music Theory. Collier, J., 72

Practical Nursing. Rapier, D., 47

Practical Sailing. Gibbs, T., 53

Practical Stage Lighting. Theatre Student Series, 75

Practical Statistics Simply Explained. Langley, R., 36

Practical Taxidermy. Moyer, J., 42

Practice for Clerical, Typing and Stenographic Tests. Turner, E., 26

Practice for the Armed Forces Tests. Arco, 27

Praise the Lord and Pass the Contribution. Bestic, A., 12

Prawdin, Michael. Mongol Empire, 116

Prayers of Peter Marshall. Marshall, P., 13

Praz, Mario. Romantic Agony, 79

Preface to Literary Analysis. Zitner, S., 79

Preface to Urban Economics. Thompson, W., 21

Pregnancy, Birth and the Newborn Baby. Boston Children's Medical Center, 51

Prepare Now for a Metric Future. Donovan, F., 29

Preparing the Classics. Theatre Student Series, 75

Prescott, Frederick. Control of Pain, 50

Prescott, Hilda. Mary Tudor, 104

Present at the Creation: My Years in the State Department. Acheson, D., 124

President: Office and Powers. Corwin, E., 26

President Makers. Josephson, M., 124

Presidential Losers. Goldman, D., 96

Presidential Power. Neustadt, R., 27

Previte-Orton, Charles W. Shorter Cambridge Medieval History, 111

Price, Eugenia. Learning to Live from the Acts, 11

Price of Glory: Verdun 1916. Horne, A., 112

Pride's Progress. Haas, E., 46

Priestly, J. B. Literature and Western Man, 79

Primer on Government Spending. Heilbroner, R., 22

Primer on Money, Banking and Gold. Berstein, P., 23

Prince; and Discourses. Machiavelli, N., 20

Principles of Arithmetic. Brumfel, C., 36

Principles of Astronomy. Wyatt, S., 37

Principles of Effective Speaking. Sandford, W., 82

Principles of Geology. Gilluly, J., 39

Principles of Mathematics. Rees, P., 37

Principles of Microbiology. Smith, A., 42

Principles of Political Economy and Taxation. Ricardo, D., 23

Pring, Julian T. Phrase Book of Modern Greek, in English and Greek, 34

Print. Adams, A., 71

Printmaking. Peterdi, G., 71

Prints-from Linoblocks and Woodcuts. Banister, M., 71

Priolo, Joan B. Ceramics-and How to Decorate Them, 67

Pritchett, Victor S. Cab at the Door, 106

———. Living Novel, and Later Appreciations, 81

———. Midnight Oil, 106

Private Pilot Study Guide. Simonson, L., 54

Private World of Leonard Bernstein. Gruen, J., 98

Pro Football Heroes of Today. Stainback, B., 77

Probability and Statistics for Everyman. Adler, I., 36

Problems of Parents. Spock, B., 19

Process of Education. Bruner, J., 28

Process of Evolution. Ehrlich, P., 42

Prochnow, Herbert V. Public Speaker's Treasure Chest, 82

———. Successful Toastmaster, 82

Producing Plays for Children. Theatre Student Series, 75

Professional Engineer's Examination Questions and Answers. LaLonde, W., 51

Profiles in Black Power. Haskins, J., 96

Profiles in Courage. Kennedy, J., 96

Prometheus. Maurois, A., 98

Promise of Space. Clarke, A., 56

Proper Study of Mankind. Chase, S., 16

Properties and Dressing the Stage. Theatre Student Series, 75

Prophet. Gibran, K., 91

Prophet Armed. Deutsche, I., 107

Prophet Outcast. Deutsche, I., 107

Prophet Unarmed. Deutsche, I., 107

Prosody Handbook. Shapiro, K., 80

Protecting our Environment. McClellan, G., 54

Protestant Establishment. Baltzell, E., 17

Proud Tower. Tuchman, B., 112

Provisor, Henry. 8mm/16mm Movie Making, 72

Prudden, Bonnie. Bonnie Prudden's Fitness Book, 77

Pruning Handbook. Sunset Magazine, eds., 66

Psalms for the Common Reader. Chase, M., 10

Psychiatry. Fleming, A., 50

Psychic Force. Angoff, A., 5

Psychoanalysis and Religion. Fromm, E., 6

Psychology of Adolescence. Horrocks, J., 7

Psychology of Human Differences. Tyler, L., 7

Public Opinion. Lippman, W., 16

Public Opinion and American Democracy. Key, V., 20

Public Speaker's Treasure Chest. Prochnow, H., 82

Publicity and Management. Theatre Student Series, 75

Publishers Weekly, 1

Puerto Rican Papers: Notes on the Re-emergence of a Nation. Lopez, A., 120

Puerto Ricans. Wagenheim, K., 120

Puerto Rico. Maldonado-Denis, M., 120

Pulaski, MaryAnn S. Understanding Piaget, 8

Pumps. Black, P., 51

Puppetry. Theatre Student Series, 75

Puritan Dilemma. Morgan, E., 108

Pushkin, Aleksandr S. Poems, Prose, and Plays, 92

Quaker Reader. West, J., 13

Quality of Mercy. Greenberg, S., 27

Quarrels That Have Shaped the Constitution. Garraty, J., 25

Queen Christina. Masson, G., 99

Queen Victoria. Longford, E., 107

Queen Victoria. Strachey, L., 107

Quennell, Charles H. Everyday Life in Pre-historic Times, 94

Quennell, Marjorie. Everyday Life in Roman and Anglo-Saxon Times, 109

Quest for America. Ashe, G., 121

Questions and Answers on Real Estate. Semenow, R., 24

Quick and Easy Way to Effective Speaking. Carnegie, D., 82

Quiet Crisis. Udall, S., 24

Quiet Rebels. Bacon, M., 13

Quiller-Couch, Arthur T. Oxford Book of Ballads, 86

Quilting and Patchwork. Sunset Magazine, eds., 69

Quinn, Arthur H. American Fiction, 84

_____. History of American Drama, 84

_____. Literature of the American People, 82

RA Expeditions. Heyerdahl, T., 94

RCAF Exercise Plans for Physical Fitness. Royal Canadian Air Force, 48

Race and Races. Goldsby, R., 40

Radiation and Life. Davis, G., 38

Radical Feminism. Koedt, A., 18

Radicalism in America. Lens, S., 17

Radio Amateur's Handbook. American Radio Relay League, 52

Radio Amateurs's Handbook. Collins, A., 52

Radio Handbook. Orr, W., 53

Rag Tapestries and Wool Mosaics. Wiseman, A., 69

Raikes, Robert. Water, Weather, and Pre-history, 40

Raising a Hyperactive Child. Stewart, M., 8

Raising Children with Love and Limits. Cattell, P., 60

Raleigh, Walter. Shakespeare's England, 87

Rand McNally. Guides and road atlases, 95

Rand McNally Road Atlas, 94

Rand McNally World Atlas, 94

Randall, James G. Civil War and Reconstruc-tion, 123

Rapaport, Howard G. Complete Allergy Guide, 50

Rapier, Dorothy. Practical Nursing, 47

Rasputin and the Fall of the Romanovs. Wilson, C., 106

Rating of Graduate Programs. Roose, K., 29

Rats, Lice and History. Zinsser, H., 50

Raw Pearl. Bailey, P., 98

Rayner, William H. Fundamentals of Survey-ing, 38

Reaction and Revolution. Artz, F., 111

Read, Herbert, Concise History of Modern Sculpture, 67

Reader's Digest Complete Book of the Gar-den. Reader's Digest, 66

Reader's Encyclopedia. Benet, W., 79

Reader's Encyclopedia of Shakespeare. Campbell, O., 87

Reader's Guide to Great 20th Century English Novels. Karl, F., 88

Readers Introduction to the New Testament. Leitch, A., 11

Readings in the Philosophy of Art and Aesthetics. Nahm, M., 64

Real Isadora. Seroff, V., 100

Real Majority. Scammon, R., 22

Reality of God. Cassels, L., 11

Reason and Revolution. Marcuse, H., 16

Reason Awake: Science for Man. Dubos, R., 35

Reason Why. Woodham-Smith, C., 114

Rebel. Camus, A., 8

Reconstruction. Craven, A., 123

Reconstruction. Franklin, J., 123

Red Giants and White Dwarfs. Jastrow, R., 37

Red Laquered Gate. Barrett, W., 12

Red Man's Land/White Man's Law. Washburn, W., 119

Red Man's Religion. Underhill, R., 15

Red Power. Josephy, A., 119

Reed, John. Ten Days that Shook the World, 115

Rees, Paul K. Principles of Mathematics, 37

Reeves, James. Short History of English Poetry, 86

Reference Books: a Brief Guide. Barton, M., 1

Reference Books: How to Select and Use Them. Galin, S., 1

Reference Books for Small and Medium-sized Libraries. American Library Association, 1

Reference Manual for Stenographers and Typists. Gavin, R., 61

Reflections on Big Science, Weinberg, A., 35

Reflections on the Revolution in France. Burke, E., 114

Reformation. Mosse, G., 111

Reformation. Simon, E., 13

Reformation Era. Grimm, H., 111

Regulating the Poor. Piven F., 27

Reich, Charles A. Greening of America, 17

Reid, George. Pond Life, 40

Reinfeld, Fred. Catalogue of the World's Most Popular Coins, 75

———. Chess for Young People, 75

———. Chess in a Nutshell, 76

———. Complete Chessplayer, 76

Reinhold Drawing and Painting Book. Jaxtheimer, B., 67

———. Easiest Way to Learn Chess, 76

Reischauer, Edwin O. Japan, 117

Reische, Diana. Women and Society, 18

Reisigel, Herbert. World of Flowers, 43

Reiss, Albert I. Police and the Public, 26

Relativity for the Layman. Coleman, J., 38

Relativity for the Millions. Gardner, M., 38

Religion: Out or Way Out. Oursler, W., 13

Religions. Haskins, J., 14

Religions of Man. Smith, H., 14

Religious and Spiritual Groups in Modern America. Ellwood, R., 13

Religious Philosophies of the West. Thomas, G., 10

Reminiscences. MacArthur, D., 104

Remodeling Rooms. Day, R., 63

Renaissance. Ferguson, W., 110

Renaissance. Hale, J., 111

Renaissance: Maker of Modern Man. Setton, K., 111

Renaissance and the Reformation. Lucas, H., 110

Rendon, Armando B. Chicano Manifesto, 19

Renoir, Jean. Renoir, My Father, 106

Repairing Small Electrical Appliances. Hertzberg, R., 59

Representative English Plays. Tatlock, J., 87

Reproducing Antique Furniture. Gottshall, F., 62

Reptiles and Amphibians of North America. Leviton, A., 45

Reptiles of North America. Ditmars, R., 45

Republican Ascendancy. Hicks, J., 124

Resistance, Rebellion and Death. Camus, A., 89

Resnick, Seymour. Anthology of Spanish Literature in English Translation, 90

Restless Earth. Calder, N., 39

Restless Spirit. Gurko, M., 105

Restoration of Antique and Classic Cars. Wheatley, R., 56

Restoring Junk. Beedell, S., 70

Retirement Handbook. Buckley, J., 19

Reunion and Reaction. Woodward, C., 123

Reverence for Life. Schweitzer, A., 12

Revised Standard Version, 11

Revolution in Learning. Pines, M., 29

Revolutionary Notes. Lester, J., 20

Rexroth, Kenneth. American Poetry in the Twentieth Century, 83

Rey, Hans A. Stars, 37

Reynolds, Graham. Concise History of Watercolors, 71

Reynolds, John. Windmills and Watermills, 53

Reynolds, Quentin. They Fought for the Sky, 112

Rhine, Louise E. Mind Over Matter, 6

Ricardo, David. Principles of Political Economy and Taxation, 23

Rice, Julius. Ups and Downs, 49

Rice, Tamara T. Concise History of Russian Art, 65

Rich Man, Poor Man. Miller H., 24

Rich Nations and Poor Nations, Ward, B., 24

Richard III. Kendall, P., 106

Richard Wright. Webb, C., 108

Richards, Stanley. Best Mystery and Suspense Plays of the Modern Theatre, 81

———. Best Plays of the Sixties, 81

Richardson, Ben. Great American Negroes, 96

Richardson, Edgar P. Painting in America, from 1502 to the Present, 71

Richardson, Emeline. Etruscans: their Art and Civilization, 109

Richardson, H. Wilmont. Freehand Lettering, 67

Richardson, Robert S. Stars and Serendipity, 37

Richette, Lisa A. Throwaway Children, 19

Richenbacker, Eddie. Rickenbacker, 106

Richter, H. P. Practical Electrical Wiring, Residential, Farm, and Industrial, 53

Riddle of History. Mazlish, B., 93

Ridley, Anthony. Living in Cities, 17

Riebel, John P. How to Write Reports, Papers, Thesis, Articles, 80

Riesman, David. Lonely Crowd, 7

Rights of Students, The. Levine, A., 25

Rights We Have. Fraenkel, O., 20

Rigney, Francis J. Beginner's Book of Magic, 76

Rilke, Rainer. Poems, 89

Rimbaud, Arthur. Selected Verse, 89

Ring Lardner Reader. Lardner, R., 85

Rise and Fall of Modern Dance. McDonagh, D., 75

Rise and Fall of the Third Reich. Shirer, W., 114

Rise of an American Architecture. Kaufmann, E., Jr., 66

Rise of Modern Communism. Salvadori, M., 24

Rise of the West. McNeill, W., 93

Rising Sun, 1936–1945. Toland, J., 117

Rising Tides; 20th Century American Women Poets. Chester, L., 83

Ritch, OCee. Chilton's Motorcycle Carburetion Systems, 55

———. Chilton's Motorcycle Electrical Systems, 55

Ritchie, Jean. Dulcimer Book, 74

Rivers of Blood, Years of Darkness. Conot, R., 20

Riviere, William A. Camper's Bible, 77

Road to Pearl Harbor. Feis, H., 112

Road to Reunion. Buck, P., 123

Robber Barons. Josephson, M., 123

Robert, Henry M. Robert's Rules of Order, 21

Robert Kennedy, a Memoir. Newfield, J., 103

Roberts, Daniel. Archery for All, 78

Roberts, Henry L. Eastern Europe, 116

Roberts, Paul. Understanding Grammar, 33

Roberts, Ron. The New Communes, 17

Robert's Rules of Order. Robert, H., 21

Robertson, Archibald. How to Read History, 93

Robertson, John G. History of German Literature, 89

Robinson, Arthur. Elements of Cartography, 38

Robinson, Charles A., Jr. Athens in the Age of Pericles, 110

Robinson, Cyril E. Everyday Life in Ancient Greece, 110

Robinson, D. B., Jr. Know Your Gerbils, 57

Robinson, Jeffrey. All of Europe at Low Cost, 95

Robinson, John A. Christian Freedom in a Permissive Society, 12

Rock, from the Beginning. Coh, Nik, 73

Rock Book. Fenton, C., 39

Rock Encyclopedia. Roxon, L., 74

Rock Revolution. Shaw, A., 74

Rockefeller Family Portrait. Manchester, W., 96

Rockets, Missiles and Men in Space. Ley, W., 56

Rockmore, Cynthia. Room-by-Room Book of American Antiques, 70

Rocks and Minerals. Zim, H., 40

Rockwell, Frederick F. Rockwell's Complete Guide to Successful Gardening, 66

Rodale Cookbook, 59

Rodgers, Dorothy. My Favorite Things, 70

Rodwell, J. M. ed. Koran, 15

Roedelberger, Franz. African Wildlife, 46

Roeing, Richard S. Auto Engine Tune-Up, 55

Roethke, Theodore. On the Poet and His Craft, 80

Rogers, Bruce A. Nature of Metals, 62

Rogers, Carl. Becoming Partners, 19

———. Carl Rogers on Encounter Groups, 7

———. On Becoming a Person, 7

Rogers, Cyril H. Parakeet Guide, 57

Roget's International Thesaurus, 32

Roman Way. Hamilton, E., 90

Romantic Agony. Praz, M., 79

Rombaur, Irma S. Joy of Cooking, 59

Rome in the Dark Ages. Llewellyn, P., 115

Romer, Alfred S. Vertebrate Body, 44

Rommel, the Desert Fox. Young, D., 106

Rood, Ronald. Animals Nobody Loves: Varmint Ecology, 46

Room-by-Room Book of American Antiques. Rockmore, C., 70

Room of One's Own. Woolf, V., 79

Roose, Kenneth D. Rating of Graduate Programs, 29

Roosevelt. Burns, J., 106

Roosevelt, Eleanor. Autobiography, 106

Roosevelt, Elliot. Untold Story: the Roosevelts of Hyde Park, 96

Rope-In Case. Beckwith, L., 88

Rose. Cameron, G., 103

Rose, Camille D. How to Write Successful Magazine Articles, 80

Rose, Herbert J. Handbook of Greek Literature, 91

Roseboom, Eugene H. History of Presidential Elections, 22

Rosenberg, Nancy. How to Enjoy Mathematics with Your Child, 37

———. Vaccine and Virus, 50

Rosenberg, Sharon. Illustrated Hassle-Free Make Your Own Clothes Book, 60

Rosenfeld, Sam. Science Experiments with Water, 38

Rosenthal, Abraham M. 38 Witnesses, 26

Ross, Ishbel. Angel of the Battlefield, 98

Ross, James B. Portable Medieval Reader, 79

———. Portable Renaissance Reader, 79

Ross, Martin J. Handbook of Everyday Law, 26

Rossiter, Clinton. American Presidency, 27

———. Conservatism in America, 20

Rostand, Edmund. Cyrano de Bergerac, 89

Roszak, Theodore. Making of a Counterculture, 16

Rotberg, Robert I. Haiti: the Politics of Squalor, 120

Rothman, Milton A. Cybernetic Revolution, 3

Rothschilds. Morton, F., 106

Rottger, Ernst. Creative Wood Design, 69

Rousseau, Jean J. Social Contract; and Discourses, 16

Rousseau, Jean-Jacques. Confessions, 106

Routh, Charles R. They Saw It Happen in Europe: 1453–1600, 111

Routley, Erik. Twentieth Century Church Music, 73

Rowe, John L. Gregg Typing, 61

Rowell, George. Nineteenth Century Plays, 87

Rowell, Thelma. Social Behavior of Monkeys, 46

Rowse, Alfred F. England of Elizabeth, 113

Roxon, Lillian. Rock Encyclopedia, 74

Royal Canadian Air Force. RCAF Exercise Plans for Physical Fitness, 48

Royko, Mike. Boss, 100

Rubaiyat. Omar Khayam, 91

Rubin, Harold. Ulcer Diet Cookbook, 50

Rudd, Rubert L. Pesticides and the Living Landscape, 57

Rudiments of Music. Castellini, J., 72

Rudofsky, Bernard. Streets for People, 65

Rue, Leonard. Pictorial Guide to the Mammals of North America, 46

Rufsvold, Margaret I. Guides to Educational Media, 3

Rugh, Roberts. From Conception to Birth, 51

Run to Daylight. Lombardi, V., 77

Runciman, Steven. Byzantine Civilization, 116

Russell, Bertrand. Autobiography, 106

———. Basic Writings, 9

Russell, Diarmuid. Portable Irish Reader, 88

Russell, John. Pop Art Redefined, 65

Russell, Robert. To Catch an Angel, 106

Russia. Harcave, S., 115

Russia. Thayer, C., 115

Russia: a Short History. Florinsky, M., 115

Russia: Tsarist and Communist. Mazour, A., 115

Russia and the Soviet Union. Walsh, W., 115

Russia and the West Under Lenin and Stalin. Kennan, G., 21

Russia Under the Czars. Moscow, H., 115

Russian-English Dictionary. Smirnitsky, A., 34

Russian Revolution. Moorehead, A., 115

Rutherford, Peddy. African Voices, 91

Ryan, Cornelius. Longest Day: June 6, 1944, 112

Ryan, Frank. Weight Training, 77

Ryan, William. Blaming the Victim, 19

Sachs, Curt. History of Musical Instruments, 74

———. World History of the Dance, 75

Sacks, Oliver W. Migraine, 50

Safe Snowmobiling. Thomas, J., 77

Sailor on Horseback. Stone, I., 104

St. John, Robert. Ben-Gurion, 98

Saint Watching. McGinley, P., 11

Salisbury, Frank B. Biology of Flowering, 43

Salisbury, Harrison E. 900 Days: Siege of Leningrad, 112

———. Soviet Union: the 50 Years, 115

———. War Between Russia and China, 21

Salter, Stefan. Joys of Hunting Antiques, 70

Salt-Water Aquarium in the Home. Straughan, R., 45

Salvadori, Massino. Rise of Modern Communism, 24

Sampson, George. Concise Cambridge History of English Literature, 86

Samuelson, Paul A. Economics, 23

Sand County Almanac. Leopold, A., 39
Sandberg, Carl. Always the Young Strangers, 106
——. Selected Poems, 83
Sandbox. Albee, E., 83
Sanderson, Ivan T. Investigating the Unexplained, 4
——. Living Mammals of the World, 46
Sanderson, R. T. Inorganic Chemistry, 39
Sandford, William P. Principles of Effective Speaking, 82
Sandler, Sandra. Home Bakebook of Natural Breads and Goodies, 59
Sandman, Peter M. Media, 29
Sands, Bill. My Shadow Ran Fast, 28
Sanford, William R. Jewelry, Queen of Crafts, 69
Sargent, Robert L. Automobile Sheet Metal Repair, 55
Sarno, John E. Stroke, 50
Sartre, Jean-Paul. No Exit, and Three Other Plays, 89
Satires, Epistles, and Ars Poetica. Horace, 90
Saunby, T. Soilless Culture, 57
Sava, Charles. How to Teach Yourself and Your Family to Swim Well, 78
Savage, George. Dictionary of Antiques, 70
Savage God. Alvarez, A., 16
Saxon, James A. Basic Principles of Data Processing, 4
Sayers, Gale. I Am Third, 106
Scammon, Richard M. Real Majority, 22
Scarisbrick, J. J. Henry VIII, 102
Scarne, John. Scarne's Complete Guide to Gambling, 76
Scene Design and Stage Lighting. Parker, W., 75
Scenery. Theatre Student Series, 75
Scenes to Perform. Theatre Student Series, 75
Scheffer, Victor B. Year of the Seal, 46
Schegger, Theresia M. Make Your Own Mobiles, 67
Scheinfled, Amram. Your Heredity and Environment, 42
Schelling, Felix E. Elizabethan Playwrights, 87
Schery, Robert W. Lawn Book, 66
Schiotz, Arne. Guide to Aquarium Fishes and Plants, 45
Schitz, Askel. Singer and His Art, 74
Schlesinger, Arthur M. Age of Jackson, 122
——. Age of Roosevlet, 124
——. Crisis of Confidence, 16
——. Imperial Presidency, 27
——. Nothing Stands Still, 121
——. Thousand Days, 124
Schmeller, Kurt E. Course of Europe Since Waterloo, 111
Schmidt, Karl P. Field Book of Snakes of U.S. and Canada, 45
Schmitt, George F. Diabetes for Diabetics, 50
Schmitt, Waldo L. Crustaceans, 44
Schoener, Allan. Harlem on My Mind 1900–1968, 124
Schonberg, Harold C. Great Conductors, 96
——. Great Pianists, 96
——. Lives of Great Composers, 96
Schopenhauer, Arthur. Will to Live, 9
Schram, Stuart R. Mao Tse Tung, 104
Schreiber, Flora R. Sybil, 51
Schreiber, Hermann. Vanished Cities, 109
Schremp, William E. Designer Furniture Anyone Can Make, 62
Schuler, Stanley. Gardener's Basic Book of Trees and Shrubs, 66
——. Householder's Encyclopedia, 63
——. How to Fix Almost Everything, 63
Schultz, Leonard P. Wondrous World of Fishes, 45
Schwartz, Alvin. Unions, 23
Schwartz, Barry N. White Racism, 20
Schwartz, Robert. Complete Homeowner, 63
Schweitzer, Albert. Out of my Life and Thought, 107
——. Reverence for Life, 12
Science and Health with Key to the Scriptures. Eddy, M., 13
Science and Sentiment in America. White, M., 9
Science and Survival. Commoner, B., 35
Science Experiments with Water. Rosenfeld, S., 38
Science for the Citizen. Hogben, L., 35
Science in American Society. Daniels, G., 35
Science in History. Bernal, J., 35
Science of Clouds. Tricker, R., 40
Science of Gems. Fisher, P., 39
Science of Weather. Day, J., 39
Scobie, James R. Argentina, 125
Scobey, Jean. Do-it-all-Yourself Needlepoint, 69
Scott, Donald F. About Epilepsy, 50
Scott, Ernest. Short History of Australia, 126
Scott Fitzgerald. Turnbull, A., 101
Scott's Standard Postage Stamps of the World. Scott Publications, 76

Screen Printing. Birkner, H., 71
Screwtape Letters. Lewis, C., 12
Scribner Handbook of English. Marchwardt, A., 80
Scully, Vincent. American Architecture and Urbanism, 67
Sculpture for Beginners. DiValentin, M., 67
Sculpture of the World. Cheney, S., 67
Sculpture with Simple Materials. Sunset, 67
Sea Around Us. Carson, R., 54
Sea for Breakfast. Beckwith, L., 88
Sea Power. Potter, E., 93
Sea Treasure. Johnstone, K., 44
Seale, Bobby. Sieze the Time, 19
Seaman, Barbara. Doctor's Case against the Pill, 5
———. Free and Female, 18
Search for Amelia Earhart. Goerner, F., 100
Search for Common Ground. Thurman, H., 10
Search for the New Land. Lester, J., 21
Search for the Past. Beerbower, J., 40
Searching for Your Ancestors. Doane, G., 108
Sears, Paul B. Living Landscape, 40
Seashores. Zim, H., 40
Seaton, Don C. Physical Education Handbook, 77
Second Arab Awakening. Kimche, J., 117
Second Sex. DeBeauvior, S., 17
Second World War. Churchill, W., 112
Secret of Dreams. Stewart, W., 6
Secret of the Hittites. Ceram, C., 109
Secret Societies. MacKenzie, N., 28
Secretary's Complete Model Letter Handbook. Eddings, C., 61
Secrets of the Great Masters. Hours, M., 71
Secular City, The. Cox, H., 12
Securities, Exchanges and the S.E.C. Tyler, P., 24
Seeger, Elizabeth. Pageant of Chinese History, 117
Seeman, Bernard. Your Sight, 51
Selected Guide to Make It, Fix It, Do It Yourself Books. Nueckel, S., 1
Selected Plays. O'Casey, S., 87
Selected Poems. Garcia Lorca, F., 90
Selected Poems. Heine, H., 88
Selected Poems. Sandburg, C., 83
Selected Verse. Rimbaud, A., 89
Selected Works. Carlyle, T., 88
Selected Writings. Stein, G., 85
Selected Writings. Valery, P., 89

Selections. Tolstoy, L., 92
Self, Margaret C. Horseman's Encyclopedia, 57
Self and Others. Laing, R., 6
Self-Renewal. Gardner, J., 16
Seligson, Marcia. Eternal Bliss Machine, 19
Sellin, Thorsten. Capital Punishment, 26
Selling of the President. McGinniss, J., 22
Semenow, Robert W. Questions and Answers on Real Estate, 24
Seroff, Victor. Real Isadora, 100
Serpico. Maas, P., 107
Servan-Schreiber, J. J. American Challenge, 21
Service, Robert. Collected Poems, 83
Servicing Modern Hi-Fi-Stereo Systems. Crowhurst, N., 52
Seton-Watson, Hugh. Eastern Europe between the Wars: 1918–1941, 112
———. History of the Roumanians, 116
Setton, Kenneth M. Renaissance: Maker of Modern Man, 111
Seven Pillars of Wisdom. Lawrence, T., 112
Seven Plays. Anouilh, J., 89
Seven Plays. Brecht, B., 88
Seven Plays. Shaw, G., 87
Seven Plays of the Modern Theatre. Clurman, H., 81
Seven States of Matter. Gottlieb, M., 38
Seven Wonders of the World. Muller, A., 94
Severn, William. End of the Roaring Twenties: Prohibition and Repeal, 8
Sewing the Easy Way. Johnson, M., 60
Sewing without a Pattern. Ficarotta, P., 60
Sex: Telling it Straight. Johnson, E., 48
Sex and Birth Control. Lieberman, E., 51
Sex Life of the Animals. Wendt, H., 44
Sexual Politics. Millet, K., 18
Sexual Wilderness. Packard, V., 18
Seymour, Harold J. Designs for Fund Raising, 28
Seymour-Smith, Martin. Guide to Modern World Literature, 79
Shackles of Power. Dos Passos, J., 120
Shadows in the Sea. McCormick, H., 45
Shakespeare, William. Complete Pelican Shakespeare, 87
———. Complete Works, 87
———. Complete Works of Shakespeare, 87
———. Sonnets, Songs and Poems, 88
Shakespeare. Van Doren, M., 88
Shakespeare: His Life, His Times, His Works. American Heritage, 87
Shakespeare: the Tragedies. Harbage, A., 87

Shakespeare Companion. Halliday, F., 87
Shakespeare of London. Chute, M., 87
Shakespearean Tragedy. Bradley, A., 87
Shakespeare's England. Raleigh, W., 87
Shakespeare's Theater. Thorndike, A., 88
Shame of the Cities. Steffens, L., 21
Shannon, David A. Great Depression, 124
Shapiro, Karl. American Poetry, 83
_____. Prosody Handbook, 80
Shapley, Harlow. Galaxies, 37
Shark. Cousteau, J., 44
Shaw, Arnold. Rock Revolution, 74
Shaw, George B. Seven Plays, 87
Sheaffer, Louis. O'Neill: Son and Artist, 105
Sheean, Vincent. Mahatma Gandhi, 101
Sheen, Fulton J. Children and Parents, 19
_____. Power of Love, 12
Shelley, Percy B. Complete Poetical Works, 86
Shemel, Sidney. More About this Business of
    Music, 73
_____. This Business of Music, 73
Sheperd, Francis P. Earth beneath the Sea, 40
Sheresky, N., and Mannes, M. Uncoupling:
    the Art of Coming Apart, 19
Sherrill, John L. They Speak with Other
    Tongues, 13
Sherrill, Robert. Accidental President, 103
Shirer, William L. Collapse of the Third
    Republic, 114
_____. Rise and Fall of the Third Reich, 114
Shoal of Time. Daws, G., 126
Shook, Robert L. How to be the Complete
    Professional Salesman, 61
Shooter's Bible. Olsen, J., 53
Short History of Africa. Oliver, R., 118
Short History of the Arab Peoples. Glubb, J.,
    117
Short History of Australia. Scott, E., 126
Short History of Botany in the United States.
    Ewan, J., 43
Short History of Chinese Communism. Houn,
    F., 116
Short History of English People. Green, J.,
    113
Short History of English Poetry. Reeves, J.,
    86
Short History of Literary Criticism. Hall, V.,
    79
Short History of Music. Einstein, A., 73
Short History of North Africa. Nickerson, J.,
    118
Short History of Scientific Ideas to 1900.
    Singer, C., 35

Short History of Sweden. Oakley, S., 116
Short History of Switzerland. Bonjour, E.,
    116
Short History of Technology from the
    Earliest Times to A.D. 1900. Derry, T., 47
Short History of the Far East. Latourette, K.,
    116
Short History of the United States. Nevins,
    A., 121
Short History of Yugoslavia. Clissold, S., 116
Short Life of Shakespeare. Chambers, E., 87
Short Season. Morris, J., 105
Shorter Cambridge Medieval History. Previte-
    Orton, C., 111
Shurtleff, Malcolm C. How to Control Plant
    Diseases in Home and Garden, 57
Sieben, Pearl. Immortal Jolson, 103
Sienko, Michell. Chemistry, 39
Sieze the Time. Seale, B., 19
Silberman, Charles E. Crisis in Black and
    White, 20
_____. Crisis in the Classroom, 29
Silent Spring. Carson, R., 54
Silent Tragedy. DeCourcy, P., 18
Silent World. Cousteau, J., 39
Silverberg, Robert. Challenge of Climate, 40
_____. Lost Cities and Vanished Civilizations,
    109
_____. Mound Builders of Ancient America,
    119
_____. World within the Ocean Wave, 40
_____. World within the Tidal Pool, 40
Simak, Clifford D. March of Science, 35
Simmons, Adelma G. Herbs to Grow Indoors,
    66
Simon, André. International Wine and Food
    Society's Encyclopedia of Wines, 62
Simon, Edith. Reformation, 13
Simon, George T. Big Bands, 74
Simon Henry. Treasury of Christmas Songs
    and Carols, 74
_____. Victor Book of Opera, 73
Simon, Paul. Songs of Paul Simon, 74
Simonson, Leroy. Private Pilot Study Guide,
    54
Simple Gasoline Engine Repair. Olney, R., 52
Simple Library Cataloging. Akers, S., 1
Simple Stage Costumes and How to Make
    Them. Jackson, S., 30
Simplified Concrete Masonry Planning and
    Building. Dalzell, J., 63
Simplified Genealogy for Americans. Kirk-
    ham, K., 108

Simplified Hydraulics. McNickle, L., 51
Simpson, George. Life: an Introduction to Biology, 41
Since 1900. Barck, O., 124
Since Silent Spring. Graham, F., Jr., 54
Sincere's Air Conditioning Service. Ewers, W., 52
Sincere's Bicycle Service Book. Ewers, W., 56
Sincere's Lawn Mower Service Book. Ewers, W., 56
Sincere's Mini Bike Service. Ewers, W., 55
Sincere's Sewing Machine Service Book. Ewers, W., 59
Sincere's Vacuum Cleaner and Small Appliance Service Manual. Ewers, W., 59
Sinclair, Dorothy. Administration of the Small Public Library, 2
Singer, Charles. Short History of Scientific Ideas to 1900, 35
Singer, E. J. Basic Mathematics for Electricity and Electronics, 37
Singer, June. Boundaries of the Soul, 7
Singer and His Art. Schitz, A., 74
Singer Sewing Book. Cunningham, G., 60
Single and Pregnant. Pierce, R., 19
Single Standard. Harris, J., 18
Singletary, Otis A. Mexican War, 123
Sinnott, Edmund W. Botany, 43
Sioux of the Rosebud. Hamilton, H., 119
Sippl, Charles J. Computer Dictionary and Handbook, 4
Sisterhood is Powerful. Morgan, R., 18
Sisters. Harris, S., 13
Sitwell, Edith. Taken Care Of, 107
Six Plays. Strindberg, A., 89
Six Wives of Henry VIII. Malvern, G., 96
Sixteen Modern American Authors. Bryer, J., 82
Sketch Book. Irving, W., 85
Skiing. Sports Illustrated, 77
Skin and Scuba Diver. Borgeson, L., 77
Skin Diving and Snorkeling. Sports Illustrated, eds., 78
Skinner, B. F. Beyond Freedom and Dignity, 7
_____. Walden Two, 20
Skinner, Cornelia. Madame Sarah, 98
Skinner, Tom. How Black is the Gospel?, 10
Skornia, Harry J. Television and Society, 29
Slavery. Elkins, S., 21
Slaves We Rent. Moore, T., 23
Sleepwalkers. Koestler, A., 10
Slide Rule Simplified. Harris, C., 36

Sloane, Eugene A. New Complete Book of Bicycling, 77
Sloane, Eunice M. Illustrating Fashion, 67
Sloane, Irving. Classic Guitar Instruction, 74
Slonim, Marc L. Epic of Russian Literature, 92
_____. Outline of Russian Literature, 92
_____. Soviet Russian Literature, 92
Small, William E. Third Pollution, 54
Small Appliance Repair Guide. Lemons, W., 59
Small Arms of the World. Smith, W., 53
Small Engines. Crouse, W., 52
Small Game Hunting. Ormond, C., 78
Small Groups and Political Behavior. Verba, S., 20
Small Sects in America. Clark, E., 13
Smallman, Kirk. Creative Film Making, 72
Smart Sewing. Doerr, C., 60
Smelser, Marshall. Democratic Republic, 122
_____. Winning of Independence, 122
Smirnitsky, A. I. Russian-English Dictionary, 34
Smith, Adam. Money Game, 23
_____. Wealth of Nations, 23
Smith, Alice L. Principles of Microbiology, 42
Smith, Bert K. Your Non-Learning Child, 29
Smith, Bradford. Captain John Smith, 107
_____. Men of Peace, 96
Smith, Carlton. Time-Life Book of Family Finance, 23
Smith, Charles M. How to Talk to God When You Aren't Feeling Religious, 13
Smith, Elsdon C. American Surnames, 108
_____. Naming Your Baby, 108
Smith, Gene. When the Cheering Stopped, 108
Smith, Goldwin A. England, a Short History, 113
Smith, Harris P. Farm Machinery and Equipment, 57
Smith, Huston. Great Religions of the World, 14
_____. Religions of Man, 14
Smith, James H. Great Critics, 79
Smith, LeRoi. How to Fix Up Old Cars, 55
Smith, Page. Historian and History, 93
Smith, Richard F. Chemistry for the Million, 39
Smith, Robert. Babe, 106
Smith, Vincent A. Oxford History of India, 117
Smith, Walter H. Small Arms of the World, 53

Smoking. Ochsner, A., 49

Smyth, Herbert W. Greek Grammar, 34

Snake Has All the Lines. Kerr, J., 85

Snook, Barbara. Costumes for Children, 30

Snow, Charles P. Two Cultures: And A
Second Look, 3

Snowmobiles and Snowmobiling. Tuite, J.,
77

Snowmobiling. Malo, J., 77

Snyder, Louis L. War: a Concise History,
1939–1945, 112

So Human an Animal. Dubos R., 16

So You Want to be an Architect. Meinhardt,
C., 66

So You Want to be a Ham. Hertzberg, R., 52

So You Want to Buy a House. Griffin, A., 24

So You Want to Buy a Mobile Home. Griffin,
A., 24

Soccer. Glanville, B., 76

Soccer. Sports Illustrated, 77

Social Behavior of Monkeys. Rowell, T., 46

Social Change and Prejudice. Bettelheim, B.,
16

Social Contract; and Discourses. Rousseau, J.,
16

Social History of England: 55 B.C.–A.D.
1215. Arnold, R., 113

Social Security and Medicare Simplified. U.S.
News & World Report, eds., 28

Social Usage. Free, A., 30

Society and Politics in England: 1780–1960.
Harrison, J., 113

Sociology. Ogburn, W., 16

Sociology of Science. Barber, B., 35

Soderman, Harry. Modern Criminal Investigation, 26

Soilless Culture. Saunby, T., 57

Solar System and Back. Asimov, I., 37

Soldier. Herbert, A., 102

Solitary Singer. Allen, G., 108

Solzhenitzyn, Aleksandr I. Gulag Archipelago,
92

_____. Stories and Prose Poems, 92

Somerlott, Robert. Here, Mr. Splitfoot, 6

Somewhere Else: A Living-Learning Catalog,
17

Song and Garden Birds of North America.
Wetmore, A., 45

Song of Roland, 89

Songs of Paul Simon. Simon, P., 74

Sonnets and Songs. Petrarch, F., 90

Sonnets, Songs and Poems. Shakespeare, W.,
88

Sorenson, Theodore. Kennedy, 103

Sorenson, Thomas C. Word War: Story of
American Propaganda, 17

Soul on Ice. Cleaver, E., 99

Souls of Black Folk. DuBois, W., 19

Soulscript. Jordan, J., 33

Sources of Indian Tradition. De Bary, W., 117

South and the Southerner. McGill, R., 124

South since the War. Andrews, S., 123

Southeast Asia. Cady, J., 118

South-East Asia. Fisher, C., 118

Southern, Eileen. Music of Black Americans:
a History, 73

Southwest: Old and New. Hollon, W., 124

Southwest Pacific. Grattan, C., 126

Souto, H. Mario. Technique of the Motion
Picture Camera, 72

Soviet Russian Literature. Slonim, M., 92

Soviet Union: the 50 Years. Salisbury, H., 115

Soyer, Moses. Oil Painting in Progress, 71

Space Age Dictionary. McLaughlin, C., 56

Space Frontier. Von Braun, W., 56

Spain. Hills, G., 115

Spain: a Modern History. DeMadariaga, S.,
115

Spain 1808–1939. Carr, R., 115

Spanish American Literature: a History.
Anderson-Imbert, E., 90

Spanish Civil War. Thomas, H., 115

Spanish Labyrinth. Brenan, G., 115

Spanish Self-Taught. Ibarra, F., 34

Spare-Part Surgery. Longmore, D., 50

Sparrow, John. After the Assassination, 26

Speak, Memory. Nabokov, V., 105

Spear, Percival. India, 117

Spector, Ivar. Introduction to Russian
History and Culture, 115

Speech Correction. VanRiper, C., 50

Speer, Albert. Inside the Third Reich, 114

Spence, William P. Architecture, 67

Spencer, Hazelton. British Literature, 86

Spengler, Oswald. Decline of the West, 93

Spenser, Edmund. Complete Poetical Works,
86

Spicer, Dorothy. Book of Festivals, 30

Spicer, Edward D. Automotive Collision
Work, 55

Spielman, Patrick E. Make Your Own Sport
Gear, 62

Spiller, Robert, ed. Literary History of the
United States, 82

Spin, Dye, and Weave Your Own Wool.
Duncan, M., 68

Spinar, Zdenek V. Life before Man, 41
Spinoza, Benedict De. Chief Works, 9
Spirit of St. Louis. Lindbergh, C., 104
Spirit of Zen. Watts, A., 14
Splendid Little War. Freidel, F., 123
Splendor That Was Egypt. Murray, M., 109
Spock, Benjamin M. Baby and Child Care, 60
_____. Problems of Parents, 19
Spoon River Anthology. Masters, E., 83
Sports and Games. Keith, H., 76
Sports Illustrated. Badminton, 77
_____. Baseball, 77
_____. Basketball, 77
_____. Better Boating, 78
_____. Diving, 78
_____. Dog Training, 57
_____. Football, 77
_____. Golf, 77
_____. Horseback Riding, 78
_____. Ice Hockey, 77
_____. Skiing, 77
_____. Skin Diving and Snorkeling, 78
_____. Soccer, 77
_____. Swimming, 78
_____. Table Tennis, 77
_____. Tennis, 77
_____. Track and Field, 77
_____. Training with Weights, 77
_____. Volleyball, 77
Sports Immortals. Associated Press, eds., 95
Sportsmanlike Driving. American Automobile
    Assn., 54
Squeglia, Michael. All about Repairing Small
    Appliances, 59
Stacton, David. Bonapartes, 96
Stage Makeup. Buchman, H., 74
Stainback, Berry. Pro Football Heroes of
    Today, 77
Stained Glass Crafting. Wood, P., 69
Stalking the Wild Asparagus. Gibbons, E., 43
Stalking the Wild Taboo. Hardin, G., 16
Stalin. Hyde, H., 107
Stallings, Laurence. Doughboys, 112
Stamm, Gustav W. Veterinary Guide for
    Farmers, 57
Stampp, Kenneth M. And the War Came, 123
_____. Causes of the Civil War, 123
_____. Era of Reconstruction, 123
Standard College Dictionary. Funk &
    Wagnalls, 32
Standard Handbook for Secretaries.
    Hutchinson, L., 61

Standard Handbook of Stamp Collecting.
    Cabeen, R., 75
Stanforth, Deidre. Buying and Renovating a
    House in the City, 63
Stanier, Roger Y. Microbial World, 42
Stapley, Ray. Car Owner's Handbook, 55
Starr, Chester G. History of the Ancient
    World, 109
Stars. Rey, H., 37
Stars and Serendipity. Richardson, R., 37
Stars by Clock and Fist. Neely, H., 37
Stars in their Courses. Asimov, I., 37
Status Seekers. Packard, V., 17
Stavrianos, L. S. Epic of Modern Man, 93
Stay Alive All Your Life. Peale, N., 7
Stay of Execution. Alsop, S., 97
Steam Plant Operation. Woodruff, E., 52
Stearn, Jess. Edgar Cayce, the Sleeping
    Prophet, 6
_____. Time for Astrology, 6
_____. Yoga, Youth and Reincarnation, 8
Stearns, Marshall. Jazz Dance, 75
Stearns, Peter N. European Society in Up-
    heaval, 112
Stearns, Raymond P. Pageant of Europe, 110
Stebbins, Robert. Field Guide to the Western
    Reptiles and Amphibians, 45
Steel, Ronald. Pax Americana, 21
Steffens, Lincoln. Autobiography, 107
_____. Shame of the Cities, 21
Steichen, Edward. Life in Photography, 72
Stein, Edwin I. Fundamentals of
    Mathematics, 37
_____. Practical Applications in Mathematics,
    37
Stein, Gertrude. Autobiography of Alice B.
    Toklas, 107
_____. Selected Writings, 85
Steinbeck, John. Portable Steinbeck, 84
Steinberg, Milton. Basic Judaism, 14
Steindorff, George. When Egypt Ruled the
    East, 109
Steiner, Jean F. Treblinka, 112
Steiner, Stan. La Raza, 20
Steinzor, Bernard. When Parents Divorce, 8
Step-by-Step Crochet. Wildman, E., 69
Step-by-Step Macrame. Phillips, M., 69
Step-by-Step Weaving. Znamierowski, N., 69
Sterland, E. G. Energy into Power, 38
Sterling. Europe-with Pictures, 95
Stern, Edith M. Mental Illness, 51
_____. You and Your Aging Parents, 19
Stern, Renee B. Club Handybook, 28

Stern, Robert. New Directions in American Architecture, 67

Sternberg, Thomas H. More Than Skin Deep, 59

Stevenson, Burton E. Home Book of Modern Verse, 80

———. Home Book of Verse, 80

Steward, Julian. Native Peoples of South America, 41

Stewart, George R. Not So Rich as You Think, 54

Stewart, Mark A. Raising a Hyperactive Child, 8

Stewart, Walter A. Secret of Dreams, 6

Still Hungry in America. Coles, R., 24

Stillinger, Elizabeth. Antiques' Guide to Decorative Arts in America, 1600–1875, 70

Stillness at Appomatox. Catton, B., 123

Stine, G. Harry. Handbook of Model Rocketry, 54

Sting like a Bee. Torres, J., 105

Stitchery and Crafts. Better Homes & Gardens, 68

Stobart, John C. Glory That Was Greece, 110

———. Grandeur That Was Rome, 109

Stockel, Martin W. Auto Mechanics Fundamentals, 55

———. Auto Service and Repair, 56

Stokes, William L. Introduction to Geology, 40

Stone, Irving. Clarence Darrow for the Defense, 100

———. Men to Match My Mountains, 122

———. Sailor on Horseback, 104

———. They Also Ran, 96

Stone, Irwin. Healing Factor, Vitamin C, 48

Stonecypher, D. D., Jr. Getting Older and Staying Young, 19

Stonehenge Decoded. Hawkins, G., 94

Stonehouse, Bernard. Animals of the Antarctic, 46

———. Animals of the Arctic, 46

Storer, Tracy I. General Zoology, 44

Stories and Prose Poems. Solzhenitsyn, A., 92

Stories from Shakespeare. Chute, M., 87

Storm, and Other Russian Plays. Magarshack, D., 92

Storr, Anthony. Human Aggression, 7

Story of Art. Gombrich, E., 64

Story of Civilization. Durant, W., 93

Story of Cosmic Rays. Beiser, G., 38

Story of George Gershwin. Ewen, D., 101

Story of Language. Pei, M., 32

Story of My Life. Keller, H., 103

Story of Philosophy. Durant, W., 5

Story of Rock. Belz, C., 73

Story of Surnames. Pine, L., 108

Story of the Apocrypha. Goodspeed, E., 10

Story of the Blues. Oliver, P., 73

Story of the Church. Bowie, W., 13

Story of the Crusades. Duggan, A., 110

Story of the English Language. Pei, M., 32

Story of the Laser. Carroll, J., 52

Story of the Plant Kingdom. Coulter, M., 42

Stout, Evelyn E. Introduction to Textiles, 62

Stoye, John. Europe Unfolding, 111

Strachey, Lytton. Eminent Victorians, 96

———. Queen Victoria, 107

Strange Career of Jim Crow. Woodward, C., 123

Stranger on the Earth. Lubin, A., 101

Strangers at the Door. Bach, M., 14

Straughan, Robert P. Salt-Water Aquarium in the Home, 45

Strecker, Edward A. Discovering Ourselves, 7

Street without Joy. Fall, B., 118

Streets for People. Rudofsky, B., 65

Strength to Love. King, M., Jr., 12

Strickland, Winifred G. Expert Obedience Training for Dogs, 57

Strindberg, August. Six Plays, 89

Stroke. Sarno, J., 50

Strong, James. Exhaustive Concordance of the Bible, 11

Stroup, Herbert. Four Religions of Asia, 10

Struggle for Indochina: 1940–1955. Hammer, E., 118

Struggle for Mastery in Europe, 1848–1918. Taylor, Alan J., 111

Struggle for the Great Barrier Reef. Clare, P., 39

Strunk, William. Elements of Style, 80

Stuart, Fredric. Fortran Programming, 37

Stuber, Stanley I. How We got Our Denominations, 13

Student Dictionary of Biology. Gray, P., 41

Studies in Shakespeare. Nicoll, A., 87

Study of Comparative Government and Politics. Hecksher, G., 20

Study of History. Toynbee, A., 93

Study of Literature for Readers and Critics. Daiches, D., 79

Subject Guide to Books in Print, 2

Suburbia. Wood, R., 17

Successful Kennel Management. Taynton, M., 58

Successful Salesmanship. Ivey, P., 61
Successful Toastmaster. Prochnow, H., 82
Succulents and Cactus. Sunset Magazine, eds.,
    66
Suetonius. Twelve Caesars, 109
Suicide. Durkheim, E., 16
Sullerot, Evelyne. Woman, Society and
    Change, 18
Sullivan, Betty. Blender Way to Better Cook-
    ing, 59
Sullivan, John W. Beethoven, 98
Sulzberger, C. L. Picture History of World
    War II, 112
_____. World War II, 112
Summer Employment Directory, 23
Summerhays' Encyclopedia for Horsemen,
    Summerhays, R., 57
Summerhill. Neill, A., 29
Summers, Harrison B. How to Debate, 82
Sun King. Mitford, N., 104
Sun Signs. Goodman, L., 5
Sunset. Ceramics, 67
_____. Sculpture with Simple Materials, 67
Sunset Magazine, eds. Basic Gardening Illus-
    trated, 66
_____. Bonsai, 66
_____. Children's Rooms and Play Yards, 70
_____. Color in Your Garden, 66
_____. Crafts for Children, 69
_____. Crafts You Can Make, 69
_____. Decorative Stitchery, 69
_____. Desert Gardening, 66
_____. Furniture Finishing and Refinishing,
    62
_____. Furniture Upholstery and Repair, 62
_____. Garden and Patio Building Book, 66
_____. Garden Pools, Fountains and Waterfalls,
    66
_____. Gardening in Containers, 66
_____. How to Grow African Violets, 66
_____. How to Grow and Use Annuals, 66
_____. How to Grow Bulbs, 66
_____. How to Grow Herbs, 66
_____. How to Grow House Plants, 66
_____. How to Grow Roses, 66
_____. Ideas for Landscaping, 66
_____. Ideas for Recreation Rooms, 70
_____. Ideas for Remodeling Your Home, 70
_____. Ideas for Storage, 70
_____. Lawns and Ground Covers, 66
_____. Macrame, 69
_____. Needlepoint, 69
_____. Papier Mache, 69
_____. Planning and Remodeling Bathrooms,
    70
_____. Planning and Remodeling Kitchens, 70
_____. Pruning Handbook, 66
_____. Quilting and Patchwork, 69
_____. Succulents and Cactus, 66
_____. Terrariums and Miniature Gardens, 66
_____. Things to Make with Leather, 69
_____. Travel guides, 95
Sunset see also, 59, 63
Super Handyman's Encyclopedia of Home
    Repair Hints. Carrell, A., 62
Super Sewing. Bishop, E., 60
Superstition and the Superstitious. Maple, E.,
    31
Supreme Identity. Watts, A., 14
Surf-Riding. Klein, H., 77
Surviving the Future. Toynbee, A., 94
Sussman, Aaron. Amateur Photographer's
    Handbook, 72
Suzuki, Daisetz T. Essentials of Zen
    Buddhism, 14
Swadesh, Morris. Conversational Chinese for
    Beginners, 34
Swahili Phrase Book. Gilmore, T., 34
Swallow, Kenneth P. Elements of Computer
    Programming, 4
Swanberg, W. A. Citizen Hearst, 102
_____. Dreiser, 100
_____. Luce and His Empire, 104
Swanson, Carl P. Cell, 42
Swanton, John R. Indian Tribes of North
    America, 119
Swift, Henry. Community Groups and You,
    16
Swift, Johathan. Portable Swift, 88
Swimming. Sports Illustrated, eds., 78
Swing the Handle, Not the Clubhead.
    Merrins, E., 77
Swortzell, Lowell. All the World's a Stage, 81
Sybil. Schreiber, F., 51
Symbol, Status and Personality. Hayakawa,
    S., 6
Symbols, Signs and Their Meaning. Whittick,
    A., 64
Synanon. Endore, G., 49
Szulc, Tad. Czechoslovakia since World War
    II, 116

Table Tennis. Sports Illustrated, 77
Take a Tip from Me. Nicklaus, J., 77
Taken Care Of. Sitwell, E., 107

Tales from Shakespeare. Lamb., C., 87
Tales Told by Fossils. Fenton, C., 40
Talese, Gay. Honor Thy Father, 28
Talmud and Apocrypha. Herford, R., 10
Tamarind Book of Lithography. Antreasian, G., 71
Tannenbaum, Beulah. Understanding Maps, 38
Tanner, James M. Growth, 48
Tape Recorder Servicing Guide. Middleton, R., 52
Tariq, Ali. Pakistan: Military Rule or People's Power, 117
Tarling, Don. Continental Drift, 40
Tarot Classic. Kaplan, S., 6
Tatlock, John S. Representative English Plays, 87
Taylor, Alan J. Course of German History, 114
———. English History: 1919–1945, 114
———. Struggle for Mastery in Europe, 1848–1918, 111
Taylor, Gertrude. America's Crochet Book, 69
———. America's Knitting Book, 69
Taylor, Henry O. Medieval Mind, 111
Taylor, John G. New Physics, 38
Taylor, Norman. Encyclopedia of Gardening, 66
———. Guide to Garden Shrubs and Trees, 66
———. Plant Drugs that Changed the World, 50
Taylor, Robert E. Feeling Alive After 65, 19
Taylor, William T. General Biology, 41
Taylour, William. Mycenaeans, 109
Taynton, Mark. Successful Kennel Management, 58
Teacher and Child. Ginott, H., 28
Teaching the Child to Read. Bond, G., 28
Teachings of the Compassionate Buddha. Buddha, G., 14
Teague, Bob. Letters to a Black Boy, 20
Teale, Edwin. Autumn across America, 40
———. Journey into Summer, 40
———. North with the Spring, 40
———. Wandering through Winter, 40
Technical Drawing. Giesecke, F., 63
Technical Publications, Inc. Outboard Motor Service Manual, 53
Technique of Documentary Film Production. Baddeley, W., 72
Technique of the Motion Picture Camera. Souto, H., 72

Technique of Wood Sculpture. Gross, C., 67
Technology of Computer Music. Mathews, M., 74
Teenage Tyranny. Hechinger, G., 18
Teenager's Realistic Guide to Astrology. Jennings, G., 5
Tegner, Bruce. Complete Book of Judo, 77
———. Complete Book of Karate, 77
———. Karate, 77
Teilhard de Chardin, Pierre. Making of a Mind, 107
Telecommunications: Booming Technology. Brown, R., 52
Telescope Handbook and Star Atlas. Howard, N., 37
Television. Brown, L., 29
Television and Society. Skornia, H., 29
Tell Freedom. Abrahams, P., 97
Teltscher, Herry O. Handwriting, 6
Templeton, George. Domestic Rabbit Production, 58
Ten Centuries of Spanish Poetry. Turnbull, E., 90
Ten Days that Shook the World. Reed, J., 115
Tennis. Sports Illustrated, 77
Tennissen, Anthony. Colorful Mineral Identifier, 40
Tennyson, Alfred. Poems and Plays, 86
Terkel, Studs. Working, 23
Terrariums and Miniature Gardens. Sunset Magazine, eds., 66
Terry, Walter. Ballet Companion, 75
Texereau, Jean. How to Make a Telescope, 37
Thailand. Busch, N., 118
Tharp, Louise H. Peabody Sisters of Salem, 96
Thatcher, William. Caring for Your Cat, 58
Thayer, Charles. Russia, 115
Theatre of Revolt. Brustein R., 81
Theater of Tennessee Williams. Williams, T., 84
Theatre of the Absurd. Esslin, M., 81
Theatre Student Series. Acting, 75
———. Costuming, 75
———. Directing, 75
———. Film Making, 75
———. Makeup, 75
———. Music and Sound Effects, 75
———. Musicals, 75
———. Practical Stage Lighting, 75
———. Preparing the Classics, 75
———. Producing Plays for Children, 75

____. Properties and Dressing the Stage, 75

____. Publicity and Management, 75

____. Puppetry, 75

____. Scenery, 75

____. Scenes to Perform, 75

Theodorson, George, A. Modern Dictionary of Sociology, 16

Theories in Social Psychology. Deutsch, M., 16

Theories of Modern Art. Chipp, H., 64

Theory of Literature. Wellek, R., 79

Theory of the Leisure Class. Veblen, T., 23

They Also Ran. Stone, I., 96

They Called Him Stonewall. Davis, B., 102

They Fought for the Sky. Reynolds, Q., 112

They Saw It Happen in Europe: 1453–1600. Routh, C., 111

They Speak with Other Tongues. Sherrill, J., 13

Thigpen, Corbett. Three Faces of Eve, 51

Things That Go Bump in the Night. Jones, L., 6

Things to Make with Leather. Sunset Magazine, eds., 69

Thinking Machines. Adler, I., 36

Thinking Man's Guide to Pro Hockey. Eskanazi, G., 76

Thinking Metrics. Gilbert, T., 30

Third Party Movements in the United States. Hesseltine, W., 22

Third Pollution. Small, W., 54

Third Voice. Donoghue, D., 87

Thirties. Boardman, F., 124

Thirty Days to Better English. Lewis, N., 33

Thirty Years' War. Wedgwood, C., 111

38 Witnesses. Rosenthal, A., 26

36 Children. Kohl, H., 29

This Age of Conflict. Chambers, F., 93

This Business of Music. Shemel, S., 73

This Cybernetic World of Men, Machines and Earth. Parsegian, V., 3

This is my God. Wouk, H., 14

This Land Was Theirs. Oswalt, W., 119

Thomas, Benjamin. Abraham Lincoln, 104

Thomas, Dylan. Collected Poems, 86

Thomas, Elizabeth M. Harmless People, 41

Thomas, George F. Religious Philosophies of the West, 10

Thomas, Hugh. Cuba: the Pursuit of Freedom, 120

____. Spanish Civil War, 115

Thomas, J. W. German Verse from 12th to 20th Century, 89

Thomas, James L. Safe Snowmobiling, 77

Thomas, Piri. Down These Mean Streets, 107

Thomas, William S. Field Book of Common Mushrooms, 43

Thomas Aquinas. Introduction to St. Thomas Aquinas, 11

Thomas Jefferson. Brodie, F., 103

Thomas Wolfe. Turnbull, A., 108

Thompson, John A. Bible and Archaeology, 11

Thompson, Paul D. Virus Realm, 42

Thompson, Wilbur R. Preface to Urban Economics, 21

Thoreau, Henry D. Portable Thoreau, 85

____. Walden, 85

Thorndike, Ashley. Shakespeare's Theater, 88

Those Damned Rebels: American Revolution as Seen through British Eyes. Pearson, M., 122

Those Inventive Americans. National Geographic Society, 51

Thousand Days. Schlesinger, A., 124

Three Centuries of Harpsichord Making. Hubbard, F., 74

Three Edwards. Costain, T., 113

Three Faces of Eve. Thigpen, C., 51

365 Days. Glasser, R., 118

Three Hundred Sixty-five Days. Irwin, K., 37

365 Shortcuts to Home Decorating. Draper, D., 69

Three Plays. Giraudoux, J., 89

Three Plays. Wilder, T., 84

3.1414 and All That. Davis P., 36

Throwaway Children. Richette, L., 19

Thurber, James. Thurber Album, 85

____. Thurber Carnival, 85

Thurman, Howard. Search for Common Ground, 10

Tillich, Paul. Future of Religions, 11

____. History of Christian Thoughts, 11

____. What is Religion?, 10

Timbie, William H. Essentials of Electricity, 53

Time for Astrology. Stearn, J., 6

Time-Life. American Painting, 71

____. "Emergence of Man" series, 41

____. Life Nature Library, 35

____. Life Science Library, 35

____. Photojournalism, 4

____. Time-Life Family Legal Guide, 26

Time-Life Books see also 95

Time-Life Book of Family Finance. Smith, C., 23

Time-Life Family Legal Guide. Time-Life, 26
Time of our Lives: Ethics of Common Sense.
Adler, M., 8
Times to Remember. Kennedy, R., 103
Timmons, Virginia G. Designing and Making
Mosaics, 69
Tin Can Crafting. Howard, S., 68
Titans. Maurois, A., 96
To a Young Dancer. DeMille, A., 74
To Appomattox. Davis, B., 123
To Be a Slave. Lester, J., 21
To Catch an Angel. Russell, R., 106
To Race the Wind. Krents, Harold, 103
To Sir with Love. Braithwaite, E., 98
To the Yalu. McGovern, J., 117
Tobacco and Your Health. Diehl, H., 49
Toboldt, William K. Auto Body Repairing and
Repainting, 56
_____. Fix Your Chevrolet, 56
_____. Fix Your Ford, 56
Today's Camping. Colby, C., 76
Today's Isms. Ebenstein, W., 24
Today's Poets. Walsh, C., 81
Toffler, Alvin. Future Shock, 17
Toil and Trouble. Brooks, T., 23
Tokle, Art. Complete Guide to Cross Country
Skiing and Touring, 77
Tokuriki, Tomikichiro. Woodblock Print
Primer, 71
Toland, John. Battle: Story of the Bulge, 112
_____. Rising Sun, 1936–1945, 117
Tolstoy, Leo. Selections, 92
Tolstoy. Troyat, H., 107
Tomkeieff, O. G. Life in Norman England,
114
Tomkins, Calvin. Eric Hoffer: an American
Odyssey, 102
Tone. Levarie, S., 73
Tongues of Fire. Keyes, F., 13
Tooley, R. V. Maps and Map-Makers, 38
Tooth Trip. McGuire, T., 51
Torche, Judith. Acrylic and Other Water-Base
Paints, 71
Torres, Jose. Sting like a Bee, 105
Torres Rioseco, Arturo. Epic of Latin Ameri-
can Literature, 90
Totten, W. Fred. Power of Community
School Education, 29
Touch the Earth. McLuhan, T., 119
Tournier, Paul. Escape from Loneliness, 7
_____. Whole Person in a Broken World, 7
Townsend, Robert. Up the Organization, 61
Toynbee, Arnold. Hellenism, 110
_____. Historian's Approach to Religion, 14
_____. Study of History, 93
_____. Surviving the Future, 94
Track and Field. Sports Illustrated, 77
Tractors and Crawlers. Eshelman, P., 55
Tragedy of Lyndon. Goldman, E., 103
Tragedy of the Chinese Revolution. Isaacs, H.,
116
Trailer Owners Handbook. Dipboye, J., 55
Trailer Owner's Manual. Eliel, L., 55
Trails of Tears. Williams, J., 119
Training with Weights. Sports Illustrated, 77
Training Your Retriever. Free, J., 57
Transformational Grammar. Aurbach, J., 32
Translations from the Chinese. Waley, A., 91
Trapp, Maria A. Maria, 107
_____. Trapp Family Singers, 107
Trapp Family Singers. Trapp, M., 107
Travel Guides. Ford, N., 95
Travel Guides. Sunset Magazine, eds., 95
Travel guides. Waldo, M., 95
Travels of Marco Polo. Polo, M., 117
Treason in America. Archer, J., 26
Treasury of Chinese Literature. Chai, C., 91
Treasury of Christmas Songs and Carols.
Simon, H., 74
Treasury of Designs for Artists and Crafts-
men. Mirow, G., 69
Treasury of Great American Speeches. Hurd,
C., 82
Treasury of Great Poems. Untermeyer, L., 81
Treasury of Great Russian Short Stories.
Yarmolinsky, A., 92
Treasury of Jewish Folklore. Ausubel, N., 31
Treasury of Russian Literature. Guerney, B.,
92
Treasury of Russian Verse. Yarmolinsky, A.,
92
Treasury of the Theatre. Gassner, J., 81
Treblinka. Steiner, J., 112
Tree Farms. Dowdell, D., 56
Tree Maintenance. Pirone, P., 57
Treece, Hency. Crusades, 111
Trees for American Gardens. Wyman, D., 66
Trees of North America. Brockman, C., 42
Trevelyan, Geroge M. English Revolution:
1688, 114
_____. Illustrated English Social History, 114
Trial and Error. Weizmann, C., 108
Trial by Jury. McCart, S., 25
Tricker, R. A. R. Science of Clouds, 40
Tricomi, Ernest. How to Repair Major Appli-
ances, 59

Trilling, Lionel. Opposing Self, 79
Triumph of Science and Reason. Nussbaum, F., 111
Tropical Fish as a Hobby. Axelrod, H., 44
Tropical Fish Identifier. Walker, B., 45
Tropical Fish in Your Home. Axelrod, H., 44
Trouble with Lawyers. Bloom, M., 24
Troyat, Henri. Divided Soul, 101
——. Tolstoy, 107
Truck and Tractor Guide. Graham, F., 55
Trueblood, Elton. New Man for our Times, 12
Truman, Harry S. Memoirs, 107
Truman, Margaret. Harry S. Truman, 107
Truman Administration. Koenig, L., 124
Truth about Contact Lenses. Baker, J., 51
Tuchman, Barbara W. Guns of August, 112
——. Proud Tower, 112
Tuite, James J. Snowmobiles and Snow-mobiling, 77
Tully, Andrew. FBI's Most Famous Cases, 26
Tunis, Edwin. Colonial Living, 121
——. Frontier Living, 122
——. Indians, 119
——. Weapons: A Pictorial History, 27, 53
——. Wheels, 29
Turabian, Kate, L., Manual for Writers of Term Papers, Theses, and Dissertations, 3
Turnbull, Andrew. Scott Fitzgerald, 101
——. Thomas Wolfe, 108
Turnbull, Colin M. The Mountain People, 41
Turnbull, Eleanor L. Ten Centuries of Spanish Poetry, 90
Turner, David R. Homestudy Courses for Civil Service Jobs, 26
Turner, Edward R. Practice for Clerical, Typing and Stenographic Tests, 26
Turner, Frederick. Frontier in American History, 121
Turner, Justin G. Mary Todd Lincoln, 104
Twain, Mark. Complete Essays, 85
——. Complete Humorous Sketches and Tales, 85
——. Innocents Abroad, 85
——. Life on the Mississippi, 85
——. Portable Mark Twain, 85
Twelve, The. Goodspeed, E., 10
Twelve Caesars. Suetonius, 109
Twelve Famous Plays of the Restoration and 18th Century, 87
Twentieth Century. Colton, J., 93
Twentieth Century American Poetry. Aiken, C., 83

20th Century Bookkeeping and Accounting. Boynton, L., 60
20th Century China. Clubb, O., 116
Twentieth Century Church Music. Routley, E., 73
Twentieth Century Drama. Cohen, R., 87
20th Century Harmony. Persichetti, V., 73
12, 20, and 5: a Doctor's Year in Vietnam. Parrish, J., 118
12-Year Reich. Grunberger, R., 114
Twenty Centuries of Christianity. Hutchinson, P., 13
Twenty-five Plays of the Modern American Theater. Gassner, J., 84
24 Favorite One-Act Plays. Cerf, B., 81
21-Day Shape-Up Program for Men and Women. Craig, M., 48
26 Letters. Ogg, O., 32
20,000 Years of World Painting. Jaffe, H., 71
20 Years at Hull House. Addams, J., 97
Twenty Years' Crisis. Carr, E., 124
Two Cultures: And a Second Look. Snow, C., 3
Two-Ocean War. Morrison, S., 112
Two Treatises of Civil Government. Locke, J., 20
Two Viet Nams. Fall, B., 118
Two Years before the Mast. Dana, R., 94
Tyil, Al. Complete Beginner's Guide to Water Skiing, 78
Tyler, Leona E. Psychology of Human Differences, 7
Tyler, Poyntz. Securities, Exchanges and the S.E.C., 24
Typing for Everyone. Levine, N., 61
Tyranny of Noise. Baron, R., 53

UFO Experience. Hynek, J. 4
UFOs Identified. Klass, P., 4
Udall, Stewart L. Quiet Crisis, 24
Ulcer Diet Cookbook. Rubin, H., 50
Uman, Martin. Understanding Lightning, 40
Unbought and Unbossed. Chisholm, S., 99
Uncommitted. Kenniston, K., 18
Uncoupling: the Art of Coming Apart. Sheresky, N., and Mannes, M., 19
Underachievers. Fine, B., 28
Underground Dictionary. Landy, E., 33
Underground Press in America. Glessing, R., 4
Underhill, Ruth M. Red Man's Religion, 15
Understanding Children. Gardner, R., 7
Understanding Drug Use. Marin, P., 49

Understanding Electricity and Electronics. Buban, P., 52

Understanding Fiction. Brooks, C., 81

Understanding Grammar. Roberts, P., 33

Understanding Lightning. Uman, M., 40

Understanding Maps. Tannenbaum, B., 38

Understanding Piaget. Pulaski, M., 8

Understanding Poetry. Brooks, C., 80

Understanding the New Testament. Kee, H., 11

Understanding the Russians. Kohler, F., 21

Understanding the Stock Market. Low, J., 23

Unfinished Odyssey. Halberstam, D., 103

Unfinished Revolution. Deutscher, I., 115

Unfinished Woman. Hellman, L., 102

Unions. Schwartz, A., 23

U.N.: the First 25 Years. Eichelberger, C., 25

United States and China. Fairband, J., 116

United States and World War II. Buchannan, A., 124

U.S. Bureau of Labor Statistics. Occupational Outlook Handbook, 23

United States Government Organization Manual, 27

U.S. Grant and the American Military Tradition. Catton, B., 101

U.S. News & World Report, eds. Social Security and Medicare Simplified, 28

United States 1942 –1877. Bradley, H., 120

United States of America. Perkins, D., 121

U.S. Service Academy Admissions Tests. Arco, 27

United States to 1865. Kraus, M., 121

Universe. Asimov, I., 37

Universe and Dr. Einstein. Barnett, L., 38

Unless Peace Comes. Calder, N., 25

Unrecorded Life of Oscar Wilde. Croft-Cooke, R., 108

Unsafe at Any Height. Godson, J., 54

Unsafe at Any Speed. Nadar, R., 55

Untermeyer, Louis. Forms of Poetry, 80

——. Lives of the Poets, 96

——. Makers of the Modern World, 96

——. Treasury of Great Poems, 81

Untold Story: the Roosevelts of Hyde Park. Roosevelt, E., 96

Up from Slavery. Washington, B., 107

Up the Organization. Townsend, R., 61

Up Your Own Organization. Dible, D., 61

Upholstery. Luna, B., 62

Ups and Downs. Rice, J., 49

Upstairs at the White House. West, J., 125

Uses of the Past. Muller, H., 93

Usher, Abbott P. History of Mechanical Inventions, 47

Utopia. More, T., 20

V.D. Story. Brooks, S., 49

V.D.: the ABC's. Grover, J., 50

Vaccine and Virus. Rosenberg, N., 50

Valachi Papers. Maas, P., 28

Valery, Paul. Selected Writings, 89

Vallery-Radot, René. Louis Pasteur, 105

Van de Velde, Theodore. Ideal Marriage, 19

Van Deusen, Glyndon G. Jacksonian Era, 122

Van Doren, Carl. American Novel, 1789– 1939, 84

Van Doren, Mark. Anthology of World Poetry, 81

——. Shakespeare, 88

Van Dyke, Dick. Faith, Hope and Hillarity, 85

Van Every, Dale. Disinherited, 119

——. Final Challenge, 122

——. Forth to the Wilderness, 121

Van Laue, Theodore H. Why Lenin, Why Stalin, 115

Van Nostrand, Albert. Denatured Novel, 81

——. Literary Criticism in America, 79

Van Sickle, Neil D. Modern Airmanship, 54

Van Zandt, Eleanor. Crafts for Fun and Profit, 69

Vanderbilt, Amy. Amy Vanderbilt's Etiquette, 30

Vanderpoel, Sally. Care and Feeding of Your Diabetic Child, 60

VanHeel, Abraham. What is Light?, 38

Vanished Cities. Schreiber, H., 109

Vanishing Air. Esposito, J., 54

Vanishing Wild Animals of the World. Fitter, R., 46

VanLawick-Goodall. Jane, My Friends the Wild Chimpanzees, 46

VanRiper, Charles. Speech Correction, 50

Vantage Point. Johnson, L., 124

Varieties of Religious Experience. James, W., 10

Varnadsky, George. History of Russia, 115

Vasari, Giorgio. Lives of the Painters, Sculptors, and Architects, 96

Velben, Thorstein. Theory of the Leisure Class, 23

Venezuela. Lieuwen, E., 125

Venomous Reptiles. Minton, S., 45

Verba, Sidney. Small Groups and Political Behavior, 20

Verdict: the Jury System. Bloomstein, M., 24

Vermeule, Emily. Greece in the Bronze Age, 110

Versailles, 1919. Czernin, F., 112

Vertebrate Body. Romer, A., 44

Vertebrate Physiology. McCauley, W., 43

Vestal, Stanley. Kit Carson, 99

Veterinary Guide for Farmers. Stamm, G., 57

Vickery, Brian. Information Systems, 4

Victor Book of Opera. Simon, H., 73

Victorian People. Briggs, A., 113

Viking Settlements of North America. Pohl, F., 121

Vikings. Donovan, F., 115

Vikings. National Geographic Society, 116

Village. West, F., 118

Violence Against Children. Gil, D., 18

Violent Peace. Mydans, C., 93

Virgil. Aeneid, 90, 91

Virginia Woolf. Bell, Q., 108

Virus Hunters. Williams, G., 50

Virus Realm. Thompson, P., 42

Vishniac, Roman. Building Blocks of Life, 41

Vitamin C and the Common Cold. Pauling, L., 48

Vittorini, Domenica. Italian Grammar, 33

Vlahos, Olivia. African Beginnings, 41

Vogt, Dieter. Complete Aquarium, 45

Voice of England. Osgood, G., 86

Voice that is Great within Us, The. Carruth, H., 83

Voices of 1776. Wheeler, R., 122

Volleyball. Sports Illustrated, 77

Voltaire, Francois M. Age of Louis XIV, 114
——. Portable Voltaire, 89

Von Braun, Wernher. History of Rocketry and Space Travel, 56
——. Space Frontier, 56

Von Daniken, Erich. Chariots of the Gods: Unsolved Mysteries of the Past, 41
——. Gods from Outer Space, 41
——. In Search of Ancient Gods, 41

Von Rauch, George. History of Soviet Russia, 115

Waddell, Helen J. Medieval Latin Lyrics, 91
——. Wandering Scholars, 91

Wadsworth, James. Glass House, 25

Wagenheim, Kal. Puerto Ricans, 120

Wagenknecht, Edward. Cavalcade of the American Novel, 84

——. Cavalcade of the English Novel, 88
——. Poe, 105

Waggoner, Hyatt H. American Poets, 83

Wagman, Richard J. New Concise Family Health and Medical Guide, 49

Wagner, Willis. Modern Carpentry, 63

Waite, Robert G. Hitler and Nazi Germany, 114

Waksman, Selman A. Conquest of Tuberculosis, 50

Walden. Thoreau, H., 85

Walden Two. Skinner, B., 20

Waldo, Myra. Travel guides, 95

Waley, Arthur. Translations from the Chinese, 91

Walker, Braz. Tropical Fish Identifier, 45

Walker, John R. Modern Metalworking, 62

Wallace, Irving. Fabulous Showman, 98

Wally's Workshop. Bruner, W., 62

Walsh, Chad. Today's Poets, 81

Walsh, Warren B. Russia and the Soviet Union, 115

Wambaugh, Joseph. Onion Field, 28

Wandering Scholars. Waddell, H., 91

Wandering through Winter. Teale, E., 40

Waning of the Middle Ages. Huizinga, J., 110

Wann, Louis. Century Readings in the English Essay, 88

War: a Concise History, 1939–1945. Synder, L., 112

War between Russia and China. Salisbury, H., 21

War of 1812. Coles, H., 122

War of 1812. Horsman, R., 122

War with Mexico. Chidsey, D., 123

Ward, Barbara. Five Ideas That Changed the World, 94
——. Nationalism and Ideology, 20
——. Only One Earth, 17
——. Rich Nations and Poor Nations, 24

Ward, Herman M. Poems for Pleasure, 83

Ward, Kay B. Feminine Fix-it Handbook, 59

Warner, Dorothy D. Adapting American Antiques, 70

Warren, Harris G. Herbert Hoover and the Great Depression, 124

Warren, Jefferson T. Exhibit Methods, 2

Warriors of God. Nigg, W., 13

Wars in Barbary. Chidsey, D., 122

Washburn, Wilcomb E. Red Man's Land/White Man's Law, 119

Washing of the Spears. Morris, D., 118

Washington, Booker T. Up from Slavery, 107

Washington, Joseph R. Marriage in Black and White, 30

Waste Makers. Packard, V., 24

Watchers of the Skies. Ley, W., 37

Water Hustlers. Graves, J., 54

Water Is Everybody's Business. Behrman, A., 53

Water, Prey, and Game Birds of North America. Wetmore, A., 45

Water Wasteland. Zwick, D., 24, 54

Water, Weather, and Prehistory. Raikes, R., 40

Water Well Manual. Gibson, U., 53

Waterloo. Howarth, D., 111

Waterman, Charles F. Hunting in America, 78

Watkins, Art. Dollars and Sense, 23

Watkins, Arthur M. Complete Book of Home Remodeling, Improvement, and Repair, 63

———. Homeowner's Survival Kit, 63

Watson, James D. Double Helix, 42

Watson, Robert I. Great Psychologists: from Aristotle to Freud, 7

Watts, Alan. Art of Contemplation, 14

———. Instant Weather Forecasting, 53

———. Spirit of Zen, 14

———. Supreme Identity, 14

———. Way of Zen, 14

Waugh, Dorothy. Festive Decorations the Year Round, 30

Way it 'Spozed to Be. Herndon, J., 29

Way of Zen. Watts, A., 14

Ways of Thinking of Eastern Peoples. Nakamura, H., 116

We Who Built America. Wittke, C., 21

Wealth of Nations. Smith, A., 23

Weapons: A Pictorial History. Tunis, E., 27, 53

Weather and Health. Landsberg, H., 39

Weather Business. Atkinson, B., 39

Weatherhead, Leslie. Christian Agnostic, 11

Webb, Constance. Richard Wright, 108

Weber, Max. Basic Concepts in Sociology, 16

Webster's Dictionary of Synonyms, 32

Webster's New Collegiate Dictionary, 32

Wedgwood, C. V. Thirty Years' War, 111

Weeds of the World. King, L., 43

Weeks, Bertha. Filing and Records Management, 61

Weeks, Edward. Breaking into Print, 80

Weeks, Mary E. Discovery of the Elements, 39

Weeks, Robert P. Commonwealth vs. Sacco and Vanzetti, 26

Weight Lifting and Weight Training. Kirkley, G., 76

Weight Training. Ryan, F., 77

Weight Watchers Program Cook Book. Nidetch, J., 59

Weigley, Russell F. History of the United States Army, 27

Weinberg, Alvin M. Reflections on Big Science, 35

Weiner, Michael. Earth Medicine-Earth Food, 49

Weiner, Peter. Making the Media Revolution, 72

Weisberger, Bernard A. American Heritage History of the American People, 121

Weiser, Francis X. Handbook of Christian Feasts and Customs, 13

Weissler, Paul. Auto Repairs You Can Make, 56

Weizmann, Chaim. Trial and Error, 108

Welding Technology. Giachino, J., 61

Wellek, Rene. History of Modern Criticism, 79

———. Theory of Literature, 79

Weller, Jack. Wellington at Waterloo, 111

Wellington at Waterloo. Weller, J., 111

Wells, Evelyn. Nefertiti, 105

———. What to Name the Baby, 108

Wells, George S. Modern ABC's of Family Camping, 77

Wells, H. G. Outline of History, 94

Wells, Jane. Name for Your Baby, 108

Welty, Paul T. Asians: Their Heritage and Their Destiny, 116

Wendt, Herbert. From Ape to Adam, 42

———. Sex Life of the Animals, 44

Wernecke, Herbert H. Christmas Customs around the World, 30

Werner, Alfred. German Painting: Old Masters, 71

West, Francis, J. Village, 118

West, J. B. Upstairs at the White House, 125

West, Jessamyn. Quaker Reader, 13

West, Richard. Back to Africa, 119

Westcott, Cynthia. Gardener's Bug Book, 57

Western Civilization. Kirchner, W., 93

Westminster Historical Atlas to the Bible. Wright, G., 11

Westmore, Michael. Art of Theatrical Makeup for Stage and Screen, 75

Westward Expansion. Billington, R., 120

Wetmore, Alexander. Song and Garden Birds of North America, 45

_____. Water, Prey, and Game Birds of North America, 45

Whale. Cousteau, J., 46

Whalen, William J. Minority Religions in America, 13

What Do I Do Monday? Holt, J., 29

What Happens in Hamlet. Wilson, J., 88

What is Cinema? Bazin, A., 74

What is Communism? Ketchum, R., 24

What is Conservatism? Meyer, F., 20

What is History? Carr, E., 93

What is Light? VanHeel, A., 38

What is Mathematics? Courant, R., 36

What is Religion? Tillich, P., 10

What Manner of Man. Bennett, L., 103

What People Wore. Gorsline, D., 30

What the Computer Can Do: a Guide for the Plain Man. Cooper, M., 4

What the Great Religions Believe. Gaer, J., 14

What to Do When "There's Nothing to Do." Gregg, E., 75

What to Do with Your Bad Car. Nader, R., 55

What to Name the Baby. Wells, E., 108

What to Tell Your Children about Sex. Child Study Assn. of America, 47

What's in a Novel. Haines, H., 81

What's in a Play? Austell, J., 74

What's Right with our Young People? Fletcher, G., 18

Wheatley, Richard C. Restoration of Antique and Classic Cars, 56

Wheeler, Joseph L. Practical Administration of Public Libraries, 2

Wheeler, Richard. Voices of 1776, 122

Wheelock, Frederic M. Latin: an Introductory Course, 34

Wheels. Tunis, E., 29

When a Child Is Different. Egg, M., 7

When Egypt Ruled the East. Steindorff, G., 109

When Love Prevails. Gilmore, J., 12

When Parents Divorce. Steinzor, B., 8

When the Cheering Stopped. Smith, G., 108

When Your Child Is Ill. Karelitz, S., 50

Where's Hannah? Hart, J., 29

Whiffen, Marcus. American Architecture since 1780, 67

Whipkey, Kenneth L. Power of Calculus, 37

Whitaker, Arthur. Argentina, 125

White, Jon M. Everyday Life in Ancient Egypt, 109

White, Leonard D. Jacksonians, 27

White, Morton. Foundations of Historical Knowledge, 94

_____. Science and Sentiment in America, 9

White, R. J. Horizon Concise History of England, 114

White, Theodore. Fire in the Ashes, 112

White, Theodore H. Making of the President 1972, 125

_____. Making of the President 1960, 125

_____. Making of the President 1964, 125

_____. Making of the President 1968, 125

White, William S. Citadel: Story of the U.S. Senate, 27

White and the Gold. Costain, T., 119

White Color. Mills, C., 17

White House Transcripts, 22

White House Years. Eisenhower, D., 100

White Nile. Moorehead, A., 118

White Racism. Schwartz, B., 20

Whitehead, Alfred N. Anthology, 9

Whitman, Walt. Leaves of Grass, 83

_____. Portable Walt Whitman, 83

Whitney, Charles A. Discovery of Our Galaxy, 37

Whitney, Edgar A. Complete Guide to Watercolor Painting, 71

Whitney, Leon F. Complete Book of Cat Care, 58

_____. First Aid for Pets, 58

_____. Pets, 58

Whittick, Arnold. Symbols, Signs and Their Meaning, 64

Whittling and Wood Carving. Hoppe. H., 67

Who Am I, God? Holmes, M., 12

Who Designs America? Holland, L., 65

Whole Earth Cook Book. Caldwallader, S., 58

Whole Person in a Broken World. Tournier, P., 7

Who's Afraid of Virginia Woolf? Albee, E., 83

Who's Who in Basketball. Mendell, R., 77

Who's Who in Boxing. Burrill, B., 76

Who's Who in Hockey. Kariher, H., 76

Who's Who in Professional Baseball. Karst, G., 76

Who's Who in Track and Field. Hanley, R., 76

Why and How to Prepare an Effective Job Resume. Angel, J., 60

Why Lenin, Why Stalin. Van Laue, T., 115

Wienandt, Elwyn. Choral Music of the Church, 73

Wigginton, B. Eliott. Foxfire Book, 57

_____. Foxfire Two, 57

Wigglesworth, Vincent. Life of Insects, 44

Wilcox, E. Turner. Five Centuries of American Costume, 30

Wild Animals of North America. National Geographic Society, 46

Wilde, Oscar. Portable Oscar Wilde, 86

Wilder, Thornton N. Three Plays, 84

Wildman, Emily. Step-by-Step Crochet, 69

Wilkerson, David. Cross and the Switchblade, 12

———. Hey Preach, You're Comin' Through, 12

———. Little People, 13

Wilkins, Ernest. History of Italian Literature, 90

Will to Live. Schopenhauer, A., 9

Willett, Frank. African Art, 65

William Shakespeare. Masefield, J., 87

Williams, E. Neville. Life in Georgian England, 114

Williams, Edward B. One Man's Freedom, 25

Williams, Greer. Virus Hunters, 50

Williams, Guy R. Making Mobiles, 67

Williams, Jeanne. Trails of Tears, 119

Williams, Laurence R. East Pakistan Tragedy, 117

Williams, Oscar. Little Treasury of American Poetry, 83

———. Little Treasury of Great Poetry, 81

———. Little Treasury of Modern Poetry, 81

———. Master Poems of the English Language, 81

———. Mentor Book of Major American Poets, 83

———. Mentor Book of Major British Poets, 86

Williams, Raymond. Drama from Ibsen to Brecht, 81

———. English Novel from Dickens to Lawrence, 88

Williams, Roger. The Bonds, 96

Williams, Tennessee. Theater of Tennessee Williams, 84

Williams, William C. Autobiography, 108

Wills, Alfred J. Introduction to the History of Central Africa, 119

Wills, Royal B. More Houses for Good Living, 67

Wilson, Barbara. Complete Book of Engagement and Wedding Etiquette, 30

Wilson, Carl L. Botany, 43

Wilson, Clifford. Crash Go the Chariots; an Alternative to Chariots of the Gods, 41

Wilson, Colin. Occult, 6

———. Rasputin and the Fall of the Romanovs, 106

Wilson, David. Body and Antibody, 50

Wilson, Dick. Long March, 117

Wilson, Edmund. Axel's Castle, 79

———. Classics and Commercials, 79

Wilson, Helen. Helen V. Wilson's African Violet Book, 66

Wilson, John D. What Happens in Hamlet, 88

Wilson, John R. Mind, 7

Wilson, Orlando W. Police Administration, 26

Wiltse, Charles M. New Nation 1800–1845, 122

Winchell, Constance. Guide to Reference Books, 2

Winchester, A. M. Genetics, 42

Windmills and Watermills. Reynolds, J., 53

Wing, Frances S. Complete Book of Decoupage, 69

Wing, Lorna. Autistic Children, 8

Winged Horse. Auslander, J., 80

Wings, Sun, and Stars. Kaufman, J., 45

Winning of Independence. Smelser, M., 122

Winslow Homer at Prout's Neck. Beam, P., 102

Winston Churchill: an Intimate Portrait. Bonham-Carter, V., 99

Winter, Elmer. Women at Work, 19

Winwar, Francis S. Immortal Lovers, 98

Wiora, Walter. Four Ages of Music, 73

Wisdom of China and India. Lin Yutang, 91

Wiseman, Ann. Rag Tapestries and Wool Mosaics, 69

Wish, Harvey. Contemporary America, 125

Wissler, Clark. Indians of the United States, 119

Witchcraft. Hart, R., 5

Witchcraft At Salem. Hansen, C., 5

With Every Breath You Take. Lewis, H., 54

With Love and Elbow Grease. Browning, E., 70

Witness. Chambers, W., 26

Wittke, Carl. We Who Built America, 21

Woddham-Smith, Cecil. Reason Why, 114

Wolansky, William D. Woodworking Made Easy, 62

Wolchonok, Louis. Art of Pictorial Composition, 67

Wold, Milo. Introduction to Music and Art in the Western World, 64

Wolf, John B. Louis XIV, 104

Wolff, Robert L. Balkans in Our Time, 116

The Woman Alone. O'Brien, P., 18

Woman, Society and Change. Sullerot, E., 18

Woman's Guide to Fixing the Car. Cleary, M., 55

Women and Society. Reische, D., 18
Women and the Law. Kanowitz, L., 18
Women at Work. Winter, E., 19
Wonder Drugs: a History of Antibiotics. Boettcher, H., 49
Wondrous World of Fishes. Schultz, L., 45
Wood, Paul W. Stained Glass Crafting, 69
Wood, Robert C. Suburbia, 17
Woodblock Print Primer. Tokuriki, T., 71
Woodin, James C. Home and Building Maintenance, 63
Woodrow Wilson and the Lost Peace. Bailey, T., 124
Woodrow Wilson and the Progressive Era. Link, A., 124
Woodruff, Everett, B. Steam Plant Operation, 52
Woods, Allan. Modern Newspaper Production, 4
Woods, Ralph L. Modern Handbook of Humor, 85
Woodstock Craftsman's Manual Two. Young, J., 69
Woodturning. Peters, G., 62
Woodward, C. Vann. Reunion and Reaction, 123
———. Strange Career of Jim Crow, 123
Woodward, R. and Bernstein, C. All the President's Men, 125
Woodworking Made Easy. Wolansky, W., 62
Woodworking Technology. Hammond, J., 62
Woody, Russell O. Painting with Synthetic Media, 71
Woolf, Virginia. Room of One's Own, 79
Woolley, A. E. Creative 35mm Techniques, 72
Worcester, Donald E. Growth and Culture of Latin America, 125
Word is Here; Poetry from Modern Africa. Kgosistsile, K., 91
Word Power Made Easy. Lewis, N., 33
Word War: Story of American Propaganda. Sorenson, T., 17
Words with Music. Engel, L., 73
Wordsworth, William. Poetical Works, 86
Working. Terkel, S., 23
Working Mother. Callahan, S., 18
World Aflame. Graham, B., 12
World Beyond. Montgomery, R., 6
World Drama. Clark, B., 81
World Drama. Nicoll, A., 81
World Food Problem. Cochran, W., 24
World History of the Dance. Sachs, C., 75

World in Flames: History of World War II. Hoyle, M., 112
World of Andrew Carnegie. Hacker, L., 123
World of Ballet. Kerensky, O., 74
World of Cyrogenics. Boyd, W., 52
World of Flowers. Reisigel, H., 43
World of Humanism. Gilmore, M., 111
World of Mathematics. Newman, J., 36
World of Musical Comedy. Green, S., 73
World of Origami. Honda, I., 68
World of Reptiles. Bellairs, A., 45
World of Rome. Grant, M., 109
World of the Formerly Married. Hunt, M., 18
World of the Frog and the Toad. Porter, G., 45
World of the Past. Hawkes, J., 109
World of the Snake. Harrison, H., 45
World Religions. Landis, B., 14
World Turned Upside Down. Leckie, R., 122
World War and American Isolation. May, E., 112
World War I. American Heritage, 111
World War II. Sulzberger, C., 112
World within the Ocean Wave. Silverberg, R., 40
World within the Tidal Pool. Silverberg, R., 40
World Without Hunger. Freeman, O., 24
Worldly Philosophers. Heilbroner, R., 22
World's Greatest Speeches. Copeland, L., 82
World's Living Religions. Hume, R., 14
Wouk, Herman. This is my God, 14
Wrestling. Douglas, B., 76
Wright, David. Deafness, 51
Wright, Erna. Common Sense in Child Rearing, 60
Wright, Esmond. Fabric of Freedom, 122
Wright, Frank Lloyd. Genius and the Mobocracy, 107
Wright, George E. Westminster Historical Atlas to the Bible, 11
Wright, Jim. Coming Water Famine, 54
Wright, Louis B. Cultural Life of the American Colonies, 121
Wright, Richard. Black Boy, 108
Write Your Own Wedding. Brill, M., 30
Writer's Handbook. Burach, A., 4, 80
Writers on Writing. Allen, W., 80
Writing and Thinking. Foerster, N., 80
Writing for TV and Radio. Hilliard, R., 80
Writing the Modern Magazine Article. Gunther, M., 80
Writings. James, W., 9

Wuoringen, John H. History of Finland, 116
Wyatt, Stanley P. Principles of Astronomy, 37
Wylie, Harry L. Office Management Handbook, 61
Wyman, Donald. Trees for American Gardens, 66
––––. Wyman's Gardening Encyclopedia, 66
Wyman's Gardening Encyclopedia. Wyman, D., 66
Wynar, Lubomyr R. American Political Parties, 22
Wyss, Orville. Microorganisms and Man, 42

Yale, William. Near East, 118
Yalta Conference. Fenno., R., 112
Yarmolinsky, Avrahm. Treasury of Great Russian Short Stories, 92
––––. Treasury of Russian Verse, 92
Yates, Norris W. American Humorist, 85
Year of Decision. DeVoto, B., 123
Year of the Seal. Scheffer, V., 46
Yeats, W. B. Oxford Book of Modern Verse, 81
Yes I Can. Davis, S., 100
Yes, World. Irion, M., 12
Yesterday's Children. Kraus, P., 29
Yevtushenko, Yevgeny. Poems, 92
Yoga for the Mind. Zorn, W., 14
Yoga Way to Figure and Facial Beauty. Hittleman, R., 48
Yoga, Youth and Reincarnation. Stearn, J., 8
Yoors, Jan. Gypsies, 16
You and Your Aging Parents. Stern, E., 19
You and Your Feet. Fast, J., 49
You and Your Pension. Nader, R., 19
Young, Desmond. Rommel, the Desert Fox, 106
Young, Donald. American Roulette: History and Dilemma of the Vice Presidency, 27
Young, Jean. Woodstock Craftsman's Manual, 69
––––. Woodstock Craftsman's Manual Two, 69
Young, John Z. Life of Vertebrates, 44
Young, Louise, B. Exploring the Universe, 37
Young, Whitney. Beyond Racism, 20
Young People and Religion. Cain, A., 12
Young Radicals. Kenniston, K., 18
Young Woman's Guide to Liberation. DeCrow, K., 17

Your Career in Interior Design. Doyle, R., 69
Your Child and Sex: A Guide for Parents. Pomeroy, W., 48
Your Children's Teeth. Berland, T., 51
Your Complete Guide to Estate Planning, Callahan, P., 25
Your First Year of Marriage. McGinnis, T., 18
Your Heart and How to Live with It. Lamb, L., 50
Your Heredity and Environment. Scheinfeld, A., 42
Your Income Tax. Lasser, J., 23
Your Inner Child of the Past. Missildene, W., 7
Your Legal Rights. Norwick, K., 25
Your Non-Learning Child. Smith, B., 29
Your Skin and Hair. Brauer, E., 59
Your Sight. Seeman, B., 51
Your Vacation Home. Hague, W., 66

Zadig, Ernest A. Complete Book of Boating, 78
Zaidenberg, Arthur. How to Draw and Compose Pictures, 67
Zeiger, Arthur. Encyclopedia of English, 80
Zelda. Mitford, N., 101
Zen Buddhism and Psychoanalysis. Fromm, E., 14
Zigrosser, Carl. Guide to the Care and Collecting of Original Prints, 71
Zim, Herbert S. Rocks and Minerals, 40
––––. Seashores, 40
Zimmerman, Elizabeth. Knitting without Tears, 69
Zimmerman, John E. Dictionary of Classical Mythology, 14
Zimmerman, Josef D. Irrigation, 57
Zinkin, Taya. India, 117
Zinsser, Hans. Rats, Lice and History, 50
Zitner, Sheldon. Preface to Literary Analysis, 79
Znamierowski, Nell. Step-by-Step Weaving, 69
Zoo Story. Albee, E., 83
Zoology. Elliott, A., 43
Zoos of the World. Fisher, J., 43
Zorn, William. Body Harmony, 8
––––. Yoga for the Mind, 14
Zwick, David. Water Wasteland, 24, 54